" 'Presence is as important as proclamation' is the theme of this book. Having worked in the inner city in Chicago with various types of poverty as well as my time working in a methadone clinic with those in and out of prison, I know the challenge of not forgetting the forgotten. These devotionals are a daily reminder of the least of these."

> — **Chad Hovind,** Lead mega church pastor, author of *Godonomics* and *Fast Track Bible*

"This book puts a human face on the two and a half million inmates in the United States. *Stories of Faith and Courage from Prison* is a powerful devotional that will capture your heart, ignite your passion, and require a choice. What will *you* do for some of the most needy in our society? If we spread the word, God could use this book to change the heart of the nation and bring about repentance, forgiveness, reconciliation, and redemption. Buy one for yourself and ten more to give away."

> — **Carol Kent,** Speaker and Author
> *When I Lay My Isaac Down* (NavPress)
> *Between a Rock and a Grace Place* (Zondervan)

"*Stories of Faith and Courage from Prison* is a profound testimony to the truth that there are no bars or chains strong enough to keep us from God's love, grace, and mercy. Indeed, God Allows U-Turns no matter how lost, broken, or bound we may be. God can always make a way when there seems to be no way."

> — **Allison Bottke,** Author of *Setting Boundaries with Your Adult Children* (Harvest House Publishers) and the *God Allows U-Turns* series.

"These true stories reveal how Jesus can radically transform hearts and lives. Jim Harris' story shares his conversion, and what a true miracle it was because he had sunk so low into the drug culture. It is amazing how he kicked his addictions and has been 'flying right' for the Lord since 1995. Jim now impacts lives through our ministry in jails and prisons as an area director and platform guest!"

> — **Bill Glass,** Founder Bill Glass Champions for Life Ministries

"God's mercies extend to the hopeless, and this series of testimonies will encourage many struggling, drug-addicted inmates as well as ministers. These stories illustrate that 'Jesus is the greatest high on this planet!' "

> — **Jack "Murf the Surf" Murphy,** former Bill Glass Ministry International Prison Director, and Founder of Sonshine Ministry.

"The diversity of viewpoints in this collection of stories is an eye opener even for someone who has been an inmate and is now in full-time prison ministry. It just shows that God is everywhere and working His will through those who answer the call and say, 'Here am I, Lord, send me.' "

— **Jim Harris**, Founder, Fly Right Ministry and Area Director for
Bill Glass Champions of Life.

"I am confident the Holy Spirit will minister deep within the hearts of our loved ones through the writings in this book. As a mom who has a son who has been incarcerated several times as a result of addictions and poor choices, I believe these devotions will be priceless to men and women around the world to offer hope, healing and restoration."

— **Sharon Hill**, Founder, OnCallPrayer.org, and author of the
OnCall Prayer Journal

"Anyone who deals with convicts or ex-convicts understands the uphill battle most face from childhood through prison. Counseling alone will not change their condition of being unwanted, abused, rejected, or abandoned; only Christ goes beyond the counseling and rehabilitation process to reconcile broken people. It is God's grace alone that can take these precious people through that long dark walk into a life of complete health and restoration. These stories from prison confirm the truth of Christ in the worst of conditions and prove the hope and healing process to be only through the blood of Christ. This book promotes the restoring touch of Christ alone . . . and gives testimony to that healing touch."

— **John Schouten**, Lead Pastor, Vineyard Grace Fellowship

"Professionally, many of my patients, and more importantly their family members, are afraid of prison as a therapeutic tool. But so many lives are turned around through the humbling, and self-reflection forces found there. Personally, prison was the turning point of my life. These stories will inspire and invite a new perspective of God's love, forgiveness, and grace."

— **Karl Benzio, MD**, Psychiatrist, Founder and Executive Director,
Lighthouse Network

"*Stories of Faith and Courage from Prison* takes the reader into a world that most people avoid. Through gripping and thought provoking vignettes, the reader is exposed to myriad aspects of prison life and ministry. These devotionals open hearts to understanding, making all of us more compassionate human beings."

— **Cleo Lampos**, M.Ed. Speaker, educator, and author of *Teaching Diamonds in the Tough: Mining the Potential in Every Student*

STORIES of FAITH AND COURAGE FROM
PRISON

COMPILED BY
CONNIE CAMERON
AND **JEFF PECK**

GOD & COUNTRY PRESS

Print Edition: ISBN 978-0-89957-168-3
EPUB Edition: ISBN 978-1-61715-292-4
Mobi Edition: ISBN 978-1-61715-293-4
e-PDF Edition: ISBN 978-1-61715-294-8

First printing, October 2012. Second printing, April 2014.

Cover designed by Mike Meyers at Meyers Design, Houston, TX

Interior design and typesetting by Reider Publishing Services, West Hollywood,
CA

Edited and proofread by Rich Cairnes, Christy Luellen, and Rick Steele

Printed in Canada
20 19 18 17 16 15 14 –MAR– 8 7 6 5 4 3 2

Dedicated to all those who have seen His light in the darkness of prison.

INTRODUCTION

FEW TOPICS dominate the public conscious more than crime and punishment. A glimpse of local and national news helps make the case. The saying still holds, "If it bleeds, it leads." We can also scan our TV program titles and count the number of dramas with durable ratings—*Law and Order*, *CSI*, *CSI Miami*, *NCIS*, *Criminal Minds*, *Blue Bloods*, *Hard Time*, *America's Hardest Prisons*, *The Mentalist*, *Bones* and innumerable docu-dramas on news and cable channels unraveling mysterious crimes. It's positively endless.

No wonder our attitudes about the guilty fall into some understandable categories. Criminals in prison have incurred our wrath by stealing from us. Stealing takes many forms—assets, such as money and property, our security, our health, our dignity, our purity, and for some, their very lives. There are no victimless crimes. Just ask the families now bereft of a mom or dad or son or daughter due to drug abuse. They are suffering everything from shame, estranged relations, and/or financial ruin.

The book before you requires putting a few things into perspective. Unlike other devotional-style books designed to aid the reader in learning something about the person and work of God, the content here begins in a deep hole. Most of the storytellers have committed crimes—everything from low-level drug use, to fraud, to sexual assault, and murder. Like passing a traffic accident, you'll find it difficult not to stare at the carnage and shake your heads. Yet it is necessary to look at the darkness into which Christ himself has descended to liberate the captives.

For anyone who has been a victim of crime, especially violent or traumatic loss, do not be discouraged that your voice is not represented. The focus of these amazing stories is the God who reaches into the ashes to redeem the unredeemable. We live with a system that makes authentic victim-offender reconciliation next to impossible. While there are a few successful mentions recorded in these pages, they are by far the exception. Most repentant prisoners strongly desire to make things right. It is our hope that you hear those cries through their stories.

One final caution is in order and perhaps the greatest challenge in reading this book. No scripture better prepares us to understand the work going on in prison than Jesus' parable of the prodigal sons. I think most modern readers have thought the focus to be on the son that exploited his father's wealth and came to his senses in the pigsty (prison) of his own making. Surely, this describes prisoners, but not all. Jesus intended this story not just for the wayward sons in the audience, but also for the morally upright "elder bothers" who are just as lost. They have fallen for the deception that they have done everything right and are not in need of the Father's grace. Yet, by the end of the story, who stands outside the party, unwilling to accept the brother whom the father has restored?

The toughest questions raised by the life and times of people in the correctional system deal with how deep does God's grace really go? Does he really forgive that? Am I in need of that same grace? How should I respond to someone who has done horrible things? What does God want me to see about his capacity to love, forgive, and send?

Our prisons collect society's worst. We tell them they are failures and no longer welcome in civil society even after they are released. Yet God is at work on the cellblocks, in the yards, in the isolation chambers, in the gangs, and in the hearts of sinners . . . just like us.

Special Note: Due to the sensitive nature of the following material, and out of respect for the victims, several names have been changed from the original as noted by asterisks (*) throughout. We have faithfully tried to capture significant stories with integrity in the context of which they occurred; however, no story is a complete telling—if for no other reason than it is the perspective of one person.

SETTING PRIORITIES

Vernon Smith, Ohio

IT'S A NEW year and time to prayerfully make some changes. I have a heart for jail ministry, especially for aftercare. It presents huge needs—helping those recently released get back on their feet and hopefully not return to jail. But, I sense God wanting me to be more committed to my family's needs, putting them before my ministry.

One New Year's morning, the first thing my granddaughter asked me was, "What are you going to do today, Poppy?"

I wasn't sure, but I told Leslie we would do something fun together since she would be out of school. I offered to pick her up at 1:30. She smiled real big.

I had errands to run, but I had no idea I would receive so many calls that day. Mid-morning a man at a local recovery center called, an ex-inmate, who told me he would have to leave the local shelter because he had stayed his limit. He had heard about the Truth Transformation House we were running and wanted to know if we had room for him. I offered to pick him up because I needed to find out more about him; the House was drug- and alcohol-free.

Next, I received a call from a man who was a resident in the House. He was being released from the hospital thirty miles away and needed a ride home. I immediately wanted to do it, but God nudged me—I still had errands to run, and—what about my granddaughter? I prayed, "Show me, Lord, how to juggle all this."

I suddenly knew what to do. I got a message to my assistant about the resident in the hospital; she handled it. I picked up the first man and interviewed him while I ran some of my errands. I discovered he was forty-seven years old, had a disability, had filed for Social Security, could hardly read or write, and had never married. The receptionist at the recovery center told me he was quiet and caused no trouble. He was a believer—trusting God to meet his needs. He would fit right into the program.

After completing a few errands I looked at my watch.

Leslie! I had more errands, but they would have to wait. I took my friend back to the recovery center and arranged his admittance into the

House, then dashed home. Leslie grinned from ear to ear when she saw me.

In the past, I would have probably postponed this time with my granddaughter. But, this is a new year and I am committed to making needed changes in my life.

> Anyone who does not provide for their relatives, and especially for their own household, has denied the faith and is worse than an unbeliever. ~1 Timothy 5:8

JANUARY 2

JAMAICAN STANDOFF
Ron Nikkel, Virginia

IN MY CAPACITY as president of Prison Fellowship International, I happened to be in Jamaica. My itinerary included a visit to the largest prison in Kingston at the time. When I connected with the senior chaplain for the institution, I learned the visit was canceled. There was a standoff between the authorities and the inmates.

The inmates were on strike for food and better living conditions. It's hard to describe the circumstances facing inmates in countries outside the United States. There are many similarities, but often non-U.S. prisoners are far worse off. The place was terribly overcrowded, dismal, and filthy. They weren't getting adequate food or medical attention. Family visits were severely curtailed. There was nothing for the inmates to do except hang out on the yard in a facility with a crumbling infrastructure. In the washrooms, everything was broken, cracked, and slimy. There was no dining hall of any kind. Inmates brought whatever tin cups or plates they had, to be served from huge cauldrons. Jamaica is also a very hot, sweltering country with no air conditioning. You put it all together and it's just a miserable place.

Correctional staff had withdrawn from the yard and refused to dialog with the inmates. The chaplain and I said, "We'd like to go in." The officers painted a grim picture of what could happen if we went in. They didn't want to give us permission. Yes, they were legitimately concerned for our safety, but also they were trying to send a message to the inmates.

That was part of the problem, this tough authoritarian stand being displayed. For anyone to break that barrier through humanizing involvement would undercut their position.

We got permission anyway.

We entered, they locked the gate behind us, and we went immediately to the first group of guys and started asking them about their concerns, showing respect, hearing their complaints. We told them, "We can't guarantee anything. We just want to hear what you have to say, because we care, and we'll take your message back out."

We walked the whole facility. It had an immensely calming effect on the place. We sensed the presence of the Lord with us in a situation that could have been violent, but neither of us felt threatened or in danger at all. Showing a personal interest in people often diffuses potential violence.

Prison officials wanted to know what we heard. They were well aware of the complaints, but it helped impress upon them the fact that something needed to be done right away, or things were going to get worse quickly. I don't know what they did, but as far as we could tell, by the next day, things were back to normal.

In some respects, presence is as important as proclamation. When Jesus showed up, he ate with people, healed them, listened to them, spent time with them, and they were drawn to him. It's no different with prisoners.

> The Son of Man came eating and drinking, and they say, "Here is a glutton and a drunkard, a friend of tax collectors and 'sinners.'" But wisdom is proved right by her actions. ~Matthew 11:19

AN ADDICTION OF ANOTHER KIND

Dawn Anderson, New Mexico

SHE STOOD in my prayer line the first night I went to minister with a team at the women's prison. I guessed her to be around thirty or so, but the lines on her face made it obvious to me, regardless of how old she was, she had survived a very hard life. When she approached me, tears burst from her eyes. Jane* was an addict, and she exclaimed that she just couldn't go on being locked up any longer. "You've got to ask God to get me out of here," she cried.

I immediately said a silent, desperate prayer: "Come, Holy Spirit." I begged God for direction on how to pray with Jane. As I look back on that night, I don't remember what I said in my prayer over Jane. I do know, however, that when I was done she wiped the tears from her eyes and thanked me. She hugged me before she turned to leave and my attention quickly went to the next woman in line.

The following month when the ministry team returned, Jane's face lit up when she spotted me and caught my eye. Her countenance was so different from the first time I saw her! I hardly recognized her. Jane made a beeline in my direction and hugged me and said, "It happened! It happened!"

When I asked her what had happened, she told me, "What you prayed for really happened; God is real."

"Can you jog my memory, please? How did I pray for you?"

Jane excitedly continued, "You asked the Lord to take ALL my addictions and replace them with an addiction for him, and that's what happened!" Her huge smile lit up her face.

Jane went on to tell me that since the night I had prayed for her, she had only missed one religious service at the prison facility. And, the awesome part was . . . she now had a hunger for God's Word. She had been reading the Bible constantly along with an abundance of other Christian literature.

We talked for a while and I prayed with her again. This time, even though the holidays were right around the corner, she didn't ask for prayer to get out early. Her only request was for more of Jesus in her life.

> Blessed are those who hunger and thirst for righteousness, for they will be filled. ~Matthew 5:6

DIVINE APPOINTMENTS

Dawn Anderson, New Mexico

"DO YOU have time to see one more?" the deputy asked as I was on my way out the door of the women's module. "Sure," I said. "What's going on?"

He reported there was a gal really struggling in lockdown, and he felt she could benefit from a listening ear and a calming voice. I followed him to her cell, where he opened the door and a petite woman with deep, hollow, bloodshot eyes came out—with a look of great relief.

The deputy escorted us to the common area and we sat down together on the cold green metal chairs. She could hardly get her words out fast enough, but with a faint and trembling voice she said, "There *is* a God—my faith has been restored." I let her talk.

Julie* (I guessed her to be in her mid-forties) went on to tell me she had got hooked on crack cocaine, was arrested, and had been locked down detoxing for three days. Five minutes before I arrived, she cried out to God and said, "If you are real, show me."

When the deputy showed up at her door, unlocking it instead of looking in at her or motioning for her to settle down, she saw it as a true miracle. And the fact that he brought a chaplain with him really sparked her faith!

Julie's bitter tears of resentment turned to unstoppable tears of joy. Her faith, lost for years, had now returned.

We talked for quite a while. I led her in a prayer of rededication to Christ before I left, but not before promising to visit her again.

It was exciting to watch Julie during the remainder of her sentence. She grew in her faith by leaps and bounds. She was such a witness to the other girls in the module, too. Julie was always the first one in line to go to Bible study or worship services and encouraged others to come with her. Because of her renewed faith and the way she shared it, several others gave their hearts to the Lord as well.

Julie went on to a halfway house a few months later. She was anxious to tell others about the miracle she had received and the new life she was experiencing.

Julie and I are both grateful, too, that God laid it on the deputy's heart to stop me and ask me to visit one more.

But God will never forget the needy; the hope of the afflicted will never perish. ~Psalm 9:18

ENJOYING "SATAN'S PLAYGROUND"

Bill Meister, California

AS AN OFFICER with twenty-one years' experience, I did it all: worked a housing unit where inmates live and sleep, took care of daily programs, showers, and medicine, watched over them in the yard at the weight pile, searched inmates for weapons and drugs; pulled central control duty where we do all the counts, control the keys, and control emergencies, and processed the intake and transfer of inmates.

One of the more interesting day-to-day responsibilities is taking care of inmates inside. This includes getting men out of the hole, searching their property, seizing contraband (which makes people unhappy), and dealing with their attitudes. We confiscate a lot of stuff, which creates a lot of confrontation.

Despite all that close contact, I never had a problem with any inmate. I didn't mess with their stuff unless I had a good reason. They are all human beings. God didn't put me there to punish them. Prison alone is punishment. My job was to take care of them and meet their daily needs.

I remember one prisoner who yelled my name across the yard, "Meister! You racist #*@." This went on for weeks. I didn't know the guy. So, I raided his cell to let him know he got my attention. He quieted down and we actually got to where we could talk to each other. In a couple of situations I had helped his brother, who was also incarcerated. Eventually, whenever he needed something, he came to me.

Another time, by an act of caring, I made as much a friend of an inmate as I'm allowed. The prisoner known as "Whisperer," because of his raspy voice, was an old alcoholic. He'd been on the yard forever. I was standing next to the medical window when Whisperer needed to check on his prescription for eyeglasses. Inmates had to endure a lot of procedures to get even simple things. He was told they were in the warehouse. Nothing can be done until the warehouse delivers them and who knows when that will be.

I overheard this and told him, "Hey, I'm going over there now, I'll look into it." I came back with his glasses a few minutes later.

Whisperer told me, "You didn't have to do that."

Why wouldn't I do it? As a Christian, I have to live out my faith with people who "don't deserve it," because, actually, none of us deserves anything from God were it not for His grace. From that day on he was very respectful and told me, "If I ever hear of any plot against you, I'll make sure you know about it."

I actually enjoyed my career working inside "Satan's playground."

> Therefore, as God's chosen people, holy and dearly loved, clothe yourselves with compassion, kindness, humility, gentleness and patience. ~Colossians 3:12

JERKS ON THE JOB

Bill Meister, California

AS A CHRISTIAN in the prison environment, occasionally other officers gave me problems. During my duty as a corrections officer I had my own desk. You don't always get a desk depending on what duty you pull. Some other officers knew about my faith and would stick confiscated porn in my desk just to mess with me.

I hated porn. Inmates get it smuggled to them. When I turned up porn during searches, I'd make the inmate rip it up himself and dispose of it, because I wouldn't touch it. However, some of the other officers would keep it for their own interests or to stick in my desk.

Ironically, the biggest time of testing I faced during my long career was not with inmates, but working under a particular supervisor. I worked for this individual as a training officer. He was senior to me by only a few months.

He went out of his way to make my life miserable. He would change my shift hours. He would have me rearrange my work area just to irritate me. He was vindictive. We routinely worked with bus teams from all over the state, and he put a wall of division between them and our teams, when we needed to work closely with them. I reached the point where I was full of hatred for this guy. During this period he was involved in an automobile accident and I prayed that he'd been hurt so badly he wouldn't be able to return to work.

I wrote a memo to the captain's office about my differences with my superior and copied all departments so it couldn't be swept under the rug.

They just figured it was a personality conflict and let it ride for a few weeks. Then he gave me a job change without proper notification and altered my schedule, which is considered punitive. At that point I requested the union's intervention. After several months, my job was reinstated and the supervisor was moved. The whole affair bothered me deeply.

People think working with inmates must be really difficult because of the attitudes, language, and violence, and it certainly can be. Yet lousy attitudes are not limited to inmates. I expected better than to have to deal with a hostile direct supervisor and fellow officers goading me with pornography. Officers should be looking out for each other in case things get dangerous, yet stuff like this goes on. It tests the faith as much as walking a yard full of tense inmates.

Still, you have to forgive people, and move on.

> In this world you will have trouble. But take heart! I have overcome the world. ~John 16:33

NOT A SCRATCH

Bill Meister, California

ATTITUDES CAN make the difference between life and death in prison, and bad attitudes don't pay off. We had an officer who was very rude and disrespectful to the inmates. He had annoyed an inmate in a very volatile situation. The general population in this facility was a mix of people with violent crime histories, gang backgrounds, and not much to lose. It doesn't take much to make such an inmate really fume and plot revenge if an officer uses his authority to make life harder than it already is. Machismo runs strong both on the inmate side *and* the officer side. Neither group wants to be seen as weak or disrespected. Unfortunately, some officers believe they have to play this same game.

So this officer had a bad attitude and prided himself on having been assaulted by more inmates than any other officer. He was always badgering inmates. When that happens it's like lighting a fuse. The officer who follows his shift gets the bomb in his face. That's what happened in this case.

It caused a major attack. About ten corrections staff went to the hospital with serious injuries, and every single one was retired early because of what happened that day. And for what? Because an officer with attitude set off a payback bomb.

Had it happened on a Thursday, I would have been one of the first to respond to the situation due to my assigned position. But the attack occurred on Friday. Fridays and Saturdays were my days off for years. It seemed like every time something big happened, it happened on Friday.

There were a few other confrontations with inmates over the years, but none ever escalated for me personally. I wasn't sure exactly where my fellow officer was on each of these occasions, but out of nowhere he came to my rescue. Two different times I hit my alarm for help—in the blink of an eye he was there. In one case he came out of nowhere and tackled the offending inmate. I went twenty-one years without ever having an inmate lay a hand on me, and I never laid a violent hand on an inmate. I've been on the edge of it and responded to many emergencies. You can't always explain why God protects some from harm and not others, but I believe that God honored my commitment to respect and treat people the way Jesus did, even his enemies.

> For surely, O Lord, you bless the righteous; you surround them with your favor as with a shield. ~Psalm 5:12

A DIFFERENT ADOPTION

Beth Michael, North Carolina

MY HUSBAND, Jesse, and I were both raised in church and became Christians at a young age. But after fifteen years of marriage and a blessed, comfortable life, we had drifted into worldliness. We had everything except children, so I prayed and asked God for a child. I was not in the habit of praying or reading my Bible on a regular basis—only when I was troubled or needed something from him. Jesse didn't take time for God either; he was busy learning ways to make money.

I was going to church, usually alone, and I was a "good" person. It was not what I did that was a sin as much as what I left undone. My weaknesses included apathy, procrastination, and little love or thought for other people. I knew God had blessed us, but I did not feel gratitude. I took God for granted, somehow thinking I deserved a good and easy life. Jesse and I were not living our lives for our Lord. We were content and going merrily on our way, unaware of our neglectful lifestyle.

Thankfully, God did not leave us there! About twenty years ago he started moving in our lives to change us. First, all my friends were taken away except for one friend from church. Then, God nudged me to begin corresponding with prisoners immediately after I read Hebrews 13:3: "Remember those who are in prison as though being in prison with them."

At first, I was not sure this was a good idea. After all, I was expecting God to give us a child to adopt. I am learning that whenever God leads us somewhere other than where we have in mind, we come up with excuses or reasons for not following his way. I thought, *I won't be able to relate to prisoners. We won't have anything to talk about. What could we possibly have in common?* But praise God, I was obedient and began writing to Richard in May 1989.

It was easy to communicate with Richard so I decided to write to two more inmates. Each of those men ended up being a real challenge. However, I found that where I was not able, God stepped in and did the work through me. It became his ministry, and I became his willing servant. Thanks be to God, who put the earnest caring for these men into my heart and equipped me for every good work.

But thanks be to God who puts the same earnestness on your behalf.
~2 Corinthians 8:16

REFINED FOR HIS USE

Beth Michael, North Carolina

I WAS EXPERIENCING the supernatural love of Jesus for these men whom God had brought into our lives. I eagerly wrote them back and prayed for them every night. The Holy Spirit prompted me to get into the Bible so he could give me the words to say to them and the Scripture passages to share. God was leading Jesse into studying the Bible as well.

We endured a time of testing that took Jesse even deeper into the Word. Soon, God led us to sell our home and property and buy an old RV. We left North Carolina and traveled to the West Coast to visit some of our friends on the inside. By this time we knew seven inmates. We enjoyed wonderful visits with them and felt God's presence among us.

A year later we returned to North Carolina. We had expected our lives to resume a somewhat normal pace, but I became very ill. God had taught us so much, blessed us with an "extended family," and made us thankful children. We longed to get back to normal with a new focus on Jesus and walking in the Spirit. Although discouraged by the suffering he allowed, we chose to stand on his promises and found him to be faithful.

God has made us more usable, and transformed our hearts through our suffering. Because of the work he's done in us, we now have great confidence and unwavering trust in him. Remembering the parable of the prodigal son, most testimonies we hear are of the younger son who left home. My testimony is that God can change the heart of the brother who stayed home as well (Luke 15:11–32). I have been healed now for more than twelve years and am off all medication! And, we currently have ten beloved incarcerated.

And remember the "child" we thought we wanted to adopt? We now have a "spiritual son," Christopher. He, with our help and God's, began the Christian Pen Pals ministry (CPP) for inmates in the spring of 1998. We look forward to the future, knowing that God has a wonderful plan for us all. Our God is an awesome God!

All Scripture is inspired by God and profitable for teaching, for reproof, for correction, for training in righteousness; so that the man of God may be adequate, equipped for every good work. ~2 Timothy 3:16–17

ALL SOULS ARE WORTHY

Beth Michael, North Carolina

RICKY, ONE of the incarcerated brothers who writes to us, once told us prison is "God's Secret Place." It is where God sets someone aside, away from the world for a period of time, to draw him to saving faith in Christ. The time for running away from God is over, it's time now to listen and turn to him.

One of the greatest witnesses to the power of the gospel is the dramatically changed life of one who accepts Jesus into his or her life. When God brings a soul out of the pit of sin and darkness and gives new life in Christ, that person has a new song of praise to him. It reminds me of the story in Luke 18:35–43 about the blind beggar (who represents the spiritually blind, lost sinner). As Jesus passed by, the beggar cried out, "Jesus, have mercy on me!"

Those around Jesus rebuked the man and told him to be quiet. They, like many of us, tended to think some souls are not worthy of God's help. But Jesus stopped and helped him. He heard the blind man's plea and did as the man asked—he gave the man his sight. "Immediately he received his sight, and followed him, glorifying God."

Not only did the healed man give praise, but the scripture says, "All the people, when they saw it, gave praise to God." After Jesus touched the man, he was no longer blind and he was no longer a beggar. We don't know what became of him, but I expect he became a great disciple and soul winner for Christ.

If your eyes have been opened by Jesus, you need to let others know, too. All souls are worthy of his saving grace.

> I waited patiently for the Lord, and He inclined to me, and heard my cry. He also brought me up out of a horrible pit, out of the miry clay, and set my feet upon a rock, and established my steps. He has put a new song in my mouth, Praise to God. Many will see it and fear, and will trust in the Lord.
> ~Psalms 40:1–3

THE POWER OF THE PEN

Beth Michael, North Carolina

THE CHRISTIAN Pen Pals outreach has been ministering to inmates for thirteen years; literally thousands of lives have been touched and changed across many states and countries. We have no idea how many prisoners have been saved or have rededicated their lives to follow the Lord. Like many of us on the outside, they don't always go back and share with people the impact those people's words or letters have had on their life. So, we don't always know where the pen pal letters to prisoners take them spiritually, and what good works they might end up doing as a result. We do know of many inmates who have started ministries while incarcerated, and others after they have been released.

God tells us we each have a ministry. "Now all things are of God, who has reconciled us to Himself through Jesus Christ, and has given us the ministry of reconciliation" (2 Corinthians 5:18). With the Holy Spirit inside us to guide us, we each have the power to share Christ with others. Most prison ministries have huge needs. We need to be faithful to do our part and prayerfully consider getting involved in, and ministering to, the "least of these."

In my book, *Your Cry Has Been Heard*, I share many powerful testimonies of the effectiveness of one-on-one personal letters with inmates. The Christian Pen Pals ministry matches more than one hundred inmates a month with a Christian pen pal or a church group of writers. Many inmates are hungry to learn about Jesus and/or anxious to have a friend who cares. There are plenty of female volunteers for female inmates, but sadly, there is a wait of one-and-a-half to two years for the men to be matched with a pen pal—we need more male volunteers.

We are the hands and feet of Jesus, and the door of opportunity is open. What a blessing it is to be a spiritual mentor to another, no matter what ministry we're feeling "nudged" to serve in.

I thank God always that I said "Yes" to his Spirit and became a pen pal he can use to bless others. The Lord may want to use you, too, as a pen pal. Pray about it, and see where he leads.

He told them, "The harvest is plentiful, but the workers are few. Ask the Lord of the harvest, therefore, to send out workers into his harvest field." ~Luke 10:2

A TRAIL OF BLOOD

Jonathan Lowry, California

IN 1989 I'd been in the special housing unit ("SHU," or the hole) for four years as a member of the Aryan Brotherhood prison gang. I was part of a group of 162 inmates plotting to acquire plastic explosives and 9-mm pistols at Old Folsom Prison. We intended to blow up the industry area (cutting the power) and kill everybody we could in the chow hall. Someone informed on us, which is how I ended up in the hole. We were going to spend the rest of our lives in the SHU as far as the authorities were concerned.

While there I received a letter from a strange lady living in New Jersey. She wrote, "Hi. I'm a Christian. God put it on my heart to write to you. I don't know how to write to inmates, but your cousin works with me and she gave me your contact info. So this is who I am. God loves you." She went on to tell me where she lived, where she worked, and what kind of car she drove. As I read this letter I was thinking, *This woman is insane!*

I wrote back, "If you want to write someone in jail there are rules: Don't tell 'em where you live, or where you work. Don't send money . . ." I gave her every rule that I've ever used to abuse other people.

She kept writing for about a year. I would never answer any of her Christian stuff. She stuffed books in big brown envelopes. I threw them away. One day I was really frustrated with her and wrote, "I do not like people. People tell on each other, hurt each other, smile in your face, and talk bad about you behind your back. I only like animals."

The next envelope arrived with a one-page letter—a miracle—and a single tract inside the letter. I threw the tract in the trash and read the letter. The first sentence said, "Do not throw this tract away (I know you did)." I have a shaved head, a giant mustache, tattoos everywhere, and am rippled with muscles. I put my hand on my hip and asked, "How did that woman know that?" The next sentence said, "Read it—it's important."

So I dug it out. The tract was made from a 1957 *National Geographic* story called "Barry the Heroic Dog." Barry is a rescue dog in the Alps with forty-one saves—more than any dog. The system is easy: An avalanche comes or a person is lost in the forest, they let the dog find the missing person while rescuers track the dog. On this outing, Barry found a lost man who was hallucinating as a result of hypothermia. The dogs are trained to lie on top of people to keep them warm until rescuers show up.

The man thought Barry was a wolf and stabbed him just as hard as he could. Barry ran back toward his master, but bled to death on the way. The owner found the dog and followed the blood trail back to the man.

The next sentence rocked me to the core: "There's a trail of blood that leads to Calvary."

Right there, I gave my life to God. My cellie, a huge Aryan Brother I'd known five years, said, "Man, you are out of your mind!"

I said, "I'm done. I'm a Christian."

> God presented Christ as a sacrifice of atonement, through the shedding of his blood—to be received by faith. ~Romans 3:25

JANUARY 13

THE COST OF LEAVING

Jonathan Lowry, California

A ST. BERNARD led me to the Lord, but I really knew very little about the faith. I started reading the Bible and I gave an extra one to my cellie, JP. I told him, "Read the Old Testament. It has war stories, it's cool." He used it under his TV to tilt the screen so the sun wouldn't reflect on it. What I did realize was that I had to leave the gang and that meant contracts would be issued for my death. To this day there are standing contracts on me.

There was a meeting in the yard with my ex-gang friends. They determined that if I so much as wrote a note or talked to staff they would kill me. I said, "No problem."

A week later they sent a youngster after me with a knife. I expected it. I didn't get hurt and no one got caught. Three weeks later, they sent two youngsters after me—one got hurt, the other ran away, I was okay. Third time, we were going through chow hall. JP told me, "Excuse me, let me get some extra bread" and he cut in front of me. One of the guys serving bread had a shank taped to his hand. His job was to kill me in line. Somehow JP knew, hit him in the throat with a tray, and put him down.

Shortly after the chow line scrape, I was invited to another gang meeting. They concluded that I was not revealing any gang secrets or flaunting my leaving. They left me alone and reminded me there would be a hit if I broke any of their rules. That was the beginning of my walk with the Lord. Several months later I was transferred to another prison and put on general population rather than isolation. The staff didn't trust me, the Christians didn't trust me, the gangs didn't trust me. I was on the yard all by myself—except for God. It took many years for people to trust me because I'd spent many years doing some terrible things with the Aryan Brotherhood.

There's a worship song with the line, "I'll never know how much it cost, to see my sin upon that cross." When I think about my background, the people I've manipulated, abused, and victimized, I just weep, because I know I'm an expensive kid . . . and God still loves me.

> For whoever wants to save his life will lose it, but whoever loses his life for me and for the gospel will save it. What good is it for a man to gain the whole world, yet forfeit his soul? Or what can a man give in exchange for his soul? ~Mark 8:35–38

JANUARY 14

FEAR GOD, NOT MAN
Jonathan Lowry, California

IT WAS THREE months before my release date. I'd been incarcerated almost eighteen years and become the inmate pastor on the yard at Calipatria.

In 1998 the California Department of Corrections ruled there would be no more family visits for lifers. The Mexican Mafia gang ordered a statewide work stoppage in two weeks in protest. No one could come out of their cells on Monday. I got caught in a crossfire. As a Christian, many other Christian prisoners came to me asking, "What do we do, Jon?"

I had a politically correct answer: "That's between you and God. Pray about it and make your own decision."

The weekend before the strike, my wife visited me. I told her about the order and that anyone who crossed the line would be stabbed. Being a gang dropout, there would be a contract on me. My stabbing would result in a homicide. I searched the Scriptures and prayed diligently. God says not to fear man, but to obey God. He told me, "Choose you this day whom you will serve." On that Saturday I had chosen to serve God and not man.

She said, "What does that mean?"

"Honey, if they open my door on Monday, the DOC rule is that I go to work. I'm going to step out of my cell." My wife broke down and began sobbing. Then she did the coolest thing and said, "Let's pray about it, because God will watch after you."

That was the longest visit I ever had. Heart-wrenching. I didn't know if I'd see her again this side of heaven. I knew I had hurt her feelings and frightened her, yet I saw great faith in my wife.

So with trepidation, I went about my business. I prayed extra hard because I determined that on Sunday I would (1) apologize to the church for giving them politically correct answers, and (2) let them know what I was choosing to do. As soon as chapel released, it meant news would be on the yard.

Sunday came. I told them my decision and specifically that God had told me not to fear man and to obey those in authority as long as they do not ask me to violate God's Word. Immediately they all stood—half were angry I had endangered the entire Christian population by my choice and the other half were mad at them for being mad at me.

I stood there wondering, *Where is their faith?* My faith was in God— not that he was necessarily going to get me through this, but that no matter what, Christ was going to be with me, as he promised.

Come Monday, the doors opened, and everybody came out— statewide. Not one prisoner went on strike.

> Therefore, it is necessary to submit to the authorities, not only because of possible punishment but also as a matter of conscience. ~Romans 13:5

CHANGING PERCEPTIONS

Jonathan Lowry, California

I WAS PAROLED to Imperial County, California. Parole agents distrusted me, and the community thought a maniac had moved in. But one guy agreed to meet me when I began searching for work. The first time I came by I noticed he had some people cutting down trees at his house. I told him the men he'd hired were "all a bunch of dope fiends. They are going to steal from you." With my background, I can spot them anywhere.

He said, "No, it's okay." That afternoon they cut a tree down that smashed his fence and snapped a telephone line. They panicked, stole all his electrical tools, and were gone.

He called the next day and asked if I wanted the job. I said, "Sure!"

I'll never forget his words when I arrived. He said, "I don't trust you, but I trust my Lord. If you've given your life to Christ, you're a new creation. You can prove it to me."

So I worked at his house for a couple of months building things. I discovered he also owned a Chevy dealership, and that they had an opening for a service manager. At a staff meeting he posed the idea of bringing me on. They agreed to offer me that job. That's kind of wild—right out of prison—to be offered a service manager position! He asked me, "Do you want the job?"

"I have to go home, ask my wife, and pray about it." He laughed at my answer in a good-natured way. Maybe I haven't mentioned that I married that lady who started writing to me from New Jersey, the one who told me too much about herself. We talked, we prayed, and I ended up working for that man more than ten years. That was an important perception change God worked out on my behalf—that a guy with my past could demonstrate to a skeptical world how I'd really changed.

Do not be anxious about anything, but in every situation, by prayer and petition, with thanksgiving, present your requests to God. ~Philippians 4:6

THE GUY FROM PRISON WORKS THERE

Jonathon Lowry, California

I'D BEEN at the car dealership for about a year when a mechanic bought a big cockatoo. He asked me to help transport the bird because he'd never touched one before and he knew I had a bunch—over a hundred, actually, plus a bunch of Rottweilers, goats, and other critters.

I arrived first at the home of the bird's seller. After knocking, a lady answered with two young kids. I introduced myself saying, "I'm here to help with the bird."

"Sure, come on in," she said in a very friendly way. When I pulled in I noticed they had a Dodge truck in the yard. To make small talk and maybe a sale, I half-joked, "Why don't you come buy a Chevy from us?"

"We can't go because the guy from prison works there," she said.

"That's me."

You could see stark terror cover her whole countenance. Instinctively, like a she-bear, she put her kids behind her. It crushed me. It was real awkward until the mechanic arrived. We got the bird and left.

When I got home my wife thought I'd wrecked my motorcycle because I had a look of total defeat. I work *very* hard for people to understand that God has changed me. You shouldn't judge a person's past. Judge what they are doing now.

The next day I was surprised when the lady called me. She invited me over to talk to her and her husband. After praying I went over, not knowing what to expect.

This amazing couple welcomed me in and explained to me they were Christians. They apologized for judging me. He's a captain in the prison and she's an MTA (medical technical assistant). All they've ever been told about ex-prisoners is to be on guard and don't trust them. I suppose they think payback is coming when an officer meets an ex-prisoner on the street.

But the apology caught me way off guard. Without faith in God, a corrections professional can't just apologize to a tattooed ex-prisoner. You can't step out like that without real faith.

"Do not seek revenge or bear a grudge against anyone among your people, but love your neighbor as yourself. I am the LORD." ~Leviticus 19:18

ALL THINGS ARE POSSIBLE

Jonathan Lowry, California

IN MY WORK as a field director for Prison Fellowship, I frequently visit the prisons in my area of responsibility, including Centinela, B yard. The number one gang member, Bo*, ran the whole yard. He was Muslim and a black guerilla family member—you don't see too many of them on the mainline anymore. He's a martial arts expert. He has been involved in homicides in the prison—all done with his hands. He's a very dangerous person. I watched as, not just me, but other Christians talked to him and planted seeds over a year. Intellectually Bo would spar with you. But he could never get over the fact that the Christians wouldn't get upset with him.

One day a white guy was on a list to get stabbed because he owed the blacks money for drugs. A volunteer named Harry talked to Bo and told him, "God teaches us to forgive one another. Sometimes it's really hard. Try something for me today. Think of someone on this yard that you just cannot stand. Go by and give them a gift, and say it's all right, I forgive you."

That night, when Bo was let out of his cell for showers, he slid a Top Ramen soup under the bar doors of this white guy and said, "Here man, take this!" and walked away.

When the white guy got out for showers, he took it back and said, "I think you made a mistake and slid it under the wrong door." In prison, it's not a good idea to just accept a gift because often there are strings attached that you cannot afford to pay.

Bo shot back, "No! I'm learning this forgiveness stuff. Take the damn soup!" The next day Bo asked to talk to me privately. He almost started crying . . . almost.

"I don't know what's going on. There's something going on inside me. I don't like this. It's like I have to forgive this guy and I've told everyone to back off of him. I'm not sure what to do."

I told him, "That's God working on your heart 'cause he loves you so much." He literally went to his knees and accepted Christ right there. That's someone you would never imagine—a Muslim, shot-caller, and hatemonger. We later worked with him when he was transferred to another prison. Today, he has led more Muslims to Christ than anyone I know. He's doing life without parole.

> Although I am less than the least of all God's people, this grace was given me: to preach to the Gentiles the unsearchable riches of Christ . . .
> ~Ephesians 3:8

LOCKED UP FOR FREEDOM

Connie Cameron, Ohio

THE APOSTLE Paul and his friend Silas were stripped and beaten before being incarcerated in Philippi, a Roman colony in Macedonia. Their charge? Teaching people some "customs" the Romans deemed illegal. Paul and Silas had commanded a demon to leave a slave girl, thereby drying up her master's source of income. Basically, they were being arrested for setting someone free from internal torment.

Around midnight, while in prison and in chains, Paul and Silas were singing and praying out loud to God as the other prisoners listened. "Suddenly there was such a violent earthquake that the foundations of the prison were shaken. At once all the prison doors flew open, and everyone's chains came loose" (Acts 16:26). Imagine the effect on those other prisoners as they heard the worship, felt the earthquake, and subsequently gained their freedom.

In 1963 another earthquake of sorts occurred in the foundation of the American church. Dr. Martin Luther King Jr., a civil rights leader from the South, was incarcerated in Birmingham, Alabama, for trying to set some people free, to help black Americans gain the same rights as whites. While he was locked up, Dr. King wrote his powerful "Letter from Birmingham Jail," an epistle addressed to nine white liberal clergymen who opposed his peaceful civil rights activities as being "unwise" and "untimely." Dr. King's well-crafted letter pointed out the lack of integration within the church, and the lack of support by the clergy for equal rights. This letter would ultimately usher in the 1963 Civil Rights March on Washington, D.C., and the 1964 Civil Rights Act.

Dr. King wrote in his letter:

One may well ask: "How can you advocate breaking some laws and obeying others?" The answer lies in the fact that there are two types of laws: just and unjust. I would be the first to advocate obeying just laws. One has not only a legal but a moral responsibility to obey just laws. Conversely, one has a moral responsibility to disobey unjust laws. I would agree with St. Augustine that "an unjust law is no law at all."

Both Paul and Dr. King obeyed the promptings of God to "go" and "do." They didn't think about themselves, they didn't count the personal cost—rather they saw the bigger picture. They were willing to be locked up for a greater cause than themselves—for the freedom of others.

> I will go to the king, even though it is against the law. And if I perish, I perish. ~Esther 4:16

JANUARY 19

USING TIME WISELY

Connie Cameron, Ohio

DURING THE five-and-a-half to six years the apostle Paul spent as a prisoner, he wrote several letters to different churches encouraging them to be more like Christ and to follow God's Word. Even though he was in tremendous pain from beatings he endured for Christianity, he still chose to help others. He could have written letters of complaint about his unfair situation, but instead his message was how to get closer to the Lord.

Much like Paul, Dr. King wanted to encourage others by writing his in-depth letter to the church leaders. Dr. King could have focused his time and energy on getting out from behind bars, but instead, like Paul, he chose to use the power of the written word to carry out God's work and to help others get free. Both men realized that even though they were in prison, they could still serve God, be a blessing, and make a difference in the lives of the oppressed. Regardless of their personal discomforts, they could still fulfill God's purpose for their lives.

For these two men, the advantage of being locked up was that they were able to gather their thoughts, spend lots of time with God, and articulate clearly the message they were given to share. As Dr. King explains in his letter to the nine leaders of Southern churches:

> Never before have I written so long a letter. I'm afraid it is much too long to take your precious time. I can assure you that it would have been much shorter if I had been writing from a comfortable desk, but what else can one do when he is alone in a narrow jail cell, other than write long letters, think long thoughts and pray long prayers?

God knows each of our situations and wants to use us to make a positive difference in the lives of others. Even behind bars we can sow seeds of peace and brotherhood.

Dr. King took full advantage of his situation, being in solitude and with no outside agenda, to think, pray, and write. He used his time wisely to craft a powerful letter that was a springboard to desegregation and helped get the church "on board" with God's truth.

> In the same way, those of you who do not give up everything you have cannot be my disciples. ~Luke 14:33

SICK AND TIRED OF BEING SICK AND TIRED

Jeannia Parsell, Ohio

I AM IN MY late forties and for twenty years of my life I lived in a whirlwind of destruction. I was a full-blown drug addict and alcoholic. I did whatever I needed to do to get my next high. There was nothing pretty about those years, or the pain and heartache I caused my family and those who cared for me.

I "thought" I had hit rock bottom on October 3, 2005, when I got pulled over for my second drunk driving charge in a year. But, a few days later, I went out on a seven-day drug binge. The world had become very overwhelming to me and I was convinced everyone was out to get me; major paranoia had set in. The last thing I remember was crying out to God and screaming, "I can't do this anymore!"

On the eighth day I awoke at the hospital. I had no idea I had overdosed on drugs. All these machines were hooked up to me, keeping me alive and functioning. When I was able, I left the hospital (against medical advice) and went home.

Extreme depression began to set in. I was so sick and tired of being sick and tired, I saw no way out. I soon became a cutter. Cutting myself helped to release all the pain I felt inside and for a short time I would feel better.

While I was hospitalized I was unable to appear in court for my charges. My husband called the court and explained to them what was going on. When I finally did appear before the judge, he said he would let me go on a bond. However, the probation department put a hold on me and I was escorted to a detox center. Our local center was full, so I was transported to a mental hospital. I was not a happy camper. After five long days there, I was transported to a rehab center where my new life in recovery got started. That was on October 18, 2005—my official sobriety date.

I learned a lot at the rehab center and did what I was asked to do. Although my mind was still very foggy, I tried to figure out why I was still alive when all I wanted to do was die. *Could God possibly have a purpose for sparing me?*

> Heal me, LORD, and I will be healed; save me and I will be saved, for you are the one I praise. ~Jeremiah 17:14

SAVED BY GOD'S GRACE

Jeannia Parsell, Ohio

AFTER SEVERAL months of inpatient care I was released and had to go before the judge for my charges. I was sentenced to thirty days in our local jail. I was terrified.

As I was being transported from the court to the jail I suddenly started praying. Except for that day when I cried out to God that I couldn't take it anymore, I hadn't prayed since I was a young child. I wasn't even sure I was doing it right or if God even existed.

I had been in jail for several long days when a group of ladies came to the facility to do a Bible study. I decided to attend the first class. One kind lady immediately asked me if I needed a Bible, gracefully handing me one and telling me it was mine to keep. As I sat there, listening to the Word of God, something started to happen inside me. I had no clue what it was. All I knew was that I liked the words that were being read and the way they made me feel.

As the week went on I kept reading more of the Bible. I didn't understand a lot of it, but I was compelled to keep reading. One of the very first verses I read was Deuteronomy 7:6: "For you are a people holy to the Lord your God. The Lord your God has chosen you out of all the peoples on the face of the earth to be his people, his treasured possession." That was the first time I realized I was a person who had value to someone.

When the ladies returned the following week, I accepted Jesus into my heart as my Lord and Savior. I began walking with him, praying, and reading my Bible every day. I had heard the Bible study leaders say, "It's up to you what choices you make when you leave here." I was determined to take it to heart.

When I got released from jail I was still on fire for what Jesus had to offer me. I immediately connected with a woman who loved the Lord and who was willing to show me his ways. Soon after, I found a church and dedicated my life to the Lord. I truly believe I was washed clean of all my sins! How amazing it was for me to know that all the things of my past were forgiven. I no longer had to carry that heavy weight—Jesus paid the price for me when he went to the cross.

Therefore, if anyone is in Christ, the new creation has come: The old has gone, the new is here! ~2 Corinthians 5:17

BIRTH BEHIND BARS

Janice Banther, Florida

IT WAS THE EARLY 1980's when I first became a doula; someone who assists a woman in childbirth. A doula does not perform any medical procedures or deliver the baby. She is there solely to support the mother.

My desire to be a doula began with an international student I knew who was pregnant and married to an American. She was scared of giving birth and clueless, so I offered to be with her and her husband when the time came. From that experience I was hooked. I knew immediately I wanted to continue being with women in childbirth and to be a doula.

I took classes and read up on childbirth to educate myself. Then, in 1991 my nonprofit organization, For the Love of Birth, was born. My heart's desire was to do more than comfort these women, though. What I really longed to do was share God's love with them and give them hope in Jesus.

Ten years later, after learning about the poor treatment of many pregnant inmates, I prayerfully contacted our local jail to inquire about childbirth classes. They did not offer such courses, but they were willing to let me teach them. Prison ministry immediately grabbed my heart, and my eyes were opened to the huge need for doulas inside prisons. Many pregnant inmates were shackled to their hospital bed with a guard (usually male) watching them through the birthing process. There was little modesty to speak of and no one to coach or comfort them.

Getting permission to assist inmates during birth was not easy, but I persevered, working hard to prove I was trustworthy. Fast-forward to today; we have a staff of ten female volunteer doulas in our jail ministry, Birth Behind Bars. We also teach women across the country how to have similar programs. Our recent classes, "Shaken Baby Syndrome Prevention" and "Happiest Baby on the Block," are now offered to both female and male inmates. Our goal with these programs is to build positive parenting skills, including infant CPR, to help inmates stop the cycle of abuse in their families.

As we help these women during one of the most important times of their life and show them love, we pray they will see Christ's love in us. Each life is precious to God, no matter the age.

Dear friends, since God so loved us, we also ought to love one another.
~1 John 4:11

SET FREE

Teresa Sewell, California

THOUGH I experience freedom in the physical sense, I have been a prisoner of my prejudices toward certain groups. One of those groups was inmates. But in 2003, my biased attitude toward inmates changed drastically when my stepbrother, Bill, was convicted of a felony. It landed him in a federal prison and caused him to lose his profession.

Some of my relatives severed contact with him. Compelled by the love of Christ, I opted to stay in touch with Bill. His letters allowed me to peek inside an inmate's lifestyle.

In addition to having a family member imprisoned, God called me to volunteer in prisons through the Mission of Grace Foundation, founded by Carol Davis. Initially her workshops helped me form my mission statement and catch a vision for the second half of my life. Our lives have continued to intersect for nearly fifteen years. Two years ago she informed me of a shift of focus to prison ministry. Knowing I am bilingual, she invited me to join her team. The team worked together for two summer months.

After successfully surviving the background check, I prepared for my first visit inside the prison. Clothing had to be baggy and in certain colors. The security check required me to remove my eyeglasses, watch, and hair accessories. Car keys were exchanged for a badge and whistle. I kept my driver's license to show at a second station.

I began to sense a loss of freedom and a taste of prison life. The tower guard controlled the opening of the chain-link fence gate. Another guard controlled the barred gates through which I passed to get to the Family Reception Center. The meeting place we gathered in featured a mural of well-known places, many of which the inmates had not seen.

Denim-clad men shuffled into the room. I greeted them with a smile, a handshake, and a simple greeting. Once they got settled in their groups I gravitated toward the Latinos and introduced myself. They seemed genuinely appreciative that I came to visit them and that I could speak their language. My compassion grew as I made weekly visits and prayed for the men and their families. At the end of the two-month tenure, sadness filled my heart. The program was over—it was time for our team to go home.

Weeks later when Carol's husband brought me a handmade thank you card from the inmates, tears gushed out. They had become my friends and I missed them.

Through family and volunteer experiences, my perception of prisoners has been transformed. Now I see Christ in them. The Lord set me free from my prison of prejudice and filled my heart with compassion!

> I will praise the LORD all my life; I will sing praise to my God as long as I live. He upholds the cause of the oppressed and gives food to the hungry. The LORD sets prisoners free. ~Psalm 146:2, 7

JANUARY 24

WHEN LIGHT PENETRATES THE DARKEST CELL

Enrique Vasquez, Texas

MY GANG name was *Chamuco*—Spanish for "devil." I was a leader of the most notorious and oldest of prison gangs in Texas. Security staff rightly perceived me as a threat to keeping order, and to other inmates, so they tossed me in solitary confinement.

This was my third time in prison. Yet I still trained gang members in organized crime and I had a vast network of contacts in gang life. And in this gang, it's "blood in, blood out."

While in solitary, I listened to my music, Metallica. One song, "Nothing Else Matters," stopped me short. I wasn't seeking God, but I was beginning to think about what my life was leading to—what I believed, what I was involved in. It wasn't what I had signed up for.

Gang life promised to be about honor and integrity. When they choose you, it's supposed to be for those qualities. We're not supposed to be recruiting soldiers and crash dummies (although that's what happened). While I was outside between sentences, I saw most of the guys were junkies, strung out on heroin and cocaine. They weren't fulfilling their duties. It discouraged me. Then I'm back inside and back in another gang war—a dead end.

So this song I mentioned has the words, "Trust and seek and I'll find in you/open mind for a different view/Nothing else matters." I realized I couldn't have an open mind—gang mentality kept me in the same cycle of lies, madness, ruthlessness, and manipulation. I couldn't trust in someone as this song was talking about.

And all for what? Death. Then what? Judgment, and then hell. I did go to Catholic church as a little kid. I was taught to fear God through tradition, not through a relationship. I thought, *There is a God and I will stand before him and give an account.* When I beat up Christians I justified it as an act for God because they were fake, and God didn't want fakers who marred his holiness. I had a really warped way of thinking.

I'm going to hell to suffer for eternity. That's what all my fighting gets me, everything I represent and believe. I started crying. Something hit my whole body and it was saying, "You weren't meant for that. There has to be an alternative, something better than that."

I felt overwhelmed with remorse and regret. The song ended and I heard a voice say, "Trust and follow me. Nothing else matters." That wasn't part of the song. I was still crying and feeling overwhelmed. I said, "God, is that you?" I'd never talked to God. I said, "If that's you, show me and I'll live and die for you. Just give me another way of life."

> "Follow me," Jesus said to him, and Levi got up, left everything and followed him. ~Luke 5:27–28

DECISION TIME

Enrique Vasquez, Texas

I TOOK OFF the headphones and snapped back to my old self. *You're not supposed to be feeling—that's weak.* I shook it off and went to bed. *This can't be happening. You just went on a trip with the music, you're claustrophobic, it's psychological, just let it pass.* As I slept I dreamed of a dirt road with two paths. I didn't know which one to take.

The next day I paced my cell and God spoke to me again: "You asked me to show you if I was real. I did. Pretend none of this happened and that will make you the very thing you hate—fake. Or, you can surrender, follow me, and you can be real."

It was the hardest struggle I've ever had. What will people think? Am I going to have to be Pee-wee Herman with a big old Bible? A monk? Those Christians I used to beat, would I be like them? I didn't know what it meant, just a lot of negative stereotypes. But I knew God was telling me, "I've reached out. It's your move."

If God is God, he's almighty, he can do anything. The way it stands now, I'm going to hell as soon as someone puts a shank in my throat. Clearly, I'm already committed to death; why not commit myself to die in the cause of God's kingdom? I didn't know anything about Christ yet. *If God is real, he'll back me up, protect me, save me, and lead me.*

I got on my knees and said, "I'm going to live and die for you. Now lead me, talk to me. What do you want me to do next?"

The next day, I told an officer, "I'm renouncing the gang, get me out of here." I also wrote a letter to the guys nearby telling them I could no longer represent the gang. They thought I was joking. The major and assistant warden called me in for a talk because it looked like games to them. I told them I had accepted God in my life. They laughed and said, "Everybody has accepted God around here."

"That's what I've done. I don't play with God and I'm not playing with you. If you put me back with my old gang and they kill me, it's on you because I've let you know." They moved me to another solitary cell block with others under investigation. They weren't sure if my decision was real or an attempt at manipulation.

During this time I learned about the faith, bought Christian books to share, sent neighbors letters, and shared with them through the bars. Six years later officers said I'm for real or a good actor. They put me back into general population.

I have revealed and saved and proclaimed— I, and not some foreign god among you. You are my witnesses," declares the LORD, "that I am God."
~Isaiah 43:12

THE SHANK FOR THE CHRISTIAN NEXT DOOR

Enrique Vasquez, Texas

WHEN THEY moved me to the new solitary cell, the guy next door cussed a lot. He saw my gang tattoo and asked about it. I asked, "Who are you?" He told me his name was Deshon* and that he was a Christian.

I shot back, "Why don't you act like one?" He started cussing me out. "Do you know who I am?" He just shouted all the louder.

Watching from the second tier, another inmate recognized me. I looked up using a mirror and he asked me through hand signals, "Is that you? You letting that guy talk to you like that?"

"Yeah. Could you send me a knife because I'm about to kill this dude. He disrespected me." I also told him I'm out of the gang because "I gave my life to God, but still, send me a knife."

Oddly, he had been writing to a Christian lady who had sent him something he really wanted me to read. He wasn't a Christian, but he challenged me: "If you really are a Christian, read this before you kill him."

He told me to look up Matthew, chapter 5, verses 23 and 24. Jesus explains that before you come to the altar to worship—if someone has something against you—you reconcile with him before you stand before God. Forgive them, or your heavenly Father won't forgive you.

This can't be real. I got angry. *I just renounced this gang, I'm out on a limb in this investigative cell block and God's telling me to forgive? You're telling me to tell that dude that* I'm *sorry? I've never forgiven anyone in my life. It's just pride.*

I felt God repeat back to me, "You said you'd live and die for me. Let's see."

I was so upset, I didn't eat. I didn't go to showers. I wanted to throw the Bible out of my cell and quit. I just kept wrestling with God in my flesh and former identity. After several days, I made my decision.

Deshon actually knocked on my wall and asked if I was okay.

"Hey, I've got to ask you something. I need to ask you to forgive me," I replied.

,"No, man, you didn't do nothing wrong," Deshon said. "God told me to tell you *I'm* sorry. All the time I've been a Christian, nobody has ever corrected me. You're the first one. I've been reading my Bible, and I'm sorry."

"Naw, dude, be quiet a minute. I need to tell you *I'm* sorry. I was about to kill you." He got quiet. He asked again, "Have you accepted Jesus?" We were both guilty of the same thing. Turns out he knew the Scriptures very well and he led me all over the Bible.

> But now that you have come to know God, or rather to be known by God, how can you turn back again to the weak and worthless elementary principles of the world, whose slaves you want to be once more? ~Galatians 4:9

THE VALUE OF A SOUL

Enrique Vasquez, Texas

VIOLENCE WAS one area of challenge I prayed to God about. I asked that I would never lay my hand on anyone again in violence, and for His protection. I didn't want to kill or hurt anybody.

One day, staff moved me from the bottom floor to the fourth floor where all my former gang buddies lived. When the cell door closed I heard an inmate say, "Somebody messed up when they transferred you here."

I was asking God, "What are you doing? Is this it?"

Soon, I will have to walk out of my cell for recreation or shower and the gang will try to kill me for my disloyalty. My thoughts were confirmed when I received a kite (message) from downstairs. The inmate wrote, "I'm praying for you. Don't come out of your cell whatever you do."

Suddenly it dawns on me. Two cells down is a gang member I knew well. Together, we used to make people "catch out." We forced inmates to choose between death or requesting protective custody. It clears a cell block of people you don't want to live there any longer.

For a year I felt God telling me to witness to that gang member. I had been telling other new converts that the minute you sense God prompting you to share your faith with someone, just do it. The results are in God's hands even if that person is your enemy. God is reaching people through us. We have to obey.

For a year I just hadn't done it, don't know why. I became determined to go down in obedience. I apologized to God. If I die, I'm going to heaven. But if he dies, that's it. He's lost. I remember thinking, *Is this what it takes to get me to obey?*

I put together a package with a Bible and slung it to him. He got it and stayed quiet. Then the call for recreation went out. I heard the gang preparing to make a hit. I felt peace. As officers began to release our cell doors we heard the "ninja turtle steps." That's what we call the special officer group that does difficult cell removals. Suddenly, twelve fully-dressed officers in pads, shields, and helmets stop in front of my cell and order me to step out. They proceed to escort me back down to my old cell. As I walked down the row surrounded by these big dudes, the other inmates cheered, clapped, and praised God.

But I wasn't a hero. It was just God trying to get me to be obedient and reach out to a soul that was lost. Later some of the guys from my former gang renounced the gang, too, and came to Christ because of my testimony. As much as I'd been studying Scriptures, I'd still needed to learn the value of a lost soul.

> "Do not be afraid of them, for I am with you and will rescue you," declares the LORD. ~Jeremiah 1:8

JANUARY 28

SPARED AGAIN

Enrique Vasquez, Texas

SOME OF the original and oldest gang members knew me well. They believed in me. I was their shining star, being the youngest to make it into leadership. Two of them said to me after I left the gang, "If we can't do any good for you, we're not going to do anything bad. We're proud of you. You made a big move. You need to represent that." They respected the authenticity of my choices. But the younger generation was different. They didn't really know me, just knew of my reputation and to young gunners, if they could knock out someone like me, it builds their own status as a rising tough guy.

One afternoon on my way to lunch—after six years of solitary, I was now back in general population—two of these young guys walked toward me with some kind of metal rods or knives, I couldn't quite tell. They were supposed to take me out now that I was more accessible. All movements are controlled within prisons. You can't go far before someone has to confirm your ID and let you through somewhere. I was heading to an access gate that would let me into chow hall after a vocational class.

I knew who they were. They had recently transferred over from the Darrington Unit and were trying to make a name for themselves. I started praying, "God, I asked to never get in this situation again, but David said you strengthened his arms for war and you made him wiser than his enemies."

I got to the gate and there were about two hundred guys waiting. They clear you through by calling out your name alphabetically. I'm at the bottom of the list because I'm Vasquez. The guys coming after me know I can't go anywhere until called and that's their opportunity to attack. I'm getting tense thinking, *I'll take the older one first then the younger* . . . then I prayed again, "Deliver me from this!"

All of a sudden I heard someone shout, "Vasquez. Vasquez!" Confused, I look around—it's the gate officer.

"Come on, boy. What's wrong with you?" He opens the gate to let me through. He started at the bottom of the list rather than the top. The crowd parted to let me through. I showed my ID, looked over my shoulder at the two dudes who were now clearly frustrated, and headed straight for my cell, where I got on my knees and thanked God.

Deliver me from the sword, my precious life from the power of the dogs.
~Psalm 22:20

34

TRYING TO PAY FOR MY SINS

Enrique Vasquez, Texas

GOD TRANSFERRED me to another prison, Ramsey III, just in the nick of time after I had challenged several former gang members to either kill me or leave me alone. While I was bold for Christ, I wasn't always bold in the right ways. If you're going 150 miles per hour and throw the brakes on, you skid for a while. It was hard for me to be forgiving, be kind, give up old tactics, and use God's tactics. Still, God has mercy.

Gangs are everywhere and transferring doesn't always fix the problem. But at Ramsey, they left me alone. That's when a volunteer came into my life, Brother Vic. He visited once a month for three years and would always ask me the same question: "Rick, you got a plan?" He meant a plan for reentering society. I joked and said, "Yeah, planning to get killed and take as many of them with me as possible." I never expected to be released, or live to see a release date. It just never crossed my mind. The seriousness of leaving an ex-gang member alive should not be underestimated. They were supposed to come after me or it would reflect on them as cowardly for not punishing my disloyalty.

Actually, I didn't think I deserved freedom. I thought I was punishing myself for all my past deeds by believing I'd never be free again. It was a subtle form of pride. I thought I was making a contribution to pay for my sins by my willingness to stay and die inside. I didn't fully understand grace yet. I learned much later the true value of those amazing words in Scripture that tell me my forgiveness was paid for once for all—it really is a free gift.

> Unlike the other high priests, he does not need to offer sacrifices day after day, first for his own sins, and then for the sins of the people. He sacrificed for their sins once for all when he offered himself. ~Hebrews 7:27

FIGHTING TO SUBMIT

Enrique Vasquez, Texas

FINALLY MY mentor, Brother Vic, thought it was time to challenge my thinking about being free and said quite soberly, "One day you're going to get out and you need a plan. You need to think of your daughter."

Not long after he gave me that thought to chew on, officers called me for a parole interview. I'd been denied ten times already. With that track record it was hard to keep from feeling defeated before I went in, but I still carried a faint hope that this time might be different. I sat down in front of the panel of judges, who asked, "Why should we let you out?"

"I have a daughter, a mother. I gave my life to God and left the gang. Why would you let me out? I have no idea, but I know that I'd like something different." They said, "Okay." and excused me. Well I was so upset for the next few days because I was sure they would deny me again. And while I was twisting inside about it, I heard the Lord say, "Ask me."

I wouldn't. I prayed for everyone else, but rarely prayed for myself. But the Lord knows me and he was saying, "I know what you want. You want your freedom, but you have to humble yourself and ask me." I bucked against it. I hated to be on my knees because the officers used to force us to our knees all the time in a position of submission and weakness. Anyway, I got on my knees, started crying, and said, "I know I don't deserve it, but if there's any way, I'd like to be free from here. But don't let me out unless you can use me, I don't want to end up back here like a failed, fake Christian."

Three days after the parole interview and my prayer, I got a note at mail call—my parole had been approved. What?! I got scared. *Uh-oh, God gave it to me. Now there's going to be new responsibility.* You can believe I got serious with Brother Vic and asked him to help me with a plan.

"For I know the plans I have for you," declares the LORD, "plans to prosper you and not to harm you, plans to give you hope and a future. Then you will call upon me and come and pray to me, and I will listen to you." ~Jeremiah 29:11–12

THE DAY OUR LIVES CHANGED

Carol Kent, Florida

WHEN OUR only child, JP (Jason Paul), was born, we were thrilled. We had such high hopes for him and he grew up to be focused, disciplined, compassionate, and lots of fun. JP had a strong faith in God, and as he matured he developed a determination to change the world for the better through military or political leadership.

In high school, JP was the president of the National Honor Society. After high school he received an appointment to the U.S. Naval Academy, where we enjoyed four years of parent visits—celebrating large and small accomplishments with him.

At Jason's first duty station in Florida, he met the girl of his dreams and they were married. She had two adorable little girls from a previous marriage. My husband, Gene, and I quickly embraced our new roles as Grammy Carol and Grampy Gene. Then, just months later, tragedy struck.

Our daughter-in-law's ex-husband had been allowed by the court only supervised visits with his daughters due to allegations of abuse. He was now petitioning to have unsupervised visits and it appeared they would be granted. There were multiple allegations of abuse against the biological father of the girls. Our son became obsessed with his fears for the girls and he began to unravel mentally, emotionally, and spiritually. One year after his marriage, my husband and I received a middle-of-the-night call telling us Jason had shot and killed his wife's first husband.

Our lives spiraled into an abyss of shock, disbelief, and mind-numbing pain. We struggled to grasp this horrible truth. *How could our son have done this?*

We couldn't forget the family of the deceased, or our precious stepgranddaughters, who had lost their biological father. Our hearts broke for them, too.

The next two-and-a-half years were a blur of legal battles. But in the end, Jason was convicted and sentenced to life in prison, without parole.

Nothing would ever be the same for any of us; our "normal" had changed forever. I now understand how someone could die of a broken heart. My heart had been shattered into so many pieces I wondered if it would ever mend.

But I was to learn, over time, that as I kept giving God the pieces, a miracle of healing would take place. Along with it came a surprise—I realized I was much stronger than I ever thought possible. As I continue this journey and give God each piece, he has been faithful to bring healing. God is truly a restorer of broken hearts, an ever-present comfort through our toughest storms.

> He heals the brokenhearted and binds up their wounds. ~Psalm 147:3

CAROL, JASON (JP), AND GENE KENT

CHOOSE TO BELIEVE

Carol Kent, Florida

I WAS RAISED in a strong Christian home with five siblings. Our parents encouraged us to pray and memorize Scripture at a young age. Early in my teens, I knew I wanted to serve God. I longed to share his powerful message of love and forgiveness with others, so I chose communication arts and speech education as my majors in college.

Gene and I were devoted to the Lord, to one another, and to raising JP to know and serve the Lord, too. We were faithful to keep God first in all areas. So, when life didn't go as planned and we were dealt such a hard blow with our son's life sentence, it was tempting to entertain thoughts of, "Where are you, God? Couldn't you have stopped this?"

During those times when the Enemy whispers the loudest and tries to convince me I have served a god who doesn't care, it helps me to reflect on Job. Job had been blessed by God and he was "blameless and upright; he feared God and shunned evil" (Job 1:1). Yet, God still allowed Satan to attack him. Job lost everything—his livestock, his servants, and even his children.

Job's immediate response was, "'Naked I came from my mother's womb, and naked I will depart. The Lord gave and the Lord has taken away; may the name of the Lord be praised.' In all this, Job did not sin by charging God with wrongdoing."

When Job's friends appeared on the scene and insisted Job had sinned, that he had brought his calamity upon himself, Job became seriously depressed. He began to believe their message and plunged into depression—wondering if he had anything to live for.

Depression over ongoing negative circumstances can wear us down until death looks more attractive than life. Job was at that point. And at one time or another each of us walks through suffering that feels intense, not unlike Job's. However, Job's story does have a happy ending; God ultimately blessed him with even more than he had before.

It comforts this mother's heart to reflect on this story. It is a reminder we *can* survive depression, we *can* make it through tough times, and we *will* know peace again.

Be strong and take heart, all you who hope in the Lord. ~Psalm 31:24

MARRIAGE MATTERS

Carol Kent, Florida

THE STRAIN of a child's incarceration on a marriage can be devastating. After our son Jason was arrested, I noticed a change in my relationship with my husband. We became short with each other where we were normally patient. Minor discussions would sometimes escalate into loud arguments.

In the past, when one of us was upset about something, the other would be there to offer comfort. But since we were both experiencing such constant pain, we were too emotionally drained to offer each other much consolation. Our lives had been shattered in a way never before experienced.

Thankfully, Gene and I were able to recognize what was happening to us. We knew that the Enemy thrives on destroying marriages; he comes "to steal and kill and destroy" (John 10:10). We vowed not to let Satan get a foothold in our relationship. Over time, we learned it's better to talk to each other frankly about the real issues we are facing than to get mad over petty irritations that become full-blown fights—all because we are dealing with a challenge that threatens to suck the life out of us. We now know that when little issues spark small disagreements that could put us at serious odds with each other, it's time to pause long enough to recognize what's happening and remind one another, "This isn't the real problem, is it?"

It's hard to see even a glimmer of light at the end of the tunnel when a loved one is facing a life sentence. But by reminding ourselves that we are both grieving and in pain, it helps us to be more patient with each other. Rather than allowing our despair to drive a wedge between us, Gene and I have become closer as we are more open and honest with each other. Knowing we will have to deal with our son's situation for the rest of our lives (barring a miracle), we are determined to keep communication open between us, and to keep God at the center of our marriage, trusting him to help us through each day.

Trust in the LORD with all your heart and lean not on your own understanding; in all your ways acknowledge him, and he will make your paths straight.
~Proverbs 3:5–6

ARRESTED BY COMMUNISTS

Kim Humphrey, Vietnam

THE COMMUNISTS arrested me June 9, Ron's birthday, just weeks after the fall of Saigon, Vietnam, in 1975. In 1970, Ron, an American with the Military Assistance Command, Vietnam, befriended me after my husband was killed in the war. After Ron's tour he was transferred to Cologne, Germany, where he later got me out of the country and convinced me to move to the United States. I couldn't leave my children, who were with my mother. I had to return. Ron set me up with documents and we thought I could get in and get out. However, standing in the embassy yard, I watched as the last U.S. helicopter disappeared.

Six weeks later my brother, Tranh, and I were arrested and taken to the Vinh Long City jail. There were already more than one hundred prisoners and most of us had been associated with the Americans or the old government in some way.

The Communists sent Tranh to reeducation camp since he had only been a low-level policeman for the former government. I was a major problem.

By linking me to Ron they suspected me of working for the CIA. They asked why I had come back to Vietnam just as everyone else was trying to leave. They thought I had been sent by the CIA to set up a new spy network.

Every day we had to listen to propaganda and communist indoctrination. I could sing so they made me learn their songs and teach them to the other women. I was forced to read propaganda lessons to the other women at night by the light of a dim bulb.

I insisted I had known Ron, but only as his girlfriend. I couldn't tell them about working with the *Van Tac Vu* (a traveling musical troupe which included propaganda messages in its program) and going up on the loudspeaker airplanes, which were part of Ron's psychological operations missions.

After three months things turned harsh. First, they isolated me in a small bamboo cage—the Americans called them "tiger cages." I was left there for three days and nights. When they took me out, I couldn't stand up. They dragged me to the old Catholic chapel on the prison grounds and locked me in there.

They had wrecked the chapel. But I found pieces of a crucifix and put them carefully back together. I had grown up Buddhist, but from some of my friends who had been Catholic and from Ron, I knew this was "Jesu," and he was supposed to be much more powerful than Buddha. I tried praying to Jesu and hoped he would understand me speaking in Vietnamese.

> Those who know your name will trust in you, for you, LORD, have never forsaken those who seek you. ~Psalm 9:10

FEBRUARY 4

TORTURED CONVERSION
Kim Humphrey, Georgia

A COUPLE OF days later, I was taken into a new room with a North Vietnamese army major. He pointed to a chair at a small table opposite him and ordered me to sit down. Then he began flipping through a large file folder. I tried to read it upside down from across the table. I was terribly scared.

I realized it wasn't my file, it was Ron's! The Communists knew everything he had ever done! I saw a name written in one corner: Khanh. We thought Pvt. Khanh was a Viet Cong defector. Instead he reported on what the Americans were doing where Ron worked. I wondered if they knew what I had done to help with Ron's mission called the Phoenix program.

The major began asking me questions about my relationship with Ron and slapped me hard several times. I stuck to my story and he beat me up, hitting my face many times, nearly closing my eyes and splitting my lips until they bled. I still insisted I knew nothing.

Then he called a couple of helpers. One of them held me down while the other used a pair of pliers to yank out my waist-long black hair, leaving painful bloody patches on my head. Finally, they tossed me back into the empty chapel.

At the next day's interrogation the major handed me a pre-written confession and a pen. If I signed, they promised to let me go home to my children.

I knew better and refused to sign. Back to the chapel, but this time the two helpers tied me up, tore off my clothes, and raped me in front of the figure of Jesu. This happened for three days. I refused to sign their papers.

One day when I was alone, a male prisoner walked outside the door, paused for a moment, and whispered, "Kim! Don't give up. We know what they do to you and your courage to resist gives the rest of us strength!"

For the rest of the week, they continued to rape me and beat me at the chapel. At last they stopped and took me back to the cell with other women. My hair was gone, my head was all bloody, and my eyes swollen almost shut. When the women saw me they quickly signed the confessions that had been prepared for them.

They were all taken away and I was the only woman left. The guards said they released the others for their cooperation, but the male prisoners reported that anyone who signed a confession had been killed. I was locked again into the small chapel where I found the broken crucifix I had hidden. I knew if I had signed their confession, my children would no longer have a mother. I held the figure of Jesu to my face and cried and cried. All I could say over and over was, "Thank you, Jesu, thank you, Jesu, thank you, Jesu."

> He will call upon me, and I will answer him; I will be with him in trouble, I will deliver him and honor him. With long life will I satisfy him and show him my salvation. ~Psalm 91:15–16

RESCUE AND A RAW DEAL

Ron Humphrey, Georgia

I MET KIM in 1970. I worked with a team of military, state department, and CIA people called the MACV—Military Assistance Command, Vietnam. I was on a province team with about ninety military and eleven of us civilians. Kim was the girl next door, a widow, and

43

mother to four children and she needed work. I hired her as a part-time interpreter.

I really grew fond of Kim and our friendship eventually turned romantic. Things got complicated when I left in 1971 to hold a diplomatic post in Germany. I was able to get Kim out a few times and work for me again while in Germany, but then the war looked like it was going to be lost in 1975. Rules forbade me from accompanying Kim home during the frenzied exit of U.S. forces. Reluctantly, I set her up with the kind of documentation I thought would get her out as the North Vietnamese closed the ring around Saigon.

My worst fears were realized when I heard of her arrest. I spent the next year pulling every string I could think of to find a way to get her out. She had served American interests at considerable personal risk and I really cared for her deeply. I knew what the North Vietnamese army could do to prisoners. I had seen their malicious work while in country. I was really afraid.

Sweden was one of the few western nations that kept a consulate in Hanoi after the fall of Saigon. They let me talk to the ambassador and send diplomatic cables to the French, who still had some presence in Saigon. The French got someone to find and visit Kim in the Mekong Delta prison. Long story short: We got Kim out of jail in 1976 and in July 1977, I succeeded in getting both her and her kids stateside.

Then came my biggest shock: I was arrested January 31, 1978, on charges regarding breach of national security. While using my influential position within international diplomatic circles to free Kim I did bend some rules, but in no way did I breach national security. I knew better than that. The main problem was a Vietnamese expatriate who had been caught for something else, and in a way to deflect guilt from himself, or at least to reduce his punishment, he fingered me as a convenient fall guy. Though my case was eventually appealed to the U.S. Supreme Court, they declined to review it.

It was a raw deal all the way around. I received a fifteen-year sentence. Kim and I had married during the long court ordeal and now I feared I would never see her again.

A bruised reed he will not break, and a smoldering wick he will not snuff out, till he leads justice to victory. ~Isaiah 42:3

MAD AT GOD

Ron Humphrey, Georgia

DURING THOSE early days, I thought I'd never see Kim again. At age forty-five, I didn't know if I'd make it through prison. A lot of bad things happened there. The federal system is a bit better than the state system, but where I was, about half the prisoners were Colombians in for drug offenses (often violent), on whom you never turned your back. So we formed little defensive cliques. I joined the group of ten Vietnam veterans. We embellished our reputations as headhunters and half-crazy from post-traumatic stress disorder.

You live day-to-day, not year-to-year, because you don't know if you have a future. I'm in here because I tried to save people from prison, torture, and death. How could God let this happen? I wrestled with that for years. As time passed we no longer feared for our personal safety. Now it was down to a mental thing. Could we tough it out? Could we maintain sanity in that environment and for how long? I would be denied parole four times—a nonviolent, first-time offender with good behavior. Others were getting out with far worse on their rap sheets.

The first week after you've been denied parole you mope badly. You had your hopes up so high. I thought, *God let me down. Here was his chance. He could have touched the hearts of those people and said, "Send him home now."* For months I was angry with God. I didn't need a miracle. I just needed three people to say, "He's done enough." But it never happened. I became the most senior inmate at that facility. Yeah, I was mad at God.

It was also incredibly stressful for Kim and the kids. They were all learning English and working. Kim became a nurse's aide in hospices and nursing homes and the kids worked odd jobs just to eat and pay bills. We had a phone call once a week and one weekend visit per year. That's all she could afford given she was in Virginia and I was in Connecticut. She'd arrive Friday night, visit Saturday and Sunday morning, then leave Sunday afternoon. I had to pull strings to get two consecutive days, which was not supposed to be allowed. We loved our time together, but didn't just chat. We had to lay out plans for an entire year: what the kids would be facing, finances, school—everything—because they were totally new to our country.

There was a long period of bitterness for me. I don't know if it showed. I didn't have many good thoughts about the government. I focused on my family and my prison job. But the bitterness lingered for a long time. I ran on fumes. Healing for me would not come until God spoke to me through several trips I would take after my release.

> I remember my affliction and my wandering, the bitterness and the gall. I well remember them, and my soul is downcast within me. ~Lamentations 3:19–20

FEBRUARY 7

LONG WINTER OF BITTERNESS

Ron Humphrey, Georgia

AFTER ALMOST nine years of incarceration I reached my maximum release date when they have to let you out.

One of the things that kept me going those years was my relationship with Prison Fellowship (PF). My family had been among the first to benefit from a new program called Angel Tree®, which helped prisoners' families receive Christmas gifts and the gospel from the parent inside. I met the founder, Chuck Colson, and he even made a personal promise to assist me when I got out.

I learned that my case manager denied my application to a halfway house in Fairfax, Virginia, which had been willing to take me. I wrote a letter to Mr. Colson and reminded him of his promise nine years ago. Three days later officers appeared telling me to pack my stuff—I'm going to the halfway house. *Okay!* For the first time in years, I sensed God stepping back in and making something happen. Soon thereafter, PF offered me a job. I told Mr. Colson I was never going back inside a prison—ever. So they assigned me to the IT department.

Several other ex-prisoners worked at PF and were conducting in-prison Bible studies. They invited me several times, but I always declined. Then came the first whiffs of spring in my long winter of bitterness.

I traveled to an American Correctional Association convention in Minnesota on assignment. An officer announced a tour of a local prison and my PF boss recommended I go. Reluctantly, I submitted. We pulled up to the modest Oak Park Heights administration building. We went through a small sally port, into an elevator, then we went down. The whole prison is underground. Inmates surface only for visits. I spent time with the chaplain and talked to many who were going to live and die in that hole.

Soon, another trip took me to Louisiana to visit Angola maximum-security penitentiary, with its famous inmate rodeo. I met a special person, Johnny Brooks. Wearing a white cowboy hat, Johnny was a tall, well-built black man who had won the prisoner rodeo many times. He really impressed me. A few years later I returned to do another story about the seminary that Warden Burl Cain allowed in the prison. I asked, "How's old Johnny doing?" Warden Cain took me to visit his gravesite at the Angola cemetery; he had died of a heart attack. His weather-beaten old hat rested atop his grave.

Not long after, I interviewed Calvin Scott, who served twenty-two years and was exonerated by the Innocence Project. He had always maintained his innocence. The DNA testing not only cleared Scott, but identified the real culprit—a fellow who had been Scott's workout partner.

After all these experiences, I looked back at the dignified Brooks, the men never getting out of that hole in Minnesota, and the injustice Calvin suffered, which reminded me a little of my own episode. God put it all in perspective. By God's grace I had finished ahead of them all—alive, healthy, married with family, with a great job and true friends. The bitterness melted away. I am a stubborn old man, but God waited for me. I still had a chance to embrace my experiences in Vietnam and in prison and make a difference. And that's what I've been working at doing ever since.

> I remain confident of this: I will see the goodness of the LORD in the land of the living. Wait for the LORD; be strong and take heart and wait for the LORD.
> ~Psalm 27:13-14

DREAM CHANGER

Brandon Duncan, Wisconsin

AS A YOUNG child I was in constant fear of my stepdad; he physically abused everyone in my family. I think that was why I liked watching gangster shows on television. It was my "escape." I would dream about becoming a "bad man," then no one would ever hurt us again.

As early as age nine I smoked pot and tried alcohol. It numbed the constant fear and enhanced my self-esteem. I also started stealing anything I could get my hands on. Between the drugs, alcohol, and stealing, I was making myself a prime candidate to become involved in a gang/criminal lifestyle.

As I got older I felt powerful when I broke the law, but it eventually caught up with me. I was convicted of armed robbery, burglary, credit card fraud, driving under the influence, and possession of drugs. I faced hundreds of years in prisons in several states. I actually served fifteen years inside some of America's bloodiest prisons.

Prison was hell. I was terrified every day, and especially at night. Each morning I woke up full of hate, rage, and violence, and went to bed with fear. But a few years after I was sentenced, a Christian man came to visit. He was an ex-inmate.

How did he make the crossover from darkness to light? I wondered.

He patiently explained to me that Jesus died for my sins and that I could have new life in him. Longing to change, I prayed the salvation prayer. But the hateful lifestyle was ingrained in me and instead of embracing Jesus and his Word, I quickly chose to go back to darkness.

My rage escalated toward those prisoners who were incarcerated for abusing children. One day, when a new inmate arrived who had violated a child, I snapped and almost beat him to death. I wish I could say I was remorseful, but I wasn't. Due to my violent outburst, however, I was moved to another part of the prison where the hatred was even worse. I became so despondent during those months, thoughts of suicide plagued my mind constantly.

All I had for a pillow was my Bible. One desperate day I opened it up and began reading the red letters. I knew those were the words of Jesus. I read his soothing messages for hours every day. Gradually I started to change. I actually began to dream about the future, something I had never

48

done before, and to set goals, too. I was actually getting excited about getting out. I even had hope I could get my family back in my life again.

Then, one day, all those red-letter words came together to convict me.

> I have loved you with an everlasting love; I have drawn you with unfailing kindness. ~Jeremiah 31:3

THE BIRTH OF A MINISTRY

Brandon Duncan, Wisconsin

I REALIZED GOD was real and I suddenly, desperately, wanted him in my life. I dropped to my knees and cried out to him as I never had before. I asked him to save a wretch like me, to forgive me of my horrible past, and to help me to love others. I was serious about it. It was all or nothing. I wasn't going to play at being a Christian—I was going to serve Jesus with my entire life.

I was amazed at the peace I began to feel and the sense of protection I had on my life. I dug deeper into the Word and I also started corresponding with those in a biker ministry. They helped me to get anchored in my new life in Christ. I found out, too, my mom had become a born-again Christian and had been praying for me to come to Christ. It humbled me and encouraged me as I witnessed firsthand the power of prayer, knowing my family had been praying for me.

As a young man striving to be a "bad man" gangster type, I had never dreamed of living past thirty. My goal, if you could call it that, was to survive each day. Prison wasn't much different in that respect, that is, until that day I gave my life to Jesus. I suddenly began thinking about my future from a Christian perspective and praying about how I was to serve God.

When I finally got out of prison I went to church regularly and worked hard at gaining the trust of my family and friends. My mom was amazing. She stood by me through everything.

Before my release from prison I prayed about what I should do for the Kingdom and how I would serve. My passion was to reach out to kids in turmoil and pain, those who were at high risk for gang/criminal lifestyles. I knew God wanted me to do my part to help prevent or end some of the suffering that goes along with being in a gang. Amazingly, doors started opening for me to begin a unique crisis intervention program to keep kids from getting involved in gangs, and to help those kids who want out, to get out.

> Therefore, with minds that are alert and fully sober, set your hope on the grace to be brought to you when Jesus Christ is revealed at his coming. ~1 Peter 1:3

FEBRUARY 10

WORTH THE RISK

Brandon Duncan, Wisconsin

IT'S TAKEN a few years, but the ministry God laid on my heart, Fierce Youth Outreach (FYO), has slowly developed roots. I constantly stress to others that the agenda of this ministry is not to police the streets or to battle gangs—law enforcement will do that. Our goal is to reach kids who are at risk for gang recruitment and to show them there is a better way— that someone cares about them. To accomplish this means giving them a place to belong and instilling in them a sense of self-worth. Those are two things all kids long for and that a gang will offer them. Part of our strategy at FYO is to teach them job skills and get them involved in church.

So, like I said, I don't work for the police, I work for God. Most gang members have an underlying respect for God. Thankfully, they tend to leave me alone to safely perform my ministry, but gangs don't discriminate against color, creed, or anything else. Prisoners are actively recruiting new gang members (especially young kids) from inside their prison cells. Incarcerated gang members are more powerful than most people can grasp. It truly is a fierce battle for our youth.

FYO now has a core team made up of professionals who have each gone through rehab and life-changing struggles. They can relate to these kids. Some team members are former criminals or gang members, but now live productive lives. We don't have all the answers, but we care about these kids. And it doesn't come without risks—to myself, my team, the kids, and their families. I have to be very careful. There are different types of gangs and the ranks within the gangs can get very complicated. We always hope a member can get out of the gang quickly and without repercussion, but there are times when the individual and his family might have to relocate out of state. We take the steps necessary to hopefully ease the suffering.

I am committed to giving my life to serve my Lord. To God be the glory!

> Then Jesus said to his disciples, "Whoever wants to be my disciple must deny themselves and take up their cross and follow me. For whoever wants to save their life will lose it, but whoever loses their life for me will find it. What good will it be for someone to gain the whole world, yet forfeit their soul? Or what can anyone give in exchange for their soul?"
> ~Matthew 16:24–26

FEBRUARY 11

BEYOND MY WILDEST DREAMS

Brandon Duncan, Wisconsin

MOST COMMUNITIES want to turn a deaf ear to the truth about gang activity. They only really sit up and pay attention after someone has been killed. God has laid it on my heart to go into schools and churches to share what's going on and how FYO can help. I speak to groups, and also one-on-one, to teachers and parents about dealing with gang involvement.

The most rewarding aspect of this ministry, though, is to gain the trust, confidence, and even love of a troubled child. One mother who was interviewed for a newspaper article about FYO said, "Brandon can relate to these troubled kids. He builds their trust and can be on their level." After her son's involvement in FYO, she and his teachers noticed a remarkable improvement in him.

Of course, all ministries require money to operate, but I don't want to ask for handouts. Instead, we've produced a Christian music CD to raise proceeds. It's titled, "In His Hands," and features more than twenty songs all donated by artists who are supportive of this cause. We chose to include all types of music in order to reach all types of kids. We're also publishing a manual that will focus on the real reasons kids join gangs, and how gang outreach extends from the prison to the streets.

I am excited about this ministry and am amazed how God is working through me and the other volunteers to touch these wonderful kids. I've been interviewed several times and recently shared my life story on *The 700 Club*. My heart's desire is not to lay blame on my upbringing or my poor choices that landed me in prison. Rather, my goal in any interview is to give glory to God. And, I want every child to know it doesn't matter where you are or what you may have been through—if you give it to God, he can make something good out of your life, for his glory. God can use us. He can wipe away everything and make us brand new. I want them to know God personally, and to know he does not make junk.

It is so wonderful now, to wake up every day with excitement to serve my Lord and Savior, instead of waking up full of hatred and rage. Today I am living a life I never imagined someone like me could. I am truly blessed.

> Truly I am your servant, LORD; I serve you just as my mother did; you have freed me from my chains. I will sacrifice a thank offering to you and call on the name of the LORD. ~Psalm 116:16–17

STAY ON YOUR KNEES

Connie Cameron, Ohio

GOD DEALS with each of us in a different way. Since he is the one who knit us together, then he is the only one who knows what it will take for each of us to surrender and turn our lives over to him. For some of us it takes being locked up to get us to look up. For others, it takes breaking our heart through the loss of one of the "created" to enable us to see our Creator. It can take feeling hopeless and desperate enough to "hit bottom" in order for us to climb out of our pit. It can take being humbled to our knees, to enable us to stand again.

While Abraham Lincoln was never incarcerated, he still experienced a form of imprisonment as a result of depression. His first documented battle with the illness was brought on as a result of being deeply in love with a woman who ended up marrying someone else. Then, a few years later, she passed away due to illness. For months Abe had no will to live.

And we are well aware of the burdens he faced in his presidency over the Civil War. A popular quotation that expressed his desperation well is, "I have been forced to my knees many times on the realization that I had nowhere else to go." With the weight of the nation on his shoulders and feeling somewhat alone with the many huge decisions he had to make, President Lincoln was wise enough to know he needed divine help. In order for him to "stand," he knew he had to first kneel, and ask for God's divine intervention.

It has often been said God is no respecter of persons. The same God who listens to a president's plea for wisdom as to how to govern a divided nation, also hears the repentant cries of a convicted criminal. And that same God hears the desperate wail of a mother's broken heart after visiting her handcuffed child in the presence of law enforcement.

Many hearts have undergone a humbling transition, both on White House floors and behind steel doors. Don't give up on your loved one. Stay on your knees—for them.

> Hear my prayer, LORD; listen to my cry for mercy. When I am in distress, I call to you, because you answer me. ~Psalm 86:6-7

MY FATHER, "BABE"

Scottie Barnes, North Carolina

MY FATHER, James Fred "Babe" Pennell, started his life in crime in what the old-timers called bootlegging. Later he moved into the drug world. We lived in the small town of Taylorsville, North Carolina, where everybody knows who you are and town gossip spreads quickly. He was a powerful and wealthy man and in prison often throughout my entire life.

During every visit there was a longing to have a father/daughter relationship. As a little girl, I wanted my daddy to love me like other daddies loved their children. So I was always reaching out in ways I thought would result in his love for me.

For example I often said, "I love you, Daddy," hoping he'd say it back. He never did. I would dream of him asking me how I was doing in school. I excelled academically and won honors, but none of that mattered to him. I think that's why I pushed so hard, so he would see he had a daughter of whom he could be proud. I'll never forget in the ninth grade when he walked into my bedroom, looked at my acne-covered face, and said, "Your face looks awful. Why can't you do something about it?"

It broke my heart. I was clinging to any hope that we could be a normal family. He missed my graduation and my wedding. I ached to see him show up at both events and be proud of me, but momma and I were a responsibility he didn't want. Every time he rejected me a wall would build up higher, topped by a razor wire of bitterness.

In spite of all this, we continued to visit him when he would go to jail or prison. I just kept hoping.

The incident that capped it for me occurred when we went to pick him up from prison (again). We arrived at the gate only to be told by an officer he had already left with another one of his women. With all his wealth, he'd begun seeing many other beautiful women. So at age thirteen I started trying to live in my own world, telling myself, *I don't need him, I'm going to be all right without him.* I really hoped I would never see him again.

> For he has not despised or scorned the suffering of the afflicted one; he has not hidden his face from him but has listened to his cry for help. ~Psalm 22:24

BREAKING MY HEART

Scottie Barnes, North Carolina

GROWING UP in the South, my momma had me in church and I acted the part of a Christian without actually having a relationship with God. It wasn't until I married that the Holy Spirit pierced my heart with the truth that my behavior wasn't adequate to make me a Christian. Though I hated my daddy, I still nursed a deep wound wanting him to love me. Coming to Christ, finding forgiveness of my sins at the cross, was my critical first step.

Although I still didn't love my dad, I started praying for him, but what's wrong with me that I can't pray with a broken heart?

One day Daddy knocked on my door, home from a four-year stint at the Atlanta Federal Penitentiary. *Oh Lord,* I thought, *what am I going to do with this man?* He moved in next door.

When I sang in the choir I could see people pointing at me and whispering to each other. A neighbor told us she didn't want to be living next to a drug kingpin. I was worried about my family and children.

Babe hadn't changed and carried on with his activities until I got a call from Myrtle Beach—he had a heart attack and probably wouldn't survive it. He put me down as next of kin. That was the first time, ever, I felt he needed me.

I drove in record time to the hospital. Entering the ICU I thought, *Daddy needs me. It's going to be okay from now on.* But he didn't have the Lord and he didn't know *how* to love me even if he finally realized he needed my help.

His health was a roller coaster. I tended to him and wanted to be there, but I still wasn't over all the hurt and rejection. He recovered enough to come home, where he had a small stroke.

He asked me one day to ride with him to a little country store. "I'm going to get me a baloney and cheese sandwich."

He sat down and began to eat. One side of his face didn't work very well from the stroke. I watched a powerful man with rolls of money in his pockets try to chew his food while pieces kept tumbling out the corner of his mouth. It totally broke my heart. I finally felt compassion for my daddy.

That's the first time I wept bitter tears over him. I could now pray for him earnestly with the right kind of heart. I got on my knees and said,

"Lord, forgive me for hating my father and tonight I ask you to save his soul. Whatever it takes I'm willing to go through it. Even if you need to take my life to reach my father, I'm willing to give it."

I have never meant anything more than that prayer. A few weeks later Daddy was arrested for the last time for his crimes as a drug trafficker.

> Forgive us our sins, for we also forgive everyone who sins against us.
> ~Luke 11:4

FEBRUARY 15

THE FIRST TIME
HE EVER SAID IT

Scottie Barnes, North Carolina

I CAN'T SAY Babe's arrest surprised anyone. One time he had popped his trunk open and I saw leaf bags filled with $100 bills. He was running a numbers racket, but I had no idea until later that he was sitting atop a drug operation incorporating organized crime. It all came out in the last arrest, and on TV. He was bringing in three drug shipments a year at $30 million to $50 million each. It was the talk of the town.

I started to have a peace that this was how God was going to get to my daddy. Out on bail he came to church one Sunday. It caused a stir to have the drug kingpin on the back row of our little Baptist church. I knew he was finally searching for something money couldn't buy. After we got home he sat on my couch and began to cry.

"Daddy? You're sixty-one years old. I don't understand why you won't give Christ a chance. You're facing forty-two years in prison."

His reply was something I've heard men across the United States say to me often in my ministry: "There's no way a holy God could forgive me, for I've done a lot of bad things."

"It's not what you've done," I told him, "but what Jesus did on the cross that gives you the right to be his child."

He said, "I can't do it," and went home. I was angry that night. I had prayed so hard and was willing to go through anything. Our family was the town gossip target. The FBI followed us everywhere we went, seeing if we would do something wrong so they could break my father by getting to us. But while I was giving up and telling God to take over, Babe gave his life to Christ.

After four weeks of trial in Florence, South Carolina, the jury found him guilty on all counts. During the trial I spent time with Daddy reading the Bible and praying at every break. They were the best four weeks I'd ever had with him.

The judge gave me time to speak at his sentencing. Looking directly at my father I told him I'd forgiven him, how much I loved him, and how much I needed him in my life.

His sentence pronounced, he stood to be handcuffed and led away. That's when he said for the first time in my life, "I love you, Scottie."

They actually let him go home with us later to get his affairs in order. We drove him to the federal penitentiary at Lexington and walked him in ourselves. We drove 800 miles round trip every other weekend to visit him. He died six months later from health complications.

At his grave I remember thinking I was done with prison, but I also told my husband that if God wanted to use this mess in some way, I'd be willing. Ten years later, I got a call.

> If what has been built survives, the builder will receive a reward. If it is burned up, the builder will suffer loss but yet will be saved—even though only as one escaping through the flames. ~1 Corinthians 3:14–15

FEBRUARY 16

PHILIPPINE EPIPHANY

Scottie Barnes, North Carolina

AFTER DADDY died, I shared my testimony at a few churches and someone made a tape of it. The tape found its way to some missionaries in the Philippines, who really connected with the theme of forgiveness. In 2001 their International Mission Board called to invite me to share my story with doctors, lawyers, and judges. I have always asked God to keep me off airplanes. Several weeks after I received the invitation,

9/11 happened. I really felt like backing out but eventually traveled in early 2002.

On the last leg of the trip I traveled to the Philippine city of Cebu. A missionary met me and said, "If you will, there is a little boy named Ezekiel who needs to talk to you. His father abandoned him at the city landfill when he was two. He's a twelve-year-old orphan now and he heard about you forgiving your daddy."

I agreed and they took me to the orphanage, which was just an alley in a street with cubby holes to sleep in. A wonderful interpreter expressed everything we had to say to each other and we prayed. I told him, "Don't you ever quit praying for your father. The Lord knows where he is. It's his will that you might have a relationship with your daddy. Wait for God's timing."

The next day I spoke inside a prison. I was there all day speaking in three different parts of the complex. We were ready to leave when we heard an old man holler. I turned to the officer, who spoke English, and asked, "What's wrong with that man?"

"He's calling you. He wants you to come to him before you leave." He escorted me down to this small cell, where I saw this very old, drawn Filipino prisoner with stringy white hair. Weeping, he told the interpreter, "I've asked Jesus into my heart."

I asked the interpreter, "Tell him I'm very excited that he did—that's why I came to the Philippines."

The old man replied, "Tell her I have a little boy. I don't know where he is. I need to tell him I love him. His name is Ezekiel."

In less than twenty-four hours God answered that boy's prayer and revealed his plan for my life. I knew then that God loves inmates and their children so much he'd send me to a third world country to show me. We returned to the orphanage and found Ezekiel. I took him in my arms and said, "God found your father! He wants to see you. He loves you! And he wants to tell you that." We threw a party in the alley that night. That was the first One Day with God Camp. Six months later, we led our first One Day with God Camp in the United States.

All this is from God, who reconciled us to himself through Christ and gave us the ministry of reconciliation: that God was reconciling the world to himself in Christ, not counting people's sins against them. And he has committed to us the message of reconciliation. ~2 Corinthians 5:18–19

RECONCILING PARENTS WITH CHILDREN

Scottie Barnes, North Carolina

WHEN PARENTS go to prison, children are forgotten. No one speaks for them. You never hear anything about inmates' children. As a child I lied every time someone asked, "Where's your daddy?" I just couldn't tell them the truth and risk more rejection. Prisoners' children are silent because they don't want more shame and ridicule by having a parent's situation become public knowledge.

They suffer everything I felt: shame, fear, loneliness, insecurity, anger, and depression. Children want to be accepted so badly. If they don't find that acceptance from their parents, they'll find it somewhere else.

After my experience in the Philippines, I understood how God was leading me to make something of the mess I had endured with my father. We can't wave a wand and make everything right again, but we have come up with a powerful two-day event that is making a difference. Remember, 2.3 million people are locked up today in America. Besides the lack of a moral transformation of their souls, the overwhelming pattern we see in prisoners is the absence of a loving father.

Our "One Day" program is actually a two-day event. The first day we spend teaching the inmate parent about the "Father's Blessing," parenting, forgiveness, and reconciliation. They pack their child's gift bag and we end with a ceremony that includes each inmate approaching a bucket of red-colored water. They write down anything for which they have harbored unforgiveness and submerge it. Then we pray for something they'd like to see God do in their children the next day. We've taught them what God expects in a parent and what children are looking for in a parent.

The second day we bring the children in accompanied by about 120 volunteers. Every inmate has two Christian mentors who assist their family for the day. They are well trained for the roles. The day is structured and we celebrate all the birthdays they've missed. They spend the last hour in quiet time, just the family. If dads don't know how to have a conversation with their children we have a list of questions we've developed to help them start.

While that's going on, caregivers and members of the child's family are at a local church going through a structured day of their own dealing with the issues from their side. We target the whole family.

Prison officials are begging for us. We can't do enough. It gives the inmates a new sense of hope and responsibility, which usually translates into improved behavior. Corrections officials appreciate it. More importantly, we're breaking cycles of family crime and self-destruction.

> But whoever looks intently into the perfect law that gives freedom, and continues in it—not forgetting what they have heard, but doing it—they will be blessed in what they do. ~James 1:25

FEBRUARY 18

A TALE OF TWO BOYS

Scottie Barnes, North Carolina

WE HAVE to buy a lot of Kleenex.

I have photos of two boys aged 16 and 13. Both attended our "One Day" camp at Pugsley Correctional in Michigan. The older boy regularly visited his daddy in prison. His father is still present in his life even though he's behind the walls. It can be done not just through visits, but keeping up through letters and phone calls. We teach a lot of those practices to the dads at our camps. This boy plays five instruments. His goals are set so high! His grades are wonderful and he smiles as if he has the world in his hands.

The younger boy had never met his dad. He was timid, shy, and withdrawn. He held his head down, avoiding eye contact. He didn't know how to communicate and we were told his grades were terrible. The child broke my heart. He looked up at me the morning we went into prison and nearly whispered with anxiety in his little voice, "I don't know what my daddy looks like. What am I supposed to do? I don't know him."

"Son, he doesn't know you either, but I know him. When your name is called, I'm going to walk him over to you." We have a ritual that as each family meets each other that first time, we all applaud. I wish I could say that we had a Hallmark Hall of Fame moment. But it's not always like that. It takes time to overcome years of absence. There is so much unspoken and uncertainty about the future. But it does give them hope that maybe they still have a daddy who loves them. We do everything we can to fan that flame and ask God to work his perfect fatherly love on them.

> He will turn the hearts of the parents to their children, and the hearts of the children to their parents. ~Malachi 4:6

HOW BAD DO YOU WANT TO SEE YOUR GIRLS?

Scottie Barnes, North Carolina

A FEW years ago I met a female inmate who caused trouble for the prison. She basically stayed in an isolation cell. We advertised we were bringing our One Day with God Camp to Southern Correctional. She let us know she would like to see her children. We have a lot of criteria for inmates to be allowed to participate. For starters, you must be trouble free for ninety days. Her children hadn't seen her in three years. Any parent knows that's nearly a lifetime given how quickly children grow and change.

We received a report the little girls cry nearly every night because they want to see their mama. Their last memory of her was watching the police drag her out of the house. That leaves a mark on children who experience a violent separation few of us can comprehend.

The prison told us she couldn't participate because she just couldn't stay out of segregation. I asked permission to meet with her and they agreed. I made the three-hour drive and asked, "How bad do you want to see your little girls?"

"I want to, sure." I could tell she lacked a strong desire. I told her, "They want to see you—really bad. What would it take for you to stay out of segregation?"

"I don't know. I can't stay out, but . . . I'll try."

"You've got three months. You can do it. Let's pray about it right now."
Well, her fellow inmates rallied to help her stay out of trouble. We took the
children in and I've never seen two happier little girls in my life. This is the
precious thing—the inmate saw her need to be a mother. She found the need
to serve a God who loved her. She never served another day in segregation
after our camp. She earned her GED. The girls' grades started going up.
They began to sleep at night and she's home with them now.

> But whoever lives by the truth comes into the light, so that it may be seen
> plainly that what they have done has been done in the sight of God.~John
> 3:21

GIVING UP THE BATTLE

Ana Ricks, Ohio

WHEN I ARRIVED in prison I had a thirty-year-old grown son and
two teenagers, a girl and a boy. I was facing a long sentence and
knew I would need a power greater than myself to endure. I turned to the
church. I am so glad I did, because I soon learned I would need the Lord
for a much greater challenge.

I had been away from God for a long time. I knew I needed to confess
my sins and be honest with him. I had even forgotten how to pray, so I
asked the Holy Spirit to guide me. Soon, I began receiving prayer books
and other literature to help me. Gradually, I was able to give God my pain,
leaving it at the foot of the cross.

My daughter, who is now twenty years old, informed me one day she
was pregnant (and unwed). What hurt the most was that I was not able
to be there for her. She felt the same way.

I began fervently praying for this unborn child. Strangely, before this
I had been praying for my grandchildren before I even knew I was becoming a grandma!

When my grandson was born everything was fine until thirty days
later. My daughter was diagnosed with lymphoma cancer. It was devas-

tating to me and my family. My emotions were all over the place. I yelled at my family over the phone and expressed my anger and despair in my letters. I was numb with pain.

Then one night, as I lay in my misery, a warm, soothing hush came over me. The Lord was speaking to me and I listened. He told me he had not brought me this far to let me down now. "Trust me," he whispered to my soul.

That night I completely gave up the battle. I prayed, "Your will be done." I even told God that if he chose to take my daughter home, so be it. God will show his glory regardless of the outcome.

Right before drifting off to sleep that night, God whispered again, "My peace I give you."

Praise the Lord my grandson was born cancer-free, and my daughter's cancer has been successfully treated! She is now on the way to being cancer-free.

The power of prayer! We are to live for the glory of God. I cannot thank him enough.

> May the God of hope fill you with all joy and peace as you trust in him, so that you may overflow with hope by the power of the Holy Spirit. ~Romans 15:13

ESCAPE THROUGH THE RAZOR WIRE

Jack Cowley, Texas

AS A RETIRED warden now in prison ministry, I've spent all my adult life in the company of convicts. While I grew up in church and understood what it meant to be a Christian, I wasn't overt in the practice. I did, however, attempt to lead by example with the belief that inmates should leave prison "better" than when they came in. I realize now that the most effective evangelistic practice is "walking the walk," rather than "talking the talk," particularly in today's skeptical culture.

When I was a warden, there was an incident that really grew my faith. I found out later that it spiritually grew the faith of the inmate involved as well. I worked at Joseph Harp Correctional Center, a high-medium-security prison surrounded by two fourteen-foot-high fences topped with razor wire. There was also razor wire coiled on the ground between the two fences—intimidating and effective.

One day, inmates John Adams* and Gerald Green* decided to escape. When I received the call that an officer had apprehended two men outside the fences, I dashed over. When I arrived it was gruesome; John had become pinned in the razor wire on his way down the outside fence. Gerald, who had made it over, was holding John up as best he could to keep the razor-sharp edges of the wire from cutting him any deeper. John was seriously bleeding and ended up needing 150 stitches.

The officer who arrived before me had instructed Gerald to drop to the ground, pointing a shotgun in a rather delicate location of John's body. Without thinking, I yelled for the officer to drop the gun and assist in getting John out of a life-threatening situation. Thankfully, both John and Gerald are alive today.

Years later I was reunited with John. He was married, raising a family, and . . . the youth director for his church. When he saw me, his face lit up.

"Thank you for what you did for me," he said. He added that although he did not come to Christ for many years, my act of urgency, along with reprimanding the officer that day, made him feel like somebody cared. He began thinking of himself in terms other than "loser." A seed was planted that day, all due to a person of my position reaching out to him in his time of need.

Actions do speak louder than words, and when we act like Jesus it can change others.

> Dear children, let us not love with words or speech but with actions and in truth. ~1 John 3:18

JAILHOUSE RELIGION

Jack Cowley, Texas

WE HAVE ALL heard the saying, "It's just jailhouse religion," meaning a convict will outwardly espouse coming to faith for worldly gain without really having a true relationship with Christ. (Lots of people who are not in prison do the same.)

Prisons do not have the reputation for being "good" places, although here in America the first prisons were under the control of people of faith. They were places for which penance of the convicts was the goal; thus the word "penitentiary." In actuality, Satan holds prisons as his own. I continue, then, to be in awe of those inmates who accept Christ into their hearts while incarcerated, and then determine to live out their faith in spite of the control Satan has inside these "houses of correction."

One inmate, Tony McMullen (aka "Tony Mac"), comes to mind because of his reputation in Oklahoma prison history. Tony had a wife and two kids and prior to his arrest, made his living selling drugs. He was a true "drug fiend" because he also used. One night while carrying out a vendetta, he mistakenly shot a friend and was sent to prison for thirty years. He quickly rose to become a leader of the prison underworld and was soon notorious. Tony Mac was not someone an inmate wanted to be confronted by. Even correctional officers turned their back on him.

But, there is no heart too far gone for the Lord to touch. Tony would be the first to say God reached out to him by having him cell with Michael, a "lifer" who definitely knew Jesus. Michael was also someone even Tony Mac had to respect.

In the beginning of Tony's new life as a born-again Christian, others couldn't figure out why Tony needed to get "jailhouse religion." What did he have to gain? In time, however, it became apparent it was genuine. Tony was indeed saved!

He served the rest of his prison term for the Lord. Now free, he and his wife Candy manage Free in Christ Ministries in Oklahoma. He travels the country, going back into prisons, sharing his testimony. His burden is to help men overcome Satan's hold on their lives.

If Christ can do this for someone like Tony Mac, then just think what he can do for you and your loved ones. Keep praying and believing that God can do all things—even turn hardened hearts toward him!

> For God so loved the world that he gave his one and only Son, that whoever believes in him shall not perish but have eternal life. ~John 3:16

MY ANGEL WAS
AN INMATE

Jack Cowley, Texas

HIS NAME was José, a reported leader of the Mexican Mafia confined inside a Texas prison. Now quiet and reserved, José was nearing the end of his sentence and giving the rest of his life serious thought. He volunteered to participate in the InnerChange Freedom Initiative, a faith-based reentry program, which I directed after retiring from the Oklahoma prison system as a warden. It is a ministry of Prison Fellowship, in cooperation with the Texas Department of Criminal Justice.

I had been raised in the church and my dad was a deacon. Baptized as a teen, I knew I was "saved," but like my father I didn't wear my relationship with Christ in public. It was becoming apparent from my work with the ministry, though, and from being tutored by Henry Brandt and Chuck Colson, my relationship with Christ was lacking.

One morning after breakfast José knocked on my door. It was unusual because we never spoke much to each other. We chatted, and then he softly, yet intently, said, "Can you tell me if Jesus is real and can he really do the things the Bible says he can do?"

I stared and blinked.

He went on, "If I allow myself to follow him, I will be putting my family and myself in danger. I won't be able to keep doing the things I've done or be around the people who expect me to do those things."

I reassured him Jesus was for real. José knew the Scriptures, so I offered to lead him in the sinner's prayer. With tears in his eyes we knelt on the floor and prayed. The Holy Spirit touched my heart, too, and thanks to José's questions, we both found Jesus that day! Neither of us has ever been the same.

Upon release, José found a good pipeline welding job. Six months later I received a call from his boss, who asked me if I had "more men" like José. He said all of José's welds were perfect, adding that before each weld José gave them to Jesus. José also leads a Bible study for the crew.

I choose to believe that José was a gift to me from God. It took a prison inmate (who many would say was the lowest of the low) to journey with me to meet Jesus. I'll always have a place in my heart for my "angel" who followed the leading of the Lord and knocked on my door.

> I will give you a new heart and put a new spirit in you. ~Ezekiel 36:26

WINNING RESPECT IN THE "HOOD"

Alphonso Spence, Ohio

MY EIGHTY-THREE-year-old aunt, Hortense Spence Williams, has been in business in Norfolk, Virginia, for about forty years. She owns a barber salon that targets professional minorities and those who live in the inner city. Her business has an amazing reputation: It's kept extremely clean, patrons must be sober to receive service (but are turned away lovingly), no swearing; most haircuts are done by ex-felons, and everyone is treated equally.

My aunt has touched the lives of countless ex-felons and their families in positive ways. She gave jobs to many of them, thereby helping keep many from returning to a life of crime. Just knowing she believed in them would often be the catalyst for them to turn their lives around. Sometimes they kept returning to her for another chance, another job. She is the personification of forgiving "seventy times seven" those who have wronged her.

On a personal level, my station in life as a successful businessman and owner of an organizational development practice is largely due to her. My aunt did not have children of her own and she chose to mentor me when I was five years old. I lived with her many summers and holidays and learned how to run a business, including how to give great customer service. She instilled in me Christ-centered values of excellence.

Her business is located in the "hood" and she has earned respect from the "hood community," along with the community at large. She would give free haircuts to kids when they returned to school and pay children to do small tasks to teach them the art of working hard. She gave the same treatment to the addict as she did the physician—with nonjudgmental respect, love, and dignity. Although addicts around her knew her daily routine (what time she came to work and left), she has never been robbed or assaulted. Businesses around her have been vandalized, but not hers. I believe God protected her because of the way she treated "the least of these."

My aunt is highly respected by those in different levels of society for her selfless giving of her resources and her time. Aunt Hortense has never expected anything in return. A devout Christian woman, she simply lives out her Christian walk in every aspect of her life.

When God nudged me to get involved in prison ministry, he used my recollections of my aunt to help me change my attitude and get involved. I am so glad he did.

> In everything I did, I showed you that by this kind of hard work we must help the weak, remembering the words the Lord Jesus himself said: "It is more blessed to give than to receive." ~Acts 20:35

AN EGO REDUCER

Alphonso Spence, Ohio

IN THE LATE 1990s, after I gave a talk to about fifteen hundred members at my church, a man asked me what type of work I did. I replied, "Organizational development work." He said he owned a corporation in Ohio as well as a division in Houston, Texas. The Houston operation was in trouble. He hired me to turn the company around, and I did.

Three months after arriving in Texas I received a call from Sharon, the CEO's daughter, and a vice president of the company. Sharon had heard of a Prison Fellowship program in Houston called the InnerChange Freedom Initiative. She asked me to go to this prison to find out more. It began under then-Texas-governor George W. Bush and celebrated fifteen years in operation in 2012.

Sharon didn't know I did not want any part of prisons. I always thought the incarcerated were getting what they deserved. I kept putting her off and eventually she gave up.

Then, two months later she suggested I at least get a brochure and "think about it." She was so nice—I caved and called for a brochure to be mailed.

Jack Crowley, the program director, answered. He informed me that to get a brochure I needed to come on a Tuesday night at 7 o'clock when the mentors visited the inmates.

Ugh.

My plan was to grab the brochure and get out of there—away from "those people." But God had different plans. When I arrived I was told I had to wait until the two-hour program was finished to get the brochure!

There were about twenty-five other "civilians" in the room. There were also musical instruments, a microphone, and chairs. Then, all at once these guys in white, starched, prison garb walked in.

Wow, these are prisoners! First time in my life I was this close to them.

Immediately everyone started hugging each other: mentors, prisoners, and prison staff. Then some of them started hugging me! The next thing I knew, it was church in that place. Songs, testimonies, tears, laughter, speeches of hope erupted.

In two hours the Lord used inmates to touch my heart. I suddenly saw them in a new light. They were no different than I—they had been caught and punished. Now forgiven, they were new creatures in him.

Before I left I became a mentor. The first man I mentored was Steve. He had arms of steel and a heart of gold.

That night was a real ego reducer. Only God can change our hardened hearts, and fill them with such love and compassion.

Do not judge, or you too will be judged. ~Matthew 7:1

BAD CHOICES

Steve Robinson, Texas

I MET ALPHONSO in 1998 in Texas. I was the first one he mentored. He signed up to be a mentor one night at the prison when he was planning on getting a brochure for someone else.

We immediately hit it off. I recognized what a good, sincere person Alphonso was, and he must've seen some hope in me, because he has stuck by me ever since. And, "ever since" includes a lot of stuff I'm not proud of.

I was one of fourteen kids in my family. It was tough, we didn't have a lot, but thankfully I was taught good morals and values. You don't see much in the way of good morals in this world anymore, especially in prison.

I married my seventh-grade sweetheart. We dated all through high school. She, too, must've seen something in me, because we've been married more than thirty years. I've put her through a lot, but I constantly show her my appreciation now. She tells me I don't have to lavish gifts and attention on her, but I want to.

When our two sons were younger I worked mostly security jobs, but fell prey to the quick easy money I could make with drugs. It wasn't without risks—I was involved in shootouts and had several near-death experiences. Besides drinking a lot back then, I also got hooked on cocaine. It turned me into a person I never wanted to be. Doing coke was an expensive habit. I drained our bank account on more than one occasion, but I never stole anything. Still, the drugs and criminal lifestyle landed me in prison—as they should have.

I was in a pre-release prison when Alphonso first came into my life. I worked hard to be a model prisoner and earned the privilege of being a first-class trustee. I never started any fights, but I wouldn't back down, either. I'm a big, strong man, which helped, as most people didn't want to challenge me.

Because I was a trusted inmate, Alphonso was allowed to come into my room. I also qualified to be part of the InnerChange Freedom Initiative, a biblically-based program where all the inmates in my section were Christians. Alphonso would sit on the edge of my bed and pour God's

Word into my life. He was faithful with his visits, and how I looked forward to them! They were one of the few highlights of my time there.

> For he has not despised or scorned the suffering of the afflicted one; he has not hidden his face from him but has listened to his cry for help. ~Psalm 22:24

SEEING JESUS IN A MENTOR

Steve Robinson, Texas

ALPHONSO WAS actually much more than a mentor; he was (and still is) a good friend. He is like a brother—a solid rock in my life. People thought we were brothers; we even looked alike. All I knew was, I wanted to be like him when I got out. I wanted to be a man whose family could respect him—a man of integrity.

When I finally was released, Alphonso did something most people would never do—he hired me to work for him. That job lasted a year or so, and then it went away due to downsizing. I stayed off drugs while I worked for Alphonso, but without the structure of a regular job and the accountability to Alphonso in my life, the old desires of drugs and easy money resurfaced. My faith and strength were tested and I was mentally weak and stressed. I was right where the Enemy likes to attack us. Even though I was a strong Christian and told myself I would not get hooked, it quickly took me down a path of self-destruction—again. I allowed temptation (Satan) to pull me back into that lifestyle, convincing myself I could keep it under control. The devil is a liar—he comes to "kill and steal and destroy" (John 10:10). I completely ignored the fact that it was the drug scene that got me in trouble in the first place.

God had given me all these blessings, but again, I took them all for granted. I kept dippin' and dabblin' in the devil's drugs. You can't straddle the fence with Satan—he'll grab your foot and pull you down. I cried and lied; I'd behave for a little while, but I'd get pulled back in. It became a horrible cycle. I ended up back on the streets—again.

A lot of wives would've left me for the things I did. I am so blessed, though, to have the wife and good friend I have. Alphonso cared about me so much he flew down from Ohio and he and my wife hunted me down. They actually came to the crack house and got me out of there. If that ain't a good wife and friend, I don't know who is.

> The thief comes only to steal and kill and destroy; I have come that they may have life, and have it to the full. ~John 10:10

A NEW DESIRE

Steve Robinson, Texas

NOT LONG after Marge and Alphonso pulled me out of that hell house, I put myself in rehab. I wanted no contact with anyone but Jesus. I needed to come clean—with Jesus, and then myself! It was during that time I saw how I'd been dancing with the devil. My eyes were being opened to the truth. I got serious with the Lord and I rededicated my life to him.

When I told Alphonso what I had done he was very happy. He would always tell me, "When man can't, God can." He'd also remind me that when things got tough, to keep calling on the name of Jesus—call on him over and over again. He didn't sugarcoat life, he told it like it was. He kept drilling it into my head how God had blessed me. And he was right. I had a great wife who stood by me, two awesome sons who are doing well in school, I'm in good health, and mentally stable. And, I had the best friend ever in Alphonso. Yes, I had indeed been blessed. A lot of mentors and "friends" would have given up on me a long time ago. They would not have wanted to bother with a wretch like me. But Alphonso's love encouraged me to get clean and I'm now devoted to living a Christ-centered life.

Marge and I are very happy now and love being with our family: our kids and grandkids. I have a great job and get to travel the world! I call Alphonso a couple of times a year to tell him how well I'm doing and that

Christ is still the center of my life. I always tell him I love him and I still thank him for what he did.

Alphonso always tells me he is just a phone call away or a plane ticket away, if I need him. Alphonso says I did more for him than he did for me and that I'm the one who has blessed him, but I don't see that. All I know is, if Jesus would bless me so, he will do it for all. God is no respecter of persons. He sees the heart and loves each of us.

I can't get those wasted years back, when I chose drugs over my family. But with God's help, I can now be the best husband, father, grandfather, and friend possible.

Then the Lord your God will make you most prosperous in all the work of your hands and in the fruit of your womb, the young of your livestock and the crops of your land. The Lord will again delight in you and make you prosperous, just as he delighted in your ancestors. ~Deuteronomy 30:9

ADDICTION REDUX

Jerry Menard, California*

I WASN'T IN the private business parking lot long. I hadn't even planned to be there, but my roommate was unexpectedly at home, and that changed my plans for the evening. Earlier that day I had met my connection to score some cocaine.

A security officer spotted me. Next thing I know, I'm cuffed and riding to the intake. They throw me in the tank with a bunch of those people who just scare you. I'm freezing. It's going to be a long night because you don't sleep in these group tanks, and I don't know how long it's going to take to get bailed out, if at all, because this time I'm facing a felony charge.

I'm thirty-four and have seen this movie before. Arrested twice for driving under the influence and drugs in my twenties, I remembered how scared and miserable I was. The court had offered me a drug diversion program, which I happily accepted. I completed the ninety-day sobriety test through Alcoholics Anonymous (AA) and found that life was really much better without the booze and drugs. I stuck with the program for the next eight years.

During that time, a friend invited me to visit an evangelical church. I liked it and got involved. Then, on a Mexico missions trip it happened. Between my Catholic upbringing and AA's higher power references I hadn't connected the dots to Jesus. Now, I understood what was meant by knowing and following him and I committed my life to Christ.

My burdens lifted and life was good. I started hanging out with my church friends a lot more, rather than my AA crowd. I also felt comfortable enough to begin drinking socially again. I just didn't see it becoming a problem—it was all in my past and few of my new friends knew much about it.

Within six months the old desires were back. Social drinking turned into binges, partying, and drugs. And even though I kept up with my real estate appraisal job, the market was disappearing, adding financial pressure to my life. I felt caught between this new life in Christ, where I could confess and gain forgiveness, and the slavery of my old addictions. It was a weird time, and I felt shame for my double life.

As I sat shivering in jail, I remembered a recent sermon. What's worse than God's discipline is when God turns you over to your sin and leaves you be (Romans 1:28). That hadn't happened to me. I thanked God for catching me and not leaving me alone—even at my worst moment—when I deserved prison time.

In the end, I was offered drug rehab and upon completion the charges were dropped. I still had to deal with the fallout of this choice: paying a lawyer, dealing with my parents, and explaining things to my new employer, who graciously supported me. That was five years ago. Now I feel like the prostitute whom Jesus told, "Go and sin no more."

> Furthermore, just as they did not think it worthwhile to retain the knowledge of God, so God gave them over to a depraved mind, so that they do what ought not to be done. ~Romans 1:28

MARCH 2

IS GOD REALLY SOVEREIGN?

Ken Cooper, Florida

I'M NOT proud of it, but I lived a double life for about thirteen years beginning with the deaths of my father and my wife. From 1969 to 1982, I robbed banks with a gun. On occasion, to buy more time or get a bigger rush of adrenaline, I took female hostages to ensure my safe exit. It ended when an off-duty police officer shot me while escaping a Tampa, Florida, bank.

I received a ninety-nine-year sentence "with a grudge." The judge said I would never walk the streets of America again. Next stop? A place called "the Rock" at Raiford, Florida, the main housing unit at Union Correctional. I existed there with murderers, rapists, and other threats to society. Now the same terror I had inflicted on others was being inflicted on me by people more deranged than I was.

I had only been a believer for six months and I was doing my best in that place of evil to allow Jesus to be in control of my life. I was a baby Christian learning what it was about.

Satan really *is* behind all kinds of evil in prison and several traumatic events would shape me into the believer God wanted me to be.

One of those events occurred within my first few weeks at the Rock. I had a new friend who was a basketball buddy—six-foot-three, 195-pound fantastic player. And more than that, Eli was a terrific Christian. In fact, although I was 45 and he was 23, he was one of my mentors because he'd been a Christian for many more years than I had.

We sat down to lunch one day and talked a lot. I enjoyed—even needed—him as one of the few friendly faces in our bizarre hellhole. Suddenly, a deranged man came up behind Eli and slammed a double-edged prison sword into his back six or seven times. I froze. I couldn't react. Amid the chaos as officers rushed in, I finally moved, wrapped him in my arms, and watched him die within moments. Officers subdued the culprit. This man already had several homicides to his credit, so what difference did one more make to his sentence? They locked him away in isolation.

It made no sense. It was contradictory to what I thought life in Christ should be. I went into deep depression and doubted my faith.

> "What strength do I have, that I should still hope? What prospects, that I should be patient? Do I have the strength of stone? Is my flesh bronze? Do I have any power to help myself, now that success has been driven from me?" ~Job 6:11–13

MARCH 3

IS GOD REALLY THERE?

Ken Cooper, Florida

HOW COULD God allow a beautiful young man such as Eli to die? He had been so important to God's kingdom in that place of hell. Wasn't God supposed to be in control and take care of those he loved—especially his own children? It's a serious question when you live in places like the Rock. It was a place where I routinely heard the screams of men being abused, beaten, and raped. If this is what faith is about, I wasn't sure I wanted any part of it.

I returned to my cell, which housed five other men. All but two had life sentences—the cell boss was a serial murderer. I considered them worse than myself and of the same ilk as Eli's murderer. For six or seven days I didn't leave my cell. I didn't go to exercise, I didn't go to chow hall to eat. I didn't want to go back to the scene of the crime. I went into a deep funk. I don't know if I was in danger of losing my mind, but I felt close to it.

The thing that changed me was that after several days, I started to smell like the guys I loathed. I had always been a clean, "Mr. Nice Guy" kind of person. I had been nicknamed "The Gentleman Robber" by the media. My first act of faith was leaving the cell to take a shower.

Then I started talking to God. I had stopped reading my Bible and praying. I cried out to God to allow me to do something to get me out of the funk. I didn't know what it would be. Then the thought hit me to clean the commode.

It was stained brown and the smell was indescribably bad. I laughed and said, "God, that is not a righteous thought." But the thought persisted. I think God wanted me to serve my wicked cellmates in a simple act. So I found some soap and during the evening while the guys watched television, I got on my knees and scrubbed. They thought I was crazy. When I finished, I felt clean, and felt hope had returned. I can't explain it to this day. I returned to my bunk and a few Christians I didn't know came over and asked if they could pray with me. We started praising God in that place, praying, and memorizing Scripture. Before we knew it, the cell boss was gone and one other insane person left.

We sang about the blood of Christ—the thing that I had made fun of all my life, even as a kid in church. Without understanding the power and impact, we sang, "Would you over evil of victory win/There's power in the blood." That became a Christian cell and it spread. Through a death I still can't explain, I had grown in my faith.

> And the God of all grace, who called you to his eternal glory in Christ, after you have suffered a little while, will himself restore you and make you strong, firm, and steadfast. ~1 Peter 5: 10

MARCH 4

SAVED TO SERVE

Ken Cooper, Florida

ABOUT 150 people became believers while I was at the Rock and one of our prayers was that the place would close. On June 15,

1985, it did. That was my big break because they transferred me to Baker Correctional, a more normal maximum-security prison.

At Baker I came to know some volunteers who believed in my transformation. They visited me and prayed that the judge would release his jurisdiction over me, which he did.

While that was in play, the president of the Florida Times Union, Mr. Whyte, came in through the Kairos ministry. As he got to know me, Mr. Whyte began petitioning the parole commission for two years. Unexplainably after three-and-a-half years of served time, they released me. To my knowledge, it's never happened in Florida, before or since, with anyone who had a sentence such as mine.

Moreover, two of the commissioners took it upon themselves to release me from parole early. I didn't request it nor did my parole officer, who was really upset. It's hard even for me to understand why God orchestrated such circumstances given I had earned the wrath of the law during my bank-robbing days. Looking back, I can see God's plan better.

I met a woman who was visiting her son at Baker and who shared my vision to help men coming out of prison. On our first visit I asked her, "What do you think you'll be doing in five years?"

"Helping men as they come out of prison," she answered. I got tears in my eyes. God put us together. We fell in love, married, and in the twenty-five years since, the four ministries we founded or cofounded have sponsored more than 2,300 men coming out of prison. Of that number, about 88 percent are still out—twice the state average of about 44 percent still out after three years.

Recently I took a break and traveled with my book *Held Hostage*, which tells the full story of my crimes and prison conversion, but I have since returned to ministry with an emphasis on helping long-term offenders with release, finding transition housing, programming, and handling the bombardment of stimulation in our environment. They are forced to make hundreds more decisions than prison allows. It's so overwhelming that many of them go back if they don't have someone for debriefing and reorientation.

For the last year I've been working with six ex-prisoners all of whom did twenty-seven years or more. God didn't just save me to show *me* his grace and power, but to send me to do the same for others.

Anyone who serves Christ in this way is pleasing to God and receives human approval. Let us therefore make every effort to do what leads to peace and to mutual edification. ~Romans 14:18–19

PRESSING PAST FEAR

Dina Zamora, California

AS I ENTERED the thick walls of the maximum-security prison, I wondered if I would die that day in 2006 with flowers in my hair and no shoes on my feet. I was completely covered in loose white Hawaiian clothing with a crown of carnations on my head. I, along with fifteen other women, was commissioned to praise and worship in Hawaiian garb behind Solano Prison's bars; however, only three dancers showed up that day. I was scared.

Once I started worshiping the Lord I forgot my fear: "All the world shall worship you! They shall sing praises to your name!" Immersed in the presence of the Holy Spirit, I almost felt invisible.

The drumming began. We chanted in Hawaiian and English; psalms and other declarations of God's glory. My prayer was that God would reveal his love to each man in the audience that day.

When we finished the song and dance, I suddenly felt vulnerable. I could not get off the stage fast enough. However, the prison ministry director, Tim, quietly approached me and said, "Do you see those two microphones on stage?"

I nodded.

He continued, "One is for you and the other is for the pastors as they take turns delivering the messages."

Tim saw my puzzled look, and then added, "You will translate all the sermons today."

I quickly came up with a million excuses as to why I could not do it, beginning with the fact that I had been saved in an English rock-and-roll tent revival church, and ending with how I did not know the name of the books of the Bible in Spanish. As much as I wanted to get out of it though, God had a plan. He had gifted me with the ability to translate, and I definitely wanted these men to hear and understand the sermons. I needed to put my trust in him to give me the right words.

But you will receive power when the Holy Spirit comes on you; and you will be my witnesses in Jerusalem, and in all Judea and Samaria, and to the ends of the earth. ~Acts 1:8

THE SECRET PLACE
OF THE HEART

Dina Zamora, California

I PRESSED PAST the fear and translated the messages. Things were going well until pastor used the word "leper." I panicked. I didn't know the Spanish word, so I had to describe a person with leprosy. As the prisoners listened intently to the vivid description of the sores and oozing wounds, I watched their eyes in amazement. The pastors were preaching about God's ultimate power of healing—especially for our souls. They spoke of how our dark hearts lead to dark choices, but how God can ultimately make us clean again with his forgiveness.

The faces of many of the men lit up as they heard God's promises in their language. It was at that moment, while witnessing their transformation, I realized my calling.

Since then, I have had the opportunity to bring in worship concerts for the men and show them the radical grace and love of God through worship and Scripture. Faith comes by hearing the Word, whether it is through sermons or worship songs. God speaks to us in our hearts.

Then in February 2012, I again toured Solano Prison maximum- and medium-security, but this time with my sixteen-year-old son. He had been dabbling in drugs and I wanted to show him the different possibilities his choices could bring. The same men I visited in 2006 were there to receive my son and show him the radical love of God. They asked him to carefully weigh his choices. They asked him to try to understand God's great purpose for him. They asked him to choose a better life than the one they had chosen for themselves.

It had been six long years since I first met with them with flowers in my hair. They had now become evangelists, trying to save our youth from inside the prison walls.

God changed my life twice through my beloved brothers: once in 2006, when he used *me* to give to them, and again in 2012, when he used *them* to give to me.

This is the true meaning of prison ministry—reaching past ourselves, through the bars that separate us—to help one another share truth.

But you have an anointing from the Holy One, and all of you know the truth.
~1 John 2:20

LIVE EVERY MOMENT

James A. Russell, Massachusetts

PRISON LIFE is very structured, regimented, controlled, and repetitive. The cell doors open and close on a set schedule. The same meals appear on our trays every week. Inmates wear identical uniforms. Every cell, in every block, is just like every other cell. It's like looking into a mirror facing a mirror and seeing your image reflected and multiplied ad infinitum. It can be a bleak and depressing existence.

When I think of Jesus, out in the desert on his forty-day fast, hungry and thirsty, surrounded by the sun-scorched, barren land, I can't help but wonder, *Why? Why would he choose to do that? Why would he subject himself to such emptiness?* When I first read James 4:14, that same emptiness appeared to me: "You are a bit of smoke that appears for a little while, and then vanishes."

It was a harsh reality to face. I didn't understand the desert fasting, and the vanishing smoke, and the blank white sheet of prison life.

But one day, an average and uneventful day, I was sitting in the cell by myself and the sun shone through the window, and . . . I understood. I realized that the noise and activity of my formerly busy life had been obstructing my ability to connect to God, as well as my ability, through God, to connect with others. Part of the reason I committed my crimes was that I thought I was the "Great Conductor"—that I was a god of sorts, twirling the universe in orbit around me.

When Jesus was alone on his fast, it was a time of preparation for his earthly ministry. He was focusing and dedicating all his senses to God, to get closer to him.

And if I hadn't come to prison, to this desert experience, I'd never have seen the truth, the wisp of smoke my life is. I would have missed the precious gift to be savored in every moment of life.

Why, you do not even know what will happen tomorrow. What is your life? You are a mist that appears for a little while and then vanishes. ~James 4:14

PUT FEET ON YOUR FAITH

James A. Russell, Massachusetts

THOUGH I attended worship services on the outside for the first sixteen years of my life, I didn't become a Christian until after I was arrested and thrown in jail. In my desperation, I cried out for God. He is faithful—he answered my cry. It was only then my heart was truly involved in worship.

I quickly discovered something, both interesting and sad, about the church. Among the body of believers, many seem to want the benefits of "membership" without paying the dues. By "dues" I'm not referring to giving a tithe; rather, I'm referring to "putting feet on your faith."

Don't we all want something for nothing? Most people, when given the option of working for something or getting it free, would choose free. But that doesn't work with faith. While salvation is free indeed, faith requires works.

The second chapter of the book of James covers this argument clearly. Faith without works is dead. Many interpret "works" as doing things for other church brothers; when someone needs a bar of soap or some food, you share from your bounty. But that's not the depth of what Christ is calling us to do.

The Bible shows Jesus healing the outcasts, the unclean, the crippled and blind. He asks us to care for the widows and orphans, and to love our enemies. He even gives us examples by means of parables, such as the Good Samaritan (Luke 10:25–37). Clearly Christians are called to go out of our way for strangers—for "the least of these."

For many of us, such actions are outside our comfort zones. We don't want to be around people who expose us as fearful, mortal, and selfish, but Jesus calls us to get over our self-important, petty selves and do our Father's will.

Some of my "brothers" are critical of me. They wonder why I hang out with those "nerds, gays, heathens, gangbangers, and atheists." I don't give them an answer. I invite them to join us.

When the Pharisees saw this, they asked his disciples, "Why does your teacher eat with tax collectors and sinners?" On hearing this, Jesus said, "It is not the healthy who need a doctor, but the sick." ~Matthew 9:11–12

83

EXCEPT FOR THESE CHAINS

James A. Russell, Massachusetts

COMING TO prison set me free. That's a pretty radical statement to issue forth from the mind of an inmate, but I believe it, and I live it.

Prior to my arrest in 2008, I was happy, or I *thought* I was happy. Maybe I was just trying to convince myself and others I was getting along okay. I spent my time and money on video games, DVDs, CDs, going to movies, riding motorcycles, and surfing the Internet for explicit images. I loved my family and spent a lot of time with my kids, but I was so loaded down with all my selfish pursuits I didn't make room for God. Prison fixed that.

Prison stripped me of everything superfluous. It left me raw, defenseless, and humble. Without the junk, I could see what I really needed and wanted in my life, and how I would spend my time and energy from then on. The prison experience freed me from my addiction, has saved me from wasting my life in pointless pursuits, and liberated me from the delusion that happiness can be obtained through things.

It also made me realize I need God. I've always had God, but I didn't welcome him, or thank him. I thought "I" was the one in charge, that "I" was taking care of myself, that "I" was everything I needed. That fallacy was overcome on my third day in jail when I wasn't sure I could go on and I asked Jesus to help me. It made all the difference in the world.

After asking Jesus' help and feeling his Spirit within me, I began reading the Bible. Shortly after, my sister took a serious Bible study course. Then my mom started seeing the hand of God at work in the subtle, impossible miracles of her daily life, and she and her sisters began working through some family issues that had plagued them for decades.

Would I try to persuade others to be a Christian as I am? Absolutely—except for these chains.

> Then Agrippa said to Paul, "Do you think that in such a short time you can persuade me to be a Christian?" Paul replied, "Short time or long—I pray to God that not only you but all who are listening to me today may become what I am, except for these chains." ~Acts 26:28–29

MY HAIR IS GROWING BACK

James A. Russell, Massachusetts

I USED TO love the Samson story. It is the stuff of adolescent male fantasy. There is violence, superhuman strength, revenge, murder—all vital fodder for modern-day adrenaline junkies. I tried to incorporate some of those extreme elements into my adult life: I raced motorcycles, fought guys in rings and cages, cranked my sound systems up to 11, played realistic and violent video games, and fed my lust on images gleaned from the Internet. I thought I was living to the max.

In the midst of my fantasy life, however, I was given unexpected and unwanted news—my girlfriend was pregnant.

When Samson's wife tricked him, he went on a one-thousand-man killing spree to exact his revenge. When I thought I'd been tricked, I bottled my rage and stored it up. Not realizing how vulgar, volatile, and diseased I was, I unleashed my anger on someone absolutely free of guile, ill will, or blame.

The Philistines seized me, gouged out my eyes, bound me in shackles, and forced me into prison. The eye gouging and Philistines are figurative elements, of course, but still applicable. I was forced by my "enemy" to become blind to my false view of self. I was not the King of the World that I clung to in fantasy. I was an egotistical, self-aggrandizing, greedy, careless, human hammer. In prison, you're thrown in with a whole bag full of hammers and your view of self changes radically.

My sincere thanks to the many Christians who volunteer to help the incarcerated. Because of them, I was able to snap out of my delusion and see how fortunate I was to be alive, loved, and capable. I am now active in the church of Christ, I am involved with my family, and I am eager to be free of these bonds so I can work to truly repay my debt to society.

My hair is growing back.

Then the Philistines seized him (Samson), gouged out his eyes and took him down to Gaza. Binding him with bronze shackles, they set him to grinding grain in the prison. But the hair on his head began to grow again after it had been shaved. ~Judges 16: 21–22

WHEN NOTHING GOES RIGHT

Chuck Colson
(October 16, 1931 – April 21, 2012)

IN THE late seventies, when Prison Fellowship was relatively new, I traveled the country to help establish the fledgling ministry. The mountaintop experience of my visit to the Atlanta State Penitentiary was still fresh in my mind. As I wrote in *Life Sentence,* we saw an amazing display of God's power among hundreds of prisoners.

Now I sought to enter a major prison in Nashville, Tennessee, to help establish more ministry opportunities in the state. The administration set up the event in their main auditorium—an arena with seats on all sides. This old prison arena could have accommodated a thousand, but fewer than a hundred showed up. They sat scattered across the seats giving the place an empty, stale feeling. Some of the inmates were bored silly. Some people fear prison for the physical threats, but I was beginning to fear that no one cared what I had to say. Once you start speaking and you're not getting engagement, you lose your edge. You get uncomfortable. I didn't feel any power of the Spirit. I labored to get through it only to receive a muted response. I gave an invitation to follow Jesus. Nobody responded—there was just silence punctuated by occasional coughs. I always looked at that moment as the low point of my ministry.

About four years later I attended the Alaska governor's prayer breakfast. Several officials invited me to visit a prison in Anchorage because there was a revival going on and they thought I'd be interested. We arrived at a sterile prison that reminded me of the modern Scandinavian designs. Despite the environment, I saw a tremendous excitement among the prisoners. The chaplain quickly introduced me to the inmate at the heart of the revival leading people to Christ. The fellow says, "I'm glad to see you, Mr. Colson. I came to Christ the night you came to Nashville. I was transferred here and God is doing incredible things."

God never strikes out. I did. I had an off night in Nashville. It wasn't working.

All kinds of things go wrong. You have as many down days as good ones. If you think speaking the way I do is easy, it's not. You have to pray hard. Yet God works especially in the non-spotlight moments. God doesn't

CHUCK COLSON

always let us see what he's doing. If he did, we wouldn't depend on him, we would get full of ourselves. We'd begin to think we're the ones accomplishing things. God's ways always confound the wisdom of the world. He uses foolish things to shame the wise and the mighty. The idea of prison being a birthing ground of revival is counterintuitive. You might think it comes from the powerful people and the beautiful churches. It doesn't. It comes from the messed-up people with scars, tattoos, bruises all over, who populate the prisons. Its authenticity is all the more evident because of the dramatic nature of God's work in their lives.

"For my thoughts are not your thoughts, neither are your ways my ways," declares the Lord. ~Isaiah 55:8

TAKE ME

Aram Hairapetian, California

IT WAS 3 a.m. when the bottom fell out for me. At forty-five, I had made an utter mess of my life. My mechanic business had evaporated. I had walked away from my family and was cavorting with "ladies of the night" who introduced me to all kinds of drugs. As a godless immigrant from Iran with nothing to lose I joined them in using and selling drugs. The life exhausted me and I really hated myself.

So, I did something I had never done. I prayed: "God, if you can hear me, if this is all there is to life—work like a donkey, then die—then take me out. I don't desire to live any longer. But if there is a way, take me and help me."

By 7 a.m., police caught me in a sting operation and charged me with drug trafficking. Together with a previous gun charge (for which I had already served two years), I got a double strike—ten years in prison.

I thought, *This must be God's way of taking care of me. He's sending me to prison, nobody will know who I am, and I'll die there.* Instead, he took me out of society and removed all my responsibilities to give me time to think.

While in the county jail, a man announced, "Anybody who wants to know about salvation, come to the gate." I was playing cards when I heard this. I dropped the cards on the table and told him, "I'd like to know." He arranged for the officer to let me come to the dorm where the meeting would be held.

I attended his meetings for several months and eventually understood why Christ was on the cross and what he did for me.

I kept my habit of playing pinochle during these months. The gang-bangers looked at me one day a few weeks after classes started and asked, "Are you okay? You're not sick?"

"No. Who said I was sick? I'm just playing cards."

"No, something's wrong. You haven't cussed in two weeks."

When I first arrived in jail, every other word I said was obscene. I now realized God had started his work. I dropped my cards that moment and told them I had to go read my Bible.

One of the first stories I read was the Parable of the Sower. I just could not understand it or what it had to do with God. So I said, "Lord, I don't know what God has to do with a farmer. If you can't explain what it means, I'll never read the Bible again. But I believe you are Lord. Teach me who you are, and use me. Amen."

I got up from my knees and felt a burden lift from my shoulders. I opened my Bible and wouldn't you know it, I saw the explanation of the parable on the opposite page. I thanked God for that and committed myself, saying, "Lord, do whatever you want with me—I'm yours."

> But the tax collector stood at a distance. He would not even look up to heaven, but beat his breast and said, "God, have mercy on me, a sinner."
> ~Luke 18:13

BOLD STEPS OF FAITH

Aram Hairapetian, California

ONE OF the first things I experienced after giving my life to Christ was a loss of all fear. I knew God was in control. When I arrived at Chuckawalla Valley State Prison, where I would do most of my time, I walked in through the gates of "A" yard. All the shot-callers of the different race-based gangs run to the gate when someone new arrives. They ask, "Who you gonna ride with?" This is a high-anxiety moment for many.

My answer was simple: "Jesus." They threw their hands up and walked away. From that day on, I knew they were watching. They love to find you in a lie so they can "take care of you."

Oddly, being the hard-headed Armenian that I was, for my first six months I picked up every book I could find *critical* of the Bible. I was looking for any possible defects. One day in chapel the Holy Spirit asked, "What are you searching for?"

"The truth!"

"You have the truth in your hand. Just read." I put all the other books away and started going to any and all Christian program offerings. After some months, some outside volunteers approached me. They noticed my studying, reviewed my homework answers, and thought I was spiritually sound. They invited me to say a word to our inmate church.

"Me? A drug addict, drug pusher, assault offender, you want me to get up and share the Word? Let me pray about it."

I got alone and prayed. The Lord just said, "I will tell you what to say. You don't have to worry or have fear. I will speak through you." So that's what I did. I found myself in the Spirit, preaching. I didn't know where this stuff was coming from. It must have been all the time I had been reading and studying the Word, and the Spirit was just bringing it from my memory. It was just flowing out.

Parallel to my studies and participation in our church, God brought my family back to me—the one I had left. Years ago during my mischief, I told my wife, "I'm stupid. I'm not a good person. You need to go and find somebody good for you." I asked her many times, "Why are you waiting?"

She told me, "God is great. And I believe he will accomplish his purpose for you." She saw a change taking place in me in prison. During visits I would minister to her and my kids, and I would also minister through letters. Before I came to Christ, I don't think I wrote or read a page of anything. I couldn't even spell. But when I got into the Word of God, within a couple of years I got my GED in prison. Through that the Lord taught me to write. You can imagine how that would impress my family after such minimal and poor communication.

Your word is a lamp to my feet and a light for my path.

I have taken an oath and confirmed it, that I will follow your righteous laws.

Your word is a lamp to my feet and a light for my path. I have taken an oath and confirmed it, that I will follow your righteous laws. I have suffered much; preserve my life, O LORD, according to your word. Accept, O LORD, the willing praise of my mouth, and teach me your laws. ~Psalm 119:105–108

YOUR GOD IS NOT MY GOD

Aram Hairapetian, California

IN 2005 I met the 85 percent requirement of my sentence to qualify for release. On my discharge date, Immigration took custody of me.

I never fought the case, but asked my wife to find an attorney to represent me. There were a lot of other Iranians on the unit who told me, "You have gun charges and drug charges? For sure you're going back to Iran." I had emigrated to California when I was twelve, but authorities revoked my green card after my arrest. My prospects for remaining in the United States did not look good.

I told them, "My God is not your god." I spent the next three months at the immigration dorm preaching to whoever would listen. A lot of Muslims and Hindus were listening. When my court date came, as I left the dorm to see the judge, the Iranians and other Muslims gathered around and said, "You'll see, you're going back to Iran."

Again, I reminded them, "My God is not your god."

The judge started the hearing by reminding me of all the wrong I'd done during my street days. She also observed that there appeared to have been a great change according to the documents submitted on my behalf by corrections officials and chaplains. I told her, "The Lord has broken my hardened heart and restored to me a loving heart."

She then asked, "Do you mind telling me about your past, present, and expectations for future life?" For the next forty minutes I explained how I had cared only for myself and not even for my family. I told of how the addiction overwhelmed me until I asked God to take my life—which he did by taking me to prison—to replace my stony heart with a new one. He has now filled me for eight years with his wisdom to prepare me to go back out on the same streets and minister to the walking dead, of whom I was one.

When I finished she simply looked up and said, "I'll be back in five minutes to deliver my decision." My attorney covered his head, frustrated I had replayed my past offenses. The DA tells me he doesn't care what my story is, I'm still an addict and he's sending me back to Iran. I told him the same thing: "Your god is not my God." Then the judge returned.

"I have reviewed your records and seen that you were an evil and angry person, but I also see through documentation provided that God has restored your heart. Therefore, this is my decision and I believe it is

the right one: Tonight, you will be with your family here in America."
After five years, I can submit paperwork for citizenship.

I didn't get to walk out of the prison then—I had to return to the dorm briefly. When I told the other inmates I was going home—not to Iran—they didn't believe me.

They do now.

> However, I consider my life worth nothing to me; my only aim is to finish the race and complete the task the Lord Jesus has given me—the task of testifying to the good news of God's grace. ~Acts 20:24

MARCH 15

SEEING PRISONERS THROUGH A DIFFERENT LENS

Jeff Peck, Virginia

DURING MY fourteen-year tenure at the national nonprofit Prison Fellowship, I had the opportunity to enter prisons of all kinds with the purpose of capturing images of prisoners and ministry. Walking into prison with camera equipment attracts a lot of attention, first from officers searching the gear, then from inmates.

I read once about some primitive tribes who refused to have their photos taken out of fear of having their souls literally captured on film. In prison, I think the fear is exposure. Yes, some already have had their photos on "wanted" posters, but who can blame them for not wishing to be further recognized behind bars? It's not a high point in life. My own photo albums contain exactly zero images of shame and failure—they're all smiles with friends, family, pets, and places.

I faced a unique and ongoing challenge in representing through the lens the work inside the prisons. Nonprofit organizations come in many forms: schools, research foundations, child welfare causes, and disaster relief agencies. It's fairly easy to appeal to people to get involved and support those causes. We all find a sympathetic connection to those suffering with disease, or poverty, or disaster. You rarely see people pull their wallets out at the suggestion of helping prisoners. Don't they deserve what they're getting? Shouldn't we help suffering people who haven't committed crimes?

So what do you say to men willing to have their photo taken? Give me "prison tough"? Show me that softer side? Not likely. Who wants to see a smiling prisoner? We'd wonder if they felt sorry for what they did and whether their punishment was having any effect. The flip side would be a photo of a sad or lonely prisoner, to which we are likely to say, "Serves him right. Did the crime, now he's doing the time!"

Stumping for prisoners is like asking people to support a despised people group like the Nazis. In a world groaning under the weight of worthy causes and little time in our busy schedules to weigh our choices, who do you think gets a quicker response, the murderer or the malnourished girl in Malawi?

As I've looked through the lens, considered the light, the angle, the story, the possible interpretations, I have learned to see each person as God sees me—fallen, in need of the cleansing blood of the cross.

> For all have sinned and fallen short of the glory of God. ~Romans 3:23

MARCH 16

THE BEGINNING OF WISDOM
John Leonardson, Texas

I STARTED DOING drugs in the Air Force and didn't stop after I left. By the time I hit my thirties I was a full-time drug dealer out of Minneapolis. The money was very good. I had a high-rise apartment, house, guns, and all kinds of stuff.

One day I did a favor for a guy by selling drugs to someone outside my normal clientele—he was undercover. Police swept in and arrested me and three of my dealers.

As I was thrown against the wall, a gun pressed to my head, I heard an unfamiliar voice speak to me internally: "This is the beginning of true wisdom." I practiced Eastern mysticism including consulting a guru and doing transcendental meditation. Supposedly, I had been seeking wisdom.

I thought, *Yeah, right. They're taking everything and I'm going to prison. Doesn't look like wisdom to me.*

Once in prison I contacted my guru for advice. He recommended I just read whatever book is popular—the Koran, the Bible, whatever. "They are all from the same source," he told me. So I picked up a Bible. Instead of being some book, it came alive. The Holy Spirit began to speak to me. It convicted me, and I realized I had been deceived—my mysticism had not been getting me closer to wisdom, but stupidity.

I got on my knees in my cell, repented, and asked the Lord into my life.

With nine months' time served, they released me. God called me to prison work immediately, though I didn't fully understand the commitment or duration of this call. I've tried to quit a few times over the years, but it doesn't work. When something's in your heart and you're called, you can't walk away without walking away from God.

Today I work for Cornerstone Assistance Network under a federal grant from the Department of Labor. We received $1.2 million to help prisoners being released. We help with food, clothes, careers, classes, training, and I do case management for up to a year post-release. I'm the president of the board of New Name Ministries, which focuses on the needs of returning sex offenders, and I also run MentorCare Ministries.

All this work generally puts me in the position of mentoring a lot of men being released, but it changes *my* life, not just theirs. I get a chance to grow as a Christian. A lot of people set boundaries and limits as to their walk with the Lord. Bottom line: I'd rather have been in prison than a fancy party or almost anywhere. I absolutely enjoy God in prison. What would you rather do: Just have the world's fun, or change a life?

For God's gifts and his call are irrevocable. ~Romans 11:29

FAITHFUL IN MISTAKES

John Leonardson, Texas

WORKING WITH prisoners on the inside is usually less messy and costly than outside. Volunteers often enjoy a special status behind the wire because prisoners realize you spend your free time in the lockup by choice. America's full of entertainment alternatives, but there you are!

Most folks who have worked inside learn that many prisoners have a real passion to change their ways. It's on the outside where the wheels come off because people lack mature Christian friendship and accountability.

Over the years I've had a lot of men live in our house with my wife and me, so we can provide that missing piece. Most of the guys have gone on to do well, but I did have one bad experience.

In 2009 I got to know John*, an ex-prisoner, by helping him find a job. He did well enough to be promoted. He attended my church and needed a place to live. We had an opening and invited him in.

He started to get an "I know what I'm doing better than anybody else" attitude. He quit his successful job and was supposedly starting his own company. A few weeks later we came home from church and were missing $7,000 worth of stuff. A month later, John parked a stolen car in a no parking zone. Police towed it and recovered my laptop in it. They also found my .357 magnum after John fired it at police in a shootout. John missed and the police didn't—hitting him three times. He was convicted of attempted capital murder and sentenced to forty years.

John was a very smart guy with a lot of potential, but he was a sociopath—he had no conscience. John was very good at telling you what you wanted to hear, and we were fooled. I hear people say, "Oh my gosh! And you're still taking ex-prisoners into your home?"

Before making a move like we have, you must consider this: My life and everything I own is the Lord's. I didn't enjoy the fact that he stole my stuff, but God took care of it. I ended up better off than before. People from seven states sent donations to help cover what insurance did not.

Bottom line: My wife and I are both committed. Our lives are in the hands of the Lord. We're not afraid to offer ourselves and what we have. God has always taken care of us.

I believe that Jesus is all in favor of the risky choices my wife and I have made. Didn't he hang out with the wrong crowd? Many churches are afraid of messes. They only want the well-dressed, well-off people. But church is meant to be a hospital, a healing place. It's meant to be where you can deal with people's sins and all, and really love them. Ex-prisoners and I have the same spiritual dad. I don't see any distinctions.

> You suffered along with those in prison and joyfully accepted the confiscation of your property, because you knew that you yourselves had better and lasting possessions. ~Hebrews 10:34

MARCH 18

HOPE RESTORED
Connie Johnston, Ohio

I WISH I could lay claims to it, but the idea wasn't mine. The inspiration behind Aunt Mary's Storybook Project actually came from a woman named Mary Best. She was a maiden primary schoolteacher for forty years; her career began in a one-room schoolhouse. Mary was the sort of teacher who nurtured her students and taught them the joy of learning. Her niece began the project in 1993 as a memorial to her aunt, and to serve the women of Cook County Jail in Chicago. Today, the successful project is available in many of the nation's penal institutions.

My husband and I began the Aunt Mary's Storybook Project at the Licking County (Ohio) Jail in January of 2007. Taking donated new and gently-used storybooks into the jail, we allow inmates to choose an age-appropriate book for their child, and then record the inmate reading the book on DVD or audiotape. The book and recording are then wrapped and mailed to the child. Inmates are permitted to participate in the project every thirty days.

Oftentimes children of inmates are the crime victims we forget about. The recording allows children suffering from the effects of a parent's incarceration to listen to that familiar, comforting voice whenever desired. To children, no matter what parents do, they are still "Mommy and Daddy." Likewise, children can be a powerful motivator for their parents. The desire to provide a quality life for their children, despite their incarceration, can cause them to seek help dealing with their personal issues.

We have found that Aunt Mary's Storybook Project helps strengthen family bonds, as well as encourage literacy. The average dad where we volunteer occasionally gets emotional when he opens up a storybook and begins reading to his beloved offspring. One man in particular came in for a second reading. After choosing a book, he opened it to read and then hung his head and began to sob. Once he was composed, I gently asked what was going on. Through tears of joy, he said he had recently learned that every time his ten-year-old daughter pulled out the first storybook recording he had made, his nineteen- and twenty-year-old sons also sat down to listen to the voice of a wayward father they had long since given up on.

Hope for new beginnings had been restored.

> Which of you fathers, if your son asks for a fish, will give him a snake instead? Or if he asks for an egg, will give him a scorpion? If you then, though you are evil, know how to give good gifts to your children, how much more will your Father in heaven give the Holy Spirit to those who ask him!
> Luke 11:11–13

MARCH 19

LESSON FROM A HARE

Connie Johnston, Ohio

STILL STUNNED that he wound up inside a jail serving time, Gary* stood staring at a bulletin board. The disheveled papers tacked all over it were for the most part long lists of rules and regulations of the institution. Included on the board were also a few "before-and-after" pictures of poor souls who found themselves addicted to methamphetamines. Gary offered up to God a quick "thank you" in gratitude that he had not been plagued by that particular evil. But, here he was in trouble with the law and estranged from his wife and two little boys, ages three and one. His heart was heavy.

Buried underneath layers of papers on the bulletin board was a bright blue paper that caught Gary's eye. He uncovered it and read an advertisement for a program available to the incarcerated, called Aunt Mary's Storybook Project. There was no cost involved to participate—a huge bonus since he had no money in his inmate account. The only requirement was to send a kite (request form) requesting a date to schedule a reading and taping of a book to send to his children. He sent the kite immediately.

As facilitator of the program, when the day arrived for the taping I went to the facility with my video camera, tripod, and a few storybooks I had chosen from our stock of donated books. Once I was all set up in a visitation room, Gary entered to read to his little ones.

After the deputy brought him in, I could tell instantly that Gary was excited to see an "outsider." And, he was eager to have this wonderful opportunity to read to his boys, whom he sorely missed.

Usually I lay out three or four age-appropriate books for the inmate to choose from. The first book Gary examined for his toddlers was a chunky, cardboard, rabbit-shaped book titled *Bailey the Bunny*. Gary's face immediately lit up with a smile that went from ear to ear.

"This book is perfect!" he exclaimed. "Our last name is Baylee."

Suddenly Gary got quiet. Tears filled his eyes and his lips quivered.

God goes to great lengths to let us know he cares about us and is watching over us and our loved ones. Sometimes he even uses a children's storybook.

> The LORD watches over you— the LORD is your shade at your right hand.
> ~Psalm 121:5

SECOND CHANCES

Connie Johnston, Ohio

NICK* CAME into the visitation room excited about the opportunity to choose a book and record it on DVD through the Aunt Mary's Storybook Project. I laid out on the table a few books appropriate for his six-year-old son. Nick quickly chose one with pictures of animated vegetable characters on the cover. He had not heard of *Veggie Tales* before, but Nick seemed to be intrigued with the title: *Jonah—Even Fish Slappers Need a Second Chance*. As he began to read about the mean and rotten Ninevites and how God sent Jonah to tell them to stop their wicked ways,

I watched from behind the camera. Slowly, his hardened countenance began to soften.

This particular *Veggie Tales* book ingeniously tells of God's amazing grace and how he is also a God of tender mercies and gentle love. It cleverly mentions how God is willing to lend a helping hand and restore anyone from dark circumstances. The story reminds us that even when we run from God, he still offers forgiveness, as well as assurance he has a better plan for our lives.

When Nick finished reading the book, there was a tear in his eye and he closed the recording by telling his boy, "I had no idea what the story was about when I started, but it sure was a good one. I love you, son."

Turning the camera off, I offered up a silent prayer of thanks for an open door that I sensed God had prearranged. Nick started asking me questions—I sensed his heart was open. He suddenly seemed hungry to know more about the God he had forsaken as a rebellious teenager, about this Savior who loved him, died on a cross for him, and never stopped pursuing him—even in the dark belly of a jail.

We had a heartfelt discussion, and then there, in Visitation Room One, a weary traveler surrendered to the extravagant grace of a loving God, One who indeed does give second chances.

> . . . and all are justified freely by his grace through the redemption that came by Christ Jesus. ~Romans 3:23–25

THE FOREMOST OF SINNERS

Bill Mothershed, California

A PAINTING of the Last Supper, painted by a prisoner, covers the front wall of the chapel at Old Folsom prison. What many people don't know is that each face in that portrait is the face of a murderer doing time at the prison. Having been baptized in the presence of this magnificent work of art, less than two years after being convicted of murder, I take some comfort in its secret. I know in my heart the love that God has for the repentant murderer.

Some of the most influential men in the Bible were repentant murderers. Moses killed an Egyptian man for striking a Hebrew slave. When Pharaoh found out about it, Moses fled into the desert, leaving his wealth and position behind. And King David, in order to take Bathsheba (with whom he had already committed adultery and who was married to a loyal soldier, Uriah), ordered Uriah to be sent out on a suicide mission. As a result, David's reign was cursed with treachery from within his own family from that day on, and the child he fathered with Bathsheba died.

Saul, who became Paul, was a powerful Pharisee who went around murdering Christians just because they had given their life to Christ. To turn him to repentance, the resurrected Christ literally knocked him off his high horse and blinded him. As a Christian, Paul suffered persecutions similar to those he had inflicted upon the followers of Jesus.

The harm Moses, David, and Paul had caused could never be healed, and the consequences of their actions did not magically disappear just because of their repentance. But this did not stop God from using them mightily. Moses was called upon to lead Israel out of Egyptian slavery and deliver God's Law to his people. David and Bathsheba went on to give birth to Solomon, who presided over the most prosperous period of the kingdom of Israel. Jesus was a descendant of David and Bathsheba through Mary. Paul went on to bring the church to the Gentiles and wrote many of the books of the New Testament.

Through these examples, I know that anyone, including myself, can be used fruitfully by God, if we come with truly repentant and humble hearts.

> Here is a trustworthy saying that deserves full acceptance: Christ Jesus came into the world to save sinners —of whom I am the worst. But for that very reason I was shown mercy so that in me, the worst of sinners, Christ Jesus might display his immense patience as an example for those who would believe in him and receive eternal life. ~1 Timothy 1:15–16

DEEPER INTO THE PIT

Jim Harris, Alabama

I WAS BORN with a rebellious nature. As early as I can remember there was always something I was mad about. One of the things I hated most was authority—any type of authority. *Who are you to tell me what I can do? What gives you the right?*

From these early memories my life in Texas became one of rebellion. I was against everything my family tried to teach me.

When I became a teenager I foolishly listened to the bad advice of others, which led to a downward spiral in my life. And . . . I discovered girls. "Sex, Drugs, and Rock & Roll" became my theme. Although it all seemed like fun at the time, those three things were leading me deeper into a pit. However, you couldn't have told me that at the time.

My first arrest was in the tenth grade for possession of speed. My parents were crushed. They longed to do whatever they could and even sent me to the first of five rehabs. None seemed to help.

The drug use escalated from weed and speed to cocaine, heroin, and methamphetamines—even IV use. The addiction became so powerful that at times I would load a syringe full of cocaine and heroin mixed together, called a "speedball." Right before injecting it, I would have a crack pipe loaded. I would do the shot, then "chase it" with a big hit off the pipe.

It's no wonder my rap sheet (list of offenses) was five pages long. I was hooked and I didn't care. Rehab and psychiatric help couldn't help fill the hole in my soul. Finally, my last "go 'round" happened in my own home. I overdosed on the speedball-and-crack-pipe routine. Thankfully, 9-1-1 came to my rescue.

When they revived me, saving my life, they also found nine grams of cocaine in my pocket. Once at the jail I had some kind of seizure and ended up back in the hospital in the cardiac care unit. When I came to, three days later, I left the hospital against medical advice. I was on a search for more dope! The law caught up with me and gave me a felony conviction. I was on my way to the Texas Department of Corrections, and a new life.

Do not love the world nor the things in the world. If anyone loves the world, the love of the Father is not in him. ~1 John 2:15

THERE IS A GOD!

Jim Harris, Alabama

SITTING IN my cell, contemplating what had happened to me, wondering if I would survive my forthcoming sentence, gave me time to ask the question, "Is there a God?" I was at the bottom of the pile, convicted of possession of a controlled substance, cocaine. The only thing I knew for certain was that if I lived I was going to prison. You really *can* taste fear.

I didn't realize that many people were praying for me. God answered those prayers through Roger, a man who came into Tarrant County Jail in Fort Worth, Texas, to do "religious services" in my housing pod. I had seen him there before and something about him drew me to him. He kept talking about how the Lord loved me and that he would forgive me if only I would accept Jesus as my Savior. Well, nothing else I had tried up to that point had worked, so I asked another inmate to pray with me when Roger asked us if we wanted to be "saved."

Even though I had a flippant attitude, at that moment something incredible happened—I will remember it forever. When I admitted I was a sinner and needed a Savior, it felt as if my entire body was encompassed in heat. It felt as if my body was blushing from the bottom of my feet to the tip of my nose! I knew with utmost certainty that God had delivered me from my drug addiction—I was sure of it! I had become a new creation. Since that day in jail, Christmas 1995, I have never had a craving for drugs again.

Prison in Texas was no vacation, but God was with me. It went by without any of my fears being realized and it turned into a period in my life when the Lord "sent me to school." Not school in the traditional sense, but every time a chaplain had a service, I was there. And I was constantly reading the Word.

God even used me while in prison to witness to a friend who later came to know Jesus. This friend wrote to me after I was out to tell me about it. His letter was the thing God used to "call" me into the ministry—a ministry now growing in amazing ways.

> But may it never be that I would boast, except in the cross of our Lord Jesus Christ, through which the world has been crucified to me, and I to the world.
> ~Galatians 6:14–16

RESTORATION

Jim Harris, Alabama

WHEN YOU know you've been changed on the inside, it makes you want to run out and tell the world! You really expect others to believe that you are a new man and that God has converted you. Unfortunately, the reality is that you've been banished by your family. Your friends are not interested in being around you. You are just an ex-con who can't be trusted. The devil will try his best at this point to steal your peace and turn you back to him.

What I did instead was this: I found new friends in church, I stuck with my wife, Fredia (who had stuck with me while I was in prison), and I took the first job offered me. It was a telemarketing job, but God had given it to me. I did my work just as if he was standing right there listening—because he was! After a little while my work ethic stood out. Before my parole ended a year later, I was promoted twice and ran several retail businesses for this corporation. My family took note and some of my old friends did also; God had begun the process of restoration.

My grandmother lived to see how God changed my life before she went home to be with Him. After she passed and my parole ended, Fredia and I moved to Alabama, where we currently live. I got a great job at a local car dealership, and then another where I did even better financially. But during this time, God also began a new ministry through me. When that letter from my friend back in prison came in the mail, I knew in my heart that God was calling me into prison ministry. He also had been giving me a vision for where to go in this ministry.

After consulting with my wife and praying for a while, I surrendered to the calling. The church we attended at that time helped me start out as their emissary to the local county jail. We had no idea what our next step would be, but we knew God would be walking with us!

> And I will restore to you the years that the locust hath eaten, the cankerworm, and the caterpillar, and the palmer-worm, my great army which I sent among you. ~Joel 2:25

BUILDING A MINISTRY

Jim Harris, Alabama

AFTER YOU step out in faith and follow the Lord's leading, the devil increases his feverish attacks against you. In my case, Satan tried to convince me that no one would ever trust me again. He wanted me to believe I hadn't changed after all, and that I would not continue to succeed.

I decided it was time to ignore Satan and trust God. It was the year 2000, right after the Y2K scare had come and gone, when I chose to follow those nudges from God and step out in faith. Even though I had a good job, working for someone else had been keeping me from having enough time to do the ministry the Lord was calling me to do. After Fredia and I discussed this and prayed over it, we began our own business.

Being self-employed meant I could set my own hours. This situation enabled me to pursue a lot of ministries: I am now an ordained minister as well as the director of evangelism for my Southern Baptist association. We started a ministry in the local jail. I worked with Prison Fellowship as a volunteer director for their project called Operation Starting Line. I was involved with Good News Jail and Prison Ministry as a local board member for the chaplain at the jail. I am currently a featured speaker for Bill Glass Champions for Life in hundreds of prisons around the country, as well as an area director, setting up prison evangelism events in the Deep South.

As long as I live I will never forget the feeling of utter desperation and loneliness I had tried to fill with the things of the world. Reflecting on my past, and knowing that others, without Christ in their lives, are just as lost as I was, compels me to keep sharing what he has done, and is still doing, in my life.

Know therefore that the Lord your God is God; he is the faithful God, keeping his covenant of love to a thousand generations of those who love him and keep his commandments. ~Deuteronomy 7:9

FLYING RIGHT

Jim Harris, Alabama

GOD PROVIDES for those he calls. This is the greatest lesson he has taught me since my salvation while incarcerated. He provides in many ways, but the most interesting method so far has been through people. When the economy crashed in 2008–09, the Lord led me to a group of men and women who helped start Fly Right Inc., a 501(c)3 organization that conducts prison ministry and school assemblies. God gave us great favor and sent us great minds to work on this.

Our name actually came from the old saying, "You better straighten up and fly right!" God also gave me the ability to fly radio-controlled aircraft to attract a crowd, opening a door for me to share my testimony, hence the name for our ministry, Fly Right Inc.

In our first eighteen months we went to six different prisons and spoke in more than forty schools. At two schools students filled out cards with their names and requests for help with any serious situation they might be facing. Three young ladies told us they were considering taking their lives and we were able to intervene with the proper authorities.

Our board has prayerfully set many goals for the next few years, including evangelism in jails and prisons, holding assemblies in schools, establishing discipleship groups to follow up in the jails and prisons, mentoring those who need and ask for help inside the institutions, establishing a reentry program for ex-cons, and, finally, to take those reformed ex-cons back into the prisons, jails, and schools to share their stories!

God has given us a great vision and we are dedicated to accomplishing it.

> But they that wait upon the Lord shall renew their strength; they shall mount up with wings as eagles; they shall run, and not be weary; and they shall walk, and not faint. ~Isaiah 40:31

SHAMED AT THE GATE

Manny Mill, Illinois

MY WIFE left me at the Allenwood Federal Correctional Complex in Pennsylvania. Everyone watched to see how I would handle this train wreck. I must confess—and confession has to be part of the Christian life—I was a terrible husband and extremely unfaithful to my ex-wife.

After fourteen years in Cuba my family fled to the United States in 1970. I didn't know Jesus, and my mother was a witch. In that environment I decided if there was a god, I was it. I became addicted to Manny Mill. I did whatever I wanted for my own glory. When I entered college in South Orange, New Jersey, to play baseball, I became addicted to sex.

I never graduated, but became one of the top life insurance salesmen for a large national firm. I was living the life: four cars, one hundred suits, and all kinds of gold jewelry. I married Cecilia at a young age and we had our first son, Manny Jr., but I was still addicted to sexual sin. I was unfaithful to my wife every single day. I provided the money my wife and son needed, but not the love and care that are essential to a healthy family.

Going from a refugee with nothing to a successful businessman with so much went to my head. I committed what I thought was the "perfect" crime for a payoff of $175,000. Sex, money, and power are the three big sins and I did them all! When the FBI began looking for me, I ran. Cecilia was *angry*.

We eventually landed in Caracas, Venezuela, because there was a Cuban community there. I opened a successful Cuban restaurant, but my sexual addiction increased during the two years we were there.

By now, my mom had become a Christian and she was praying for me. In a desperate phone call from my parents, who were still in New Jersey, I ended up coming to Christ through the witness of my mother. Then she asked, "When are you coming back?"

I *really* wrestled with that one, but decided by faith I had to. The whole family met me at New York's Kennedy Airport where the FBI arrested me right off the airplane. I pled guilty to federal charges of possession of interstate stolen property.

While out on bond for a short while before going to prison I told Cecilia, "Now might be a good time for you to leave me." I knew she was *really* wounded. But she said, "No, I want to stick with you." She visited me a few times with the kids early on, which encouraged me (as it does any prisoner).

Then in my tenth month, chaplain Manny Cordero and I hosted an in-prison marriage seminar. With around 85 percent of inmate marriages ending in divorce we really believed in bringing this material to the guys. As the head elder of our in-prison church I organized it all and asked Cecilia to join us. She said she would.

The day of the seminar I was at the gate with the chaplain welcoming all the wives—mine never showed up. The chaplain discovered she had moved to Miami without saying anything. It was a tremendous blow. Here I am teaching this seminar expecting not only that she would come, but that we were going to beat the statistics. I remembered the verse my mother gave me over the phone when I became a believer, Hebrews 13:8. I really needed that. I needed to trust He would show up in that adversity. I was finding out that a true Christian's character is revealed in adversity.

> The Lord will never leave you nor forsake you. ~Hebrews 13:8

MARCH 28

ALL THINGS ARE NEW
Manny Mill, Illinois

TWO WEEKS later inmate #07592 received an envelope in the mail— my divorce papers. I couldn't contest it because she rightly accused me of abandoning her. I went to prison due to my own sins. That weekend was so significant in breaking me. I knew the guys were watching me. I was leading three meetings a day and planted the first Spanish-speaking church (75 guys) out of a general population of 400 at that time. My life was all about church. I did a lot of damage to my ex-wife and I take full responsibility. She remarried and I don't blame her.

Even though I had come to Christ, decided to own up to my crimes, and even worked to save what I had damaged so badly—my relationship with my wife—in the end I could not outrun the consequences of earlier decisions. I still went to prison, I still lost my marriage. God does not wave a magic wand to fix everything. Prison is a stripping-away experience of identity, family, everything. It was no different for me. But what got me through was that precious hope that I could not be separated from Jesus. That's it. I had to take the shame, the disappointment, the embarrassment, the loss, and let Jesus do something with it in His timing.

It's worse when you know that the adults are not the only ones damaged. Children are hurt by divorce. The biggest battle we face in America is not the economy, or war in Afghanistan. It's the war we don't know how to fight—saving the broken family—that leads to crime. I would be a liar to say my adultery throughout my marriage didn't affect us, or contribute to my decision to steal. Sin is corrosive and it spreads. I ached during the five years my ex-wife kept me from speaking to or seeing my two children. What could I do?

Years later, God did not *restore* anything. He made everything *new* for me. We want to recover, but Jesus did not come to be a mechanic and fix things up. He came to make us new. I have a new wife (married 22 years now) with whom I have two sons and a daughter. I also have two other new children, because both my kids with Cecilia became "born again" after I went to prison. It's all about Jesus plus nothing else. God never grows tired of new beginnings. He gave me a new life.

> Therefore, if anyone is in Christ, the new creation has come: The old has gone, the new is here! ~2 Corinthians 5:17

MARCH 29

FURLOUGH FOR A FUGITIVE?

Manny Mill, Illinois

ABOUT A year into my sentence, Prison Fellowship asked Chaplain Cordero to recommend two guys to be a part of the last Washington Discipleship Seminar (WDS). You cannot imagine how exciting this program sounded to us inmates. Prisoners left prison for two weeks! They traveled to the Prison Fellowship headquarters in Virginia to get trained and equipped for ministry inside prison. Chaplain Cordero wanted to pick me. I thought I had a great chance because of my status as a leader in the church and a perfect disciplinary record with the Department of Corrections.

He went to my case manager and counselor. Both agreed I was the perfect guy to go. They also both rejected our petition because of my former status as a fugitive from the law.

"Yeah, he's a Christian, but we've seen this game played before and we don't know what he'll be like when he's out," one of them said. I ran from the FBI for three years before my conversion to Christ. The WDS was six weeks away and you have to have enough time to get all the paperwork done if selected.

I was really discouraged, but we went to prayer with the chaplain and three church groups. During those days of prayerful intensity I had to check myself. Many times we want God to act for our own benefit. That was a great lesson for me. I had to be sure I was examining my motivations. *Why do I want to go to WDS?* Is it for two weeks' vacation, good food, and time away from the cellblock? The Holy Spirit convicted me that I was to be there to be an equipped disciple. It was a good tune-up for my motivations. I was beginning to experience the cross in my prayers.

Four days later both the counselor and case manager were transferred out of the prison and two new people were assigned to me. We *did not* see that coming. Even though it's the same case against me, the chaplain said he was going back to the new guys and try again. We got an immediate reversal. This is God! A miracle is when God answers our requests without human manipulation, orchestration, influence, politicking, or money. Usually we want to pursue all these avenues and offer short prayers. But here, God got all the glory.

We finished the paperwork; people donated money for my flight and program. I received a two-week furlough to go out of state. I even saw my parents, who made a delicious Cuban meal for all the guys. We try to be good Christians doing things in our own strength without God. But this time, it was simply all God.

I am the Lord; that is my name! I will not yield my glory to another.
~Isaiah 42:8

109

FIRST EX-CON
ATTENDS WHEATON

Manny Mill, Illinois

THE DAY before I returned to prison from the wonderful two-week furlough to study at the Washington Discipleship Seminar, I was invited to a fundraising dinner for Prison Fellowship.

God is precise toward those he purchased with his blood. My hosts sat me next to someone I didn't know. "Nice to meet you," he said, "what are you going to do after you leave prison?"

I said with intense charismatic enthusiasm, "Sir, by faith, I'm going to Wheaton Bible College!"

"That's a very noble objective, but let me correct you, it's just Wheaton College."

"Sir, I know what I'm talking about. I just applied for the Charles W. Colson scholarship. It's Wheaton Bible College, I know that's right!" We go back and forth and finally in a humble way he tells me, "Manny, my name is Ken Wessner and I'm the chairman of the board of Wheaton College."

Where was I going to hide? I felt like a fool, completely embarrassed. But he was so gracious. We moved on and became real friends. I discovered Ken also founded the Institute for Prison Ministry at the Billy Graham Evangelistic Center and found a donor to fund a scholarship chair in Colson's name for people like me. Ken Wessner became my spiritual guide.

When I returned to prison expecting another year before I could be paroled, the news came: I qualified for early parole! Again, this was completely outside my control, except through prayer. Another work of God allowed me to travel to Chicago while on parole to settle the details of my attending Wheaton.

Ken greeted me warmly and took me to dinner when I arrived on Wheaton's campus. I'll never forget as he pointed a finger at me. "Manny, I'm going to help you, but you have no room to fail." He put the fear of God into me! I still had to interview with many people to see if I was the caliber to come to Wheaton. I had the desire. However, a lot of people have good intentions and desires, but they don't qualify.

I had many things against me: One, I was on parole and I needed a transfer approval. Two, I haven't been to college in a long time, and I have to learn how to study again. Three, I knew English, but not at a university level. Even today, you can clearly hear my Cuban accent. So I remembered three things: Ken's challenge to me, that God will never leave me, and that he answers prayer.

I entered Wheaton in July 1988. A local church adopted me and they still support me today. Some of my prior college credits transferred so I started as a second semester sophomore. By December of 1989 I finished my B.A. and made the dean's list twice. I took it seriously. I was convicted that I was representing many guys and gals who would come after me. I had to be a good example and was the first ex-convict to complete a bachelor's and a master's at Wheaton.

> Now it is required that those who have been given a trust must prove faithful.
> ~1 Corinthians 1:2

THE DAY MOTHER DIED

Joe McDonald, Alabama

ONE OF MY most humbling experiences in prison came in July 2009. I drove with a trailer full of gear from my home in Alabama to help with a "One Day with God" camp in a Beaumont, Texas, prison. A shadow followed me. A few days prior I visited my mother in a nursing home in Mobile. At 93, she had been slowly fading with Alzheimer's disease. She gave me a look that said, "You're not going to see me again." She wasn't particularly lucid. Though both my wife and I were scheduled to be out of town the same weekend, four of our six children were local, should anything happen.

I decided there was nothing to be done but to go forward with my commitment to the Texas prison.

Thursday night my cell phone rang. Mom had only a few hours at best. If I wanted to get home, I had better make it quick. I couldn't drive or make a flight in time given my location. I was leading a program for the kids on Saturday as well as volunteer training. God had called me to a purpose to

111

help restore relationships with fathers and children still living. I had a peace about that. So I let them know I'd be home as quick as possible after the event. My kids called later that same evening. "Dad, she passed."

I didn't say anything about it, but someone on our team found out and leaked it to the inmates who were going through the program with us that weekend.

Most inmates live with a fear that someone close to them—usually a mother or grandmother—will die while they are stuck in prison with few, if any, options to be there. They usually can't be with the family and share in the loss. I had a choice the day before, but decided God had wanted me to see this through.

About twenty-five inmates in their white uniforms gathered in a circle around me, laid hands on me, and prayed for me and my loss. They just couldn't get over it. Though I felt separated from my family it seems God placed me among the most empathetic group of people I could have been with that day. God established a strong bond between me and the prisoners because of their prayers for me. It made for a special weekend for us all.

I'm hardly a super saint, but it's a powerful message to prisoners when you're not paid and still show up in their world and tell them God loves them. They've been cursed all their lives. Most of them were raised with a steady diet of people telling them they would never amount to anything. All anybody wants is to hear someone say, "I love you. You're valuable. You have worth in this world." I think God used my loss to really push that message home into some hearts.

"Truly I tell you," Jesus replied, "no one who has left home or brothers or sisters or mother or father or children or fields for me and the gospel will fail to receive a hundred times as much in this present age: homes, brothers, sisters, mothers, children and fields—along with persecutions—and in the age to come eternal life." ~Mark 10:29–30

HASSLES

Joe McDonald, Alabama

GETTING INTO prison as a volunteer isn't as simple as you might imagine. I almost think it would be quicker to commit a crime than to go through everything we do just to spend a few hours with prisoners for their benefit.

You learn from experience that whatever agreement you made on Thursday with whichever staff member, doesn't mean anyone on Friday will have a clue about that plan. People come to work late and miss the memo. You hope to have it in writing so when you show up you've got paperwork to give the officer who says, "You're bringing a trailer full of what in here?"

It's a tough spot for officers because your security is their responsibility. Anything that adds to that difficulty by bringing a bunch of folks into a secure area can make their job more complicated and stressful. If anything goes wrong, it's going to fall on them. Sometimes officers come in not because they love Jesus, but because someone said, "You're working today to accommodate this event."

The time schedule is always tight. You always have a limited window to do your thing and lots of things happen to make that window even smaller. Instead of thirty minutes you now have fifteen. We have to be ready and willing to adjust. If it's an outside event, you factor in the weather—we don't want the inmates squinting into the sun. *Where's electricity coming from? Do we need a stage? How are we going to set it up?* You have very little control and you're always trying to please the staff. Officers working through counts and meal schedules will stop everything in the middle of your program. Then there's the Transportation Security Administration (TSA) slowing things down at the airports, and the airlines losing your luggage.

The closer you get to God the more barriers the Enemy is going to throw down to thwart you, get you aggravated, and make you feel like quitting. I recognize it better now, so I can step back and say, "I must be fixin' to get blessed because I'm having an extra hard time with this process or person today."

When you *choose* to look at it that way, you can fight through the discouragement and frustration. Often people want to hear about the mountaintop rather than all the time we spend in the valley, such as fourteen hours of windshield time in the pouring rain with no place to sleep and no supper. We get 4 a.m. wakeup calls to get to the prison gates by 6 a.m. to start the clearance process.

Actually, we spend most of our time in the valley with only brief glimpses on the mountaintop. When we see a person understand redemption, hear about Jesus for the first time, or hear that God loves them, that justifies all the valley hours invested to get to that point.

> I consider that our present sufferings are not worth comparing with the glory that will be revealed in us. ~Romans 8:18

WANTING GOD'S WILL

Bernice Hayes, Ohio

I BECAME A Christian at age seventeen while living in West Virginia, and attended church sporadically until my late twenties. Then I moved to Ohio, where I was drawn to visit a local Baptist church. During that first worship service the Lord spoke clearly to me that this was the church he wanted me to attend. I had never experienced the Holy Spirit like that before, but there was no mistaking it.

A new peace and joy filled me as each week I listened to the Word of God being preached. Then, a woman at that church started mentoring me, helping me get even more grounded in my faith.

I was still single and longing to marry a godly man. I prayed about it regularly. One evening, while working at my waitress job, a nice-looking guy came in. I was immediately attracted to him, although he appeared to have been drinking. I did not want him to leave the restaurant in that condition so I offered him some coffee. We struck up a conversation and I introduced myself. He said his name was Scott and he lived in the area.

We started dating and quickly fell in love. Scott even started attending church with me. In less than a month we were engaged.

When Scott shared that he had served time in prison, I assumed he was over his drug addiction. But then I noticed he would disappear, sometimes for several days. I soon discovered how bad his addiction was—and knew he needed help. He wanted to quit, but the pull of the drugs was strong. I immediately made an appointment with my pastor.

"I'm sorry," the pastor said. "I can't marry the two of you while Scott is involved in such a destructive lifestyle. Once he is clean for a year, then I will agree to perform your wedding ceremony. In the meantime, we will keep praying for him and helping him in any way we can."

Scott desperately wanted to quit, but the stronghold of his addictions was intense. We prayed together often about it.

The church and the pastor helped Scott a lot, too. They mentored him through his habits and taught him to turn to Jesus. It wasn't easy, and change didn't happen overnight, but it did come. Scott's love for God increased and he began serving by getting involved in different ministries at church. He even got a job in church maintenance.

Finally, after a year had passed, I had peace about marrying Scott. I sensed the Lord was telling me it was okay. This time the pastor agreed to it, too.

Neither Scott nor I had any idea how the Lord was going to work in our future. We only knew we were committed to following his lead in our lives.

> Then he said to them all: "Whoever wants to be my disciple must deny themselves and take up their cross daily and follow me." ~Luke 9:23

APRIL 3

SEARCHING FOR IDENTITY
Scott Hayes, Ohio

I WAS JUST sixteen months old when my parents divorced. I have an older brother and our dad wasn't a positive influence in our lives or very involved with us. My mom did a wonderful job as a single mother and she later married a man who became a great stepdad, but there was always something missing in my life.

There were times we were on welfare and lived in low-income housing. We moved about once a year, making it hard to fit in and make lasting friendships. Add that to the fact that I was usually the smallest kid in the class and the other kids seemed to enjoy reminding me of that.

I had a close relationship with my mom's mom. She was the only grandparent involved in my life and I loved her dearly. Sadly, she committed suicide when I was eleven years old. Back then, and even now, I sometimes wonder, *Did she think I didn't love her?"* and, *Did she not love me?*

I started drinking alcohol when I was fourteen, mostly to fit in. I didn't feel good about myself and didn't like myself. I was searching for significance. Not long after I started drinking, I experimented with smoking weed. From there, my drug use escalated to LSD, PCP, cocaine, heroin, and my favorite, meth.

I soon found my identity in my addictions, violence, and trying to "outdo" my peers through wild and crazy behavior. I had lived this life for so long I convinced myself this was who I really was.

In the sixteen years that I struggled with my addictions, I overdosed twice. Both times paramedics were unable to find a pulse. In actuality, I should have died. Which was okay with me; I didn't care most of the time. In fact, I had suicidal thoughts on a regular basis.

My life became centered around drugs and partying. As my tolerance grew, it took more and more dope just to feel "normal." I continued to care less and less and became depressed. Once, after a five- or six-day binge on meth, unable to eat or sleep at all, I locked myself in an unfinished basement. As usual I became extremely paranoid, anxious, and delusional. I tied a dog chain around my neck, stood on a chair and looped the other end of the chain around a gas pipe next to the ceiling. My plan was to end my miserable life by kicking the chair out from under me, but the thought of the pain and devastation I would cause my mom kept me from going through with it.

God had another plan, a plan for my life I would have never guessed in a million years . . .

> The LORD will accomplish what concerns me; Your loving kindness, O LORD, is everlasting; do not forsake the works of Your hands. ~Psalm 138:8

THE VALLEY OF THE SHADOW

Scott Hayes, Ohio

I FELT MY life was taking me down the wrong road, that I would probably end up in prison or even dead. So when I was eighteen I joined the Air Force. I continued to abuse alcohol and drugs while in the service.

One night, while home on leave, my brother and I were partying and getting drunk. A confrontation between us and police broke out at a bar and we were arrested and taken to jail. We were released on bond, but decided to go back to the police station to get even, this time with survival knives, slashing the tires on the cruisers. We then went to the home of one of the cops and threw a concrete block through his picture window. After that, we decided to go back to the police station and slash the tires on their personal cars. The grand finale happened when we went to a sergeant's house, where I fired four shots from a 9mm handgun right into the living room.

As a result, my brother and I were both sentenced to the old Mansfield Reformatory. It was a dumpy old prison, now thankfully closed. It had been condemned even before we got there, with broken windows, leaky plumbing, crumbling walls, and cockroaches that seemed to be the size of a small cat! It was an intimidating and scary season of life for me. There were chaos, violence, and screams heard 24/7. There are no words to adequately describe that experience.

In the midst of my being in what seemed to be hell, God saw to it someone handed me a pocket-sized Bible. I didn't know a lot about the Bible because I didn't believe in God much. But one day, while flipping through the pages, I remembered the Twenty-Third Psalm. I received two of my grandma's possessions after she passed away, both of which I still have and treasure today: a plant that fortunately is impossible to kill, and a copy of the Twenty-Third Psalm on a magnetic clip that she kept on her refrigerator.

I read that twenty-third chapter of Psalms over and over again, receiving great comfort and peace: "I will fear no evil, for you are with me . . ."

There were times in prison I wondered if I would make it out alive, but, thankfully, God had plans for me here.

Even though I walk through the darkest valley, I will fear no evil, for you are with me; your rod and your staff, they comfort me. ~Psalm 23:4

GOD HAD ANOTHER PLAN

Scott Hayes, Ohio

I T DIDN'T take long for me to return to the old lifestyle after being released from prison. I continued with my pattern of abusing drugs and alcohol. I dealt drugs, I lied, stole, and cheated. I robbed dope dealers, shot at people, and was shot at. I struggled more and more with the thought of taking my own life. While on drugs I felt guilty, miserable, and depressed. I was hopeless, believing I could never live life without using. My life felt out of control.

Then, one night in 1995, I was falling off a stool drunk at a local restaurant. A beautiful waitress approached me and offered me coffee and food to sober up. Her name was Bernice and there was something incredibly different about her. She had a genuine peace and joy I never knew existed. I wanted what she had. I later learned what it was—the saving grace of Jesus. After a couple of weeks and through the involvement of a mutual acquaintance, she invited me to church.

I wasn't interested in church or God. God was not real to me. And I always thought of Christians as weak-minded and weird. But, I was drawn to Bernice and wanted to impress her, so I went. Our first date was at a local church.

God used Bernice and her pastor to reach me. Long story short, I have been called into ministry and am now a pastor at the very same church. I am also the chaplain at the very jail where I was first incarcerated.

After coming to Christ I was convinced we would have to move away in order for me to have an effective ministry. *I know so many people here and have done a lot of things,* I thought. *If there is any possible way for*

this new way of life to succeed, I would surely need to start fresh some-
place new. Right, Lord?

But it was that very change in me that God wanted others to see. That "new creation" was, and still is, a testimony to him and his remarkable power to transform lives. God can and will use any one of us if we just let him. It's amazing to me that he uses the most difficult and painful parts of our lives to minister to those who are in the same places he brought us out of!

God had another plan for me—and he has a plan for you, too!

For we live by faith, not by sight. ~2 Corinthians 5:7

JAIL CHAPLAIN
Scott Hayes, Ohio

AS A CHAPLAIN at the county jail in the same city where I grew up, I frequently see inmates who are old acquaintances. Many are from my past when I lived another lifestyle.

One day, I ran into a female inmate I used to do drugs with. I had not seen her for several years. As I walked through the module where she was housed she stopped me.

"Scott? What are you doing here?" She looked me over, noticing I wasn't wearing an inmate uniform; rather I was dressed in casual business attire. She then asked, "Are you a social worker or something?"

I smiled slightly, and answered I was now drug-free and God had changed my life. I went on to tell her I was a pastor. After she finally picked her jaw up off the floor, I told her how God had sent me this amazing wife who pointed me to Christ, and how my wife's pastor took me under his wing and helped me with a job, showing me how to do life drug-free.

The following Sunday I was back in her housing area when she asked to talk in private. We went into a classroom where she let me know she had watched the morning sermon I had preached via closed-circuit tele-

119

vision. She asked if the forgiveness I talked about was available to her. Does God really care about *her*? Could he really change her life? Could God really forgive and release her from the bondage of her past? I assured her that God loved her and wanted to have a personal and intimate relationship with each one of us.

She told me she noticed a difference in my life—that I was different. She said she wanted a life full of peace, too, as I had.

"Seeing you in the jail and hearing your story is no accident," she said. "Scott, did you know that the first time I ever tried cocaine I was with you?" She then held up both hands and put her thumbs and fingertips together so they formed a circle.

"I started my drug use with you and I want to end it with you. I've come full circle. Will you pray the salvation prayer with me?"

Vicki's name was entered into the Lamb's Book of Life that day and her life has not been the same since.

Moments such as those have helped me understand why God did not want me to move away and start over. I'm glad I obeyed and stayed.

Before I was afflicted I went astray, but now I obey your word. ~Psalm 119:67

APRIL 7

DREAMS AND VISIONS
Scott Hayes, Ohio

YEARS AGO, God repeatedly gave me the same dream. Although details were unclear, the mission was not. He said, "Reflect my love and light into the darkness of the community, pointing those who are lost to me." Secondly, I heard, "Bring my church together." I can't explain it, but I knew I was to start a Christian community center in my hometown.

After much prayer I began an amazing journey. I actively searched for local property to either lease or purchase. I formed a nonprofit organization, recruited other believers, and began networking with other churches and organizations. God closed the doors on many prospective sites, teaching me lessons along the way as I tried doing it on my own. In short, he reminded me he was God and I was not!

Eventually we were able to purchase an old elementary school through an auction. Funny how most of the other buildings that *I* so desperately tried to make happen would fit in just the gym portion, a fraction of the 25,000-square-foot facility. I had been putting God in a box. He taught me he is bigger than any building (or anything else) in this world. God has provided for all our ministry needs!

I didn't like the name that God gave me for the community center: "The Look Up Center." Maybe it was because of my street kid mentality or my sinful pride, but I wanted a masculine, tough-guy name like "Samson's Place" or "The Slingshot of David"—anything but "Look Up"! However, God was persistent and I gave in. "The Look Up Center" has grown on me and now I think it's pretty cool.

We opened in 2006 and our first ministry was a free monthly meal offered to anyone in the community. It was a success and is now offered every Monday evening. We facilitate many areas of ministry: an after-school club, a household goods and clothing ministry, a food distribution service, and sports ministries. In 2010 we expanded off-site by opening a Christian coffee house downtown, The Psalm Café. It's another dream and vision that God gave me while I slept.

The latest vision that has come to fruition is a free dental clinic offering urgent dental care to uninsured patients. Professional volunteers joyfully share their gifting and talents to serve those less fortunate. Many churches and denominations partner with us, thus fulfilling God's instruction to "Bring my church together!"

Having gone from a hopeless drug addict locked in a cell from hell, to being used by God to point others to him, I encourage you to allow yourself to be used by God, too. Let him give you the vision and strength to fulfill the calling on your life. Nothing is too big for our God!

> For God does speak —now one way, now another —though no one perceives it. In a dream, in a vision of the night, when deep sleep falls on people.
> ~Job 33:14–15

THE JUVENILE EXPERIENCE

R. Steve Lowe, California

THERE ARE roughly 1,200 juvenile facilities in America. About half a million kids will be run through those institutions this year. In 1899 a law was enacted to make juvenile places as home-like as possible to differentiate them from institutions for adults. This is my life's work as a chaplain.

Juvenile halls today are very much like jails, with maximum security and lots of razor wire. It's very different from when I began forty-two years ago. They were not all felons then. About one-third were misdemeanors and one-third status offenders—truants, incorrigibles, and runaways. But today, it's *just* felons and hard-core felons. When I started and a kid stole a car, he was arrested, sent to juvenile hall, and sentenced to a boy's ranch in San Bernardino County for six months with four months of aftercare. Today, if a kid steals a car, he won't even see the inside of juvenile hall because it's full of kids who have committed much worse crimes.

Juvenile detention is serious. Kids come into a scary environment. Often they are fourteen or fifteen and some states have reduced the age of eligibility to be tried as an adult from 18 to 14. A kid can be sentenced to life without parole.

The California Youth Authority, which started in the 1940s—and through the 1960s and 70s was the Cadillac of all juvenile systems—fell into disrepute in the 1990s. The state has been closing all its facilities, going from 12,000 youth locked up to about 800. They are ready to close everything by 2013. The state is broke. Youth that would have gone to juvenile hall now stay at the county level. And counties are scrambling to figure out what to do with these kids. How do we treat them? What programs do we have? The body of Christ really needs to be aggressively involved—*now*.

These kids are still wet cement. They haven't settled into antisocial criminal activity as a way of life—yet. They still cry themselves to sleep at night when no one is looking. They are afraid, they miss their home and family. They're asking existential questions: *Why am I here? Is this a cruel joke? Am I destined for a crummy life because my dad and uncles are all locked up? I need to figure out some things for myself. What do I believe?*

Every year we make about 14,000 contacts just in Orange County, where our ministry is focused. We're getting feedback from youth almost every day that's encouraging to us. But I do worry about juveniles on a national scale. Most facilities don't have a chaplain. Counties don't pay for them. If there is one, he or she has to be a home missionary.

And the scale of need is enormous. You have to figure out where your philosophy is to manage that task without feeling as if you're failing every day.

First thing I did when I was chaplain for Orange County was to pray at my empty desk. The Lord told me to draw a line down a sheet of paper. One half is face-to-face ministry, the other half is reproducing yourself; it's fifty-fifty. That insight from God changed everything about how I did ministry.

> When he saw the crowds, he had compassion on them, because they were harassed and helpless, like sheep without a shepherd. Then he said to his disciples, "The harvest is plentiful but the workers are few. Ask the Lord of the harvest, therefore, to send out workers into his harvest field."
> ~Matthew 9:36–38

APRIL 9

THE SOBBING PROSTITUTE

R. Steve Lowe, California

I REMEMBER meeting a 17-year-old prostitute. She was pretty, red-headed, tall, statuesque, and very bright. She entered the girls' unit for six months with all of the Latina girls, black girls, and "white trash" girls. She also felt superior to everyone else, causing her peers to hate her. Her attitude really stunk up the place.

One evening she asked if we could talk about God. We did for about an hour and she put her trust in Christ. At 5 p.m., the dinner bell rang. A new ruling forbids chaplains from eating with minors so I had to leave. She seemed fine and normally I would have checked back on her in two days to see how things were going.

After my own dinner an officer left this message: "Steve, you've got to come down here. We can't get her to *stop crying*. Mental health can't stop it. We don't know what you've done to her, but come down and fix this thing."

I entered the unit and walked down the long hallway. When security electronically popped open her door, she burst out and ran down the entire hallway into my arms crying, nose running, makeup running all over her face, and then makeup smearing all over my shirt.

We go into a quiet meeting room. She tells me, "I'm really a horrible person. What I've been doing is *horrible*. I've been having sex with married men. Married men have cheated on their wives with me. I may be responsible for homes being broke up! I've been stealing money off their credit cards . . ." and she went on sobbing and shaking. I let her talk for a good hour. Clearly the Holy Spirit had begun to work on her after I left. She poured out everything in her life that was off. I then began to explain more about forgiveness and the finished work of the cross so she could understand what had been covered by the blood of Jesus when she prayed to receive him earlier that day.

The next day she stopped looking down at the rest of the girls. She helped them with their homework. She became a tutor to many struggling to break out of third- and fourth-grade levels. After she finished her unit chores she would help the others with theirs. She began to be loved by the other girls.

When she left the unit, the girls insisted on having a good-bye party for her. Everybody wept at her leaving, including the staff. Her change was so complete, she had endeared herself to everybody.

We found her a family to live with because she could not go back home. She went to work for a lawyer as an assistant. She paid off her restitution at twice the level required. That's what God can do. He broke her, convicted her of her sin, showed her the reality of it, and, in that place of tremendous need, she could experience his love and forgiveness.

Godly sorrow brings repentance that leads to salvation and leaves no regret, but worldly sorrow brings death. ~2 Corinthians 7:10

CAN VICIOUS "ANIMALS" CHANGE?

R. Steve Lowe, California

YEARS AGO I taught a Bible study at the boys' intake unit. No matter what the crime, they all go there initially. A 15-year-old boy attended who had been arrested the day before. He committed a savage, brutal stabbing of his neighbor. It was all over the newspapers. As I remember it, he was loaded out of his mind and tried to burglarize the house in the middle of the night. The owner woke up and starting screaming. He stabbed her to death, put her in his car, drove down the street, and ran into a tree, where he was arrested.

Now he was in my Bible study. His entire countenance was clouded with darkness, like a fogbank surrounding him. It happens I had also invited a volunteer to join me that day. It was her first time experiencing ministry inside a correctional facility. She was scared.

I've been in this work long enough to have seen plenty of hard-core felons showing up to hear the chaplain talk about God. I opened the Bible, taught through the gospel, and invited them to make the decision that would change their lives.

I shouldn't have been surprised, but sometimes God does take your breath away. I saw this young man pray to receive Christ. Immediately his countenance physically changed. This surprising manifestation made such an impression on my first-time volunteer she would become my right-hand helper for the next seventeen years. God moved in and everything dark moved out.

Here's a case where the born-again experience was so visual and visceral, you had to be there to believe it. A light just came in like a sunny day, instantly. The young man had a dramatic experience of the reality of God and felt the forgiveness immediately. He knew it.

Today, he's living for Christ in prison realizing he's never getting out. I still correspond, take his collect calls, and have visited him all over California. He's still experiencing the consequences of his past behavior, but God's going through that process with him. It's part of sanctification. God doesn't participate in a lot of sentence-changing because he doesn't want people becoming Christians to try to get their sentence changed. It's the same with physical healing. Sometimes yes, but often no, because God's ultimate goal for our lives has much more to do with the light that shines in our lives even through suffering, than with temporary fixes that turn him into a vending machine.

> For he has rescued us from the dominion of darkness and brought us into the kingdom of the Son he loves. ~Colossians 1:13

FACING MY SIN

Henry Nelson, California

THE YEAR before I was incarcerated my life and marriage were in shambles. God was gently tugging at me to come back to him. As I took stock of my life, I realized that all the parts of my life that I had held back from God were ruined, a real mess. And I knew that the only way my life was going to work was if I returned to God with my entire self and committed my life completely to him.

As I journeyed back into the loving embrace of my God and started confessing (and surrendering) all my sins, giving God the broken pieces, a strange thing began to happen. I began to be filled with the Holy Spirit. I say "strange" because of the way it happened; driving to work one morning, listening to Christian radio and just ten minutes from my destination, I started sobbing uncontrollably. This same scenario played out many times over the course of a year, and in my heart I could feel the change. During those experiences God was filling me with a long-term charge of power and courage (and conviction). He was preparing me for the future.

When the time finally came for me to step out and speak up, I knew it. I told God, "Okay, I'm ready and willing to do this." That was pretty remarkable since the skeleton in my closet was . . . a sex addiction that led to a sexual relationship with my thirteen-year-old stepdaughter.

I confessed to a family member first, and then to the police. There was no trial; confessions have a way of negating those. I received a sixteen-year sentence, having to serve a minimum of 85 percent before becoming eligible for parole.

The Bible says that if we confess our sins God is faithful to forgive us and cleanse us from all unrighteousness. But we still have to pay the consequences for the wrong choices we make. I ended up losing my family and my freedom—for a while—but I gained the most important relationship of all, the eternal one with my heavenly Father. His presence carried me all the way through. God used those years in prison to teach me and train me. I grew up in many ways. And he allowed me to serve him the entire time by being a good neighbor to my fellow inmates and witnessing to many men.

> If we confess our sins, he is faithful and just and will forgive us our sins and purify us from all unrighteousness. ~1 John 1:9

APRIL 12

FISH ROW WELCOMING COMMITTEE

Henry Nelson, California

WHEN I GOT to my first prison yard at Corcoran State Prison in California, I found the Christians and started worshiping and fellowshipping with them right away. They met on the yard daily to sing, share testimonies, have Bible studies, and even preach and teach. I learned how important it is to gather together, and that God gives each of us gifts and abilities others need so we can encourage and bless each other. Those gatherings were a highlight of my day.

I know I have the gift of teaching and I was given the opportunity to practice in prison. I also got to learn how to reach out to others. One of my extrovert brothers, "Preacher," asked me to help him start a ministry on Fish Row, where incoming prisoners were initially housed. When you arrive at Fish Row it takes two weeks or more to get processed in. You sit there, isolated, and often scared. He planned to visit the new guys and welcome them on behalf of the Christians on the yard, offering them prayer, some reading material, and small toiletries.

"Preacher" requested permission from the captain to have a memo made up about his new ministry inside the prison. I told him I would pray about it to see if God was leading me to that ministry. The next time I saw him he enthusiastically said, "We were approved!"

"We? I didn't say yes, yet!"

"Well, it's done now," was his reply.

At first, I was not happy with him, but then God did wonderful things with that ministry. I was scared the first time I walked up to a stranger's door. I would tell them I was with the Christians on the yard and ask if I could pray with them. The funny thing was, I had an encouraging effect on people, especially the "scared, meek folk," like me. When they saw me, a soft-looking white guy without tattoos or muscles walking around confidently, it gave them hope that they, too, could live there and be okay. Many people asked for prayer, and some of the guys came to the church circle when they got off Fish Row.

We don't need a special invitation from God to step out and be nice to people. We're already commanded as Christians to love our fellow man. It is God who will produce the fruit. The Lord truly blessed me and "Preacher" those four years at Corcoran.

> And let us consider one another to provoke unto love and to good works: Not forsaking the assembling of ourselves together, as the manner of some is; but exhorting one another: and so much the more, as ye see the day approaching. ~Hebrews 10:24–25

APRIL 13

ANGELS WATCHING OVER ME

Henry Nelson, California

THERE WAS a time, just prior to my going to prison, when I was very worried about my future. Even though I knew I had done the right thing by confessing my crime, facing the time was daunting. I was out on bond, awaiting my sentencing. My future was unknown and scary.

One day while visiting my mom, I sat alone on her porch praying. I was asking God for comfort. I immediately felt, more than heard, that still, small voice say to me, "Look up."

I looked up at the large elm tree. It had a whole bunch of birds I hadn't noticed before. More words were spoken to my heart: "You see all those birds flying over that tree? In the same way, angels are preparing every step of your journey."

That peace that passes understanding flooded me. Somehow I knew in that moment that all my cellmates were going to be hand-picked for me. And even the judge, the prisons, the cells, all would be sifted through God's fingers. The Lord would have an active role in my life, no matter where I was going. What a huge comfort that was!

Fast-forward to my very first night locked up. I was in a little county jail in Oregon. I was scared to death—not just because I was locked up, but also because I did not know what the future would bring. I prayed hard. Never had I been so scared.

Sometime during the night I finally made it to sleep. I was in a cell by myself, but as I was waking up the next morning I immediately heard the sound of a heavenly chorus singing the most beautiful worship songs. Still sleepy, I knew it just had to be from a dream or another world. As I slowly woke up, however, I could sense another being in the cell with me. The door was still locked shut, but I knew I was not alone—an angel, a good angel, was with me. I couldn't clearly make him out, but I could sense his presence. There was no mistaking it.

I just barely opened my eyes, afraid it would immediately disappear. Its glorious translucence was amazing!

My cell was about twelve feet long and ten feet high. This powerful, protecting angel was bent at the waist, with one wing covering me and the other wing to the side. He was huge—he completely filled my cell!

What a wonderful gift from God! Not only did he allow me to see my guardian angel, but he also gave me the knowledge I would not be alone. And in fact, I did make it all the way through prison without harm. That was no accident—that was God's faithfulness.

For he will command his angels concerning you to guard you in all your ways.
~Psalm 91:11

THE BLESSING OF THE WORD

Henry Nelson, California

ONE MORNING at church, and before I knew for certain I would have to go to prison, my neighbor told me God had spoken to her, saying I was going to have a prison ministry. I remember the excitement on her face as she shared this wonderful news. I was not at all excited—I didn't want to go to prison! I was still trying to convince God there was a better way for me to be disciplined. It turns out there really wasn't a better way for me. And God did give me a prison ministry—several, really.

The first ministry started right away. I asked "Rooster," my first cellie at reception, if he minded me reading the Bible out loud. I explained that it was hard for me to concentrate and "absorb" what I was reading without hearing it. Speaking God's Word aloud aided me in focusing on its meaning.

"Not at all—go ahead," he responded. And so I read to him every day. In those early days I read too monotone and it would put him to sleep. Whenever he wanted to take a nap, he'd holler, "Hey, cellie, read the Bible to me, I need a nap!" I was happy to accommodate him, as I loved reading the Bible.

When I hit the main line I did the same thing with all my future cellies. It turned out for the seven years I lived in a cell only one person would not let me read to him. It was a wonderful blessing and an enormous honor to be permitted to read God's Word in prison, and to share it with others.

When I moved to dorm living it was no longer feasible to read out loud because of the noise, so I ended up getting an audio version of the Bible on CDs. There were seventy CDs; each one lasted more than an hour. I could only listen to one at a time so I put up a sign in my building offering them to anyone who wanted to listen to them. Several people listened to all seventy CDs. I listened to them many times during the ensuing seven years and in all that time none of the CDs ever got lost.

Each time I listened to the entire Bible I was amazed at how fresh and new God's Word was.

I'm happy to report I'm out now, but those CDs are still there being loaned out by my replacement. I keep praying over those men listening to them because I believe that God's Word never returns void.

One thing God has spoken, two things I have heard. ~Psalm 62:11

THE SINGLE RED PANE

Timothy James Burke, Ohio

IT IS IRONIC that in prison, where I have very limited freedom of movement, I often feel lost. The distractions and temptations inside these walls are every bit as powerful as the ones outside, and staying focused is just as difficult.

In the chapel at Lebanon Correctional, we have all varieties of inmates attending the services. Most are there for the right reasons, but some guys use the worship time to talk with their friends from other blocks, pass contraband, or just get out of the confines of their six-by-eleven boxes.

One Sunday, during a service in which I was having a tough time with my feelings and the distractions around me, I looked up and noticed that all the chapel's stained-glass panes were yellow, blue, or white—all but one pane. The following poem came to me:

Sunday, each Sunday, I sit in these pews
And listen to preachers dispensing their views.
Doing my best to ignore and deflect
All the talkers around me that won't show respect . . .
Trying to tell if the sermon I heard
Matches up with the lessons I learned in the Word.
Trying to quiet my anger and violence
So I can hear Jesus alive in the silence.

Forgive me, God, for my negative mind
For the times when I don't trust the plan You designed,
For the nights when my faith flies away on a breeze
Cause I'm too weak or stubborn to drop to my knees.
Dear God, my thoughts are full of disease
So I sit in these pews and I pray, "Father, please
Help me to walk on the path of pure light
With my eyes always forward and Jesus in sight."
Tears wet my cheeks in a lachrymal flood
When I think of the Savior shedding His blood.
I look to the heavens for God to explain
And there . . . in the stained glass . . . a single red pane.

"I have not left you, My Word's never lost;
The blood I gave freely has covered that cost.
That single red pane is there to remind you
Whenever you wander . . . I can still find you.
The blood that I gave left a permanent stain,
A sign and a promise, My love will remain."

God has said, "Never will I leave you; never will I forsake you."
~Hebrews 13:5

THIS IS ETERNAL LIFE

Timothy James Burke, Ohio

THE PRISON cell I'm sitting in is about six feet by eleven feet, or about the size of the average household bathroom. I share this space with another man. The walls are concrete, the ceiling is concrete, and the floor is concrete. There are steel bars on the windows, steel doors lock us in—just like in the movies. This is nobody's vision of heaven.

However, that doesn't mean it isn't heaven. I was very excited the first time I read an overlooked bit of Scripture (John 17:3) because it very clearly presents an idea I've believed all along: If you know God, you already have your "reward." That's so simple, powerful, and beautiful! So why do we keep *waiting* for the "return," and the mansions with many rooms?

I think most of us, prisoners especially, want to believe there has to be something better than *this*: this material world, this wasteland of lost souls, this habitat of fear, pain, and danger—and there is. But, it requires a new outlook, not a new location.

I prefer seeing the world through Jesus' eyes, through God's eyes. This is the world he created, his chosen place for us—for now. There are works of great beauty here to inspire us, and there are dangers and challenges to help us grow. It is all here to help us become closer to our Father. But, just as we resisted our chores, our spinach, and our piano lessons, we continue

132

to resist those parts of our lives we don't like, and we wish for something better instead.

Maybe I have it wrong—plenty have already told me so. But I don't believe so. When God says, "I AM," he makes a statement for being in the *now*. Jesus says in John 17:3, "This is eternal life, that they may know You." He doesn't say, "This *will be* eternal life . . ." It's all in the present, in the now, just like we are, with God.

It's a wonderful thing to know.

> Now this is eternal life: that they know you, the only true God, and Jesus Christ, whom you have sent. ~John 17:3

CHURCH LADY GOES TO JAIL
Myra McMillian, Maryland*

I PROBABLY SHOULD have experienced jail much earlier in my life, but God led me there through a different door I would not have imagined. I was attending an annual missions conference at our church in Maryland when I heard a gracious lady talk about her work in the local jails. Something inside me just snapped and I said, "That's it!"

My health had recently forced me to retire early from my job as an executive assistant to the CEO of a hospital. I had developed a serious liver disease and would endure more than seven years of treatment. It was not easy to leave work, which formed so much of my identity given I had never had the role of being a mother. I really struggled against the effects of the treatments—exhaustion and nausea—and suffered anxiety about my prognosis. I was asking God, *What do you want me to do with the rest of my life? How long do I really have?*

I'm not the first person to be hit with a life-threatening disease, but that's not really the whole story, either. Though I probably look like a sweet 58-year-old church lady who had a nice job and has been married to her husband for twenty-two years, in reality I'm a walking miracle of

God's grace. When I was younger, I had a heroin addiction, then a divorce, followed by the loss of just about all my material possessions. God found me in that pit and set me on his path of life.

During the years of my liver disease treatment, I developed a habit of walking my neighborhood and looking for ways to serve my neighbors and tell them about Jesus. I didn't have much energy, but I kept praying for opportunities to somehow serve in spite of the limitations on my body.

So there I was with this background when I heard about going to jail for Jesus. My liver treatments were ongoing, but I had enough energy to complete the training offered through Good News Jail and Prison ministry. My new partner Janice* and I headed to a large Maryland correctional complex.

I confess to being a little scared of the stereotypes, the walls, and the steel doors. I remember looking at Janice as officers cleared us in saying, "What did we get ourselves into?" That first night triggered many old memories of my decadent past, then reminded me of how Jesus had healed me and was about to use that past in the lives of female inmates. I regained my boldness for speaking and looked forward to what we would see when we sat down with the orange-clad inmates.

Then I heard the voice of the Lord saying, "Whom shall I send? And who will go for us?" And I said, "Here am I. Send me!" ~Isaiah 6:8

APRIL 18

INSTITUTIONALIZED

Myra McMillian, Maryland*

OUR WEEKLY mission at the prison complex is to conduct Bible studies within a strict time limit. We journey through five locked gates to a small back room. Inmates attend voluntarily. Some women are interested, but others just want a change of scenery. It's not Hollywood dramatic once you sit down and start studying. And we often ask ourselves whether anything is really happening in their lives as a result of our simple efforts. You just don't get to see the end of many of their stories.

Dana* is a good example. She knew all the Christian jargon. Someone raised her with some church background. She had a few other inmates who looked up to her. Sometimes we would have to remind her *we* were leading the study. She was smart and outgoing, and quoted verses and showed off her Christian expertise. We got attached to her, though. We encouraged her to disciple the other ladies since we're only present one hour a week. I wondered, *If she has all this knowledge, is she really applying it in her life?* Soon she was discharged home. Two months later she was back.

The first time I saw her she almost turned her face away due to embarrassment and shame. I could tell she wasn't going to come to our group so I walked up to personally invite her back. She came, but kept quiet. Halfway through the session she walked out. This repeated itself the following week, so I pulled her aside.

"Dana, how long have you been coming in and out of prison?" She looked at me funny. "I love you and I'm attached to you. Forgive me if this hurts, but I think you're getting comfortable."

"What do you mean?"

"You're getting institutionalized. Here you have a following. Women look up to you. You know how to get by and people look to you for leadership. You don't pay bills and all your meals are free. Aren't you tired? What kind of legacy do you want to leave for your children? You have so many natural leadership gifts. You could be doing what I'm doing! You are so much more than this place."

I'm about 5'3", 100 pounds. She is about 5'8". Her rough face reflected years of drug abuse. She looked older than in her forties and the way she looked at me I thought she was about to throw a punch.

"No one's ever told me that before," Dana said in her low, rough voice. She seemed to soften, hugged me, and whispered, "Pray for me." She's been released again since our conversation and I haven't seen her in two years. I don't really know what's happened to her, but she hasn't been back.

> I beg you that when I come I may not have to be as bold as I expect to be toward some people who think that we live by the standards of this world.
> ~2 Corinthians 10:2

GETTING THE EYEBALL

Myra McMillian, Maryland*

A LADY came to our Bible study group from a Muslim background. She was disruptive, threatening, mocking, and a leader. While we taught one evening she interrupted and made the claim that all these Bible stories are fairy tales. But God gave me boldness. My partner Janice could sense what was coming and whispered to me, "Myra, let it go."

"We have this privilege to come here and have only one hour," I began with an even but firm tone. "It's a volunteer session. Any woman who wants to hear about the God of this Bible is welcome and even those who don't are welcome, but please save your questions and comments until I've finished."

She got quiet and eyeballed me the rest of the time. I don't recall the specific lesson that night, but often we study people like Rahab the prostitute, the outcast Samaritan woman in John 4, the woman of questionable morals who washed Jesus' feet with her tears, and the tax collectors, who were shunned. We love those stories. Our time ended and nothing else happened that night.

Yet month after month this Muslim woman kept coming. Gradually she stopped mocking. Her questions became more respectful. Finally after five months she said, "I think what you're saying is truth." That was a big breakthrough for her. Seeds were planted, but we never saw her again.

I'm just doing my small part. It's not about me getting satisfaction about lots of people coming to Christ. I don't control that. I don't take it for granted I get to go into prison and share who God is and how he changes hearts. And personally, I don't have to be ashamed anymore of sharing my past. I can boast like Paul of that former life and my current weaknesses, and treasure the promises I have in him. When I do this, I find we get to the heart of things.

I share transparently about my drug addiction and having suffered sexual abuse, which has such a stronghold on most of the ladies. Even though I'm forgiven, I know there are consequences to wrong choices. When I was hooked, I would do anything for a high and would put myself in situations where I was used and abused. That was hard to get past. When I gave my life to Christ I still couldn't put those men and places in my past behind me. But Jesus washed away those memories over time.

I remind the group of this, and while they are in prison, I ask them, "How many of you would be attending a Bible study if you weren't in prison?" Most of them laugh. Of course not. But God now has their attention and they can be set free.

> Then you shall know the truth, and the truth shall set you free. ~John 8:32

DISRUPTIONS AND QUARRELS

Myra McMillian*, Maryland

WE JUST ARRIVED in our room at our usual evening time and some kind of altercation broke out nearby. Immediately the alarms went off, they went on lockdown, and the male officers came running in. A lot of the ladies started to scatter away from the incident, which meant about twenty-five ended up packed in our room. Quickly a lady officer entered and locked us all in. It was standing room only and nobody is allowed to go anywhere until officers give the "all clear."

Well, the crowd started buzzing—about the male officers, who did what to whom. Some are taking sides. Apparently some witnessed a portion of the incident, which became the basis of their arguing. They were really getting worked up and becoming hostile. The noise level became louder and the situation felt a little out of control. My partner and I looked at each other with wide eyes and I started praying, "Please make your presence known in this room."

Then I said loudly, "Don't you see this is the Enemy? We've come in here to teach the Bible and the Enemy wants to disrupt it any way he can. Let's hold hands. We don't want anything to interfere with what we're doing." Everyone held hands and we prayed. They quieted down and we shared the gospel with a lot of people who hadn't planned to be there. There were some crossed arms checking us out, but by the end they all hugged us. What a great, unexpected opportunity, and I was reminded how much I enjoyed this in spite of my health.

> For I am not ashamed of the gospel, because it is the power of God that brings salvation to everyone who believes. ~Romans 1:16

APRIL 21

SERVING THROUGH GRIEF
Myra McMillian, Maryland*

NOT MANY weeks after the prison scuffle, a truck hit my husband while he rode his bicycle and he suffered a serious spinal cord injury. It was a heavy blow to us both because I had developed another health problem. As a result of my liver treatments, I now had a rare form of incurable cancer. The chemotherapy treatments sapped my energy, but I usually recovered enough to go in for our weekly prison visits.

Immediately I dropped out of the group to take care of my husband. Just like that, the ministry I enjoyed so much was no longer available to me. We didn't know if my husband would walk again. It was a dark, difficult time.

His recovery was slow, agonizing, and uncertain, but he finally reached a point where we agreed I could return briefly to prison as circumstances allowed. On my first night back since the accident I decided to share about my recent trials. Usually we talk about their trials, but I was still grieving with some of the heaviness of the accident and my cancer. My heart was crushed, but God says he's close to the broken-hearted.

A lady thanked me and confessed she probably wouldn't come to prison to be with us if roles were reversed. I think they saw that even though you may have some horrible crisis in your life, you can still hope in him. They all put their hands on me and prayed for me and really encouraged me that night. I had not expected that. I reminded them God will one day turn their prison trial into something that will glorify him.

I thought I had it all together as a Christian with victory over my past, but new trials come. Yet I love Jesus more today than ever.

> My soul is weary with sorrow; strengthen me according to your word.
> ~Psalm 119:28

THE PRODIGAL CHRISTIAN
Bill Mothershed, California

THERE IS a period in my life I call "the wasted years." Not the years before I was saved, but later, when I had grown comfortable with my salvation and just didn't want to be bothered with it. I still "believed," but wanted to live life my way. If you asked me, I would tell you I was a Christian, but if you didn't, you would never suspect it. I was the devil's favorite kind of Christian—undercover and useless.

But the Holy Spirit was tugging at me and I finally realized I needed to get back to a real Christian life. The problem was, I just couldn't bring myself to walk back into the prison church. I didn't want to have to explain the spiritual tug-of-war going on inside me. So, I prayed and asked God to bring me back to him. And, of course, the first thing he did was get me fired from my job. My initial reaction was to do what I had always done—find a way around it and stay in my comfort zone. But somehow, I just absolutely knew, deep down where you can't ignore it, this was God's answer to my prayers. So I let go. I had asked God to take control of my life and bring me back to him; who was I to complain about the way he did it?

Almost immediately I was offered another job in prison industries, a place I had not been allowed to work because of the length of my sentence. I let them process the application not really expecting anything to come of it. It took three separate classification hearings and a signature from the warden, but to my amazement they actually approved it. Because this process took so long, the job I had been offered was already filled, so they assigned me to be a clerk in the maintenance department of the factory.

Why did God go to such trouble to bring me to that job? Because that was where the Christians were. Out of a sixteen-man crew, the boss and eight of the men were Christians, and four of them were elders in the church.

The Lord saw me turning toward him, and instead of shaming me for having been away, he came running to meet me. He wanted me surrounded by strong men of faith to mentor me. That is how much he loves us.

"My son," the father said, "you are always with me. Everything I have is yours. But we had to celebrate and be glad. This brother of yours was dead. And now he is alive again. He was lost. And now he is found." ~Luke 15:31–32

THE SUN STILL RISES
Bill Mothershed, California

A YOUNG BROTHER sat beside me in the prison chapel. New to the faith, he was feeling trapped by the expectations of unbelievers in his life. He shared how they were pressuring him to "put in some work" by attacking someone who had violated their idea of proper prison conduct. He knew that what they were demanding was not something a Christian should be doing, but he was also understandably scared. If he didn't do what they demanded, then he would be the next target.

While God is simply asking us to focus on doing what is right, the devil wants us to focus on what the consequences might be. Satan wants to neutralize us with fear, keeping us from being fruitful for Christ. How often do we let fear keep us from doing the things we know God wants us to do? And not even the fear of violence, but just the fear of disapproval from people whose opinions matter to us more than they should.

This young man wanted to do the right thing, so I told him the hard truth—the same hard truth Daniel's friends embraced when they were threatened with being thrown into the furnace for not worshiping the king's idol. "If we are thrown into the blazing furnace, the God we serve is able to save us from it, and he will rescue us from your hand, O king. But even if he does not, we want you to know, O king, that we will not serve your gods or worship the image of gold you have set up" (Daniel 3:17–18 NIV 1984).

Whether God saves us from consequences or allows us to suffer as martyrs, the important thing is that we are working boldly for his kingdom. We need to see past the momentary fallout and look to God's promise. No matter what happens, the sun will still rise the next day.

When we bow to fear, we show the world a pitiful and insignificant faith not worthy of its respect. But when we do what is right and let God handle the rest, we show a faith the people can respect—a faith that may lead them to embrace the path to salvation. This is the witness upon which the church was founded.

In the end, my young brother did what was right and he was attacked; but he passed the test by boldly representing the Lord, serving as an example of a faith that is real and true.

And the sun did still rise the next day.

> If we are thrown into the blazing furnace, the God we serve is able to deliver us from it, and he will deliver us from Your Majesty's hand. ~Daniel 3:17

APRIL 24

THE FAITHFUL STEWARD
Bill Mothershed, California

IT IS AMAZING to me the number of men who, after coming to Christ, feel the need to do something great to serve him. They all want to be the next Billy Graham. I always tell them they need to readjust their focus. Billy Graham, and now his son Franklin, are great men of God. Their events draw tens of thousands who come forward to receive Christ. But they, themselves, didn't bring most of those people to Christ. Out in the audience are the many people who prayed for and brought those people who came forward at the crusades. It was one soul reaching out to another soul in the name of Jesus. Even in the largest crowd, God still works one soul at a time.

It can be hard to convince an aspiring evangelist it's the little things that really matter in a ministry. It's a great privilege to be allowed to preach the gospel before a large group, but it is also a great privilege to be allowed to deeply touch one soul in private. There are few privileges greater than being trusted by God to be the hand that bestows his comfort on a soul in turmoil; to be the lips that speak his words to one lost sheep who desperately needs to hear them.

I've been blessed to do both, giving sermons in the prison chapel and at other events. It was often fruitful, and I believe many were helped, but these were mostly men who were just coming to receive their daily spiritual bread, a spiritual tune-up. The most important sermons I've ever given had an audience of one—one soul on the edge of his personal spiritual cliff, desperate to understand what was happening in his own life. This is when I have felt the Spirit of God most powerfully. These are the moments when I felt truly used by God to do his work on this earth, to help one soul see God through the drama and trauma blinding him. I will always love giving the big sermons, and I take seriously the responsibility and privilege of feeding his flock. But the privilege of truly touching one soul, of sharing God's love in a deep and profound way that can lead from turmoil to peace in Jesus Christ—that is true evangelism.

> His master replied, "Well done, good and faithful servant! You have been faithful with a few things; I will put you in charge of many things. Come and share your master's happiness!" ~Matthew 25:21

IT BEGINS WITH A CHOICE

Connie Cameron

AS A VOLUNTEER in women's jail ministry, I like to share with the women how none of us is immune to sin. Those on the outside who might seem to have it all together, the highly intelligent or famous, can still fall from grace. Sometimes I give the ladies examples, such as Lisa Nowak, a U.S. Navy officer and former NASA astronaut.

Ms. Nowak gained international attention when she was arrested for confronting her romantic rival in the parking lot of Orlando International Airport. Lisa was a highly intelligent and respected person, but she allowed her emotions to get entangled in a bad situation. Involved in a love triangle, Ms. Nowak became obsessively jealous of the other woman. On February 5, 2007, she acted on those thoughts, which ultimately led to her downfall. Her career was destroyed, her family was embarrassed, and she was put behind bars.

We often hear this same theme of falling from grace with politicians and celebrities. Yet none of us is exempt. We are each just a choice away from committing a sin of huge proportions.

Sometimes when I share with the ladies that all actions, good or bad, begin with a single thought, I witness them having a "light bulb moment." I then encourage them to trace their arrest all the way back to what led up to their crime. Usually they can go back to where it all began—with a single thought—a poor choice they had made.

The lesson is, while we can't always help what is thrust before our eyes, or a thought that pops into our brain, we can, with God's help, control what we choose to dwell on and linger over. The secret is: Keep God first in our lives. He will help us make wise choices. And that, too, is a choice. By choosing to spend time with the Lord and in the Word, first thing in the morning, we will build our faith, and hopefully spare ourselves and our loved ones a lot of pain and embarrassment.

Everyone can have a life that glorifies God, even behind bars—it begins with a choice.

> Above all else, guard your heart, for everything you do flows from it.
> ~Proverbs 4:23

APRIL 26

ARRESTED AT THE BORDER
David Reyes, Texas

MY FAMILY left Chicago's inner-city ghettos and moved to Texas my senior year in high school. I was never a troublesome kid. In fact, because I was big I broke up fights; sort of played the peacemaker role. Friends thought it peculiar, but I was a leader. I charted sun spots as a hobby and prayed at Nineteenth Street and Racine. I knew the Lord had something for me back then. He was always real to me.

A homicide took place in the town we used to live in near Chicago. Somehow, someway, I was implicated. In a move unrelated to my legal situation, my family decided to move to Texas while the investigation continued.

My father's side of the family is from Mexico, so after we settled into League City near Houston, we visited relatives in Reynosa over the Christmas break. The Border Patrol stopped us coming back and arrested me. The state of Illinois had a warrant for my arrest in connection with the sixteen-year-old homicide. I waited 119 days in that little jail to be extradited.

There are a lot of poor people in jail. They can't read or write. I knew that the Lord wanted me to help in spite of my circumstances, so I'd write letters to their families and teach them to read. I even gave one of them my winter coat. I knew that God was with me the whole time.

Then suddenly an officer said, "You're free to go home." We hired an attorney to clear up this mystery. The only thing we learned conclusively was that the case had taken a different direction. I thought that was it. I went to night school to make up for lost time and graduated.

I had every reason to pursue my dreams now. I'd loved the stars since I was a kid. I thought the Air Force could get me closer. They sent me to tech school at Lowry Air Force base in Denver, Colorado, where I trained on the F-4, then the F-16. I'm three years in and waiting on my top secret clearance when it comes back saying I will be discharged from service.

Confused and disappointed, I asked, "Why?" It seems Illinois still had a warrant for my arrest; it never went away. Attorneys called again, and again the answer came back that Illinois didn't want me right now. The state appeared to be keeping its options open on an unsolved case, but it was preventing me from pursuing my life. We demanded our right to see charges and answer them, but the state wouldn't do anything.

Something just wasn't right, but no one could solve it. Sadly, I had dreamed about retiring from the military. At that point, I was back to Square 1.

Why, my soul, are you downcast? Why so disturbed within me? Put your hope in God, for I will yet praise him, my Savior and my God. ~Psalm 42:5

LIFE INTERRUPTED

David Reyes, Texas

RETURNING TO League City, to pay for school I resumed the moving business I had begun. I won some NASA contracts, worked hard, and employed a few college friends. We grew rapidly. Some of the contracts were huge—like moving aerospace companies.

We're a close family and I know God has his hands on my life. I thought that my plans for the Air Force were good, but I could trust God to have a better plan. I was thirty-one and business was good when the phone rang. It was the local police department. I knew them well because they hired me often for moving jobs. Sergeant Dan started first.

"David, we got a problem here. I don't know what's going on. This thing here doesn't fit you, but I need you to come down."

"No problem. I'm in the middle of a major move but I promise to come tomorrow morning, 9 a.m."

My pickup truck wouldn't start so Sergeant Dan comes by and picks me up with a few other gentlemen in suits. At the station there are six guys from Illinois and federal marshals. They explain there had been mob activity back in Cicero, Illinois. The mayor had been indicted; other officials were going to prison. A special cold case unit came in to clean up all the records and my name came up.

"Yes, I know all about it and I'm more than willing to answer any questions."

They asked me about my life from the time I was a little boy through the present. Everyone who knew me in that station agreed something was wrong there. The shoe didn't fit.

"We have to clear this matter up," said an officer. "Right now, we have to arrest you because Illinois does have an outstanding warrant."

"You're kidding! Based on what? This is ridiculous!" I snapped. For several months a spiritual battle had been going on inside me. My spirit was not at peace with things I was doing. My business success distracted me from the things of God. I was looking for a sanctuary, a place I could pull away from the world and just seek him.

As the cuffs came out, I realized God would use my arrest to answer my prayer. I thought, *God's hand is on this and it's for my benefit.*

Officers even wrote in the report that I was a Jesus fanatic; that I was not normal. They thought I'd need a psychiatric evaluation. The Lord told me not to worry, to just stay close to him.

> Rejoice always, pray continually, give thanks in all circumstances; for this is God's will for you in Christ Jesus. ~1 Thessalonians 5:16–18

APRIL 28

STUCK IN THE SYSTEM

David Reyes, Texas

THE VERY next day I was on a flight to Illinois in ankle and hand shackles locked to a wheelchair. It's embarrassing to sit like that in an airport. Just yesterday I was a respected member of the community. People steered clear and gave me strange looks. A little boy walked up and said, "Why do they have you like that?"

"Because they're making a big mistake, but they're taking me someplace to fix things up." I think he may have been the only one besides my family who believed me for the next four years.

Some of the Illinois detectives had known me since I was a kid. One attended grammar school with me. They assured me they just needed to close this up. They're not saying, "You're the guy." I tried to get details and learned there was political corruption; my name was implicated, and nobody pursued it properly. We had to go through the motions required by the system.

We demanded a right to a speedy trial—rejected. So another right was violated. I continued to hold on to the fact that the Lord allowed this to be. I was sent to the high-security Division 9 in the Cook County Jail—a massive facility. My family was exasperated. I closed the business and sold everything to pay expensive attorney fees. The case was continued and continued until the money ran out. Then my lawyers dropped out. I went to a public defender who suggested I plea bargain for thirty-five years.

"What do you mean "thirty-five years? Thirty-five years for what?" The state wanted to pin me with sixty-five to life. My lawyer told me I needed to take a deal.

"You have to be out of your mind," I told him calmly, but firmly. "I will not take any deal for something I didn't do. My Lord tells me that is not the answer. I tell you what, you're fired. I no longer need your services."

"But the court appointed me."

"You and I are not on the same page so we'll need to go before the judge." I believe without a doubt the judge was a Christian man. "David, do you understand why you're here?"

"Yes, your honor. It's technically about my case, but I'm here because the Lord Jesus has me here. That's the truth."

He said, "Be patient," and smiled. That comforted me some.

I know the system. It's a numbers game for the state. Guys take plea bargains all the time because they can't afford a good defense. They feel they have no options. With Jesus, I knew I always had options.

> The Lord your God is with you, the Mighty Warrior who saves. He will take great delight in you; in his love he will no longer rebuke you, but will rejoice over you with singing. ~Zephaniah 3:17

APRIL 29

REFINING FIRE

David Reyes, Texas

IN PRISON I put my nose in the Bible from morning until night. The more I read, the more he empowered me. He performed divine surgery on me. We embed so many things within us throughout our journey from childhood to adulthood. He showed me who he was and how filthy I was, even at my best. He crushed me, then showed me who I should be in Christ.

Underneath the success, business, church, fishing, and golfing on the weekends, there was a lot of pain. I was drinking alcohol more than I wanted to admit. My parents owned bars and I grew up in that environment from birth. Even the priests bought their brandy from mom's business. It wasn't okay that I drank profusely, which started in childhood after school, at a park or picnic. We drank beer and got drunk.

Even though we went to Catholic church, my mother was an alcoholic. Raising six kids by herself, it's no wonder she drank. We weren't the greatest kids. I have some brothers in prison today. When I was eleven, my stepdad left, and Mom's habit became severe. She became abusive to one of my little sisters. I had to protect my sister a lot. It's a shame to have to call the police on your mother, to have her arrested because she's beating your little sister. I had to have her put in jail. They never did take us to Child Protective Services. There were a lot of wounds with that—anger, resentment, and embarrassment.

I also thought about some people I'd hurt emotionally with my mouth and attitude. I still believed my prison time was no mistake. I belonged here so God could have his way with me. That's what these places are for. Incarceration is either a detriment or a help to you. People come here because they can't live in society. Laws are intended for lawbreakers. Every human being has the potential to break the law. Laws are helpful to stop you from hurting yourself and others. God's "Thou shalt not" is part of the mirror to show you your dirty self alongside his holiness.

At first I prayed for God to help me when I arrived. I didn't want to be blind and ignorant as to how to act in prison. Then I prayed for everyone around me and that God would do for them what he did for me.

> Many will be purified, made spotless and refined, but the wicked will continue to be wicked. None of the wicked will understand, but those who are wise will understand. ~Daniel 12:10

APRIL 30

ACQUITTED

David Reyes, Texas

AFTER NEARLY four years, my case was still in limbo. I decided to write a letter explaining my case to a professor at Northwestern

University School of Law. A few months later a team of six attorneys—some from Northwestern Law and others from the Winston & Strawn law firm—greeted me on a surprise visit and took my case at no cost.

Finally my trial date arrived. The state presented its case first, and the next day my defense lasted for about five or ten minutes. The judge said, "Case dismissed," and shook his head. He apologized and said this hadn't needed to happen. He was so upset at the state. At the time of the crime they had physical eyewitnesses who saw me in lineups and sketches and they said, "This is not the man." Almost twenty years later the answer was the same.

I walked out penniless in 2002 and went home to Texas. Even my clothes didn't fit me. I mismanaged God's blessings before my arrest. Now he equipped me to properly handle what was about to happen.

I went back to Calvary Chapel. The church wrote me a check for $200. They saw my inmate boots and ill-fitting jeans, which is all I had. I was content and didn't feel I needed clothes per se. So I prayed over the $200 and asked the Lord to use it in a way to benefit others and not just myself.

I spent it on flyers, turned on a cell phone, and bought business cards. To advertise my moving service, I distributed these pieces to the business community I had left years ago. Immediately phones rang off the wall. I could not keep up with it. It hasn't stopped. I had tenfold the business I did before. I didn't even have a truck to move anything yet! I hired fifteen employees almost immediately.

The Lord must have marketed my business. People called me at midnight! What people may not know about the moving business is that a lot of it involves people in a crisis—divorce, job loss, etc. People open up, tell me personal things, and I get a chance to encourage them, having been through a crisis myself. I look back on all the arrests and disappointments, and I praise God. He made me a better man and my faith was not disappointed.

And hope does not put us to shame, because God's love has been poured out into our hearts through the Holy Spirit, who has been given to us.
~Romans 5:5

TEMPORARY MOMS

Carol Davis, California

LUCY IS HER *name, a young girl shackled in regret and shame. She wishes she could return to her former life, the one without court trials, turmoil, and strife.*

She started hanging out with the wrong crowd. Now in hindsight she can't see how. She had a loving mother and friends, but chose to hang with others living on the fringe.

Now the life she has is living accused of stabbing someone. Her new friends are nowhere to be seen, and she's in the process of being reamed. She knows they don't really care. Now she's alone and very scared. She's worried about her mom, and has yet another bomb.

She has a baby in her womb, who's headed for a tomb, because she doesn't feel that giving birth during her incarceration is an option. Even if she has the child, she doesn't have a caretaker for such a long while, leaving her feeling she has no options, for she can't bear the thought of adoption . . .

I penned the story above in my journal after a visit to the local county jail where I taught a women's Bible study. Lucy's story broke my heart, for I couldn't imagine giving birth while incarcerated, let alone having an abortion while being shackled to the bed.

I tried to visit Lucy one-on-one to talk with her about her situation. Unfortunately, she had already had her maximum number of visits for the week so it was not allowed. The following week Lucy wasn't in our Bible study because she had been transferred to the state prison to begin serving her sentence.

Lucy wrote me from prison, thanking me for making a difference in her life while she was at the jail. She never mentioned anything in her letters about what happened with her baby.

While talking with people about this tragic situation, I learned of a church that takes in babies of incarcerated mothers whose only options are abortion or adoption. They care for the infants until their mothers return home from prison so they won't be raised by the state.

It is a significant investment of time, energy, and money to care for a child who's not their own, but what a lifesaving mission! How comforting it is for the mother, too, knowing her child is being loved and cared for in her absence.

The ministry needs for inmates are many, providing many different ways for us to express the love of Jesus. Imagine, without this ministry, the number of infants who never would have made it safely out of the womb.

> He will defend the afflicted among the people and save the children of the needy. ~Psalm 72:4

PLEADING GUILTY WHEN YOU'RE INNOCENT

Keb Johnson*, Illinois

I GREW UP in Chicago's ghettos. It seemed as if everyone in that environment was blind and lost. As a child I thought I was doing okay. This is how people live, they manage it. Yeah, people get shot and killed, but there are old people, so apparently you can survive.

It wouldn't matter though if I grew up in a castle or a dungeon. I can't blame my environment for my downward spiral. My ego, overconfidence, and rebellion were all rolled up in my sin nature.

I graduated high school with honors and was on my way to college, but decided to delay just a bit so I could do some things I wanted to do. That's when my downfall started. I pursued pleasure and approval of others. I didn't follow good counsel. I hung with the wrong company, and tried to find happiness in it. I wasn't into drugs or alcohol, but neither was I focused on pursuing something positive.

What happened next was never fully investigated. A friend's ten-year-old son accused me of sexually molesting him. It never happened, and conjecturing on the motives for such a serious charge with no basis in reality doesn't change what happened or my life today.

I tried to figure out who said what about whom as several weeks passed, and I was given the impression that the accusation was all coming to nothing. Still, nobody was at ease, including myself, after this kind of accusation had been raised. It shocked me when police arrested me for a nonexistent crime.

My legal counsel advised me he was not going to be able to fight this kind of case. It's a child's word against an adult's, it's a sexual crime, and no jury is going to buy my story. I should rather plead guilty, take the least amount of judgment, and move on with my life. That's the advice a lot of young men get in the system. Out of ignorance, a big fear of losing my freedom, and not understanding the full impact of my decision, I pled guilty, not realizing it would ruin my reputation. I really believed the lawyer's word that I had no chance.

I received the deal they promised: two years of probation (no prison time), therapy, and being registered as a sex offender for ten years.

I moved back in with my mom, started therapy, and had no idea that the trouble was just starting.

> Acquitting the guilty and condemning the innocent—the Lord detests them both. ~Proverbs 17:15

GUILTY, BUT INNOCENT

Keb Johnson, Illinois*

I DECIDED TO pursue college as a way to move on with life, but the obligations of my probation were so restrictive my grades suffered. I left after one semester with nothing but a small student loan debt.

I returned home to my mom and the old neighborhood—who had known me as a boy. My community now believed I was out to hurt their children. One afternoon coming home from the mandatory counseling program, twelve guys jumped me. I couldn't get away from them until some security officers a block away arrived to break it up.

They picked me up and said, "Time to go, you're under arrest."

"For what?"

"You should already know. Let's go." I told them I didn't feel very good from the beating. They didn't care, as if it were something I deserved. An unmarked police car took me downtown, but officers there didn't care either. My lip was so swollen I could barely talk, I was dizzy, I felt like passing out, and my wrist was swollen.

"You'll be just fine, just sit up and talk to us," was always the answer to my complaints. After many hours of interrogation—"fishing" is a more accurate term—they finally took me to the hospital. After treatment, the police asked if I would take a polygraph, which I readily agreed to. They claimed I failed the test, but wouldn't show me the results. *I'm twenty—what did I know?*

They charged me with another sex offense claiming I fondled a young lady living in my complex. I decided then and there I wasn't going along this time, even if they gave me the thirty years that went with this crime.

When I was younger, I had made a clear decision to follow Christ; however, it was based on some flawed information. I believed Jesus died for my sin, so maybe God honored it because I really was seeking him honestly. However, I followed the same path Israel did: When I could pursue my own pleasures, I forgot all about being delivered from Egypt. The important details I lacked about my faith were about to be supplied during my two-and-a-half-year ordeal.

Sitting in my jail cell, the first thing I realized was that I was a wretched sinner, and I was disgusted. I wasn't saying, "I can't believe I'm locked up like this! I've been wronged, twice!" *No, you did this to yourself,* I thought. I was humbled rather than filled with anger or desire for revenge for being wrongly charged, again.

Everyone has turned away, all have become corrupt; there is no one who does good, not even one. ~Psalm 53:3

GETTING PLAYED

Keb Johnson, Illinois*

Nobody enjoys strange company, and it's worse in jail.

My first cellmate on a regular deck was a gang member. He was shrewd, cunning, and clever. I just thought he was real nice. I had no idea he had an agenda. He made me feel welcomed. I was worried about beatings and violence, but he said he was going to protect me.

"Nobody's going to bother you. You're a nice guy. Where you from? How'd you get in here? What are you charged with?" He was real nosy. He was trying to get enough information to know how to manipulate the situation. I had no idea.

He worked his game: He told me about his past, showed me pictures of himself and his gang buddies, told me he's a big shot and that he ran the whole compound.

"If you need something, let me know. I got you."

He coached me on how to avoid trouble, like going to chow with the "neutrons" (those not affiliated with a gang), not when the gangs go out. When I returned, he asked, "What you got on your tray? Why don't we trade? You take this and I'll take that . . ."

As time went on he started playing his tricks. He'd say, "Let me show you how to play a game." He always won and I'd owe him stuff from the commissary or clothes. I went along for a while. Soon I owed him a lot of stuff. I got myself in a trap. And he knew it.

He warned me that if he told the cell block that I wasn't paying what I owed, "They gonna jump down on you. You don't want to be caught in the showers by yourself." He said a lot of things that made me think, *It's time to walk.*

I tapped on the window of the security guard booth. "My life is threatened and I need to get out now."

"You're telling me you need to go to PC (protective custody)?"

"You can take me wherever you want, but I don't want to be here." Immediately I was told to pack my stuff. My cellmate called out, "I'll find you. You know you owe me."

When I arrived in PC I had a cellmate because of overcrowded conditions. He informed me he was HIV-positive. It's stressful to be thrown into a cell with complete strangers and you don't know their state of mind or heart. Would you guess he gave me a Bible? He let me keep it the day they moved him out. Then I was alone—a chance for solitude and to connect with the Bible twenty-three hours a day, no one threatening me.

God gave me a month to decompress and to find him in his Word.

> Do not drag me away with the wicked, with those who do evil, who speak cordially with their neighbors but harbor malice in their hearts. ~Psalm 28:3

THE MAIN THING

Keb Johnson, Illinois*

WHEN AUTHORITIES transferred me from the small jail to Cook County, my first questions were: *Where's a Bible? How am I to get right with God? Who are you, God?*

I got those answers beginning in solitary confinement, but also as I was transferred to a special deck called "The Life Learning Dorm." Who God was, what he'd been doing, and what he was going to be doing were key themes for me. I learned about the church, that God is personal, not in the middle of nowhere casting spells on people. He's intimate with his creation. God deals personally with man, loves man, and sees him as his prized possession. I didn't know any of this stuff on the street and can't see how I would have, given my selfish nature.

His Word to me came across like this: "Keb, you really need to get on my page. I'm trying to restore man. I'm restoring you."

He wants a broken spirit. I had a proud, cocky spirit and there's no room for a spirit like that in the presence of God Almighty. You have to surrender. You have to be broken of your arrogance. Before jail, I left people no room to correct me. You can't learn a thing while pride is in the way. You can't repent if you don't acknowledge wrong.

I spent many nights crying to God. I wasn't doing *that* in the street, either. I saw what kind of fool I had been . . . how wretched mankind is as a whole . . . how much God was displeased with me. It tore me to pieces.

156

I said, "God, you got a raw deal out of this creation you call man, whom you're so in love with." There was a lot of crying and pain. "Why do you deal with us instead of wiping us out?"

Eventually, God got around to showing me his mercy, grace, patience, longsuffering, and forgiveness. He introduced true redemption. That's what God did with me for two-and-a-half years.

> When I consider your heavens, the work of your fingers, the moon and the stars which you have set in place, what is mankind that you are mindful of them, human beings that you care for them? ~Psalm 8:3–4

MAY 6

THE BULLPEN
Keb Johnson*, Illinois

WHENEVER YOU need to go to court you're transferred to a bullpen. Usually sixty to seventy guys sit in a tight box so close your knees are touching. Guys talk about their cases, what they're going to do if they get out or if they don't. To some it's a little game or joke.

Others are worried, twiddling their fingers, smoking cigarettes down to the nub so they burn their fingers just trying to get the last drag. I sat in a corner and asked the Lord, "What do you want me to do? What do you want me to say? Do you just want me to pray?" I was quite uncomfortable. God was going to have to give me the boldness to pray the kind of things he wanted me to pray.

Working for God is sometimes scary. He's telling me to stand up in front of sixty guys with different personalities—some who are huge and could not care less about anybody. And God is telling me to get them quiet. *Lord, how does that work? Not to mention what's going to happen to me?*

By the grace of God and by his own Spirit inside me he shut everybody up every time.

"Good morning, gentlemen. I just wanted to get a time in where we can all reflect and pray." I heard a few say softly, "Good morning, sir," and other mumblings. Some would ask for prayers to fix circumstances, but I couldn't. That takes boldness because I was opposed to what they were asking me.

"Lord, thank you for today and that we can trust you with our lives. I want to ask, if you want us to go to prison, send us there and prepare us to understand you and your will. Help us be humble before you and not complain or murmur. Whatever you want to do with us, do it. If you want to break us down, break us down. If you want to build us up, build us up. Cause us to repent and feel guilt if we need to feel guilt. Don't allow us to live the lies we're living now. Help us to break the curses in our families."

I heard, "What is he talking about?" But I wasn't being nudged to pray, "Lord, help us get home, catch a blessing, have favor on my case, make my life easy." It wasn't a "fix everything," but a "fix me" request. Some guys would come to me afterward and ask, "Man, can you pray for me?" We had real conversations, not just sloppy talk.

I was grateful to be obedient in spite of my own fear. I grew in my faith, my prayers, my courage, and my character.

> And Isaiah boldly says, "I was found by those who did not seek me; I revealed myself to those who did not ask for me." ~Romans 10:20

WHEN NO ONE BELIEVES
Keb Johnson*, Illinois

MANY DAYS passed with continuances from the court. Many more days passed with my attorney trying to advise me to plead guilty, take a lighter sentence, and get going. He didn't believe I was innocent. I don't think he wanted to put in the necessary work for a guilty sex offender.

I couldn't pay him much. My minister friend pled with him to help me. I think the attorney took it mostly pro bono for his own motives. He said I didn't stand a chance. He told me he'd practiced law for thirty years and, "I will tell you, I've never won a case such as yours, where you are accused by a child of abusing them. It's an uphill battle and you're about to get crushed."

Honestly, I didn't doubt his facts. He brought in different legal people to find out why I was fighting the charges. They all said the same things—I was about to get destroyed.

"I'm innocent and just want to fight the case." They walked away frustrated and angry because I wouldn't listen to counsel. I knew God would prepare me for any outcome.

My day in court arrived and I took the stand in my defense. I was in a nice shirt and tie, giving the appearance of a free man (so as not to prejudice the jury). Everybody did their thing for about two hours of back and forth. Then something happened.

The young girl who alleged that I did these things testified that the person who violated her had an eye that twitched all the time. I don't think she was supposed to say that. The state pulled her off very quickly with "No further questions, Your Honor." It came out of nowhere.

Attorneys immediately arranged to put me in front of an eye specialist. The doctor's professional judgment? No problems whatsoever with either of my eyes. The jury deliberated.

I spent the waiting time alone praying and singing songs to the Lord. Though I didn't know the outcome, I felt gratitude to God. Suddenly my attorney rushed back, "The jury reached a verdict! It's not been very long. That's not a good sign. You're in trouble. Let's go."

The bailiff brought me in first. The judge asked, "Has the jury reached a verdict?"

"Yes, we have, Your Honor." That's when I thought, *Now I'm going to find out what God has planned*. I felt a slight twinge of fear—fear of the unknown.

Then I heard the words, "We find the defendant . . . not guilty."

> I will maintain my innocence and never let go of it; my conscience will not reproach me as long as I live. ~Job 27:6

ANOTHER PAINFUL MOTHER'S DAY

Allison Bottke, Texas

WHEN I STARTED writing *Setting Boundaries with Your Adult Children*, my son was living as a free man. By the time I proofread the first copy, he had been sitting in jail for almost six months, awaiting trial and sentencing. When the book was released, Christopher was serving a five-year sentence in a Minnesota state prison. He will be almost forty years old when he gets out.

As another painful Mother's Day comes and goes, I am reminded that I can choose to see my life as half-full or half-empty. I can replace the feelings of guilt, blame, anger, and lack of forgiveness with feelings of peace knowing that God is in control, that he has a plan—for my life and the life of my son. In the midst of disappointing times, we can have freedom to enjoy life, embrace good friends, and encourage ourselves in the Lord.

Life isn't always going to be pleasant. Sometimes we need to remind ourselves of that.

I am comforted by a story in the Bible about King David. In 1 Samuel 30, David tells about his mighty men and how they had been away from camp fighting a battle. While they were gone, the Amalekites had come to the Israelite town of Ziklag. The Amalekites destroyed everything and even took their women and children. In verse 18, it says, "David was greatly distressed because the men were talking of stoning him; each one was bitter in spirit because of his sons and daughters." Ever been there? As the stoner or the stonee?

In moments of anger and confusion, we don't always pause and ask ourselves, "How would the Lord like me to handle this?" Or, "What lesson is God trying to teach me in this horrible mess?" Yet, when we read further in the same verse, we learn a lot about how David handled his mess: "But David found strength in the Lord his God." In other translations it says, "He encouraged himself in the Lord." Even in the midst of discouragement, facing the loss of his family and the possibility of being stoned—he "encouraged" himself. He remembered the times before when God had pulled him through.

This Mother's Day, if you have a child who is incarcerated or even just far from the Lord, encourage yourself by remembering the times when

God came through for you, too. It will not only give you strength to face another day, it may even enable you to enjoy the day, *knowing* he is in control.

> But David found strength in the LORD his God. ~1 Samuel 30:6

WE ALWAYS HAVE A CHOICE

Allison Bottke, Texas

ONE OF MY friends chuckles at me, because I'm often whistling a tune, or breaking out in dance when I hear music. I do it frequently without thinking, and many times I do it to encourage myself, to keep my mood upbeat. I am also careful not to use negative words about my son, myself, or others. I surround myself with people who are cheerful and positive. I've made conscious choices to always see the glass as half-full—in spite of the painful situation—even on a day when mothers around the country are celebrating with their children but I'm separated from mine.

I've spoken with my son several times since his sentencing. While the outcome wasn't what we had been praying for, he has been positive and optimistic because the sentence could have been much longer and also because he can now move on to the next stage. He's accepting the consequences of his actions and is trying to make the best of the present and future situations. I'm proud of how far he's come in his journey of accountability. I know God has a plan for him.

More importantly, *my son* now knows God has a plan for him. Christopher has found freedom in a disappointing time. He's making new choices that will change his life.

Does your present situation seem insurmountable? If so, find a nice quiet place, and reflect on what God has already brought you through. Look for the good where you are now. Find a Scripture passage, a song, or a poem, something that encourages you. Read it daily, hourly, every minute if necessary—whatever it takes to help you take another step for-

161

ward. Surround yourself with positive people, people who will support and encourage you.

If you are in need of setting firm and healthy boundaries with your children, I encourage you to lift up your voice in praise and thanksgiving—no matter the disappointments or pain. Enjoy the newfound sanity that comes when you discover that you have a choice to see life as half-full, and not half-empty.

We always have a choice.

> Do not grieve, for the joy of the LORD is your strength. ~Nehemiah 8:10

LOVING OUR ADULT CHILDREN WITH OPEN ARMS

Allison Bottke, Texas

IF YOU ARE walking a journey to set healthy boundaries with your adult children, you will need to be strong in your convictions—strong as well as loving. We need to learn about our own choices—and how we must change our responses to the choices our adult children make. We need to learn we can't change our kids—and that they may never change. It's a sad thing to acknowledge—but it may be true. However, the opposite may be true as well. When we develop a backbone that is firm, straight, and loving, there's no telling how it may change the people we love.

And we do love them. No matter how angry they make us. No matter how they break our hearts. That's why we may have made so many poor enabling choices along the road. But no more—our enabling days are behind us. We've learned we are not bad parents if we say, "No." We've learned the critical need to be strong and loving at the same time.

Throughout Scripture, the Lord was often quite firm in the lessons he taught his followers. His firm hand came with a loving heart. I know what it feels like to want the pain to stop—to want to turn my back on my son and never have to deal with his issues ever again. But he's my son and I love him. That doesn't mean, however, I have to accept his choices with open arms, nor does it mean I have to bear the acute financial responsibility for them.

It can be a life-changing moment when we realize our adult children may need to walk their own Damascus roads to be the people God intends for them to be.

Let us not become weary in doing good, for at the proper time we will reap a harvest if we do not give up. ~Galatians 6:9

THE TRUTH ABOUT CONSEQUENCES

Allison Bottke, Texas

THE LAST time I was able to wrap my arms around my adult son, Christopher, he was getting out the passenger side of my car. I leaned over to hug him, knowing he would be spending the evening sleeping under a bridge, or in a laundromat, or in a halfway house shelter—if they had room. I could have taken him home with me; he could have slept on my sofa. Yet, for us that option had long ago been exhausted. He got out of my car and I drove away. I was only able to drive a few blocks before the tears in my eyes made it impossible for me to see. I pulled over to the side of the road and wept.

That night, my son turned himself in to the authorities, tired of running from numerous outstanding warrants. By the time the book I was writing was published, he was serving out his sentence in a state prison. He was thirty-six years old.

My "mother's heart" was broken—it had been broken for many years. I ached for a "normal" relationship with my son, but I wasn't sure what normal was anymore. I wasn't sure I would recognize normal if it stared me in the face. The past few years my relationship with him has become considerably more painful, if that could even be possible. Why? Because *I made a choice*. I made a choice to change my life—to stop accepting responsibility for the choices Christopher was making, allowing him to fully experience the fallout from his own actions.

We must be willing to set healthy and appropriate boundaries, and to accept the consequences of those choices, whatever they may be. Deciding to parent differently is a key ingredient in making the changes needed to stop our enabling behavior. Seek professional help if necessary.

No matter how old we are, it is never too late to parent differently. It's never too late to turn around—remember, *God Allows U-Turns*!*

> With God all things are possible. ~Matthew 19:26

(*Allison Bottke is the author of the God Allows U-Turns series.)

GOD WINS THE BATTLE

Allison Bottke, Texas

SETTING HEALTHY boundaries with my son has brought consequences that vary from peace to panic. I wish I could say that when we begin to set those boundaries, our lives will be instantly transformed to pleasurable places of peace and tranquility; however, that's not likely to happen.

On the contrary, things are likely to blow up all around us. That's why it's imperative that we look at all the possible consequences, insofar as we are able, once we begin responding differently to the choices our adult children make.

And who knows, maybe the changes we make will be the catalyst to help our adult children make positive changes as well. Maybe when we stop trying to be God in the lives of our adult children, they just might find the real God.

When we stop accepting the consequences for the actions of our adult children, for some, the outcome may barely register as a blip on the radar screen of life. For others it may be a cataclysmic jolt of seismic proportions. When their hand is forced, some adult children may choose to get the professional help they so desperately need and do what it takes to turn their lives around. Yet others may die from drugs, violence, or criminal behavior. It's difficult to write that, let alone consider it as a possible consequence. So varied are the possibilities—is it any wonder we are afraid to rock the boat? Is it any wonder we have allowed things to get so bad by perpetuating the craziness?

Only God can erase the bitter and painful memories our adult children might be carrying in their minds and hearts—you and I are not God. We must get out of the way and let God do what only he can. We must temper compassion for our children with wisdom, and we must not confuse compassion with sentimentality.

Although it's often too late for prevention when it comes to our adult children, it's never too late for redemption. Our only refuge is in God's grace and mercy. Our child might not be a "good kid" at this point in time, but he is still "God's kid." Though the devil may seem to have won a skirmish or two, the battle is still the Lord's.

Because—lest we forget—God loves our kids even more than we do.

> Then they cried to the LORD in their trouble, and he saved them from their distress. He brought them out of darkness, the utter darkness, and broke away their chains. ~Psalm 107:13–14

PARENTS, DON'T BLAME YOURSELVES

Christopher Smith, Minnesota

IT HAS taken me almost forty years to come to this conclusion: I alone am responsible for the wrong choices I've made in my life. I spent years blaming my mother (Allison Bottke), the police, and society. I spent years behind bars and I have no one to blame but myself.

I know my mother loves me and she continues to hope and pray for me. She had to set some firm boundaries with me, but never failed to tell me how much she loved me. If you have a loved one making wrong choices, don't give up hope—don't stop loving them even when they seem unlovable. They need to be set free from your hands so they can learn some lessons on their own.

Set your adult children free to make their choices and live the consequences. But please, don't deadbolt the door entirely. Someday they may show up and knock and ask for forgiveness. Hopefully they will have some life experiences under their belt to realize they need caring people in their life. It's much easier to live with people who genuinely care for you. One day they will admit they didn't know everything—I know I did. It may take longer for some adult children, but I believe the day will come. It wasn't easy, but it finally came for me.

Parents, don't blame yourselves for the actions your kids choose to take. Many successful, positive, and important people learned the hard way, but they did learn. You need to trust that God can restore a messed-up life. He's changing mine and I pray to him every day for the strength and wisdom to make better choices. As I said, it's not easy. I can't change the past, but I can make better choices in my future.

My mom always says, "God Allows U-Turns." And I say there's no statute of limitations on turning to him—no matter what we've done.

> Therefore if anyone is in Christ, he is a new creation; the old has gone, the new has come. ~2 Corinthians 5:17

MAY 14

GOD'S TIME

Travis Newell, Ohio

I HAD SIGNED up multiple times over the years to attend a Kairos event. Out of the blue one day, the pass arrived announcing that it was my turn. It had completely slipped my mind that I had applied months earlier. I was given a two-week notice to reschedule my personal visits and other appointments, but I was glad to do it! The excitement and anticipation escalated with each passing day; time seemed to slow to a snail's pace.

Kairos is an ancient Greek word meaning "God's special time." Highly trained Christian volunteers come to the prison for three days and stay at local churches or in private homes at night. Dedicated brothers in Christ minister to us, sharing with us God's Word and his love. We learn how to love one another and to accept our differences. I had seen the changes it made in many inmates and couldn't wait for my turn to finally come. But, I was also nervous about being around a bunch of people I didn't know. *What will I say? Will I have to speak in front of a lot of people? What will people think of me?* For two weeks the questions wouldn't stop going through my anxiety-ridden brain.

And then, the day finally arrived. That Thursday was the first day of the rest of my life. After having been around so much negativity and despair for so many years, I was a little skeptical of the genuine love and sincerity of these people. I kept thinking to myself, *Is this real? Are these people real?*

I came to realize I was actually projecting the build-up of fear and anxiety from years of my hostile prison environment. It had become part of my own perspective. Now I had to ask myself, *Am I the one who's being real?* Fear had dictated my life for so long—I had forgotten what it felt like to be truly free and receptive to the love. "Agape" is what they call it. I was amazed at how these wonderful people kept giving to us, how they kept pouring the love of God into each of us, expecting nothing in return.

> Finally, brothers and sisters, rejoice! Strive for full restoration, encourage one another, be of one mind, live in peace. And the God of love and peace will be with you. ~2 Corinthians 13:11

MAY 15

RENEWED FAITH

Travis Newell, Ohio

THE NEXT three days at the Kairos event were unlike anything I have ever experienced. It was by far the most positive, life-changing event I had ever been a part of. We feasted, we cried, we sang praises to God, we grew and learned more about God than we knew about ourselves. My eyesight, sense of touch, hearing, and taste and smell—all my senses were alive to the fullest. I was much more aware of God's touch and his presence than ever before in my life.

My faith had been renewed. Before, I knew God existed but I had become comfortable with my own fleshly desires and had put God on a side burner. But no more. God deserves to hold first place in our lives—not second, to anyone or anything.

The change in me was instant and dramatic: love, hope, and a positive outlook radiated from my being. I had a glow about me noticeable to my friends. Without a huge effort on my part, I was drawing in others who were "looking" and "searching" for something, like moths drawn to a flame. This was my calling—to be a light in a dark world. I felt at ease and at peace, a feeling that in the past, I only felt when I was high or drunk. I found my new and permanent "fix"—it was God's Word, including his love, and fellowshipping with other Christians.

"God's special time." I was on it and now realize the blueprint was already drawn up. It's up to me to build my life as *God* has intended. Every day I learn a little bit more and I continue to make improvements in my life, staying sensitive to the Spirit in me. I keep reading the Word and spending time with the Lord daily. I also stay alert to how I can help others.

I wish every person could have the same Kairos experience—several days locked up with strong believers who love on you and show you how to go deeper with God. It can change your life—it did mine!

> Know therefore that the LORD your God is God; he is the faithful God, keeping his covenant of love to a thousand generations of those who love him and keep his commandments. ~Deuteronomy 7:9

MY WORST DAY

Corey Bush, Illinois

IN MARCH of my senior year in high school I expected to graduate even though I had become a gang member. My academics were decent, but in my mindless thinking, I continually got into it with rivals. I thought I was so bad, so tough. Predictably, police arrested me for my criminal activities.

When I first arrived at the Cook County Jail I had no idea what was expected of me. I thought it was a badge of honor to be going to prison at nineteen. My crime was the ultimate expression of loyalty to the gang. My first day, I went to my assigned tier housing with about 100 other guys. I dropped my mattress in the cell and started doing my gang "thang," yelling out my gang ID.

It was my idea that fellow members would come up and greet me. An older guy did show up. "Yo, good to see you. First thing I need you to do is apologize to that sheriff you just disrespected." I was shocked. I thought prison life would be "us versus them" chaos. There was chaos, but it was organized through leadership. I could have set the tier off in a riot if there had been a few more gang members with a different affiliation.

I'd been incarcerated a few months awaiting trial when my mom came for a visit. She just looked tired, worn out. It dawned on me: I'm causing it. Returning to my cell I had a deep sense of loneliness, shame, and embarrassment. For the first time I realized the promises of street life and the friends I ran with didn't pan out. I began to have serious doubts about who I was and what my life was about. It was my worst day.

About that time I met an older gentleman called "Preacher" who was awaiting a trial of his own. As I tried to sleep I would hear him singing gospel hymns. Earlier someone had given me a New Testament, which I tried to read. One day Preacher asked me, "Do you understand what you're reading?"

"Not really." So he began talking to me about it.

In the midst of trying to understand the Bible, Joseph, a former gangster, saw me about to get into a fight. Afterward he came to me and said, "Satan wants to kill you. I thought you might like to know. God loves you and he wants to do some things with your life." I thought he was nuts and he looked a little weird, too. He gave me a copy of the devotional *Our Daily Bread* and soon I was transferred, so I couldn't talk to Joseph much after that.

Be alert and of sober mind. Your enemy the devil prowls around like a roaring lion looking for someone to devour. ~1 Peter 5:8

HONEST CONFESSION

Corey Bush, Illinois

I AWAITED TRIAL almost sixteen months. My mom, dad, and sisters were ready for me to come home. I was fixated on getting out at all costs, but they had no idea what I was experiencing inside. Once I arrived at my new cell, Preacher came down again and explained the Bible to me. I was fascinated and childlike in my understanding—stories such as Adam and Eve that I had never heard before!

I get transferred yet again to a special wing for younger inmates or those interested in going to school. Who do I see? It's Joseph again. He continued to tell me more about what God would like to do in my life. Soon thereafter, a volunteer pastor came in to hold a church service. He offered an altar call and I accepted the Lord.

Immediately I had a sense of gratitude and hope, as well as a new dilemma. I no longer wanted to go to court and tell a lie. But I still prayed and hoped something would happen that would allow me to be released. I dropped the news on my family that I was not going to take the stand. I knew if I went up there I would lie. One older inmate I talked to about this gave me a verse: "He who seeks to save his life will lose it, but he who loses his life for me and the gospel will save it, for what does it profit a man to gain the whole world but forfeit his soul?" (Matthew 16:25–26).

It was confirmation. No matter what happens, I'm going to walk with the Lord, and I'll be okay with the outcome. The stakes were high. I had two cases involving guns—attempted murder and aggravated battery. One case could net me four to fifteen years, and the other six to thirty years.

I also told my parents I had become a Christian. They thought I was crazy or having a nervous breakdown. My elderly father told me he wasn't sure he'd be around if I got out in ten years. That fear hit me. His subtext was clear: Do whatever it takes to get free.

After some months passed, I told my lawyer I was guilty and asked him to get me some time I could do. He was shocked, but didn't want to know the details. The state offered ten years and we negotiated to nine. At least I didn't get double digits. It was tough to hear, but I knew this was the right thing before God. I remember praying, "I don't want to go to prison, but if you'll go with me, I'll go."

An honest witness tells the truth, but a false witness tells lies. ~Proverbs 12:17

YOU CAN'T BE BOTH

Corey Bush, Illinois

GOD ALWAYS provides pockets of light. It might seem strange, but every deck or tier I lived on had a pretty strong cohort of Christians, sometimes called "neutrons"—inmates not affiliated with a gang.

I knew I had to get out of my gang. One Scripture verse hounded me: "No one can serve two masters. You'll love one and hate the other." Gangs met to talk about "nation business" including money, what's going on in the street, and how to better organize the tiers; however, I was trying to slowly withdraw. If a meeting was called and a church service was scheduled, I'd go to church every time.

As the coordinator for my tier, tension was building. I'm supposed to be more involved, not miss meetings. I talked to other gang members with positions on our deck to feel out the situation. They said, "We saw it comin'. We respect that. We just hope you're not faking it so you can bypass assignments." They told me to talk to the man in charge of the entire gang for the Cook County system. I sent him a kite indicating I wanted to go "off count."

While waiting on a decision I went to church one day and asked God to not let me mess up my faith and not let me get stabbed. I didn't so much fear for myself, but how it would impact my parents. The service ended and I headed back to my cell.

Lots of people go to church for different reasons and often gang members pass kites and do business. On this day, there was a large gang crowd hanging outside the tier. I didn't have any fear, but a tremendous peace like I was walking on clouds. I walked right through the crowd back to my cell. Later, I found out the word was to leave me alone. I could no longer use them for protection, but I didn't have to fear them, either. It had been about three months since I came to Christ and frankly, leaving the gang was a relief.

When I first became a believer, it seemed as if everything God did for me was a miracle. As years passed, it changed to trust—you don't see him working, but you know he's moving. And I noticed I had more tests to trust him than I did in those early months. My prayers also changed so I didn't *need* to see big miracles. My prayers were less self-centered, such as, "Help me abstain from things and be disciplined in [this area]."

I'm thankful to God I never allowed pornography to enter my cell. It would have been very easy. People's cells were littered with it. My cellmates respected my faith and wouldn't post it around me or they would leave the cell to look at it.

> Do not be misled: "Bad company corrupts good character." ~1 Corinthians 15:33

WATCH YOUR ASSOCIATIONS

Corey Bush, Illinois

MY FIRST stop after leaving the Cook County Jail to begin my sentence was the maximum-security Joliet, where I received my classification. They determine the kind of prison to which you'll go. I made a brief stop at Menard, and then another transfer to Shawnee, a medium-maximum prison. My walk with God was really strong throughout my prison sentence—even through my one near miss.

I have an older brother by fifteen years. When he was my age, he too was caught up in the gang life. One of his street enemies killed my brother's best friend. My brother testified in court and the perpetrator got more than forty years for the crime.

When I showed up at Shawnee I ran into a guy who said, "You look familiar, where you from?" He was huge, 6'3" and just ripped. He had already been inside for close to twenty years. He was completely out of touch with the outside world and glad to meet anyone familiar with the area where he had lived.

We worked out together. He would spot me lifting weights while we talked. Of course, we ended up knowing some of the same people back home. Afterward, I had a chance to call home and my brother happened to pick up. I told him about this new workout buddy. He just panicked.

"Don't you ever say your name, or talk about me. That is the man I testified against!" By God's grace I had not given up my last name. My brother was really afraid for me.

One day I went to the gym and saw this man watching a basketball game. He was in a mood. This happens to people who've been incarcerated a long time. He was bitter. I said, "Hey, what's going on?"

"Nothing, Shorty. They goin' to put me away for all this time! I get tired of being up in here, making me pay for it. I ain't forgot about how I got in here," and he used a nickname that my brother used to go by. It caused me some concern, but I stayed prayed up and kept up my schooling and church. This meant we didn't cross paths much.

This incident was one of the two worst things I worried about—walking around on eggshells not knowing if something was going to jump you like a riot or a fight, and not knowing how my parents would be when I got out. I stuck to Jesus, did my routine, and never got involved with the gang violence that occasionally flared up. I ended up doing four years and three months and was released to parole in June of 1995. I was twenty-four.

> Whoever strays from the path of prudence comes to rest in the company of the dead. ~Proverbs 21:16

MAY 20

A FRIEND IN THE STORM

Mryrien A. Jenkins, Georgia

IT WAS August 3, 1982, when my world came crashing down around me. My heart did not want to accept what was being explained to me by the arresting detectives; my seventeen-year-old son, Mark, was being charged with murder in North Carolina.

I was crushed and hurting so deep inside—no one but God could enter in. I desperately called on him over and over, begging him to give me strength to carry on. I did not ask God for Mark to be released, but I asked that Mark would accept the truth of what he had done. I also asked he would not get the death penalty.

Gradually the fog in my mind began to clear. I had never been more grateful for knowing God's Word; he came through in amazing ways and at JUST my moment of need with perfect Scripture verses. The two that helped me breathe were 1 Peter 5:7: "Cast your cares on me for I care for you," and 1 Peter 5:10: "But the God of all grace, who hath called us unto His eternal glory by Christ Jesus, after that ye have suffered a while, make you perfect, establish, strengthen and settle you."

Mark was in jail with no bond, charged with first-degree murder. I looked for lawyers to take his case. One attorney, supposed to be very good, wanted $25,000 up front and couldn't promise me anything but life in prison. I didn't have the money. Those I thought might help either wouldn't or couldn't, including Mark's father.

I was forced to accept the court-appointed lawyers. I felt all alone in this battle. Again, I cried out to God and immediately I heard, "Is anything too hard for the Lord?" (Genesis 18:14).

The Lord gave me songs in the night, too, to softly rock me to sleep: "He lives, He lives, Christ Jesus lives today . . ."

I thought I was a strong Christian before, but as the weeks turned into months and I walked this battle out, I discovered a depth of God's love for me that I had never known. He proved to be faithful. He truly is "a friend that sticketh closer than a brother" (Proverbs 18:24).

One who has unreliable friends soon comes to ruin, but there is a friend who sticks closer than a brother. ~Proverbs 18:24

AGAINST THE ODDS

Mryrien A. Jenkins, Georgia

WE ENDED up getting two very knowledgeable lawyers to defend Mark. They encouraged me to hold on and they worked hard to save his life. One day, the female lawyer approached me, looking a little disturbed. She said the district attorney was asking for the death penalty.

I firmly responded, "Mark will not get the death penalty."

She stared at me and said, "This is serious."

"I know," I confidently replied. "The Lord has reassured me Mark will live. God showed me in a dream Mark getting a life sentence and being led out of the courtroom to enter a bus to carry him away."

Eight months later, Mark's trial began and the young man who committed the crime with Mark turned state's evidence (against Mark). But the jury couldn't reach a verdict. Ten were for the death penalty, two were not. And thankfully, those two would not give in. According to the state of North Carolina, when the jury can't reach a verdict the judge is responsible for setting the sentencing for the crime. The judge gave Mark life with parole and he was shipped to a youth facility twenty-seven miles from where we lived. Mark would be eligible for parole in twenty years.

My son ended up spending twenty-six years in prison. God redeemed that time; Mark gave his life to the Lord—a huge answer to prayer! While in prison he went to college and maintained a high grade point average, making the Dean's List several times. He also won many awards.

Mark was released December 1, 2008. The Lord has called him into ministry. I am an evangelist and we sometimes have the joy of working together serving our amazing Lord.

Every promise God made in his Word came to fruition. He *is* the God of all grace and comfort. Thanks to God we have a Savior who knows the end from the very beginning and who takes this journey with us. If we trust him and him only, he will see us through every storm that comes our way.

> You, dear children, are from God and have overcome them, because the one who is in you is greater than the one who is in the world. ~1 John 4:4

MAY 22

VALIDITY IN CHRIST JESUS

Mark Jenkins, North Carolina

AFTER BEING sentenced to life in prison, when I walked through the rusted and ragged gates of the correctional facility I felt a heavy condemnation. Then, as I was being processed in, I was met by inmates who had a copy of the newspaper with my picture on the front page. I hung my head even lower.

But there was one scenario that will be forever etched in my soul. There were two correctional staff members standing behind a desk. As they looked at me they shook their heads. Then, one of them said to me, "If I were you, I would not try to do that 'life sentence.' I would just jump the fence." He said this more than once.

I was unaware that just weeks prior to my transfer to that facility an inmate had "hit the fence," as it is called, and he was shot. At that moment

I sunk to the level of seeking the validation of man. I wanted to be accepted by others and not judged for the horrible crime I had committed.

I lived under the spirit of condemnation and became enslaved to every criticism, whether just or unjust, tossed my way. I was vulnerable and felt unworthy of anything good. It would take years for me to become untangled from this mind-set. After going before a review board, I struggled, feeling like a failure. I would talk to people who meant well, and I would leave with that same heavy sense of foreboding hovering about me.

I fully committed my life to Christ some nineteen years later and began to walk according to the Spirit and not the flesh. I became sorrowful in a godly way and that's when true repentance took place. I realized that my worth as a human being is in Christ alone. I needed to care about what *he* thinks of me.

I found that when I humbled myself before him and began to do that which was pleasing in his sight, he silenced my accusers. My prayer to God became, "I'm guilty of my crime, but that's not who I am." I held on to God's Word, which boldly declared who I was in him.

I challenge anyone who may be feeling less than they really are, or worthless, to make this same cry to God. Ask him to forgive you, begin to walk in the Spirit, grasp hold of who you really are in him, and be free of condemnation. You can experience a whole new way of life—a victorious life.

> There is therefore now no condemnation to those who are in Christ Jesus, who do not walk according to the flesh, but according to the Spirit. ~Romans 8:1

MAY 23

LETTING GO OF THE PAST
Mark Jenkins, North Carolina

NOT LONG after I was transferred into the North Carolina Department of Corrections, I vividly remember sitting in my dormitory and reading Philippians 3:13. Although I did not have a true understanding of that verse at the time, or the context in which it was written, still, I held on to ". . . *forgetting those things which are behind and reaching forward . . .*"

Little did I know that in the years to come this would become the verse that best described all I had overcome and where the Lord was taking me.

In some instances it had been difficult for me to forget about many of my accomplishments and failures. However, once I made up my mind to follow Christ, that verse in Philippians took on new meaning. God began to give me revelation after revelation of how my life paralleled those men in the Bible who had accomplished great things, but were also guilty of horrendous acts. There was Moses, who killed an Egyptian for beating a slave. There was King David, who killed Uriah after he had an affair with Uriah's wife and she became pregnant. And there was Paul, who, when he was known as Saul, killed lots of Christians just because they were Christians.

I read how each one of these men, like me, was guilty of murder, yet God redeemed them and had an awesome plan for their life. God ultimately used each of them for his glory.

It was in those moments of revelation I began to seek more after the Lord and desired to have his favor upon my life. To do this, I realized I could not allow myself to be held a victim of my past. I needed to walk in my forgiveness.

The apostle Paul, in essence, is telling us, in spite of all, to pursue Christ-likeness. If we pursue Christ there will be little or no time to rest on our laurels, or to dwell on the disappointments of our pasts. In this glorious pursuit, it becomes all about him and where he wants to take us. Our part is to let go of our past and trust him with our future.

> Brethren, I do not count myself to have apprehended; but one thing I do, forgetting those things which are behind and reaching forward to those things which are ahead. ~Philippians 3:13

MARK JENKINS AND HIS MOM, MRYRIEN A. JENKINS

SOME THINGS, YOU NEVER GET OVER

Joe Avila, California

THE MEMORIES from twenty years ago are fresh like a scar that still stings—the crash, the sadness and void in my daughter's eyes, while I paid the price in prison. The memories of my crime and failures hurt a lot, yet I am also able to trust and glorify Jesus, who sustained us and molded us into who we are today.

In 1992, at the age of 42 I lived with my family in the Central Valley of California. I was an *acute* alcoholic, but functioning as a professional at a communications company. I started drinking in high school in a small town and it became a way of life. Alcohol motivated me to get up early in the morning, get my job done, and have adequate time left on the clock to go out drinking. Everything I did was to get to alcohol every day. I spent thousands per month not only on drinks, but on the environment of drinking. When you hit a bar, you're buying drinks for those around you, too. It also led to cocaine use, which became extensive (and expensive).

Every day on the highway I drove impaired to some extent. It's surprising I didn't do more damage. I had several driving under the influence charges on my record, plus others that I had beaten.

One Friday evening I was driving drunk as usual. I hit a car driven by a seventeen-year-old young lady, Amy Wall. The force of impact spun her car several times until it hit a tree.

Amy died at the scene and her passenger was hurt.

I remember panicking, "Oh, God, what have I done?"

Authorities first took me to the hospital to be treated for minor injuries and then TO the Fresno County Jail. For the first four or five days I looked for a way to kill myself. I was angry and so ashamed. The accident was the top news story in a community where I was known. People were angry and I couldn't blame them. I just looked for a way to end it. But in the infirmary it is very hard to pull anything because of their 24/7 oversight.

Initially, because of my prior DUIs, the state charged me with second-degree murder, a conviction which carried a sentence of fifteen to life. We never asked to have that charge dropped, and to this day we can't be sure why it changed to vehicular manslaughter, which carried a twelve-year maximum.

> You may be sure that your sin will find you out. ~Numbers 32:23

A SERIES OF FIRSTS

Joe Avila, California

MY NEIGHBOR asked the jail chaplain at his church, Les Lyle, if he would see me. Les pulled me into his small office and we talked a long time about what I'd done, and about Christ. I was profoundly struck by his counsel.

"Joe, hear me on this: Christ died even for what you did five days ago."

Be sure I was desperately looking for a way out, including suicide. It may look phony or like an evasion of responsibility to some, but I actually came to understand that Jesus was the only true way out. No one including myself believes I deserve any mercy. Yet the gospel seems to shout it from the cross. I decided then to follow Christ. My suicidal thoughts fell away.

The court reduced my bail from $1 million to $50,000, giving me a pivotal opportunity to go directly to the Salvation Army rehabilitation center while my case waited to go to trial.

I desperately wanted to see my young daughters, but it would not look good for me to disrupt classes for a visit. Instead, my wife Mary drove me to rehab for my intake interview to see if we could secure the one opening left.

In my mind I was still functioning as an alcoholic. My behavior had not completely been transformed in a few weeks. So during the interview I asked, "Can I start in two days? Tomorrow is Thanksgiving and my daughter's twelfth birthday."

The counselor shot back, "How bad do you want to get sober?" I decided I had to go in now without seeing the girls.

In the program we delved into the Scriptures. In the book of 2 Corinthians, Chapter 5, much is written about reconciliation. That became my heart's wish—to be reconciled to God and Amy's family.

Then, through study and conviction I accepted my guilt for the first time. Of course I knew it all along, but it was a perverse guilt—the kind that made me suicidal and to enter a plea of not guilty. In litigation, time is your friend—the longer it drags out, the better the chance of getting some deal. I couldn't drag Amy's family through court any longer and prolong their pain. This meant no plea deals.

After finishing the twenty-eight-day program, Mary drove me to court. We knew I'd be remanded immediately back into custody when I changed my plea to guilty. Pausing outside we talked; then, for the first time, we prayed to have a triune marriage—me, Mary, Christ. We were going to base all our decisions on Christ. We made it a sacred vow before walking into that courtroom. The day before Easter 1993, I received the full twelve-year sentence.

> You shall not give false testimony against your neighbor. ~Exodus 20:16

MAY 26

THE GREATEST MOMENT OF MY LIFE

Joe Avila, California

REGARDLESS OF their resources, prisoners who care about their families seek ways to communicate and reach out. My children were the center of my life. I tried corresponding with my daughters early on in my prison sentence daily using a 3-inch pencil and whatever scraps of paper I found. My appreciation for prison chaplains also grew because as I left one service the chaplain passed out two greeting cards to each inmate. They were like gold. I could finally send my daughters something less ratty.

Some inmates paint or draw, but I could write. During Christmas I made a special effort to pen a unique children's story for each of them. And there are plenty of prisoners with artistic talent so you barter and purchase cards or pictures whenever you can.

Before I went behind the walls a friend told me I needed to journal. I agreed, but decided it would be in the form of my daily letters home to my family. Mary kept all those letters in chronological order, eight volumes. I described everything that happened in an acceptable way—my progress, not all the bad stuff you see in prison.

In 1993 around September, I was transferred to the California Men's Colony. Because I was discipline-free, along with other factors, I was eligible for family visits. Families drive in, often hundreds of miles, to stay in torn up trailer-like bungalows that have a kitchen and two rooms. I tried to have the girls up as often as I could.

Something began to happen that I didn't perceive until my twelve-year-old, Elizabeth, said something. Both Mary and I were new Christians. The drinking had stopped, but the girls experienced what kids of alcoholics do. They'd suffered in ways not visible to us.

On a Saturday visit around the lunch table we talked about how God was changing me. Then Elizabeth said, "Grace and I have been talking. We really like what you and mom have become. And we want what you guys have."

We talked about sin, repentance, the cross, and the grace of God and I led them both to the Lord in the prison visiting unit. Today they'll laugh and tell you they met Jesus behind bars, too, just like Dad.

That was the greatest moment of my life.

Fathers, do not exasperate your children; instead, bring them up in the training and instruction of the Lord. ~Ephesians 6:4

FINDING PURPOSE IN PRISON SOCIETY

Joe Avila, California

THE SYSTEM determines your custody level based on points. A twelve-year stint equals a lot of points, which automatically sent me to a maximum-security prison.

I first arrived at Corcoran. I'm Hispanic, not covered in tattoos, and sticking out like a sore thumb. California prisons are highly gang infested. Even at forty-two, I had to claim north or south Hispanic gang affiliation. Staff didn't know what to do, so they threw me into solitary—a creepy place holding people like Manson and Corona. Officers feared I would be taken advantage of in general population.

Finally a captain reduced me from level 4 to level 3 and shipped me to the California Men's Colony. They bunked me with someone from the north. Soon, I was called to interview with a high-ranking gang member. I told him I'm a Christ- follower and that was what I was going to do. This gangster either really liked me, or knew I was sincere. He gave me a pass and promised to leave me alone as long as I keep to the chapel system and don't backslide. Prison culture has an odd respect for authenticity inside—fence sitters and hypocrites don't do well.

I'm assigned a high-trust job in the hospital doing procurement of all kinds of medical supplies. In an overcrowded prison the job required I have a single cell because I was pulled out at all times of day and night to change oxygen tanks. It gave me space to let my guard down, pray, and meditate.

I then found the specific thing God wanted me to do in that hospital—the hospice wing. That's where I started sharing my story, which is really God's story, and tried to lead terminally ill inmates to Christ. That became my mission field.

Compared with patients in other hospice wards, men dying in a prison hospice are among the most hopeless of all men. Most don't have family because they are dead or have rejected the prisoner. Many die of AIDS, hepatitis, and tuberculosis. They have no visitors and expect to die alone in prison, completely forgotten.

I remember officers asking me, "Why do you want to go in there?" People feared catching something in such a sick place. It was never a con-

JOE AVILA

cern of mine. God protected me. A chaplain friend reminded me Christ embraced the lepers and so should we.

Like most testimonial experiences, some listened, others told me to get lost. When they said that, I'd ask to pray for them and they never protested. Many just wanted to die. Others were joyous because they knew they would be with the Lord.

Those were my most gratifying prison experiences.

> But the Pharisees and the teachers of the law who belonged to their sect complained to his disciples, "Why do you eat and drink with tax collectors and sinners?" Jesus answered them, "It is not the healthy who need a doctor, but the sick. I have not come to call the righteous, but sinners to repentance." ~Luke 5:30–32

PACIFIC KINDNESS

Joe Avila, California

AFTER SIX years, my time at CMC East ended. As you do time, your points go lower. The facility lieutenant had already kept me from going to the lower-security camp twice. He liked the job I was doing, and I felt good about all that I had—great job, single cell, and hospice care.

Finally, the lieutenant could hold me no longer. I gave most of my stuff away because at the new place I'd have only a small locker in an open dorm setting.

I hated my new situation and decided to try to work my way over to the fire camp, which gives you a chance to work for the Department of Forestry. I scored an interview with the fire chief and my new job would be feeding thousands of deployed men fighting fires.

For six years I'd lived with thirty-foot walls, tower guards with guns, high-density lighting all night, and lots of bars and locked gates. Now I live in an old military camp, unsupervised, around vehicles with keys in them, yet I'm still living with a higher-security mentality, waiting or asking for permission to do things or go places I didn't know I was already free to do or go.

That's when I met Officer Bill Hartman, who operated heavy machinery. He came out and said, "Avila, come with me. I heard you spent the last six years across the way at level 3?"

"Yeah."

"Get in the truck." We exited the camp and pulled into an In-N-Out Burger drive-thru.

"What do you want?"

"What do you mean? I don't know." I'm really caught off guard by all this. So he ordered two meals and drove on.

Next he parks near a summit I recognized from years ago. We stepped out with our lunches and walked to the edge, where I saw the vast Pacific Ocean.

I don't think Bill realized how his act of kindness overwhelmed me. You live under the correction officer's boot, and officers don't usually go out of their way for an inmate. To see, feel, and smell the salty ocean air after years of concrete and metal bars . . . I hardly have words to describe it. What a tangible example of kindness given to someone deserving none. I'll never forget it.

We became great friends. After that, we got involved with fighting fires and I would see the ocean again. We set up camps and ran the mobile kitchen unit feeding two thousand people three times a day. It really made the last year go by fast. After fire season I only had a few months until release.

> You gave me life and showed me kindness, and in your providence watched over my spirit. ~Job 10:12

CAN WE TALK MAN-TO-MAN?

Joe Avila, California

AFTER SEVEN years I was paroled out and started putting a life back together. I'd always wanted to reconcile with Amy's family since I read about the concept in my study of 2 Corinthians. My long-time friend Ron Claason and I had worked on this issue while I was still inside. I'd written a letter and Ron hand-delivered it. The family opted not to read it. We had never had contact since I last saw them in court.

I started a window-washing business to help pay bills while volunteering with Prison Fellowship, and continued to talk to Ron about reconciliation options. There really were none. I had to go on with life, accepting that this was just going to be a missing component.

About seven years later the Fresno chief of police called me to participate in an anti-drunk driving campaign. I didn't hesitate since I'd been sharing my story as opportunities arose. We secured a spot on Frank Pastore's drive-time radio broadcast.

During the broadcast Amy Wall's dad was looking for a sports game, but couldn't find a station in the boondocks where he was driving, except ours. He called his son Derrick to tune in also. I didn't refer to Amy by name because I didn't have permission, but I let everyone know my heart. The next day, Ron called me. Derrick, Amy's younger brother, had asked to meet. God kind of ambushes you. I'd given up hoping that the possibility still existed.

Reconciliation is a sensitive process, from venue choice to when people arrive. You don't want victims and offenders meeting in the parking lot for an awkward moment. You agree to ground rules in case something goes wrong. For example, if he says something, I must paraphrase back to him his statement so the victim knows I'm listening and correctly hearing his meaning. We agreed I'd have my wife and Ron attend and Derrick brought his pastor. Anybody can call time out, no questions asked, and reschedule.

Derrick started talking and I would paraphrase, when he said, "Stop. I just want to talk to Joe man-to-man." Ron looked at me and I agreed. We talked two-and-a-half hours. He told me what Amy meant to him, about the night she was killed, how he thought I was a monster. He hoped I would get the electric chair.

Then I talked about my history, my faith, and I asked him to forgive me. He said he did.

"I really feel good about this meeting today," he said, then pulled out a key chain and wrote something on it.

"I want you to have it," he told me. It was a picture of Amy. Printed on the back was, "Somebody drank and drove and Amy died . . ." and next to it in his writing, "so others could live."

He looked at me. "I guess what I'm saying is that it's our charge to tell our story so others may live." And that's what we've done ever since.

> And forgive us our debts as we also have forgiven our debtors.
> ~Matthew 6:12

MAY 30

A FATHER'S FORGIVENESS
Joe Avila, California

THE CHANCE to meet and reconcile with Amy's brother meant a lot to us both. It was God's timing, not mine, and that would hold true for Amy's dad, Rick. We met at the same place as Derrick under similar ground rules. Having experienced my heavenly Father's forgiveness years earlier did not change the emotional impact of facing Mr. Wall for the first time. Nothing I could say would ever change the fact that he had lost a precious daughter.

Rick came in carrying a legal pad with all kinds of writing. He first started talking about the Amy he loved and described the two days a year he visits the cemetery—on her birthday and the day she died. He looked at me and said, "You know, Joe, I've been following you. I know what you've been doing since you got out and even before you got out. I just want you to know I approve. And I also want you to know that I forgive you."

This man *forgave me* for killing his daughter before I could even ask him. After we prayed he came around the table and gave me a hug.

Not long after, I was invited to a reconciliation conference in Fresno. Before I realized it, the whole event pivoted around a panel featuring Derrick (who has earned his PhD) and myself. Several hundred people packed the room because the community knew about me and the story.

So Derrick and I shared our experience. After finishing we returned to our table and lingered while people came to talk. Among the people who came over was Linda, Amy's mother, who shook my hand. Then out of the side of my eye I saw a big guy coming over—it was Rick. I thought he was coming to talk to his son. Instead he came directly to me, gave me a big hug and said, "I love you, Joe." That was huge. It's true forgiveness. The offense has been dropped.

We all feel the void left by Amy and will the rest of our lives, but we can also move on to what God would call us to do in his service and find joy in that.

> As far as the east is from the west, so far has he removed our transgressions from us. ~Psalm 103:12

MAY 31

WE NEEDED TO BE CHANGED
Mary Avila, California

I WAS SITTING on the front lawn with neighbors enjoying a summer Friday evening. Around midnight I saw Joe coming home driving erratically, steam pouring from the hood of the car, and the highway patrol right behind him. I knew he'd been drinking.

At least I assumed Joe was driving. Around 3 a.m. with Joe dazed in the back of a squad car and unaware of his actions, police were finally able to tell us what happened at the accident scene barely a mile from our house.

Shock set in followed by the realization I'd have to tell our two young daughters that their daddy had killed someone and wasn't coming home for a long time.

Drinking and driving wasn't unusual for either one of us. I grew up in a family of alcoholics, so it was no surprise I married one. I remember family members drinking cocktails before and after dinner, and nightcaps before bed. Neither one of us could really talk sense to the alcoholic we married. This criminal tragedy was bound to happen.

When I had a chance to talk to Joe a few weeks later from the county jail he started telling me about how he'd found Jesus. I'd heard all the excuses before. This was a new one—it really looked like jailhouse religion. I was skeptical. But the more we talked and I observed him during visitation at the Salvation Army rehab program, there really was something different. I couldn't explain the extreme change in his character in such a brief time. I was fighting fear and anxiety about the future, which led me to want what he had. That's when I came to Christ. It was like getting married for the first time.

We made a 180-degree turn. We did so many things for selfish reasons in our first thirteen years of marriage. Now there was a real sense of love. We were covering each other, we were kind to each other, we'd help each other up when we stumbled. We discussed all major decisions together either on the phone or during face-to-face visits.

The alcohol had been so much of the picture. With that eliminated, we had a brand new relationship. When Joe came home years later, he would vacuum! He brought home a new love of cooking and took over the kitchen. Pre-prison I did all the finances and he didn't know or really care where we were financially. There was so much ugliness in those years. I couldn't trust him about money. When he came home from prison, we started paying the bills together.

Our lives needed to be changed. Our marriage would have been shattered otherwise. I couldn't have taken that length of time away from him or found the grace to forgive him had we not each been truly changed by Christ.

No, in all these things we are more than conquerors through him who loved us. ~Romans 8:37

SINGLE MOM

Mary Avila, California

ALTHOUGH JOE and I had begun a new spiritual life and a new marriage, I was still facing single motherhood for possibly twelve years. Any single mom knows the anxiety, fear, and exhaustion of doing it all by yourself.

Our income was cut significantly, as was our lifestyle. Our wonderful church provided scholarships for the girls to attend summer camp. We'd find envelopes with gift certificates to grocery stores. But when kids got sick or I got sick, I had no backup, and no adult to talk to at the end of the day.

I had plenty of hard choices every month about which bills to pay. There was a civil suit against us, but because we had nothing they could only collect from insurance. We rented a house and I had to call the landlady to tell her what happened. She was a Christian. She couldn't lower the rent and we didn't ask, but she allowed a revised pay schedule because I didn't have it all at the front of the month. It always hung over us, but she never raised the rent in seven years.

I did have my meltdowns figuring out how to pay our bills, or how to schedule everything with work, school, and medical and dental appointments. I'd get frustrated and go off on the kids when it wasn't their fault. They would be watching TV instead of folding their clothes—normal kid stuff.

We didn't have Disney trips, but we did fun things when we drove 150 miles one way to visit Dad in prison. I'd promise a trip to the outlet to get some school clothes and sometimes I'd tell them we needed to check on "our" beach. We had many picnics at the coincidentally named Avila Beach. I needed to coat some of these visits with a little sugar given the distance and how they caused the kids to miss a lot of weekend activities.

I became part of a support group, all of whom had a relative in prison. Often I'd walk away thinking, *I don't really have it as bad as they do.*

I had a great neighbor who used to hug me after work. One day she came over and I burst into tears, because my car had broken down and I was going to be laid off after twenty years. *Now what am I going to do?* Instant panic.

She prayed with me and told me, "It's going to be okay." And it was, with unemployment insurance, the landlord lowering the rent temporarily, and a severance package God provided.

God only gives you what you can handle and provides everything you need.

> Be joyful in hope, patient in affliction, faithful in prayer. ~Romans 12:12

WHAT WOULD HAVE HAPPENED IF . . .?

Grace Avila, Texas

YOU HAVE to wonder how I didn't end up like the kids I work with at a special center for traumatized youth. These children have had abusive parents, divorced parents, and incarcerated parents, and all of them have been forced to deal with "icky" topics at a young age—infidelity, drug abuse, the horrors of a hostile divorce. Young children are simply not mature enough to shoulder that weight.

I don't remember much before my dad went to prison when I was only six. We went to Catholic church on holidays; my parents smoked, drank, and fought. But something clearly changed after his arrest. Mom quit smoking cold turkey after twenty-five years. We visited Dad almost every other weekend for years. I remember the two-and-a-half-hour drive each way, celebrating birthdays in visitation, talking on the phone with Dad a lot during the week.

When my parents decided to make Christ the entire focus of our family, it turned a disaster into something really positive. I learned about God through the changed life and behavior of my Dad in prison. That's not normal. I told new friends, "Don't feel sorry for me. Let me tell you about what amazing parents I have!" They really did a lot of things right, shielding us from much of the negative stigma. They were open to our teachers and coaches so they understood why we missed weekend games or why I drew prison bars in my pictures.

That's not to say there were no rough spots. I sensed a shift as Dad came home and I became a teenager. There's a man in the house. I sensed lingering guilt on his part, because he wanted me and my sister to have everything and do what made us happy when sometimes we needed restraint. He never hid his past and would invite me to ask questions, but I didn't really know how. Teens like me are trying to figure out the world and default to believing we are the center of the universe. It takes a while to grow up and process. I struggled with the fact that I didn't have a normal dad and worried about having to dodge questions about it in my social circles.

I'm really so proud of who my Dad has become. He's dedicated his life to service. He raised two successful daughters. He loves my mom. That can't happen without something transforming the vicious cycle. People may ask what would have happened if the accident never occurred? But what would have happened if that chaplain hadn't shared Christ with my father when he was suicidal? It's bad enough one family had to experience their loss. God in his mercy saved my entire family out of the ashes of that moment.

> May your unfailing love be with us, Lord, even as we put our hope in you.
> ~Psalm 33:22

JUNE 3

GOD'S PERFECT TIMING

Steve Osborne, Ohio

I HAVE BEEN a pastor for thirty-five years. I have received a lot of correspondence over the years from people in various situations. One letter I still cherish is from Tim, who was a young man during the 1970s and 80s. Tim was incarcerated at the Orient Correctional Facility in Ohio. I was a student attending Asbury Theological Seminary and pastoring three churches in the rural area of Sugar Tree Ridge, Ohio. As a young teenager, Tim had found himself on the wrong side of the law several times. Seems he enjoyed partying with his friends and playing around with recreational drugs, but once he turned eighteen he soon learned that the judicial system was not as forgiving.

We planned a family camp for one of the churches down on the Ohio River in the summer of 1978. There were about fifty people, including kids, and Tim decided to join us. As was our practice, we had a group Bible study every night around 8:30. I had chosen to share on the topic of our Lord's return. As the evening progressed, I noticed that the teenage boys, sitting on a hillside, were only half paying attention.

The Scripture I read was Matthew 24:7: "Nation will rise against nation, and kingdom against kingdom. There will be famines and earthquakes in various places." Jesus was describing the "times" in which we could expect his return. Even in the late 1970s I was convinced the Lord could return at any moment. Many people back then, like today, were asking questions about his return.

Strangely, as I read, "and earthquakes in various places" my stomach became queasy. At the same time I heard a soft rumble and thought maybe it was a semi passing by, but there was no road close enough for that to be the case. I glanced over by the creek bed and saw that it was shaking. One of the ladies let out a squeal— creeks don't shake! It ended almost as fast as it began, but we all knew we had experienced our first earthquake.

> So you also must be ready, because the Son of Man will come at an hour when you do not expect him. ~Matthew 24:44

TIM'S "EARTH-SHAKING" EXPERIENCE

Steve Osborne, Ohio

THE HOT topic after the quake was the timing. Was it a "coincidence" that the rumbling and shaking happened at the exact same time that I was reading those words? What did it mean? Could it be a direct message from God, and if so, what was he trying to tell us?

Everyone went to bed that night still amazed by it. As I approached my tent, Tim asked if he could talk with me for a few minutes. I said, "Sure," and we sat down at one of the picnic tables. I remember Tim poured his heart out that night. He shared about his drugs, alcohol, and partying, and how he had never really believed the Bible. However, earlier that night he had prayed that if God was real and that if anything I was saying was true—to please show him. Then, when the earthquake hit, Tim knew God did it just for him.

That night Tim gave his heart to the Lord and we both rejoiced, talking late into the night. As I headed back to school that week I prayed and rejoiced over Tim's surrender to the Lord. I was looking forward to discipling him on the weekends when I was home.

So, when I came back to that area the very next weekend, I was shocked to read the Hillsboro paper. It seemed there had been a drug bust the night before and . . . Tim's name was listed as one of the guys picked up. I was crushed. As soon as I could, I went to visit him at the jail.

Tim hung his head as he shared with me he wasn't guilty. He wanted to reach his friends with his new faith so he went where he knew they'd be on a Friday night. He was hauled in, and because he had a record he was detained. The judge chose to make an example out of him to the other young men, many of whom were under age. Tim was charged with trafficking and sentenced to three to five years in prison.

> God is our refuge and strength, an ever-present help in trouble. Therefore we will not fear, though the earth give way and the mountains fall into the heart of the sea, though its waters roar and foam and the mountains quake with their surging. ~Psalm 46:1–3

JUNE 5

FROM SERVING TIME TO SERVING JESUS

Steve Osborne, Ohio

TIM'S FIRST letter from prison was heartbreaking. I knew I had to see him. When I arrived he looked at me sadly, and asked, "Why,

Pastor Steve? Why would God allow this to happen to me? I was just getting my head on straight. I know I deserve what I'm getting for all the times I didn't get caught—but, why now?"

I pointed out to him Romans 8:28: "And we know that in all things God works for the good of those who love him, who have been called according to his purpose." I told Tim that God was going to use this whole situation in his life and that something good would come out of it. I then encouraged him to read in his Bible the letters Paul wrote while in prison. I also asked Tim to go to chapel services, get to know the chaplain, and be willing to share his faith with fellow prisoners.

A month later I received a wonderful letter from Tim. He was so enthusiastic, his first line practically shouted his excitement!

> *Dear Pastor Steve,*
> *I know why now! God wants me here for a reason. For the first time in my life I know what I want to do with my life. God wants me to be a prison chaplain. I have been meeting with the Chaplain . . .*

His letter went on and on about all he was learning and how the chaplain had made him an "Assistant Chaplain" already. I never had the opportunity to meet that chaplain, but I know he was an answer to prayer. My next visit to the prison was nothing like the first—it was a joy!

Tim served his time, was released, and went back to school. He was making great headway toward his calling into the ministry when I was moved to another city. Tim's dream was eventually realized, although it took nearly ten years. We've since lost contact, but I am convinced he's out there somewhere reaching the world for Jesus.

Tim's experience led me to have a heart for those caught on the wrong side of the law—whether guilty or innocent. I rarely enter our local county jail without the encouragement of knowing that God is already at work—we get to just go along for the ride!

And we know that in all things God works for the good of those who love him, who have been called according to his purpose. ~Romans 8:28

THERE'S ALWAYS HOPE

Nikola Matesic, California

I HAD JUST been transferred from the county jail to the Solano Prison in California, and was a baby Christian, in 2001. This was a strange place. Somebody was fighting somebody all the time.

It was my first time in a cell with another man and there were loud conversations going on through the pipes between the inmates housed upstairs and downstairs. Actually, strange communications were taking place all across the entire building. Some were speaking with pride about their crimes.

I kept wondering, *How do I deal with all this? How do I get through this?* I lay on my bunk under the blankets and began to cry—and pray. I was fairly new at praying and my prayers were scattered all over the place. But I ended with, "Dear God, come and live in me and let me live in you."

I thought this was an interesting prayer, so I wrote it down with the date, 5/5/01. The next day I looked at that prayer and the date and thought that those numbers looked like a Bible verse. So I decided to open my little pocket Bible and wherever it opened I would search for 5:5. It opened to Romans. When I went to Romans 5:5 I read, "And hope does not disappoint us, because God has poured out his love into our hearts by the Holy Spirit, whom he has given us."

Right then and there I knew all would be well. I knew that God was with me. It is hard to put into words, but I was suddenly encouraged and liberated at the same time! Romans 5:5 was the power of God's love being poured into my heart. His assurance of his love never left me. Even when I was a Level 3 inmate and I was going to be moved to Level 2, and another inmate told me I did not want to go to Level 2 because it was no good there, I was not afraid.

"Wherever I'm going, God will be there," I responded.

This man did not believe in God, but when he heard my answer, even though he was puzzled, he still affirmed it. "Yes, God will be there."

I knew I had nothing to worry about—God had set me free.

Through him you believe in God, who raised him from the dead and glorified him, and so your faith and hope are in God. ~1 Peter 1:21

THE BATTLE IS HIS

Nikola Matesic, California

I WAS STILL tormented by the fact that I had hurt my wife. To hurt her on any level is not my way of dealing with life.

And now in prison, I knew there was violence. I thought long and hard and I prayed for God to show me what to do if I was engaged in a fight or attacked (Philippians 1:21). I came to accept the fact that I was prepared to die, rather than ever hurt another human being. Then God opened my heart and mind to new understanding (Psalm 28:7). He pointed out to me that I do not have to fight anyone, because "the battle is His" (2 Chronicles 20:15). I chose to trust God completely. I understood that there was this shield of Jesus all around me as if I was encapsulated in Jesus and I no longer had arms, nor did I need arms for protecting myself.

Then, one morning, a man stood in front of me with his fists ready, angry, saying, "Let's settle this right now!"

I looked at him quick, hard, and precise. And at that same time I thought, *Jesus is my protector. I have no arms to fight . . . remain calm.*

These were all split-second thoughts, but thanks to the power of God, I remained calm, keeping my arms down and relaxed. I was not going to add any fuel to the fire.

And then—the man just dropped his arms and walked away, without a word.

I knew I could trust my Savior completely, but I was also ready to let my body die, rather than to hurt another person ever again.

I was in prison for eleven years and had two close calls where I almost got hurt, but not even a hair went missing from me. God was with me all the way through, just as he is with me now. And in him, my freedom is complete. There is no fear, no confusion. All is clear, all is beautiful. Not even a fiery furnace can touch us—we are in God's care.

For to me, to live is Christ and to die is gain. ~Philippians 1:21

196

BLESSED BEYOND MEASURE

Nikola Matesic, California

MY ARREST at age forty-nine was like dying and I was there to view my own funeral. People came to watch out of curiosity, wanting to know what happened.

Thankfully, my friends stood by me. Almost all my wife's family, though, distanced themselves. Some of her family sought legal protection against me. I am never to see them again, except my daughters, Courtney and Michelle. Courtney was nine years old at the time, and I was allowed to write to her, but indirectly.

I wrote many letters to Courtney; on average fifteen to twenty letters per year. I received three letters back in eleven years—all true blessings. One year I wrote more than 180 letters to my daughters and others. I didn't complain to them—rather, I encouraged them in the Lord. God had filled me with such peace, love, joy, courage, and hope, I wanted to let everyone know how free I was—right there surrounded by an electrical fence.

Prison actually became my sanctuary and I was not anxious for anything, not even about getting out of prison. God had transformed me into a new creature and I was enjoying this newness of life. My family would even tell me they didn't think of me as being in prison, rather somewhere on a retreat studying. And they were right. I was investing my time in growing in the Lord. God had made sure I had everything needed to serve him fully and to honor him with my life. "Bloom where you are planted" became my motto.

Many men in prison did not write to their children because they wrote one letter and did not get a response. I kept writing letter after letter without an answer because I knew I was at fault. I am the father. I must let my children know I miss them, I love them, and I think about them all the time. I have been blessed with a wonderful family.

Now that I am out of prison, I live with my daughter Michelle and her husband, Matthew. I also get to enjoy my wonderful grandsons, Benjamin and Desmond. Family is so precious to me and they are so good to me—I am blessed beyond measure!

Rejoice in the Lord always. I will say it again: Rejoice! ~Philippians 4:4

GET OUT OF THE COMFORT ZONE

Russell Walthour, Florida

THE CHURCH needs to serve in difficult places and on battlefields. I've learned that if we just go, God will take care of things once we get there. You have to get out of your comfort zone. Even a combat veteran turned businessman like me can be stretched and called into something unknown and uncomfortable.

Many years ago, a group of men from Miami decided to take the Kairos weekend experience into a Florida prison. The first one they held would be at the Rock at UCI—a very tough unit with hardened men. *Kairos* is a Greek word for "in God's time," and the program is designed to encourage the spiritual growth of followers of Jesus. As it happens, it also becomes a place where many meet Jesus for the first time.

My phone rang and it was Jack Meeks, a close brother in Christ and someone with whom I had gone through the same weekend experience, only in the free world. Jack told me he planned to lead a Kairos weekend at UCI and asked me to join his team of volunteers.

"That's not me, Jack. I don't have any ties to those men. I don't know how I would relate to them." I didn't see a connection. Growing up I always had everything I needed and more. My mother was born with a silver spoon in her mouth. My father was a regular army officer. We were upper middle class and never wanted for anything.

Jack didn't buy my excuse and so out of a sense of duty I agreed to attend in the spirit of helping him, rather than being useful to the prisoners.

My concerns about entering a maximum-security facility were really the same I had going into combat—a fear of the unknown, of how the system works, of how men would respond to me. I discovered it was a place full of people who needed God.

God gives us each different talents. He gave me a talent for dealing with young men. West Point trained me in the middle of the Korean War. Three months after graduation I was sitting on the front line leading a platoon. I was twenty-four and the average age in my platoon was nineteen. I was a kid leading kids.

After leaving the military I worked with high school kids from meager circumstances. They needed a male parental influence. That's what a lot of prisoners need, too.

We have different gifts, according to the grace given to each of us. If your gift is prophesying, then prophesy in accordance with your faith; if it is serving, then serve; if it is teaching, then teach; if it is to encourage, then give encouragement; if it is giving, then give generously; if it is to lead, do it diligently; if it is to show mercy, do it cheerfully. ~Romans 12:6–8

JUNE 10

LOVE AND VULNERABILITY
Russell Walthour, Florida

THE KEY factors for a successful Kairos weekend are love and vulnerability. I watched and practiced those qualities as I continued to go in with the team over the years. You'll never reach these men without being vulnerable yourself. You have to be transparent, and tell them your heartaches. That probably sounds ironic when you think about going into a tough environment like prison, but inmates have to know we don't think we're better than they are. We're all sinful people moving in the direction of redemption.

The first night, most prisoners come with walls up, hard looks, and a question on their minds: *What do you want from me?* We also bring in more than 10,000 cookies. Outside food is dynamite as far as prisoners are concerned, and word spreads like wildfire.

These men are blown away by the love we demonstrate, because they've never had it. Half of them don't know what the word means apart from sex. There is a closing ceremony on Sunday night. The inmates are encouraged to express what the experience has meant to them. The majority of comments shared by prisoners touch on the impact of the love they've been shown. Once they understand that the ground is level at the foot of the cross, then they open up to you and to Christ. They become vulnerable.

It humbles me to attend these weekends knowing all the advantages I've had over these men, yet God still teaches me through them.

I've learned that young men in combat share some similarities to young men in prison—they think they're tough, they don't know what they're doing, they're wet behind the ears, and they're looking for someone to lead and love them. I also quickly realized no one is going to stab or rob me. There is a special understanding between volunteers and prisoners.

As I mentioned, most inmates can't understand why we come in. I can't tell you how many times I've been asked, "Why do you give up your weekend to see us?" Sure, I play golf, fly airplanes, and have weekend soccer with kids. Why would anyone give those up to be with offenders?

They're struggling with their first experience receiving unmerited favor—no strings attached—what we call "grace." And that can change anyone's world. Christ wants me to serve him. That's why I do this. I can play golf some other time.

> Serve wholeheartedly, as if you were serving the Lord, not people, because you know that the Lord will reward each one for whatever good they do, whether they are slave or free. ~Ephesians 6:7

JUNE 11

CAN'T CHANGE ON MY OWN

Lance Herst, Texas

I DIDN'T START on the mean streets or in gangs. My wonderful mom and dad raised me in an average, middle-class home. They provided for us all of our time growing up. My father even led me to faith in Jesus when I was thirteen.

However, during the time I was twelve to fourteen years old, our church went through a major split. The Enemy used that mess to twist my ideas about God, church, and religion. And I wanted nothing to do with it. By age sixteen I started my drug use. Deep down I knew it wasn't the way I was supposed to live. I knew God wouldn't tolerate this kind of life, but it made me feel good and took away a lot of the dark feelings I had about myself.

At seventeen, I started a one-year sentence for my first felony conviction. Things got rough. An inmate came up to me my first day and said, "I'm giving you twenty seconds," and he started counting. I hit him instantly, but he pummeled me. He saw I was willing to fight and that's all that mattered. When you're working out in the fields as a human lawn mower in the middle of a Texas summer you can't help but have a testy attitude at times, which led to more incidents.

Nothing changed. I still had no desire to serve God and returned to my old ways for two more rounds of arrests and prison time. By the third arrest, I hit the bricks.

It had been ten years since I opened a Bible or spoke to God. I was eager to talk to God, but also extremely angry. A lot of my animosity and resentment came straight from the Enemy's message that I could live any way I wanted without consequences. It was all God's fault I was not able to have my fun.

Over the next week my anger subsided some and I just talked to God more openly. About two weeks into my third stint one of my prayers became, "Lord, if I get out of here, I'm going straight back to the same things. If you don't change me, give me new desires, then there's no hope."

One night I decided to read my Bible and remembered a letter from my grandmother encouraging me to read through Philippians. Sitting on my bunk I stopped cold at, "For God is working in you, giving you the *desire* to obey him and the *power* that pleases him" (Philippians 2:13 NLT). I almost dropped my Bible. God told me through that verse, "I'm going to give you what you asked for and I'm going to be with you the whole way."

The next day, marijuana was smuggled into the cell—my drug of choice—which I smoked from sunup to sundown. The guys invited me repeatedly and I said, "No"—I just didn't have the desire. That was just the beginning for me.

> For God is working in you, giving you the *desire* to obey him and the *power* that pleases him. ~Philippians 2:13 NLT

NO GOOD CHOICES

Lance Herst, Texas

EARLY IN my prison sentence I was assigned to a tough cellblock. There were guys doing twenty-five to life who had no regard for life. It's hard to make good choices around people like that even if you're keeping your nose to the grindstone.

It always starts off casually, especially if you're small or young. I'm a 170-pound "pretty boy." Predators want to see if you're willing to just give it up first. They don't want to have to take it. So it starts with innuendo. Someone will look at you a certain way. I'd been in prison twice already, so I knew the signs. Other people you know are informing you of what these people are like. They do obscene things out in the open— nobody cares, nobody does anything about it. Then predators put themselves in close quarters with you to test you. The guy stalking me was big. I knew I'd need a shank to defend myself. He'd already been in for ten to fifteen years and was staring at another twenty.

I knew he was going to make his move soon. If you don't fight you have no other good choices: give in, pay somebody for protection, or go into protective custody (isolation that only delays the inevitable).

I feared the outcome if God didn't intervene. I was quite immature as a believer and prepared to defend myself, but I always held out the hope that God would intervene. Quite honestly, in preparing, I considered a lethal first strike—turn the tables before he hurts me on territory of his choosing.

A real nice, big black guy had seen me read my Bible. He couldn't read, so often when he saw me in the day room we would talk. I shared my faith and story with him. He knew what was about to happen as well. He told me point blank, "This guy will rape you. He done it befo'. He got his eye on you."

One night out of the blue, officers came to my cell. They just told me to pack—in minutes I was moving. I never had to deal with my stalker or anyone else like him again. I later discovered that my illiterate friend let officers know there were going to be problems and that one of the elements needed to be removed—that was me.

The LORD protects and preserves them— they are counted among the blessed in the land— he does not give them over to the desire of their foes. ~Psalm 41:2

RACIAL RIOT

Lance Herst, Texas

DURING THE 1990s Texas went through a huge prison-building explosion. A lot of those facilities looked like large sheet metal barns holding between sixty to one hundred prisoners. They just lined up bunks along both walls and put a razor wire fence around it. At the same time gangs were also increasing in numbers, almost exclusively along racial lines. Officials assigned me a job at one such facility during my third sentence.

When you're in a place without separate cells and tiers, you're forced to choose friends quickly. You get asked, "Are you riding with the Mexicans? White boys? Blacks? Going solo?" I was able to hang with a few friends, but we didn't call ourselves anything. It's really a strange "neighborhood" to live in. Just like outside, there are certain bunk areas that you want to avoid either because you're not welcome by virtue of your skin color, or suspicions run so high you just don't want to risk a misunderstanding. Even so, without any real physical barriers, belligerent prisoners find a way to raise the threat levels for everyone.

I remember one night the racial tension was so thick you could have cut it with a knife. It was just a matter of time before a riot took place. It was getting so bad people were bringing in nails, pieces of metal, anything to make a weapon.

The night before it happened I got another job assignment—out of the blue. I hadn't made any request or complained to anyone about my current situation. They moved me from one big dorm to another, similar facility. That night, the riot went off. Dozens of people were stabbed and cut, and I believe a few people died.

There's no other explanation for those close calls except the hand of God.

> Though I walk in the midst of trouble, you preserve my life; you stretch out your hand against the anger of my foes, with your right hand you save me.
> ~Psalm 138:7

PRISON ROMANCE

Lance Herst, Texas

EVERY PRISON I ever spent time in I saw women guards, but they did not have roles where they could be near showers or other places alone.

One day a female officer took me to the infirmary because my job at the time was as a nurse's station orderly. Whenever you travel between cellblocks a guard escorts you. So it just started with friendly conversation. Then one day she slipped me a note. It was all very innocent. Then it became clear she liked me and wanted to get to know me better and I liked her. In an all-male prison, a good-looking female guard is a prize and a power trip. You have something nobody else has. Yes, other guys may have wives or girlfriends out there from whom they get letters or phone calls, but to be seeing an actual person—who is a guard—it's a power thing. You've crossed a line.

We fell deeply infatuated with each other. We were not in love. We never had physical contact or anything inappropriate. This went on about seven months. But something happened. I prayed asking for God's approval. Everything looked right—she was nice, we're not doing anything wrong, we like each other. That's when he spoke in my prayers.

"Lance, I designed free will so you could make choices. I won't stop you, but understand this: You can't see down the road. You can't see five or ten years from now. What you settle for now may bring you grief and not be my best for you. You can settle or taste my goodness."

When that happens it's always a crossroads choice. If we're genuinely seeking God I believe he'll speak in a way we can hear. I was ignoring the fact that she was in violation of the authority under which she served. Guards are not allowed to have these kinds of relationships. It's unethical and dangerous because of the potential it opens up for manipulation and blackmail. Our feelings for each other don't trump God's Word. We should have been aware that breaking with the civil authority she had pledged to uphold could not be twisted to mean God's will for the relationship.

I broke up with her. She was broken-hearted, told me she would resign, and wrote me some notes. Within two weeks of that conversation, I was moved to a different facility. I never saw her again.

I developed a mantra at that time. I've carried it with me for twenty years: "You are defined by your choices. Choose wisely."

Do not forsake wisdom, and she will protect you; love her, and she will watch over you. ~Proverbs 4:6

GIMME THAT HAT!

Lance Herst, Texas

I'M SURE it's different for each person, but from my own experience, some prison mentality follows you out to freedom. It did for me one night while I worked at a hotel in downtown Dallas near the grassy knoll made famous during the JFK assassination. I was a bellman and valet.

I worked the overnight shift the night the Cowboys defeated the Steelers in their last Super Bowl victory. Of course I wore my Cowboys championship ball cap. People were driving up and down the streets going crazy. It was a big party downtown.

I exited the front of the hotel to look around when a little car pulled up in the drive. A Mexican guy pops out with a crowbar and says in Spanish, "Give me your hat!" He's already wearing *three* Cowboys hats on his head. I quickly surmised they'd been knocking people on the head and taking their hats. Instantly my brain goes into prison defensive mode. Not recognizing how many other guys were in the car I said, "You're going to have to take it."

He swung and missed. I knocked him down and started doing jumping jacks on his head. Then I noticed little flashes on the wall behind me. The car was not thirty feet away, and it suddenly clicked: *They're shooting at me!*

At that point, I ran. I made it around the corner, stopped, and prison mentality took over again. I was so angry I wanted to fight them all . . . for my hat! By the time I ran back around to the front they were gone.

I have to laugh when I remember who I used to be coming out of prison. Today, I'm married with three children, so if a guy comes at me

205

with a crowbar demanding any of my clothes, I'll get naked. I don't care. They can have it all. Life is more important than hats with logos.

Someone might wonder, if God was really in my life, how I could react so recklessly over a stupid hat? We're all in a process of shedding the old self and putting on the new. Yes, I began that process in prison, but it really wasn't until I met and married my wife it really went deep. Within that special relationship there was love, accountability, and all the other dynamics that make it a mysterious complimentary relationship. It's just another example of God's unmerited grace protecting me from myself.

> Do not lie to each other, since you have taken off your old self with its practices and have put on the new self, which is being renewed in knowledge in the image of its Creator. ~Colossians 3:9–10

CLINGING TO A PROMISE

Lance Herst, Texas

WE WERE not prepared when police notified us our teenage son had been arrested for burglary. We were stunned, numb. I worked in the corporate world, but I also was a lay minister within our church. We were very active there. Our close family read the Bible together, took vacations, went fishing, played soccer, and did all the things you imagine a healthy family doing. I even had the high privilege of leading Lance, my oldest son, to accept Christ. Honestly, I didn't see this coming. Lance wasn't perfect, as any father knows about his own children, but I never dreamed our family would be touched by a crisis like this.

I searched my heart asking the obvious questions: *Am I responsible for this? Did I miss something that pushed him into it?* I tried my best to lead my family in the way we should go. I grieved for my son and my family. My wife was very distressed, as I was, grieving with a mother's heart. The younger children didn't really understand it all.

Lance is proof that no matter what upbringing a child has, whether he has parents who are derelict due to alcohol or too busy making money, or godly parents trying to live the faith, sin penetrates every person, every family.

I didn't know it initially, but Lance would make three trips to prison before turning things around. But from the beginning my wife and I really clung to one promise in the Bible above all: "Train up a child in the way he should go, and when he is old he will not depart from it" (Proverbs 22:6). I really believed prison would push Lance back to Jesus in time because of the promise of this verse.

For ten years we walked through Lance's repeated incarcerations, wrote letters constantly, visited him when we could, and prayed for God to work his will and timing so the whole family could heal and grow out of this mess.

Without a doubt it sensitized me. As I've ministered to countless people in the church, and as a police chaplain on the street, I've certainly become more compassionate, understanding the stigma of being in the fishbowl. God worked on me as a father to really empathize rather than criticize or judge. I don't compromise on the basics of faith, but I understand temptation and shame that people feel when they fall.

Most of all, my faith was strengthened as I saw our promise play out. We are extremely proud of Lance, his new role as a pastor to youth and assistant pastor, and the family he has raised. That's the promise of God, and one he mercifully gave to parents to keep them through turbulent times.

> Train up a child in the way he should go, and when he is old he will not depart from it. ~Proverbs 22:6

JUNE 17

CONVICTION
Nanette Friend, Ohio

THE DEPUTY who transported me to the women's state penitentiary that brisk October morning appeared to be confused. My wrists and ankles shackled, I was still clad in black dress slacks and heels, a white polyester blouse trimmed in small pearls, and a black suit jacket.

He commented, "You don't seem the kind of person who would be going to prison."

I sheepishly realized this would be the last day, for a very long time, that I would be wearing make-up and jewelry. I couldn't answer him—I was hanging my head in shame.

Convicted for aggravated theft, he inquired how much time I had been sentenced to. I choked back tears and softly answered, "One year."

As we turned onto the long gravel driveway and approached the massive, tall silver gates in the huge barbed-wire fence, I silently gasped to myself, *What have I got myself into?* The sickness began deep within the pit of my stomach and traveled to every part of my body. I ached with fear; only beginning to understand what I had become, and where I had taken my life. I had truly arrived at the end of a long and twisted road— a road of my own choosing. I was filled with shame and humiliation— struggling to grasp it all.

I was escorted to "Admissions." The rules have since changed, but back then I was allowed to bring a pair of tennis shoes and a sealed copy of the Bible.

Days turned to weeks. Alone and isolated from the outside world with nothing but time on my hands, I eventually opened the Bible. Having never read it, I soon couldn't get enough of its wonderful, soothing messages, and read for hours every day. For the first time in my life, my eyes were opened to how much God loved me. I had never before realized a love like that existed.

I don't believe God brought me to prison. It was my own bad choices, but I knew he had a purpose for allowing me to be isolated from the outside world. For it was there on the cold floor of a prison cell I was *truly* convicted and gave my life to Jesus. I went from conviction by man (who sentenced me to prison), to conviction by God (who made me free while in prison). I thank God for the first conviction because it grasped my attention and prepared my heart to receive the powerful, life-changing conviction of the Holy Spirit. Praise God for his Spirit who opens our eyes to the truth!

Yet the LORD longs to be gracious to you; therefore he will rise up to show you compassion. ~Isaiah 30:18

ACCEPTANCE

Nanette Friend, Ohio

ARRIVING AT the office of the prison psychologist, I knew this appointment was a matter of determining what was going on in my criminal mind and how I was going to own up to my actions. Actually, I was relieved to have the opportunity to speak with someone. Possibly she could help me understand my irrational and unethical behavior these past few years.

On the wall of her office was a large poster with faces showing several different emotions. Under each face was a word describing the accompanying expression. The psychologist asked me to review the poster and pick out the "face" that would best describe my current feelings.

I reviewed each one carefully, pondering several of the choices. I certainly didn't feel happy, confident, or hopeful. Possibly I felt ashamed, overwhelmed, or even anxious. I *knew* I felt guilty, embarrassed, and frightened. But the face that caught my attention most was "determined." When I announced my choice, the psychologist asked why I had chosen that particular feeling. I explained I didn't understand why I had made the choices in my life, but I was "determined" to find out. I was determined to change the things in my life that had threatened to destroy me.

The psychologist then inquired if I had accepted responsibility for the crime I had committed. I realized right then . . . I hadn't. *I couldn't.* That would mean admitting and accepting that everything I had done was my fault. Certainly I was the victim. If my father, husbands, and the other men in my life had not abused me—beating me, lying to me, cheating on me, or stealing from me, I would have never been forced to do the things I did! This wasn't fair. Why should I have to pay for the sins of others?

During the next several months I kept learning more about Jesus and the love he had for me. I learned that his love was so great he paid the ultimate price for me—a sinner, a criminal. He didn't do anything to deserve what I had chosen to do, and yet he suffered the indescribable and inhumane cruelty of beatings, torture, and eventual death on a cross so I may have a new life. In prison, the hardest thing I ever did was to understand and accept the sin I had committed. The greatest thing I ever did was to accept Jesus as my Savior.

In him we have redemption through his blood, the forgiveness of sins, in accordance with the riches of God's grace. ~Ephesians 1:7

FAITH

Nanette Friend, Ohio

THE CHAPLAIN at the women's prison instructed us to select our favorite verse and explain why it was important to us. Having read the Bible only a few months, I didn't have a favorite verse. Besides, I wasn't sure I could believe anymore; I had started questioning my new-found belief in God and struggled with unworthiness.

Having been sentenced in October to serve a one-year mandatory term, my only hope for an early release had been the opportunity to go before the parole board four months later, in February. I could then request release to a halfway house after serving a total of eight months. I missed my family and desperately longed to step outside the prison walls. But in the end, the parole board turned it down.

"Lord, have I not been faithful? Have I not read the Bible daily and prayed regularly?"

Excited as a new believer, I had grown closer to God. I had seen his hand move repeatedly the past few months, amazed at the answered prayers and favor I was experiencing. I knew God was real. So why now was I being denied the one thing I desperately wanted?

I called to tell my boyfriend of five years the crushing news. His response? He wasn't surprised. Oh, and he was leaving me for someone else.

Crushed again by someone I thought loved me.

Suddenly, I recalled Hebrews 11:1: "Now faith is the substance of things hoped for, the evidence of things not seen." I looked it up and read it over and over, trying to convince myself of its truth. "Please, God . . . why have you left me? I don't feel your presence anymore. I am alone and scared."

Two months after my prayer I was called to the corrections officer's desk. "Do you want to go home?" he asked.

"Sir?"

"You have ten minutes to get your things or you're not going any-where!" he half laughed.

I literally ran to gather my belongings. Had there been a mistake? I didn't understand, but I sure wasn't going to question it any further!

Having served only seven months total, the judge had called for me to come home . . . *home*, not a halfway house. Once again, God showed me he had a plan for me all along—far and above anything I could have ever imagined or hoped for. I only needed to have *faith*, and to trust him.

> Now faith is the substance of things hoped for, the evidence of things not seen. ~Hebrews 11:1

AN UNEXPECTED END

Nanette Friend, Ohio

WALKING OUT the gates of the state penitentiary for women, I took several deep breaths, absorbing the fresh scent of freedom. My heart pounded with excitement, humility, and gratitude, as I realized I was leaving this place of retribution a different woman than I arrived. God had made his presence known to me, over and over again. What plans did he have in store for me now?

Convinced I would never be able to get a job with a felony record, I spent the first few weeks sheepishly searching, but not believing anything beneficial would transpire. Who would hire me—a convicted thief?

As the days went by, God kept whispering to me to call my previous employer. It seemed ridiculous, but I finally succumbed and called. When I was told there were no openings I heard myself convince my ex-boss John that he needed to meet with me.

The day of the appointment God was persistent: "Tell him the truth."

"But I couldn't possibly do that, Lord. John would never consider hiring me back!"

Sitting across from John in his office, though, I again found myself obeying that nudge and poured out my entire story. When finished, John stood up, shook my hand, and said he would get back with me. I cried all the way home.

Not long after I returned to my small apartment, the phone rang. It was John. He asked me to come in the next day—there was a job for me! And to top it off, I had been hired to serve as his personal assistant, as payroll clerk and backup accounting clerk, and as an advisor within the operations department! I was stunned. In my obedience to God, he blessed me with a job, a raise, and a promotion!

That was more than twelve years ago. I have since been employed at a doctor's office and an insurance company. I was manager of a youth facility and student manager at a college campus. I have also been blessed to serve as a mentor for at-risk teenage girls in a court-ordered program; a volunteer at the local women's shelter; and a board member of our local jail ministry. I teach Bible studies in the jail and mentor female inmates, besides working in the jail library. I recently graduated from college with honors, and I am currently writing a book to tell the world of the promises and mercy of an amazing, loving, and faithful God.

> May he give you the desire of your heart and make all your plans succeed.
> ~Psalm 20:4

MODERN-DAY LEPERS

Chuck Brown, New Mexico

OH, NO! I KNEW *there was something strange about that guy. Now what do I do? He just spent the entire weekend with all the Cub Scouts, had kids ride in his car, and now I learn he is a registered sex offender? I can't believe this.*

That was the nightmare unfolding the evening I came home after a wonderful weekend in the mountains camping with our local Cub Scout troop. Fred, a live-in boyfriend of the mother of one of the Cub Scouts, had come along with all the other fathers as a guardian.

Throughout the weekend I sensed there was something not quite right about Fred. There was nothing tangible to point to—just a gut feeling—which made it confusing. He was a really nice guy who liked to talk a lot, and the kids seemed to enjoy his company.

When I came home I prayed about it, then felt led to do a search with his name on the Internet. Bam! To my horror, he was on the state Web site as a registered sex offender!

My mind went wild. Could he have done anything to any of the boys? Does his girlfriend know he's a sex offender? Are she and her son safe? Do we need to call the police?

Thankfully, it turned out his crime had nothing to do with children. He had no restrictions on where he was allowed to live or with whom he was allowed to associate. He had a one-time conviction from more than thirty years earlier related to a domestic dispute with his ex-wife, requiring him to register annually with the state for the rest of his life.

Seeing my own knee-jerk reaction to this situation made me acutely aware of how quickly I can jump to conclusions. I immediately assumed the worst—that he was a predator.

When I told him I knew he had been in prison, he wanted to bolt. He thought sure I was going to condemn and reject him just like everyone else had, including family, friends, churches, landlords, and employers. But as my wife and I chose to reach out and embrace him, he poured out his life story, including the struggle of being permanently branded as one of today's society's lepers—a sex offender.

Since then, Fred has been coming to church with us along with his girlfriend and her son. There are still things he needs to change in his life, but he is making progress one step at a time. Feeling our love, acceptance, and compassion has been the key to his motivation.

> Filled with compassion, Jesus reached out his hand and touched the man.
> ~Mark 1:41

JUNE 22

WORKING WITH MY FATHER

Bill Mothershed, California

I AM SOMETIMES troubled by the fact that I have never "officially" led anyone to Christ. I have never sat down with someone who was not yet my brother, explained to him his need for salvation through Jesus Christ, received his confession of faith, and experienced the joy of witnessing his new birth. As an inmate with a ministry and many years of witnessing to my brothers in prison, you would think it would have happened at least once. But somehow, I've never been there, one-on-one, for that wonderful moment when the light comes on inside and someone says "Yes" to Jesus for the first time. Others have told me of having had this experience and, I must confess, I get a little bit jealous.

I realize, of course, this is just pride peeking out from behind a mask of self-righteousness. It comes from a desire to say, "This one is mine, I caught him—I did this." But we know the truth: No matter how much we sow seeds, water, and nurture, it is the Holy Spirit of God who draws us to salvation. It took a long time, but I've finally figured out my role in this great work of bringing people to Christ. It's a lot like when I was a child, and my father would have me help him build a bookcase or fix the car. It wasn't that he needed my help; he could have done the work himself. I was probably in the way more than I actually helped. What he wanted was the joy of sharing the experience of the work with me. He wanted to watch me learn and grow by doing the work. He would give me tasks I could handle—hold this, turn that. He would encourage me when I did it right, and he corrected me when I did it wrong. But there was never any doubt the work was his. I was a guest, privileged to be allowed to participate in the work.

Today I am privileged to help in God's great work, and behind this barbed wire there's a lot to be done. He lets me do the little things I can handle—hold a hand, turn a phrase. Whether I plant seeds, water, nurture the new growth, or harvest—the work is his. He alone gets all the glory.

And I am so very grateful he loves me enough to let me get in the way and help.

> So neither the one who plants nor the one who waters is anything, but only God, who makes things grow. The one who plants and the one who waters have one purpose, and they will each be rewarded according to their own labor. ~1 Corinthians 3:7–8

GOD KNEW

Terry Mapes, Iowa

AT THE first prison I worked at, the personnel director smoked a big cigar. On my first day he looked at me and said, "So, boy, you done got yourself a college education and you want to work in a prison?"

"Yes, sir."

"Why in the h*** you wanna do a thing like that?"

I get that question from time to time. Why corrections? In fact, I probably never would have applied except for what happened when I was thirteen.

In 1971, my farmer father died of cancer. *I* was going to be a farmer, until he passed. That ruined my plan. It led me to attend Western Illinois University, where I majored in law enforcement administration. Before my father's death, there was no plan for college.

I thought I'd like to be a state trooper and applied at the age of twenty, but they won't consider you until twenty-five. They advised I try the military for four years as an MP or work in prison for two years. I applied to the nearby maximum-security prison and started in corrections seven days after graduation. During this time I had only a superficial knowledge of God, having attended a traditional church growing up. But through college and my early corrections career, he didn't matter much to my life until a fellow staff member invited me to a party.

I walked in, danced with a girl, and thought, *She's the one I'm going to marry.* Five years later, I did. Brought up in a strong family of faith, she would be the instrument God would use to call me to himself.

We settled into a Methodist church and started our family. Somewhere along the way, my then ten-year-old son informed me he had invited the pastor over to our house. I said, "For what?"

"To talk to him." I was still young in my faith, but okay, he's welcome. So I listened to my son visit with our pastor. My son wants to be baptized and someday be a pastor! That's when I decided to get baptized—we would do it together. That was a small step.

My faith grew stronger with a move to Newton, Iowa, and a church that emphasized missions. I learned tithing, giving firstfruits—not just money—but everything.

God is so much bigger than me in his infinite omnipotence. He put my story together before I existed. How did I get into corrections? God had a plan and it wasn't just so I could have a job. Had my father not died, I would not have gone to college, worked at the prison, gone to the party, met my wife, had the son who has a passion for lost souls and is now licensed to be a pastor.

When you think about how big he is . . . as much as I hated that my dad died, it had to be that way. Otherwise I would not have listened to God's plan for my life.

> All the days ordained for me were written in your book before one of them came to be. ~Psalm 139:16

JUNE 24

CAREER HAZARDS

Terry Mapes, Iowa

I LOVE WORKING with people. My first prison post at Fort Madison looked like an old castle—dingy, dull, overcrowded, and full of guys doing life for murder. Many inmates died there, stabbed at the hands of others. I don't always know how to explain why I enjoy my job—it's in your blood. You don't get paid just for what you do on a daily basis, but what you might have to do in an emergency.

Corrections professionals deal with tremendous stress. This stress contributes to obesity, high blood pressure, heart trouble, and all the things that go with heart conditions. You live on the very edge and your adrenaline kicks in many times a day. As incidents occur, it's a rush. You get used to that. Adrenaline goes up and down, which contribute to high blood pressure and heart disease.

You go home mentally exhausted from interacting with people: being a problem solver, a fireman, a paramedic, and a counselor; helping prisoners with family problems, and dealing with violence. The only thing you want to do when you go home is to be away from people. You eat a bag of potato chips and drink a six-pack of Pepsi and vegetate in front of the TV, which contributes to obesity, heart trouble, and high cholesterol. Younger officers, low on the totem pole, work afternoon shifts. For them, life begins at 10 p.m. Alcohol abuse is not uncommon. The average life expectancy of a career corrections officer is fifty-eight.

Nobody ever brings good news to the warden. Nobody ever calls to say, "I've got something that's going to bless your day." The issues that reach my desk include: guys with mental health problems, the most aggressive violent offenders, and employee problems.

There is no insulation. I cannot take these things home to my wife. I can't take them to another staff member. You keep them to yourself in the solitude of sitting in your chair and meditating and praying for some kind of wisdom and guidance to help people.

People look to me for help. I'm the last stop shop, the emergency room. The day-to-day work is managed by others. I don't get the call from personnel until someone's been gone for five days without checking in, or the union's not happy about something and is filing grievances. Until it boils over the top it doesn't get to my desk. My supervisors have observed that I seem to function best when everything is boiling over. The louder it gets, the more arrows shot, the calmer I become.

> For the Lord gives wisdom; from his mouth come knowledge and understanding. He holds success in store for the upright, he is a shield to those whose walk is blameless. ~Proverbs 2:6–7

JUNE 25

NO PLACE BUT UP FROM HERE

Terry Mapes, Iowa

THE VISION of the Iowa Department of Corrections is, "No more victims." Yes, we put people in prison, but then put them back into society where they can victimize more people, or the same people. Currently 65 percent of those released are incarcerated again within three years. Besides locking them up and throwing away the key, what is our role?

Like me, they have their weaknesses and failures. I can't judge them simply because they failed again. I can only offer them the hope that this time we will give them something, some treatment, program, or opportunity that will cause them to change. It's not my role to preach, lead treatment programs, or deliver any other offering. My role is to ensure that opportunities are available to those ready to make the effort to change. I think people might be surprised at how many prisoners do wish to change, but just don't know how or where to start.

It's as with my faith—I didn't deserve Christ's death. Even though I've failed and may be experiencing the consequences, Jesus still says, "I took it. Let's do better tomorrow." For inmates, I can't let them out until the courts or the parole board say so. While they're serving their sentence, I can give them another chance to make this life different. If they fail today, I'll promise to give them another chance tomorrow. Most will be our neighbors again. They are someone's son or father, and future taxpayers.

Prison is unique not just because of bars and guards, but for what it symbolizes. Prisoners have nowhere to go. There's no place down from prison. It's only up from here. Sometimes it takes several trips to learn that, just as it has taken me a lot of trips to learn certain lessons in life. What grace I can show to any offender is so small compared with the grace I've been given. How can I not show that grace?

For a few years we partnered with the Retired Thoroughbred Foundation. We had an African American inmate from Chicago with thick dreadlocks who was scared to death of animals—particularly big ones—but we taught him to work with horses.

At first, he tried to bully them around like he bullied people. He quickly discovered that doesn't work. Horses kick and bite. It forced him to change his approach. He's connecting with concepts like gentleness, confidence, and firmness without aggression or anger. He really figured it out. As the learning progressed we worked on translating those lessons over to people.

Eventually he returned to Chicago and six months later I received a call from his mother, in tears. "You have no idea how much impact you had on him in changing the way he deals with people. It's the best thing that ever happened to him. He's the most wonderful son."

For me, in this tough job, that's a joy.

> So whether you eat or drink or whatever you do, do it all for the glory of God.
> ~1 Corinthians 10:31

WHEN INMATES ATTACK

Terry Mapes, Iowa

IF THE Lord's ready to take me, then I will die today. If he's not ready, there's nothing man can do. He'll take care of it. That's the only reason I survived the incident with Mr. Gruber back when I worked as an officer inside the cell block.

As I was coming onto the work unit, I was told an inmate—John, who was part of a motorcycle gang—had been caught with homemade hooch in his cell. Procedure required I padlock him in his cell. I work with these same inmates every day. So I walked up to the third tier called E range and put the padlock on the cell door. An intoxicated John wanted to know why.

"Every time you get a good party going, one of us comes along and ruins it for ya," I told him. He laughed and I laughed.

Two of his friends missed the context of our conversation, but heard us laughing and thought I was laughing *at* John. Then Ron Gruber and Mike Howell rushed me. They began beating me and were trying to throw me off the third tier. I took a blow that knocked me unconscious. It took forever for backup to get there, given it was the third tier. When a fellow officer showed up, he was hit and knocked down. I really don't know how long it took to regain control.

Next thing I know I'm in the supervisor's office, wearing an inmate's t-shirt. I assume they took my bloody uniform shirt as evidence. Then I rode to the ER, where I discovered bruised ribs, stitches in my nose, chipped teeth, and a concussion. They released me late the next day.

After two days off I returned at 2 p.m. on Wednesday—stitches in my nose, bent glasses, chipped teeth, ribs hurting. I didn't have second thoughts. My family did. My mom sure thought I should find a different job.

My legs were like jelly climbing the stairs. I was jumpy for six months. Ron loved to take the wooden stool in his cell and slam it every time I walked by. It sounded like a bullet and I'd jump. He'd laugh at me. Years later, by God's divine appointment, I'd be the warden where Ron was again incarcerated. Only this time, we shook hands. He was following Christ now and asked for my forgiveness and my wife's, too.

There have been other situations involving riots and violence, but that was the closest personal encounter. Through it all, I've never felt fear for my safety. It's in God's hands. I just have to help staff, officers, and inmates stay safe regardless of the risks to me.

> He is my loving God and my fortress, my stronghold and my deliverer, my shield, in whom I take refuge, who subdues peoples under me.
> ~Psalm 144:2

JUNE 27

CAN EVIL BE GOOD?

A. Raymond, Georgia

IN THE 1960s my friend, Katie Rose, lived with Ed and their four children in a small Midwestern town. Ed was a race car enthusiast. Between work and racing, he was rarely home. Katie was lonely and neglected. Overwhelmed with caring for the children, in time she found a boyfriend. Something went terribly wrong, and—she killed her boyfriend.

Ed and Katie lost custody of their children and Katie went to prison. She couldn't live with what she'd done and day after day she refused to eat. One day, the aroma of fried chicken drifted into her cell. Hunger took over and she decided to eat. The strange thing was—no food had arrived yet at the prison. The cooking was done off-site and the meals had not been transported. But guess what ended up being served for dinner? Fried chicken! It was also a luxury—rarely did they get such a treat.

God got Katie's attention and she started sensing his presence more. She began attending a Bible study held by a local church at the prison. God's loving message of forgiveness took root. It wasn't long until Katie was convicted of her sins and drawn to asking Jesus into her heart.

Ed never abandoned Katie through this whole ordeal. When she told him about the Bible study and her salvation, he started coming to church on Sunday, which was also visiting day at the prison. In time, he got saved, too.

At Katie's first parole hearing she was not expecting to be released, but she was! There was great celebration at the church for Ed and Katie. Everyone knew this was the hand of the Lord.

While Katie was in prison, Ed went to college and got a degree in Spanish. They moved to Texas, where Ed studied to be a minister. Then, they began their ministry working with Spanish-speaking people in the United States and Mexico. Before heading to Texas they spent a couple of days at our home and my heart was so touched by Katie. Even though she was filled with joy for what God had done in her life, behind her eyes was such sadness over the loss of her children, and the fact that she had taken someone's life. She lives with the consequence of her sin, but knows she is saved by the blood of Jesus.

Can evil be good? No, it can't, but God can take something evil and turn it into good. Look at the gospel Ed and Katie are preaching. They are telling of a sinless Messiah who was crucified by evil men. However— he was resurrected and Satan was defeated!

> Praise be to the God and Father of our Lord Jesus Christ! In his great mercy he has given us new birth into a living hope through the resurrection of Jesus Christ from the dead. ~1 Peter 1:3

JUNE 28

THE SUITCASE
Bobby Griswold, California

I REMEMBER the first time the Lord showed me he was real and that he loved me and that he was there for me. I was thirteen years old and had run away from another boys' home. I would get caught for being a runaway and I would go from the police station to the children's shelter. I would stay in the children's shelter until I could escape or until they found another place I could go to, where I would run away again.

One night after being on the run for a while, I was dirty, cold, and hungry. But I'd rather be all of that than be in another one of those homes. I had nowhere to go. I sat on the curb and prayed to Jesus—whom I'd met through one of the boy's homes I had been in.

I prayed for a warm place to stay. I prayed for some food to eat and some clean clothes and a shower. After praying I got an idea to go to the house of a friend whose family had just moved away and no one lived in the house. I tried the back door and it was open. The place was totally empty except for a couch—and next to the couch was a suitcase.

I sat down and opened the suit case. The very first thing I saw was a 9" x 12" picture of Jesus. That took my breath away— I was shocked! Under the picture there were clean clothes that fit me perfectly and new shoes for my sore feet. Also, in a tiny plastic snap case, was a neatly folded two-dollar bill.

So I got in the nice warm shower and put on my new clean clothes and shoes and I went to the 7-11 down the street and bought two chili dogs, then went back and slept on the couch.

I always remember that part of Hebrews 13:5 that says, "He will never leave you nor forsake you." When I had no parents, no one at all in this world who cared about me, Jesus was there for me. In such a way that no one could ever tell me any different, he showed me he was real and that he loved me.

> Yet he has not left himself without testimony: He has shown kindness by giving you rain from heaven and crops in their seasons; he provides you with plenty of food and fills your hearts with joy. ~Acts 14:7

JESUS CAME TO MY CELL LAST NIGHT

Tom Beatty, Nebraska

IN 1974 I moved to Nebraska to start a career in nuclear engineering at a power plant. It lasted three years before someone found out I was a drug and alcohol abuser. You can only keep it under the table so long. They promptly fired me.

This was neither the first nor the last time my habits cost me more than I wanted to pay. I was only twenty-five, but already had lost count of the times I'd been arrested for something involving my drug and alcohol abuse. I got more involved in crime for several years after losing this job and managed to get back into jail again.

I really hated the way I was living. I noticed my cellmate reading his Bible. I'd seen lots of people read Bibles in jail—it's a popular thing to do. I didn't have much respect for religion. I wasn't raised in a Christian home. I asked my cellmate, "Why are you reading that book?"

"Because my wife's a Christian and she and her Christian friends are really neat people."

That was the first time I'd ever heard someone refer to Christians in a positive manner. He also had a pastor visiting him on a regular basis. I asked if the pastor would talk to me. Our first conversation lasted twenty minutes. He told me I needed a relationship with Jesus. I was pretty skeptical, but I listened to what he had to say. Then I did something for the first time—I read a Bible.

I had a King James Bible, which is not the easiest reading material, but I was interested and determined. I started in Genesis and persevered through Leviticus before I managed to get tossed into solitary confinement as a disciplinary measure.

Now I had nothing to do. I requested a Bible and this time got one in modern English. It was nothing like I expected it to be. It became the most fascinating thing I ever read. I couldn't get enough. We were nearing Christmas and some Gideons came to visit. They gave me a pocket New Testament. In it they inserted a section that had Scripture to look up by topic. For example, if you were scared, worried, or critical, they listed relevant verses. I looked them all up because they all seemed to apply to me. There was also a prayer, which I prayed one night and I added, "Jesus, take my life, do whatever you want with it." Then without bells or whistles I went to bed.

In the morning I knew something significant had changed about me. When they unlocked my cell on the second tier I went down the catwalk and banged on the door of a friend a few cells down.

"Keith, Keith, you'll never guess what happened to me last night!" He looked at me matter-of-factly and said, "Okay, what?"

"Jesus Christ came to my cell last night," and into my heart.

Yet to all who did receive him, to those who believed in his name, he gave the right to become children of God. ~John 1:12

GARBAGE MAN

Tom Beatty, Nebraska

WHEN I got out I knew I needed a job or I'd go back to my old ways. My first temp agency assignment was helping on a garbage truck. It paid $125 a week, working Monday to Friday and half day Saturday. By the hours it was less than minimum wage.

Also a few days after I got out of jail, my wife lost her job. So the two of us were about to be living on less than she had been making. At the same time I got a crazy idea to start tithing, which we did on my miniscule income.

Strangely, because I no longer drained our income on alcohol, cigarettes, or other drugs, we had more than we thought. It was still very tight, but when we needed stuff, I started praying for it.

I began seeing answered prayers in the garbage. We prayed for screens for our windows so we could open them in the summer. We had no air conditioning. I found curbside enough expandable screens for the whole house.

We started going to a church and I joined the men's softball team to get to know some other men. I didn't have a mitt, but soon found one in the garbage. I prayed specifically for badminton gear to play in our little front yard—found a complete set, in the garbage.

It was an incredible time on the truck, too. One day each week the company hired an extra man from the temp agency to get through the extra streets. Once a young man named Tim joined us. I shared my story and quoted some verses from the book of Romans, but I couldn't remember things exactly. At the last stop we found a Bible sitting on top of the garbage can. I grabbed it and showed Tim the verses we had talked about. He became a Christian that day.

I spent most of my time on the smelly end of the truck. When the truck got full, I'd ride in the front seat with the driver on the way to the dump. Our driver talked like I used to—every other word was profanity. I asked him about it. He told me it wasn't any of my business. I said, "You know, the Bible says, 'From the overflow of the heart, the mouth speaks.'" That was the last garbage I picked up. He told the boss he wasn't going to drive with me in the truck anymore. You win some, you lose some. You just have to be faithful.

To go from a nuclear power plant operator to jail to hauling garbage probably doesn't seem like the dream career path to most people. But God used each experience to prepare me for a life apart from the haze of drugs and alcohol. Every bit has proved valuable: working in jails, prisons, and rescue missions, reaching other men not only with the gospel, but with how to live it out.

For we are God's handiwork, created in Christ Jesus to do good works, which God prepared in advance for us to do. ~Ephesians 2:10

HOW I AVOID BURNOUT

Bob Potter, Nebraska

MY FIRST tour of the jail I would work in, I remember an officer telling me, "Now, Rev, you need to know one thing. If you ever get taken hostage, it's just you and God, because we don't negotiate for hostages." *He must have the gift of encouragement!*

Certainly working daily in a jail or prison has its hazards. I once observed a huge fight breaking out in the chapel, but in thirty years I've never been involved in a single act of violence directed at me save for one prisoner who spit on me. People still wonder, "How do you keep it up in such a place?"

First, I really trust God. This is where I'm supposed to be. So why worry?

Second, I coined a line that has guided me after someone asked that same question years ago. I said, "I go to jail, I do what I can do for the Lord that day. I go home, then come back the next day and do it again." Every job has its downside, but if you're doing what you love and you are equipped to do it, those peculiar challenges don't strike you as insurmountable. I can't imagine how brain surgeons do what they do with the stakes so high. I think the real burnout factors cross job lines—too much need, not enough you.

I like talking to people. I'm a very gregarious person, a big extrovert, so talking to people is not a big deal and that's a big part of a chaplain's life. My other secret weapon has been my wife, who has been a great one for not allowing me to bring all the junk home. She's always been my greatest cheerleader and supporter. She really helps me stay in balance.

I'm not burned out. I've seen other ministers doing stupid stuff and I made up my mind I would not be married to my ministry. I put in some extra hours when I had to be at the jail at 3 a.m. to deal with something. But basically, when I go home, I'm done. I raised my kids, and loved my wife. Maybe that's too simple for some, but it has worked for this tuba player turned servant of God.

Who of you by worrying can add a single hour to your life? ~Luke 12:25

HOMICIDE NOTICE

Bob Potter, Nebraska

THE PHONE rang about 3 a.m. I don't get many calls at that time, but it's one you have to answer.

"Chaplain, this is Officer Campbell*. Sorry to disturb you at this hour, but we've got a situation we need your help with."

"Go ahead."

"We need you to come in. It's about an inmate we took into custody yesterday. The hospital just notified us his three-year-old son died of injuries."

"Okay. You need me to give him the death notice?"

"Yes, but there's one other thing you should know."

"What's that?"

"The inmate is responsible for his son's injuries. He killed his own boy."

I wasn't prepared to hear that. My own son was three years old. I have delivered many death notices over my career and, while they are not easy, I often find those times to be opportunities for God to show up in their grief. This was different.

This inmate had beaten his own child to death. Part of me drew some satisfaction from knowing I'd tell him that he'd be charged with first-degree murder the next time he went to court. I wanted to see justice. Having ministered to many prisoners, I can tell you, they all have fatherhood issues. But I had a hard time finding a shred of sympathy for this one.

I started some serious praying before leaving for the jail because there was no way in my own strength I could minister to him in a way that would honor the Lord.

He didn't deserve anything, but then, who does? The most despicable person in jail is a person Christ died for. Sometimes this aspect of grace confronts my pride. I revert to the all-too-easy comparison game. I would never do something such as that to my own children. Yet, when it comes to the holiness, majesty, and glory of God, I have no better standing than this man. I'm either covered by the blood of Jesus, or I'm under his righteous wrath.

You have heard that it was said, "Love your neighbor and hate your enemy." But I tell you, love your enemies and pray for those who persecute you.
~Matthew 5:43–44

"YOU'VE GOT TO SEE THIS GUY!"

Bob Potter, Nebraska

OFFICERS BOOKED John* into our facility charged with murder for the third time. The first two times he had gotten off with a lesser charge and just did a little time. This time, however, he was struggling emotionally with all kinds of problems.

An officer came to me one day and said, "Chap, go see this guy in Iso 2." When officers notice certain behavior that worries them, I'm a resource they turn to. When I looked through the narrow sliver of security glass in the door to his isolation cell I saw a guy sitting on the edge of his bunk rocking back and forth. There was no light in his eyes. He looked totally disheveled.

It was late in the afternoon, and quite frankly I wanted to get home. No matter how important a task might be, humanly we probably all feel that way at times. I don't say that by way of excuse, but as a confession to reality. With that frame of mind, I entered the cell. We talked for a little bit—the usual routine really. He didn't jump at anything I had to say and I excused myself as soon as possible. I just wanted to end the day. Before exiting, I turned and handed him a pocket New Testament.

The next day I came to work and the same officer approached me excitedly. "You've got to go see this guy. He's changed!"

Curiously I looked in through the same window. He sat on the same edge of his bed, hair combed, light back in his eyes. That little New Testament looked as if he'd been reading it for six months. It was all chewed up and dog-eared. He had come to faith during the night—just him, the Holy Spirit, and that New Testament.

He stayed at the jail for quite a while until he received a sentence of death by electrocution. The younger inmates, who thought they were cool and tough, would look up to him almost as a hero because he'd killed three people. They feared and respected him. But John took advantage of that status to share his faith.

The people walking in darkness have seen a great light; on those living in the land of deep darkness a light has dawned. ~Isaiah 9:2

MAIL CALL

Kym McNabney, Illinois

AS THE coordinator of the Christian Pen Pal program for my church, Willow Creek, one of my duties is to handle any mail that comes into the church from the prison and jails. We sometimes receive general inquiry pieces and in many cases I address their issues and never hear from them again. On more than one occasion, though, I've responded in a way that caused them to write back.

As much as I would love to honor requests to be a pen pal with many of the people who have written Willow over the years, it's often just not possible. But every now and then, God decides differently.

In July of 2011, Willow received a letter from an inmate requesting a pen pal, one who could meet his needs and not be scared off by his crime. I read the letter and knew I was not that person. Sadly, due to his requirements and situation, I feared he'd have a hard time being matched with a volunteer pen pal.

I wrote this man back, letting him know the situation, but encouraging him to have faith. God will give him the right pen pal in his perfect timing. In return I received a letter from him saying he thought I was that person.

My life was full of responsibilities; I had to put this solely in God's hands. Before long, though, it became unquestionably clear to me God was calling me to write this prisoner.

I have a heart for the least of these, and sex offenders are no exception. Who am I to say what crimes should be forgiven and which should not? So I took on God's challenge.

Paul* and I continue to write each other. His words have broken my heart on more than one occasion. He spoke of his family's abandonment, and the harsh treatment by staff and inmates alike.

Two of Paul's letters particularly stand out. The *first is* after he received a book I sent him. He told me, step-by-step, how he was called to the mailroom, bewildered. *No one sends me anything,* he thought. Then Paul went on to express his joy when he discovered it was from me, and how he had never received anything from anyone.

The second incident is when he wrote to express his thanks for a birthday card I'd sent him. He said in the twenty-some years he'd been incarcerated, no one had ever sent him a birthday card.

Paul just recently gave his life to the Lord. I am grateful, now, that I obeyed God and wrote to Paul. What a blessing I would've missed out on!

> But blessed is the one who trusts in the Lord, whose confidence is in him.
> ~Jeremiah 17:7
>
> Trust in the Lord with all your heart and lean not on your own understanding.
> ~Proverbs 3:5

WE'RE NEVER ALONE

Tara Hupp, Ohio

IT WAS November 25, 2008, and I was supposed to appear for my trial for passing bad checks. However, due to some unforeseen health issues, I ended up in the emergency room. My devoted husband contacted our attorney to let him know what was going on. The attorney informed the judge, who unfortunately did not see my illness as a valid reason to excuse me from court, and he issued a warrant for my arrest. I ended up going directly from the hospital to the justice center.

Sitting in a jail cell is not only physically isolating, but mentally and emotionally isolating as well. *I've never felt more alone,* I thought. Unfortunately, this was only the beginning. . . .

While I was incarcerated the unthinkable happened—my husband passed away. That was the most empty and alone I have ever felt in my life.

But after weeks of grieving and battling depression, I realized I had a choice. I decided I was not going to let this get the best of me. Instead, I began to do something I hadn't done in a long time—I began to pray. And as I continued to pray, something amazing started to happen. Things began to get a little easier. Life just didn't seem quite so hard. I sensed a glimmer of hope with each new day.

I also started doing something else I hadn't done in a while: I started attending church and going to Bible study at the jail. The more I attended, the less alone I felt. Before too long, I realized that those times when I had thought I was alone, I never was. The Lord was always there with me—I just needed to open my heart to him and allow him to carry my burden.

After my sentencing and my arrival at prison, I enrolled in correspondence Bible study programs and started attending church services at the prison. I didn't eagerly give up control of my life—it took a lot for me to let go of the reins and let the Lord have control, but the church services helped my broken heart begin to truly heal.

This is a journey I continue to struggle with. But thankfully, I have a strong family who honors God by giving him first place in their lives. I feel like my old self again—the Tara many people said had been lost for some time, but thank the good Lord—he brought me back!

> Then you will call, and the Lord will answer; you will cry for help, and he will say, "Here am I." ~Isaiah 58:9

JULY 6

DEFENDING A BROTHER

Kelon Williams, California

PRISON HAS its own social structure and balances. It was due to these "balances" I happened to witness God's power radically change one man's life.

When I first met him, he introduced himself as "Slimeball." The overall consensus from others who knew him seemed to validate that name.

There was another young brother who was constantly getting himself in a bind over drugs and debts. He always seemed depressed. This young brother became an easy prey for slugs the likes of Slimeball.

Within the prison community there was a growing concern about the plight of this young brother. He was giving away his personal belongings to cover debts he had already paid. Yet, out of fear, he kept giving more.

When I was made aware of this situation, I knew I was to pray for him. I also struggled with being angry and sickened that the other brothers would allow something like this to get so out of hand. I knew I had to act.

I believed God called me to be a protector of the weak and the helpless at any cost. (I had also used that "calling" to justify my crime.)

The next morning, I waited for the young brother and told him not to worry about anything because, "I got your back on this and I'm going to make sure you're not bothered again." As we walked to our building, I listened to him share about all the stuff he had "given away." He only had a few items left, some things his mother sent him, and he did not want to give away what little he had left.

Hearing all this only added to my fury. Right before we came to the cell where the young brother resided, Slimeball appeared. He grabbed the young brother's arm and asked for the rest of his stuff—not too subtly.

Reading the "save me" plea on the brother's face, I positioned myself between them.

"He's paid you already," I said.

Slimeball responded, "Who are you? This is none of your business."

I told him it *was* my business.

Slimeball proceeded to unleash all the "claims" he had and who he ran with. He added that the young brother was not claimed by any specific group and that I'd better stay out of it.

I stared him down. When I opened my mouth I was not sure what I was going to say, but the words that came out and the force they held surprised even me.

> He defends the cause of the fatherless and the widow, and loves the foreigner residing among you, giving them food and clothing.
> ~Deuteronomy 10:18

FROM "SLIMEBALL" TO MY "BROTHER"

Kelon Williams, California

I'VE NEVER experienced God taking over my mouth before, but that day I was certain he had. When Slimeball said that no one "claimed" my young brother, something arose in me, a power and authority I had not known was in me.

"I claim him 'cause he is my brother, my brother in Christ," I calmly said.

And that was it. That was all I said. But, it was spoken with such authority Slimeball backed away. He was momentarily speechless. Finally, he agreed there would be no more deals transacted with the young brother.

I was amazed, and so was my young brother.

Not long after that encounter, Slimeball was sent to confinement for dealing drugs in prison. When he returned he was no longer the same person. Suddenly, he refused to let people call him Slimeball.

"My name is Brother Hammond," he would say.

Then one day, Brother Hammond approached me, asking me questions about the Lord. It happened again—and again. Each time he came near me I braced myself, but he was always sincere. His eagerness to learn more about the Bible was genuine. And what probably astounded me the most was, when he was placed in certain situations that could have easily led him back to his old "Slimeball" character, he would come to me and seek my guidance. Every time this happened God would show his goodness and deliver Brother Hammond, or fill him with more strength and understanding to comprehend God's perfect will.

The day before Brother Hammond was to be transferred to another facility, he slipped a note in my pocket. It had lots of Scripture verses on it, along with this message:

Brother Williams,
You have proven to me over and over that you are my brother in Christ and I appreciate and thank you. God gave you your job to be a man of peace, and you are serving him well.
God bless you,
Brother Hammond

The change in Brother Hammond not only brought God's healing and restoration to Brother Hammond, it also brought God's comfort to the young brother. And I was regularly blessed, too, with a clearer vision of who God is and how I'm viewed through his eyes. We serve an amazing God.

So he said to me, "This is the word of the LORD to Zerubbabel: 'Not by might nor by power, but by my Spirit,' says the Lord Almighty." ~Zechariah 4:6

CAREER CHOICES

Terry Hamilton, Colorado

I THINK 90 percent of the corrections staff I know would tell you that when they were kids they never dreamed of growing up to work in a prison. Likewise, I think 100 percent of inmates never wanted to go to prison when they grew up. So how did I end up as an officer?

I grew up in Buena Vista, Colorado, in the shadow of a prison reformatory. It was one of those necessary evils in the community. It provided some jobs, but the big money in the area was the local mine. My father, grandfather, and future father-in-law all worked there.

After finishing high school I planned to work at the mine for a year, save money, and go to college. But during that year I decided to delay college and get married.

Not long after that, the mine business collapsed. I talked my way into a new job working for Associated Groceries (AG) in the big city—Denver. I was promoted to district manager, and we relocated to Canon City. My wife initially didn't want to move there because it's known as a prison town. Then AG went bankrupt.

I found similar work, which became a road job, with SuperValu. I spent 60 percent of my nights in hotels. I had a company car and a nice expense account to wine and dine grocery retailers. My weight went from 160 pounds to 190 pounds. However, my two children were growing up without me. I was missing sports, AWANA scripture memory club, and church life. That's when my wife suggested I consider resigning and working in corrections. I never wanted to do that.

I explored the topic of prison as a career with my men's Bible study group. We talked about the idea that true believers can have purpose wherever they work. That clicked with me. I didn't want to be on the road anymore.

To even apply you had to have a year of experience or a college degree in a related field. With neither I enrolled full-time in school, taking twenty-eight credit hours to qualify while still working my grocery job. One year later I had enough credits to file my application and was the last officer hired at a brand new facility at Arrowhead.

I told the Lord, "If I'm going to make this kind of commitment in order to be back with my family, make it purposeful."

After thirty days in the Academy and working graveyard shift, which messes up your sleep and eating habits, I had lost forty pounds. With my little experience I started to make a difference in inmates' lives. I helped an inmate see his dying mother. I showed God's compassion to families of prisoners. I try to live my life in a way people know what I stand for, and if they ask me, I'm ready to share.

I went back to school and finished my degree in applied criminology. I now have a twenty-two-year career in prison work. That's where God wanted me, not because I planned it. It saved my marriage and made my relationship with my children better. I don't think most people imagine that result, given what they think prison is like. It just shows that God can put purpose and joy into any career.

> As a prisoner for the Lord, then, I urge you to live a life worthy of the calling you have received. ~Ephesians 4:1

JULY 9

WHAT LARRY* SAW
Terry Hamilton, Colorado

I DIDN'T know anything about Larry, including his charges or background, when we first met. He saw me and some fellow officers one day and came over with a question.

"Excuse me, Mr. Hamilton. Whether you're by yourself or with Lieutenant Black, I notice that you guys always take time to say a short prayer before you eat. Isn't that crazy? You're in chow hall surrounded by inmates. Doesn't that make you vulnerable?"

"On the contrary, I think it lets everybody know I believe in a greater power."

"What do you pray about then? Not getting beat up? That you don't have to break up some fight or shoot somebody?" I could tell Larry wasn't mocking us. He really wondered.

"Yes, we pray that staff go home safely, but I spend a lot of time praying for inmates—that more of you will find the Lord and not come back to this place." We parted.

236

I observed him steadily decay over twelve months, from a picture of health, lifting weights on the yard every day, to a shell of a man. He was homosexual and came in with AIDS. This was early on, when people didn't know much about the disease. Then one day after a year he stopped me and asked, "Can you teach me how to pray?"

"Sure, let's talk about this." Over the next nine months he started attending church and Bible studies. He stopped me from time to time to ask me what a particular Scripture passage meant to me. He continued to wither away physically. Three weeks before he passed, we talked of his acceptance of the Lord, the forgiveness for his past sins, and what he was looking forward to.

He looked at me and said, "Had I not seen you praying in chow hall, I don't think I would have ever started asking questions."

I was one of the last people he talked to before he passed. I made the call to the coroner that night. Even if I go to work and it is my last day, it's okay as long as I've done it right, living my life in such a way people like Larry start asking questions.

> Always be prepared to give an answer to everyone who asks you to give the reason for the hope that you have. But do this with gentleness and respect.
> ~1 Peter 3:15

HAIRY AND SCARY

Terry Hamilton, Colorado

I HAVEN'T spent any time on duty in maximum-security settings. Most of my time has been spent at medium- and low-security facilities. I've broken up some minor fights. In one rare incident when an inmate had been stabbed, shots were fired, but by the time I arrived on scene things were over and other officers had handled things.

Credit goes to the Lord on my lone hairy-scary moment a few years back. Usually when I come up on a fight I'm able to bring the situation under control with a little pulling and tugging and a lot of verbal commands. But one time up at Fremont we had a gang-related fight between whites and Hispanics.

It's a large facility and there were probably four hundred prisoners on the yard that day. I was there as a captain and had been assigned to the facility the prior year to clean up a lot of personnel problems. By the end, nearly forty staff had resigned or transferred due to our changes. We really tried to change the way business was conducted. My task was to change the culture in those two big monster cell houses.

I was walking back to the cell block in the midst of a number of inmates with Lieutenant John Skillen*. We began to hear grumblings behind us. Then we heard shouts back and forth. We turned around to see the inmate mob continue to move toward us as men began to square off against one another. Without us realizing it, the blacks had hung back in the yard to see what developed. The nearest backup was about one hundred yards away in a different crowd of inmates. We had about eighty men evenly divided with just the two of us to respond.

Then it broke loose with fists and horseshoes flying between these gangs. Neither group seemed prepared for the fight because later we did not find any shanks. Rather than retreat, we waded into the middle barking orders. At that moment only six or eight men had engaged each other. I knew two of the Hispanics really well and Skillen knew two of the whites well. We start shouting their names and getting them separated. Within a few minutes we diffused it and the rest decided to back down.

Inmates told me a week later, "Had it not been you and Skillen that day they would not have been able to stop it." I can't say for certain, but when you treat people right, they often give you respect, even if you're their jailer.

> The authorities are God's servants, who give their full time to governing. Give to everyone what you owe them: If you owe taxes, pay taxes; if revenue, then revenue; if respect, then respect; if honor, then honor. ~Romans 13:6–7

THE FAILURE OF CHUMMY DAVIS*

Terry Hamilton, Colorado

THE REFORMATORY at Buena Vista housed about five hundred inmates under the age of twenty-three. Growing up, I played in a youth baseball league. From age eleven to fifteen all our umpires were inmates from the reformatory. I got to know one of these umpires. Chummy Davis was not tall, but extremely athletic. This young black teen had a good sense of humor and was serving time for some low-level drug and burglary crimes. Officers let him hang out a little after games to talk to us, run us through some drills, or take batting practice. I might have learned as much or more about baseball from Chummy as my coaches.

About fifteen years later, I worked the graveyard shift as a sergeant at Colorado Territorial. The captain and I were moving inmates to chow hall at 6:30 a.m. An individual passed by and the captain said, "Morning, Chummy. What are you doing back here?"

"Just passing through. I'm headed up to DRDC for some medical tests."

I turned to the captain asking, "Did you just call him 'Chummy'?"

Sure enough, he'd spent his whole life in the system. After release from the reformatory he'd gone back to his old ways. Hopped up on drugs, he severely injured a nun during a crime.

Three years later I was a case manager when Chummy's file hit my desk. I had looked up to him as a young teen because he was an older boy who played baseball really well. Chummy knew I was now a father coaching my young son through baseball. He liked to talk to me because of our common bond years earlier. He married while inside and I believed this new family was his best chance for a successful release.

Parole gave him a shot after serving twenty-two years. He went to work at a grocery store. Seven months later his wife found him a new job buffing the floors at a hospital. He broke into its narcotics cabinet and went on the run. Four months later police caught him in Arkansas and extradited him back to us. We crossed paths after he'd had some kind of surgery. His health was fading. That was the last time I saw him before reading his obituary. He died of unknown causes.

Chummy had a sad life. At many points along the way he had chances. The nun visited years later to forgive him. I had a personal connection and tried to encourage him toward useful programs and faith, but you can't force transformation on anyone. I live in the regular presence of failure, but I don't let it get me down. God's in control of it, not me.

> For those who find me find life and receive favor from the Lord. But those who fail to find me harm themselves; all who hate me love death.
> ~Proverbs 8:35–36

LEARNING TO OBEY GOD

Scott Parsell, Ohio

A FEW YEARS ago, as I sat in our local county jail during one of my many different incarcerations there, I realized that things were not going according to plan. I had spent nearly twenty-five years of my life wrapped up in alcoholism and drug abuse. I tried many self-help groups and even thought I had the ability to fix myself, but none of that worked. It was during my last stay at the jail God truly decided to meet me right where I was.

I was court-ordered to participate in a program in the jail, and that is where God put some Christian men in my path. After listening to their stories, I realized they were just like me. They assured me I didn't have to continue living this way—that Jesus could change my life. I was tired of the way I was living—there had to be more than this. As I called out to God that evening to come into my heart, I knew with certainty he was there. I made the decision right then to give my life to him. God truly had not forsaken me.

Jesus will take the worst of the worst, forgive them, and bless them if they simply choose to truly believe and follow him. I left that facility with a plan to never go back.

However, God's plan for me was all too different from my own. Because . . . I am now part of a ministry team in our church that goes into the jail and teaches the love of Jesus to men. We laugh, cry, discuss, and share his Word. I have truly been blessed by God as I see the men transformed right in front of me, led by the Holy Spirit.

I am now seven years clean and sober and a true lover of Jesus. He is the One who has molded and shaped me into a child of God, instead of a drug addict or alcoholic. God has forgiven me and used my past for his glory and for that I am truly blessed. He has also given me the ability to go on two missions trips to Honduras with my church to use my talents to help his people. I am not sure what else he has in store for me, but I know, thanks to him meeting me in the jail that night, that my life is not the same and that I am never going back to being the person I was before.

> See, the former things have taken place, and new things I declare.
> ~Isaiah 42:9

WINNING THE BATTLE

Joshua B. Smith, California

ONE DAY, while in lockdown, Satan began to attack me. I am not talking about some small, easy-to-deflect attack; rather, this was a serious full-fledged assault over mind, body, and spirit. Stuck in my cell and not able to even think straight, I knew what to do to combat it—at least, these things had worked in the past.

I began praying out loud, reading Scripture out loud, singing worship songs, and—nothing worked. I was still miserable. Realizing I was horribly losing this battle, I began to break down (easy to do in prison). At my lowest, darkest moment I began to do something that shocked me, as soon as it came out of my mouth. I began to simply praise God for who and what he is.

I cannot tell you how long it took, from when I began praising God until when Satan fled, but what I *can* tell you is that not only was the battle won, the plunder was great! I was left with a peace that, until that moment, I had never experienced in my entire life! I felt wrapped tight in a cocoon of love—like liquid love was flowing through my veins. The heaviness in my spirit was gone, and in its place were peace and indescribable joy!

241

I believe this battle was won by living out and applying Philippians 4:4–6. I began to "rejoice in the Lord," and then he took away my "anxiety." In turn, he granted my supplication in my thanking him and praising him. When all was said and done, I was left with the "peace of God that surpasses all understanding."

So, next time you are in a battle and overwhelmed, let God do the fighting for you. Simply praise him, rejoicing in the fact that he is holy, mighty, and true. Know he loves you and lift up to him your heartfelt love. You just might be amazed at the fallout—when the battle is over.

> Do not be afraid or discouraged because of this vast army. For the battle is not yours, but God's. ~2 Chronicles 20:15

FROM SERVING TIME TO SERVING JESUS

Santana Acuna, California

AS A NINE-YEAR-OLD kid I was bullied at school a lot. It didn't stop until one day I hit one of the bullies with a rock. All the kids saw the blood and ran. At that age, I didn't know if they were staying away from me due to fear or respect, all I knew was—it worked. This was how Santana became a vicious person who did not care about anyone or anything.

As I became a teenager I hung around four other guys, two of whom, by the age of fifteen, had become murderers. I was the same age the first time I entered the corrections system. At seventeen I began using heroin and continued using it because I thought it made me bolder; it made me feel significant.

Then, in 1960, came my first time in an actual prison—Soledad. I was there because of a homicide that was reduced to an assault with force. By then I had already become a very vicious person whom many feared. I was in and out of many prisons after Soledad. I went to San Quentin, Folsom, Corcoran, and Tehachapi. In 1985 I was picked up again for attempted murders and robberies. I was now a habitual criminal facing one hundred years.

242

One day, fed up with myself, I called out to the Lord, "I have heard that you are a good God. How come I am always going through all this?"

Then, three days later I knew he had answered me. I had not had any drugs, and—it was the first time I hadn't gotten sick when I was without drugs!

From that time on I began to serve the Lord behind bars. God got me out in five-and-a-half years! I was released in 1991 and have been serving the Lord ever since. I am now a pastor and founder of a small church and rehab which I call Special Forces Discipleship Church.

Life in prison is a whole different world. Many cannot survive it. I thank God I have found the key with which, even in prison, you are free.

> For whosoever shall call upon the name of the Lord shall be saved.
> ~Romans 10:13

"HEY, BOSS! GOD LOVES YOU!"

Santana Acuna, California

AS AN HISPANIC, while in prison I would not converse with other races and especially guards of other races; it seemed to cause problems. But that all changed after 1985 when I gave my life to the Lord. I started to call out to the guard towers, "Hey, Boss! God loves you!" I started doing this constantly to all the guards, but more to the guards in the yards.

I kept yelling, "Hey, Boss, Jesus loves you!" and one of them started answering me. He would just say, "Hey, Santana Acuna," like he was mad at me (they were not supposed to call us by our first names). But as time passed and he would say my name back to me, it didn't seem like he was mad anymore.

I took advantage of him not being mad at me and started sharing with him how Jesus had changed me. Of course he already knew because he had personally witnessed the "before" and "after" in me on a daily basis.

One day he called me to his office. He simply said, "Acuna, I did it."

243

"Boss, what did you do?" I asked.

"What you've been talking about. I did it. I gave my life to Christ."

From that day on, he called me "Brother Santana," and we would talk about the Lord. God continued to be gracious to me and allowed me to lead a lot of others to the Lord.

My current ministry on the outside invites people to come as they are. We also encourage people to evangelize where most people would not want to go. Our slogan is Jeremiah 16:16: "But now I will send for many fishermen," declares the Lord, "and they will catch them. After that I will send for many hunters, and they will hunt them down on every mountain and hill and from the crevices of the rocks."

I have many wonderful stories of people coming to Christ as a result of the ministry God gave me. One man had just come out of prison and was on parole. He came to a Bible study and felt the presence of the Lord that day so much he began to cry, and fell on his knees, and accepted the Lord. Within a few years he married a young widowed Christian woman who was Hispanic and he is Caucasian. He only knew a few words of Spanish, yet he and his wife moved to Mexico and started a ministry. I am so thankful for the way God changes us and fills us with his love!

> "But now I will send for many fishermen," declares the LORD, "and they will catch them. After that I will send for many hunters, and they will hunt them down on every mountain and hill and from the crevices of the rocks."
> ~Jeremiah 16:16

IDENTITY CRISIS

Keith Krantz, Arizona

FOR YEARS I thought I was better and smarter than everybody. For the most part I successfully evaded the cops from the age of fourteen until my arrest at thirty-one. My addiction started in my teens and I figured out how to sell drugs to keep up with my habit without getting caught. I believed nobody did it better.

244

Despite my cocky attitude, I did hide a little fear inside. I carried a .45 handgun everywhere I went. When you're selling drugs you always have a lot of cash and drugs on you. That means a lot of people will look for an opportunity to relieve you of your stuff, by force if necessary.

The way the game goes, everybody works overtime to portray an image that they are "badder" (tougher) than the next guy. I was small, 140 pounds soaking wet. Because of my stature, the people I dealt with always knew what kind of gun I carried, including the exploding hollow-point bullets loaded in it. Any attempt to get one over on me would be a costly mistake. While I presented this front, however, I was scared on the inside. I'm pretty sure they were, too—at least I hoped so.

I did my thing as a typical "street pharmacist," then went into the Navy for four years, where I traded drugs for alcohol. When my Navy contract ended, I returned to the same drug-dealing business I had before.

But things had changed both in me and in the drug world I thought I knew. Six months before my final arrest I told God—whom I had never spoken to—"I don't know who I am, I don't know who you are." It was my way of reaching up from my exhausted dead end and wondering if there was anything else in life.

Be careful what you ask for—sometimes you get it. God would soon give me almost four years to figure it out. He taught me first who he was as I read through the Bible, and second, who I was, using the same method.

The truth that captivated me and changed my heart read, "I will never leave you nor forsake you." That was important given where I was. All the crimes and sins I'd committed were plain to me, but somehow he would never leave me or forsake me.

For I am convinced that neither death nor life, neither angels nor demons, neither the present nor the future, nor any powers, neither height nor depth, nor anything else in all creation, will be able to separate us from the love of God that is in Christ Jesus our Lord. ~Romans 8:38–39

PLAIN TALK WITH THE "DUDE"

Keith Krantz, Arizona

SOMEONE I did drug business with cooperated with police, who waited for the right moment to pick me up. That landed me in Sheriff Joe Arpaio's jail in Maricopa County, Arizona, on my third offense. In Arizona we didn't have the three-strikes rule yet, but I knew I was looking at ten-to-twenty years, at least.

Those numbers put my so-called search for truth in the drug life into perspective. I just knew I would do a long time. I still had a lot of pride, although at that moment it had taken a serious blow. Still, I started talking to God again, calling him "Dude." I told him, "I'm done. You win. I'm tired, I can't run anymore. I give you my life. Whatever you want, that's what I'll do." In my heart I knew he was real. I'd been searching many years without the Bible.

So it was a process over the next few months to get off the drugs. I don't have the greatest memory on the planet due to nineteen years of drug abuse. I've done enough drugs to kill a herd of horses. I was an extreme user—meth, coke, pot, more than 150 hits of LSD—way too much. If I was going to be coherent and start following Jesus this had to change. I started praying, reading through the entire Bible, and attending Bible study; however, every time drugs arrived in the jail, I showed up for my share. Jail is not the easiest place to quit a habit, which is quite ironic—they can keep people in, but they can't keep drugs out. I couldn't get away from it on my own. It was too easy to get.

Finally I called out to God, "Dude, the drugs come in, they're in front of me. I'm going to do them. That's the way it is." I felt as if God could handle my plain, direct way of talking and that he understood my intentions.

Two days later, the drugs dried up. Officers confiscated all our hooch. God stopped it all. The authorities got fancy new equipment to see through everything and stop the flow.

Two months later when I went to prison I'd have access to drugs again. But those critical two months were enough for me to get sober. God gave me grace and space long enough to get a clear head and to be able to say "No" on my own.

Watch and pray so that you will not fall into temptation. The spirit is willing, but the flesh is weak. ~Mark 14:38

246

DOING THE IMPOSSIBLE

Keith Krantz, Arizona

WHEN I arrived at Yard 2, I met Frantz. He knew the Word well and I was attracted to his knowledge. He brought up an idea during a Bible study. He told us, "Let's all pitch in for sodas and doughnuts, and I'll write Scriptures on paper. We can hand out a snack with Scripture attached to everyone on the yard."

Everyone agreed in principle and pitched in a little something, but in the end only he and I showed up for the actual delivery phase. You don't give gifts to gangs and racial groups. There's also concern with religious overtones like Christians giving stuff to Muslims. The yard at Yuma Correctional Institution was evenly divided. They try to keep it that way so no one gets an upper hand. Not only do corrections staff frown on this sort of gift-giving activity, but a lot of inmates simply fear what could happen if someone takes the gesture the wrong way.

Franz and I did it anyway. We just knew God promised to never leave us—"What can man do to me?"

We didn't get any flak. The inmates were cool with it. However, after our third successful attempt, officers noticed. After investigating where we got all the stuff—which we all donated out-of-pocket—they simply gave us the cease-and-desist order.

The next idea Franz came up with was to write plays. He wanted fifteen guys and two months to practice and learn lines. Each play revolved around a theme like AIDS, or domestic violence, and somebody always finds Christ in the end. We even wrote a play about two thieves.

Predictably, the staff said "No." They saw too many security issues: Can't have one hundred-plus guys of different races in a single place, can't give opportunities for cross-communication between gangs for hits or doing business, too dangerous.

We kept practicing anyway.

They caved in because God is bigger. We prayed through it. We put on the first show for the staff and warden to be sure they approved. They did and everybody loved it.

We raised the bar by asking to take the show to Yards 3 and 4. Again we heard "No way." Those were higher-security prisoners. We weren't supposed to mingle with those guys. We prayed and kept talking about it. Frantz had the worst record of us all. The staff worried about him the most. Eventually they let us do it—on both yards! It took four months of praying and asking before they let it go. We always played to a packed house with a warm reception.

> Ask and it will be given to you; seek and you will find; knock and the door will be opened to you. For everyone who asks receives; the one who seeks finds; and to the one who knocks, the door will be opened. ~Luke 11:9–10

JULY 19

NO COMPLAINTS

Keith Krantz, Arizona

FROM THE moment I turned my life over to God, it was good from then on. It will probably sound crazy to someone who never went to prison. Yes, there was a lot of boredom because of lockdowns. Yes, there were struggles, but compared with the destructive nature of my former life, I can honestly say I never had a really bad day.

We were very busy in prison. Each one has his job. I worked in the motor pool fixing cars and tractors. There's not a lot of hanging around looking at each other. Of course everyone works out to stay fit. And for Christians, we had a regular stream of volunteer-led services and programs to attend. To me it was one of the best times in my life because it's where my life began. Before, I had no life. You can't call what I had had a life.

It doesn't matter what's going on around you. God is bigger. Guys coming to prison who didn't know me would pull me aside and ask a personal question: "What did you do to get in here? I can't see what you possibly could have done to get in here." They couldn't grasp it—my attitude, I guess—my lack of that hard prison look. God did it all. I did none of it.

When I first invited God to take over, I didn't know anything about the gospel or what it would mean to live a Christ-filled life. I didn't trust what anybody else was telling me about it, either, given they were probably naive like me. We were all in prison! My understanding came from reading the Word. I started in Matthew. The first time I read the entire Bible it took less than a year. I had to do that. I knew I needed to read every word in case somebody tried to tell me something different. People did so all the time, and still do.

I'm a little different. I see my time in prison for what it was—a gift from God. Prison was where he brought me to him, the only place we could meet. In the world, I was too busy being stupid. I can't complain about prison for that reason. I don't want God to hear me say anything negative given what he did for me.

> I will give you thanks, for you answered me; you have become my salvation.
> ~Psalm 118:21

THE STORY OF "Q"

Callie J. Bond, Illinois

I'VE BEEN writing to those behind bars for many years. When I tell others what I do, they often say how nice it is that I do so. What they don't understand is, I am doing what God has called me to do. Because I've obeyed him, he has blessed me in ways I could never have imagined.

One of my first pen pals, TJ*, was a tough case. He was clearly angry at God, as well as the entire world. For whatever reason, TJ chose to give my information to another inmate, whose name was Q*.

Q and I corresponded for about a year before he wrote something inappropriate. With kind, yet firm, words, I informed him it wasn't acceptable conversation. I received a couple more letters from him before they stopped completely.

Inmates often sign up for the pen pal program for the wrong reasons. My church is affiliated with Christian Pen Pals. CPP connects volunteers with inmates who have gone through the same organization. Q had not done that. One of the dangers in not being screened by CPP is the lack of knowledge of the guidelines, including the reason for the ministry, which is for Christian friendship and spiritual guidance.

One Sunday morning, two years after Q's last letter, I stopped in the mailroom to pick up my mail. I thumbed through the stack of letters and my hand froze. In the upper left-hand corner was a name I had not expected to ever see again: "Q."

I immediately opened the envelope. I pulled out a homemade card and anxiously read it:

"Thank you, thank you, thank you sooo much. Thank you so much for your prayers, I've finally got it right. God is WONDERFUL and you'll never be forgotten. Q."

My feet were glued to the floor. Tears welled up in my eyes. *Who am I, God, that you would go through me to touch the life of another?*

Though I knew we should be obedient to plant seeds in the hearts of others, God had now given me amazing proof of the results. We should never pass up an opportunity to do his work. If the Lord whispers to us to carry out an act of kindness, or nudges us to be a friend and mentor in his name, we need to pray about it, check it against Scripture, and then act. You never know the impact you may have on the life of another—or when the seed might sprout and take root.

> If you keep my commands, you will remain in my love, just as I have kept my Father's commands and remain in his love. ~John 15:10

BUNYAN'S DUNGEON

Jeff Peck, Virginia

NEAR THE end of the classic *Pilgrim's Progress*, the reader finds the characters Christian and Hopeful locked in the dungeon of Doubting Castle, held there by the impossibly huge Giant of Despair. Earlier they had taken what seemed like a fairer path that ran parallel to the true path they were on and figured the two roads would meet somewhere further ahead. But the author reveals through powerful symbolism that this was a massive error on their part.

After their capture and imprisonment off the wrong path, Christian and Hopeful are surrounded by bones indicating the fate that awaited them—indeed anyone who starts down a path of sin.

Author John Bunyan, a Puritan in the 1600s, keenly understood how sin works even in the life of true believers. Christian and hopeful had already come through many dangers and trials and now, near the end of their journey, they have essentially been deeply entangled by the roots of sin that yet existed in their flesh.

The apostle Paul wrote the strongest statement of his frustration with sin near the end of his life while chained to a Roman guard, exclaiming, "Christ Jesus came into the world to save sinners; of whom I am chief."

Bunyan could sharply describe their sense of hopelessness and shame as he himself wrote the book during his twelve-year imprisonment for preaching without a license. The characters struggle with the question of whether Christ's blood is actually sufficient to save their souls. After all, they've messed up badly, and have done so knowing the truth.

Many prisoners in *Pilgrim's Progress* wrestle with the same despair, the same longing to know for certain whether their deeds are beyond redemption. Many wish to die—which is what sin would accomplish if it could. It seeks to destroy our lives and take us further than we desire or imagine.

As the characters discover, the answer to their doubts are found in the "key" of God's promises—not the depth of their feelings or even the nature of their sin. Bunyan would himself be released and called to a local pastorate to passionately proclaim the truth of Scripture as he had experienced it in prison.

Whether in a metaphorical prison, an English jail, or a modern American penitentiary, God's Word penetrates and sets free the slaves of sin—both children of God and the lost who are now found.

The Spirit of the Lord is on me, because he has anointed me to proclaim good news to the poor. He has sent me to proclaim freedom for the prisoners and recovery of sight for the blind, to set the oppressed free. ~Luke 4:18

GREEN PASTURES

Tom McCullough, Ohio

I LEAD A men's group Bible study at the Licking County Jail, and one week we focused on the Twenty-Third Psalm. Usually when I read about how God makes us to lie down in green pastures, I visualize being outside on a beautiful sunny day, the wind softly blowing and no one around; it's just the Lord and me. It can be easy to imagine hearing God's voice in such an atmosphere.

But during this particular Bible study, an inmate shared an interesting perspective with the class that gave additional insight into and application of that passage.

He shared that while the Lord is his Shepherd, he believed that the Lord had provided this jail time as his "green pasture." He explained that the time he has spent in jail has allowed him to get a clear head, without the distractions and influences of the outside world. He was thankful God had allowed him this time in jail to think and reflect as to what and who were important in life. It had given him time to prayerfully contemplate the choices he would make now, and in the future. He said God, making him spend time in (or lie down in) the jail green pasture, had changed his life.

I couldn't help but consider other passages from the Bible that reflect a similar message. In 2 Samuel, the eleventh and twelfth chapters, David's fleshly and worldly temptations inevitably lead to his decisions to sin. Later, in Psalm 51, David describes reflecting and repenting due to his "green pasture." Then there is the book of Job. Throughout that book is the similar theme of being alone with God to enable us to change our perspective. And then the parable of the prodigal (the lost son) is shared in Luke 15:11–32.

Each of the aforementioned was made to lie down in various "green pastures," and after reflecting on his circumstances, "came to his senses" (Luke: 15:17). Each eventually realized his need to place his faith and trust in the Lord.

Whether we are made to lie down in a jail cell, hospital bed, or a hog trough, we have the opportunity to reflect in our circumstance and come to our senses. It is our choice. Today you can place your faith, hope, and strength (Ephesians 6:10) in the Lord Jesus Christ, the One who can and will provide for you.

He makes me lie down in green pastures. ~Psalm 23:2

ANGOLA FOOT-WASHING

Callie J. Bond, Illinois

IN 2006 I found myself entering the gates of Louisiana State Penitentiary at Angola—not as an inmate, but with a small group from my church. I spent the next eight days on the grounds of what used to be the bloodiest prison in America.

The first night, although tired from the long trip, when offered the chance to attend church with the inmates, I didn't hesitate. The spirit of these men was so evident; God's presence was nearly tangible.

In the following days we visited Hospice, were given a tour of the grounds, visited the prison museum, attended the funeral of an inmate, visited a radio station run by inmates, attended church services, saw the grounds of the rodeo, had cell visits, and sat in at a class of the prison's Bible College.

But if I had to pick the most memorable experience, I'd have to say the washing of feet. On our final day at the Bible college our group leader decided to teach about the story of Jesus washing the disciples' feet. She had talked to us the night before about her idea. She suggested we could wash the feet of the inmates. I was swarmed by emotions.

My biggest hindrance was—I'm easily turned off by feet. So, this was no easy "feat" for me. But, knowing God wanted me to do this, I chose to set aside my uneasiness for obedience.

At the end of our leader's talk she invited the men to have their feet washed. I guess it shouldn't surprise me God took over and everything I was struggling with disappeared. I can't begin to explain how moving and humbling the entire experience was.

Later that night we went to one of the several churches on the grounds. As I walked into the building a man was sitting on a table with a huge grin on his face. He was looking directly at me, and said, "You washed my feet. I called my mama and told her a white girl washed my feet. Imagine that!"

It was as if my washing his feet put us on even ground. It didn't matter who was white and who was black; who was incarcerated and who was not. In Jesus' eyes, we are all loved equally.

To this day the image of that man sitting on that table grinning is as clear as if it happened yesterday. What that man didn't realize was, he blessed me far more than I blessed him.

> Now that I, your Lord and Teacher, have washed your feet, you also should wash one another's feet. ~John 13:14

RACE-BASED REARING

Jose Seals, Minnesota

I GREW UP in Ventura, California, in the predominantly Hispanic West-view Village projects. I was the third-born son of a Mexican mother and a Scotch/Irish father. My parents divorced before I turned two and until age twelve, I believed my stepfather Alberto*—a Mexican national—was my biological dad.

In my house and our community the police were "bad" as were the social agencies, even though the family used their services when possible. The whole environment was tainted by fear. More than half the people I grew up with were illegal aliens, and it was a high-crime neighborhood. It was all normal.

Alberto was a hardworking man, and jack-of-all-trades. I was grateful that he took care of us. We had a roof over our heads, clothes on our back, food in our bellies. He was a good father who taught me my work ethic. I went everywhere with him as a young boy.

I didn't realize just how light my skin looked compared to my family until I turned twelve. Then one day I got sick at school. Alberto tried to pick me up, but school administrators refused. He was not my legal guardian. That had never been explained to me so I started asking, "Who is this man?" and "Who am I?" With my identity as a son, a family member, a member of a culturally distinct group of people in doubt, I was ripe for trouble.

Racial prejudice was instilled in all of us toward whites and blacks. We don't go to college like whites. Race-based gangs surrounded us. Within that mix, I built a habit of putting my enemies down to a subhuman level. This made it easier to harm them just like soldiers do in war. Blacks live on their side; we live on ours, and we don't mix.

We always lived in a state of chaos. Stealing was permissible if you were helping the family. I fully understood the right way to acquire things. In fact, I frequently looked for ways to earn money, but there was an undertone of, "We have the right to steal because we need it."

As I got older I started stealing to be accepted by my brother and cousin. My parents didn't know I had an issue with how I looked. I remember mom telling me that she thought I was embarrassed of our family. She didn't realize I felt shame and unsure of my place in the family and the way we lived. In my heart I knew all the illegal activity was wrong. I think God puts that in everybody.

> Do we have any advantage? Not at all! For we have already made the charge that Jews and Gentiles alike are all under the power of sin. As it is written: "There is no one righteous, not even one; there is no one who understands; there is no one who seeks God. . . . there is no one who does good, not even one." ~Romans 3:9–12

SOLVING PROBLEMS THROUGH VIOLENCE

Jose Seals, Minnesota

AS I GREW older my identity with the culture and geography of the "Avenue" increased. The Avenue is your life, so you're mad at everyone else. The attitude is, "I'm tough. You're not going to keep us down!"

Like a military operation, I always wanted to be on point as we roamed our streets. I have a hard time even now learning how to relax. We fought with our nemesis from Oxnard all the time as well as with the white guys down at the beach. I spent the rest of my teenage years making a mess of my life, and barely finished high school.

The day after graduation I boarded a plane to South Carolina to meet my biological father for the first time and spend a few months getting to know that side of the family. I thought, *Wow! I look like these people.* I learned he was a truck driver, and served in Vietnam. After he came home the second time he was violent in ways he hadn't been before. He drank and smoked cigarettes until he died of cancer.

He and my paternal grandfather proceeded to expose me to some hard-core racist culture. My grandfather introduced me to some black people with the last name Seals. I didn't understand why he was doing this. When we returned to the truck he told me, "Just so you know, if you meet an African American with your last name, you be kind to them . . . we used to own them."

What do I know of the history of slavery in the South? I grew up with an illegal alien perspective even though I was born here. I loved my grandfather who visited me in prison years later, but he believed racism was justified in Scripture.

When I returned home, things got serious in the street. A buddy of mine killed a black man who came to an all-Hispanic party. It was seen as racial. My friend was acquitted on self-defense. As a result, the authorities let us know they were going to get us eventually so I moved to Alaska.

After two years, I got drunk in a bar one night and was arrested for fighting. I lied in court, was acquitted, and decided to move again.

I had a buddy in Moorhead, Minnesota, where I lasted two weeks. The first week I landed a job at a printing place. An employee recognized my work ethic and told me he wanted to invest in my training to keep me long term. The second week I turned twenty-two, and some guy invited me to a party. As soon as I reached the front door I immediately ran into trouble regarding my light-colored skin. Heading down the racial identity road—which ties in with my childhood, which ties in with the reason why I began fighting in the street—did not sit well.

When I left the party there was a fight, and I ended up taking a man's life. That's how I went to prison. I spent the first five years of prison fighting trying to create the same kind of structure I understood out in the world.

The violence of the wicked will drag them away, for they refuse to do what is right. ~Proverbs 21:7

SOLVING MY IDENTITY CRISIS

Jose Seals, Minnesota

IN 1998, a white inmate tried to sit at my table in the prison chow hall. According to the insane rules, that's clear disrespect, and I almost killed him. Officers sent me to the hole for a long time. Without any distractions, I started to think for the first time. *Why am I doing this? Who am I? Why am I here?* I didn't get any answers. I didn't know God. I knew about him as a kid in a Catholic family. I never personally read the Bible. It would be eight years before I found any answers.

When I got out of segregation, I tried to change on my own. I went to school. I earned two two-year degrees, one of them in applied science. I became a tutor and a network administrator building computer networks inside the prison—a lot of what people would consider good things.

But doing good things doesn't mean you *are* good. The day I finished school, I beat a guy who had been bothering me a long time.

I also tried to stop hanging with my old crew in prison. I was in good standing, but they still expected me to violently defend the group.

I finally got tired of it and told them I was done, but they wouldn't let it lie. So I went out to the yard one day and waited until they were all congregated in one area. I readied myself to stab as many of them as I could at once. They had no idea what I planned.

I believe God spoke to me at that moment. People may call me crazy; I don't care. I heard, "If you do this, you have no part with me." That scared me.

I returned to my cell and decided to never carry a weapon inside prison again. Then some of the Christians inside started witnessing to me. They were mostly lifers. I became interested in how these Christian men lived. I believe God puts that in you, too. I didn't understand at the time why I felt that way.

A Christian inmate who was released sent me a Bible and told me to call him from inside. He told me how he got "saved." I didn't know what that meant and it sounded a little crazy. Now, I always had Bibles; they sat in the cell as coasters but I never read them. One day I opened the Bible my friend sent me and started reading in John. I didn't just read it straight, but I looked up all the cross-references in the margins. I didn't know it, but I was doing a type of hermeneutical study. On March 24, 2005, at Stillwater—a closed/maximum–I reached John 11:40. Alone in my cell, I got on my knees and begged Jesus to save me.

> "Take away the stone," [Jesus] said. "But, Lord," said Martha, the sister of the dead man, "by this time there is a bad odor, for he has been there four days." Then Jesus said, "Did I not tell you that if you believe, you will see the glory of God?" ~John 11:39–40

JULY 27

REAL CHANGE
Jose Seals, Minnesota

ALL I KNEW was eleven chapters of John, and I realized Jesus Christ is real. That was a revelation. The next day I walked out of my cell with a Bible under my arm. My old friends still invited me to join them in illegal activity and I said, "No, I'm going to church." The contrast was stark: for years I'd been steeped in wrong beliefs, illegal activity, and surrounded by those who did the same things. Then, suddenly I was going to church. Since you would seldom see guys from other blocks except at church, sports, or school, my friends thought I was just going to church to conduct business.

Within four months officials moved me to the medium-security Lino Lakes where I entered the InnerChange Freedom Initiative program, which was surprising for someone with that much time left. I was really changing, and I suppose others noticed, too. I witnessed to the gangs. One gang member told me, "We respect the God thing you're doing, but you can't be talking to our recruits."

"God told me to do it, so I will. If you want to do something [to me], that's on you, because I'm not going to stop." I took the boldness I had as an unbeliever and used it differently. The transformation in my life was night and day.

I had found the truth. My whole life I wondered, *Who is right? Was my grandfather right? Is my Hispanic side of the family correct?* In the end, they were all wrong. God's right. I had never read the Bible before. I told my mom through tears of joy, "I got saved! I got saved!"

"What are you talking about? You sound like a crazy person," she said to me.

"Well, I am crazy, crazy for Christ."

I lost half my family when I became a believer, and the other half when I got married because of the racial background of my wife.

In Galatians Paul talks about the equality of Jews and Gentiles in Christ. It helped my heart to read that. Now I have friends of all colors. Who cares what color you are? Who do you believe in? What is your character? That's where I'm at.

After almost five years of studies and learning, I made parole on February 21, 2012. Even though I work as an electrician and I'm stressed to the max about paying bills, God always gives me time to help somebody—always. I volunteer at the halfway house; I mentor anyone who wants to be mentored. I stretch myself thin—that's true—but my wife helps reel me back and rest when I need to. God's given me a fresh energy I've never had before, even though I'm a hyper person naturally. Everything is brand new.

I used to think being bi-racial was a curse. That's what I fought about. Now I see it differently. I speak two languages, which gives me more opportunities to cross more bridges. God's making me useful for his kingdom. Now I'm a child of God. I'm a *family* member. He's brought me from death to life (John 5:24). That's why I have a compassion for people of all walks.

> I will not die but live, and will proclaim what the Lord has done. The Lord has chastened me severely, but he has not given me over to death. ~Psalm 118:17–18

JULY 28

TESTING AT THE FIRST JOB

Jose Seals, Minnesota

LIFE REALLY speeds up when you reenter the free world, and one of the first things I did was land a bussing job at a restaurant. The staff at IFI (InnerChange Freedom Initiative) prepared and warned us about the tests waiting upon release—a bunch hit me immediately. My new wife fell so ill that she could not work. Suddenly we were dependent on my meager income. I quickly found a second full-time job so I was running one hundred-miles-an-hour to keep up with both jobs just so we could eat and keep our little apartment.

Then a female employee at the restaurant began to flirt with me. The biggest thing I try *not* to do out here is lie to myself. It's the easiest thing to do. As soon as you qualify a lie, you're toast. I could see only two ways to go if I stayed—tell management, or get sucked into it. I'm a man who's been down seventeen years. I had to draw a firm line for my wife, my faith, and myself.

The harassment didn't stop. This put me in a very stressful corner. As a newly-released ex-prisoner, I absolutely didn't need this kind of trouble. It can be hard to find work with my status. I lack credibility in the eyes of many people. If it weren't for all the brothers and sisters in Christ that checked on me, my freedom would have been over before it got started. My family is not here; my wife's family lives down south. Our family consists of fellow inmates who've gotten out and their wives.

I talked to my mentors: my wife more than anyone, and my brothers (in Christ) at the halfway house. Everyone concluded I needed a different job. There was also little upward mobility anyway that was desirable to me. It took three months to finally decide I had to leave. Before I left, God provided another job.

Many months after the restaurant episode, I watched a brother I love return to drugs and he "fell off." I had been mentoring him, but no matter what I said, what help I offered, he ignored it. I told him I knew what he was doing and that his so-called friends are leading him back to prison and death. He didn't want to hear it.

It's sad. You feel it. The kingdom feels the loss. He isolated himself from God's community. You've got to do things that make you uncomfortable in the right way—keeping company with your community helps a lot. Now I can't be around him. He's back in the system and my hands are tied by legal restrictions. Imagine if I showed up while he's involved in that stuff and the police arrived with me there, even though I haven't done anything. It's one of those boundaries that when ignored become very serious very quickly.

> Flee the evil desires of youth and pursue righteousness, faith, love and peace, along with those who call on the Lord out of a pure heart.
> ~2 Timothy 2:22

CONFRONTED BY VIOLENCE

Jose Seals, Minnesota

IT WAS A relief to land another job, and I worked as hard as I could. The company manufactured things and I had a few different bosses. One of my bosses called me to bail him out, regularly. I worried that by bailing him out I'd get fired because I'm not doing my job. And I saw he was getting ready to be a manager. I was brand new and didn't know anything. I started realizing this guy wasn't pulling his weight. Finally I said to him, "Look, if you do your part I guarantee I'll do mine, but I can't do yours *and* mine."

Nothing changed and the tension got worse. One day he came up, pushed me, and got all in my face. All my thinking suddenly stopped.

I know that feeling. I've been there many times. It wasn't a push with his hands, it was his chest and up in my face. He challenged me. In the past he would have had the fight he was looking for.

Instead I caught myself, looked him dead in the eye with all sincerity and said, "You don't have the heart for this brother. When you're ready to deal with reality I'll be glad to sit down with you."

It messed him up. He didn't know how to react. I made a decision long ago never to hurt anybody again in a violent manner. I'm trained now to not respond violently. I learned that in the Word, through the state's restorative justice programs, and at IFI. God has forgiven me for so much that I can't imagine going back to that way of life. In hindsight it's interesting to see how my faith was tested in the exact same area of my greatest downfall. This time, by God's grace and His power, I resisted the pride in me that knew I could fight.

People want to see if you're real and they test you... and so does God. Our relationship changed and this man started asking me for council about life stuff, and his drinking problem. He also asked about my time in prison. I could tell he wasn't ready to let go of his pride. He wouldn't humble himself. So I told him how I was in the same position and what happened. Things had to get so bad that I couldn't see any other way but to scream out for help from God. I could not do it by myself. I implored him not to wait that long.

From the fruit of their lips people enjoy good things, but the unfaithful have an appetite for violence. ~Proverbs 13:2

SHOW ME THE MONEY

Connie Cameron, Ohio

IT WAS October 2006 and I was deeply discouraged. I had been writing inspirational personal experience articles for more than a decade and was despondent over the lack of income. Sales from my book and books I had contributed to had slowed down, and I had recently received several rejections of magazine articles. With two kids in college, thoughts of walking away from writing and getting "a real job" bombarded my mind. It was a time of genuine self-doubt. But what it really boiled down to was, I was losing my focus on souls—the true reason I write.

While driving to the post office to mail a letter, I vented my frustration to the Lord. After mailing the letter I remembered I had not checked my post office box for a month. I initially got the box so readers could contact me. As a regular contributor to *Chicken Soup for the Soul* books, I did not want to give out my home address in the biography section. However, so far, no one had written to me. I occasionally included my children in my writings and *they* had received letters, but I never had.

Of course that thought only added to my despair, "God, is anyone even reading my material? What good does having this gift of writing bring to anyone—including me?"

Inside my post office box was the usual junk mail, but embedded in the papers was an envelope—from Marysville, Ohio. It was stamped, "Inmate Correspondence."

I stared at it for several seconds. I didn't know anyone in prison, and quite honestly, I didn't want to—I was afraid of prison ministry. But then I suddenly recalled that for the past several months, every time I drove by the local county jail I had a strange desire to go inside the facility and visit someone. I had not shared with anyone this desire to go behind steel doors and give hope to the hopeless.

I got back in the car to open the letter. With trembling hands, I somehow knew my attitude about inmates was about to change. But I had no idea how drastically.

No one can serve two masters. Either you will hate the one and love the other, or you will be devoted to the one and despise the other. You cannot serve both God and money. ~Matthew 6:24

IT'S NOT ABOUT MONEY— IT'S ABOUT MINISTRY

Connie Cameron, Ohio

THE LETTER was from a woman named Michaelene. She shared that she had served four years of a fourteen-year sentence, and that both her parents had died in the past year. The last time she had seen them was prior to her incarceration. Michaelene had not been allowed to attend their funerals and had been battling depression ever since. Despondent, she had attempted suicide twice.

I dug in my purse for a tissue, my eyes suddenly filling with tears.

Michaelene went on to say that due to her suicide attempts she was now a resident of the mental health ward at the prison. While attending a therapy class, the group leader encouraged the ladies to read inspirational writings. The leader had handed Michaelene a copy of *Chicken Soup for the Grieving Soul*, suggesting it might help.

Michaelene wrote she'd just read my story, "I Still Choose 'Mom,'" about the loss of my seventeen-year-old stepson, Conan. Even though she had never been married and did not have any children, the way God revealed himself in the story deeply touched her. She went on to say her relationship with the Lord had been strained. God had used my story to encourage her—to get her to turn back to him.

Thank you, Lord, for using my story to help a hurting inmate.

And then came the clincher: "Even though I have never been married and never had children, God used you to comfort me with your story. For whatever reason, I feel led to *encourage you* to keep writing because your inspirational works are needed everywhere, especially in prisons."

Oh, my. The floodgates opened and I wept all the way home.

All I could think was: *A despondent inmate is encouraging me—to keep writing?*

Michaelene had also shared that she had not received any mail since her mother's passing except for an occasional note of encouragement from an overloaded priest. Her seven siblings and many nieces and nephews had never visited or written.

I glanced at the date of the letter; it was dated almost a month earlier. *She probably thinks I'm not writing her, too.*

I showed the letter to my husband and he responded, "You are going to write her back and send her your book, aren't you?"

God was already nudging me to do so, but I was hesitant. I wanted to believe the sincerity of the sender, but needed confirmation. It took me a day or two, but finally I tucked a letter inside my book and sent it on, praying it would arrive in God's perfect timing.

Then the LORD replied: "Write down the revelation and make it plain on tablets so that a herald may run with it." ~Habakkuk 2:2

GIVING BEYOND OUR MEANS

Michaelene Duffy, Ohio

I HAD JUST finished reading a story in a *Chicken Soup* book that unexpectedly touched me. I saw the author's address in the back of the book and for some reason I wrote to her. I'm an avid reader, but I've never written to an author before. Her grief over her loss struck a chord with me.

I've always been a giver, and back when I had a good job at a university, giving nice gifts wasn't a problem. Now I receive a few bucks a month from the state. At least I can give free words of encouragement to another and get my mind off myself.

Back when I had money, though, I always wanted to outdo myself. My spending got out of control with bigger and more expensive gifts. When I lost that good university job and was unable to find another one, I still wanted to keep up appearances (including giving items to my church), so I stole someone's identity. I rationalized that it was for a good cause and only planned on doing it once, but I did it again—and got caught.

When I realized my crimes were catching up with me, I let the paralyzing fear of being incarcerated lead me to committing another, even worse, crime to cover it up. It earned me fourteen years behind bars.

I wasn't in prison long when I realized most inmates argue they are innocent, or that someone "made" them commit their crimes. The abuse of drugs plays a big part in most crimes, with the pull of the drug seeming to own them. Many are simply out of their mind when they commit their crimes. Some inmates say that they would do *anything* to get the drug so they could feel their version of "normal"—which is anything but normal.

I'm not the typical inmate in that regard, I didn't have a drug problem. And I'm not typical in another category, too: I'm highly educated. I have three college degrees. I guess I'm proof that no matter how smart you are, you can still fall. I thought my stealing was for others. However, I am learning through counseling I was trying to impress people by pretending to be someone I wasn't. It was my "extreme giving" that landed me in here doing some hard time.

I am finally learning how to be content with just giving from the heart as Jesus did. Jesus didn't give big gifts to show his love, he simply gave from his deep, sincere love for others. Small things, such as words of encouragement, prayers, and even smiles, can go a long way, especially in this place.

> "Do not plot evil against each other, and do not love to swear falsely. I hate all this," declares the Lord. ~Zechariah 8:17

AUGUST 2

DISAPPOINTMENT AND DENIAL
Michaelene Duffy, Ohio

I DID NOT blame my family for disowning me—I completely understood. I tried to imagine if it were one of my seven siblings who had done what I did. I'd probably keep my distance from them, too, for a little while. What I still don't understand, though, is how they can all continue to forsake me; my crimes were not committed against any of them. We were raised to be there for each other. It's been ten years now and I haven't heard a word from anyone except my mom. She passed away a couple of years ago, and my dad passed the year before.

To be completely cut off from family is tough. They are, after all, part of my roots. Add that to losing my parents and I was devastated beyond words. Mom and Dad were elderly and their health wouldn't permit the long drive for a visit. My dad wouldn't have visited me anyway, as he had completely disowned me. I received a few letters from Mom, but otherwise nothing. I never saw them again. I couldn't even attend either of their funerals.

I had worked hard on my education; my life held such promise. I know my parents were greatly disappointed in what I did. It's ironic how, because of my concern over not wanting to disappoint people by discontinuing the nice gifts, I ended up disappointing them much more by committing crimes to keep up the farce.

To say that the abandonment hurts doesn't begin to cover it. As I said, I fully expected them to add to my "punishment" by staying away for a while. I truly felt I deserved it because the embarrassment alone for them had to be huge. But as time went by, and especially when my parents passed and no one contacted me about their passing, I became very sad. We should be there for each other, no matter what. I mean, if your family isn't there for you, who is?

I tried to seek peace in the Bible. With my Catholic background and lots of Bible knowledge, I never really witnessed any "divine moments," per se. I knew *of* Jesus, but I did not really know him personally. At least, not until one night when I was at my lowest point ever.

> The LORD himself goes before you and will be with you; he will never leave you nor forsake you. Do not be afraid; do not be discouraged.
> ~Deuteronomy 31:8

AUGUST 3

A DIVINELY-TIMED PACKAGE

Michaelene Duffy, Ohio

DESPONDENT, I attempted suicide twice and was moved to the mental health unit so they could watch me and try to help. It looks real bad on a prison's record to have an inmate kill herself, so they brought in all kinds of therapists and social workers. Nothing worked—I had no desire to live.

And then, in the middle of the night on October 24, 2006, at 1:15 a.m., while I was planning another suicide attempt, I heard a piece of heavy mail drop through the cuff port in my door. I flicked on the dim light and plodded across the cold cement floor, curious as to what it was.

I didn't immediately recognize the return address on the package. When I opened it, I saw a letter tucked inside a book. I had written to the author of a touching *Chicken Soup* story I had read, and this was a copy of a book she had written. I was shocked! First, I had not received any packages or letters since my mom died, just an occasional card from an overworked priest. Then, knowing that prison rules mandate that all mail is screened through the mailroom (*especially* for the mental health unit), and this package was unopened, floored me. The sender had used her post office box return address; books are only allowed from publishers or bookstores, definitely not from a post office box. And lastly was the timing of it—arriving while I was planning my (hopefully) final attempt at suicide!

Red flags were all over this gift. It should have been intercepted and returned to the sender. I knew there was no way I should ever have received this package—but I did.

Goosebumps broke out all over my body. I dropped to my knees, tears streaming down my face. The dim light glowed in a way that warmed me from the inside out, as if the heavens were parting and the Lord himself were shining down on me, saying, "Michaelene, I love you. You matter to me. I have plans for your life."

> He will take pity on the weak and the needy and save the needy from death.
> ~Psalm 72:13

AUGUST 4

THE QUESTION MARK

Michaelene Duffy, Ohio

I FINALLY COMPOSED myself and read the letter. The author *thanked me* for writing to her, saying God had used *me* to encourage *her* to keep writing. The final sentence, though, pushed me over the edge, because it ended in a question mark. That simple question mark told me the author wanted me to write back. It told me someone on the outside wanted to hear from me. Someone out there cared.

There's no way I could sleep that night, so I read the mysteriously delivered book, *God's Gentle Nudges*. I was touched by how God had shown up in the author's life daily. In story after story God comforted her in simple ways.

As soon as they unlocked my door and I was allowed to make noise that morning, I did! I don't think I shut up about God's divine intervention for several weeks. That's about how long I remained in the mental health ward, too. The staff realized a true, permanent change had taken place and I was put back into GP (general population).

When a person experiences a miracle, I don't see how they can stay quiet about it. I truly believe God himself divinely intervened and instructed his angels to transport that package to my door, at just my hour of need. It boggles my mind and fills my heart with joy each time I reflect on it.

I shared with other inmates what had happened to me, and I began Bible studies with anyone willing to listen and learn. Some were hearing for the first time that God was not another mean judge mad at them and punishing them. Instead, they heard that God loved them and would forgive them. A few inmates and a staff worker came to the Lord as a result of what happened to me.

Word spread fast all over the yard, too. I was surprised when I got back to GP at the number of inmates who already knew about what had happened. Some had seen the squad transporting me to the hospital after my suicide attempts and they were amazed at how God had changed me.

God showed me his love for me and that I mattered to him. While life will always be hard in here, I know now I don't go it alone.

> He performs wonders that cannot be fathomed, miracles that cannot be counted. ~Job 5:9

A LOVE FOR PRISON MINISTRY

Connie Cameron, Ohio

ABOUT TEN days after sending Michaelene the letter and book, I received a twelve-page letter from her. She shared about the timing of the gift and how she should never have received it. She knew prison rules—I didn't.

The excitement in her writing was unmistakable. She kept repeating that I had no idea the impact this had on her and many others around her. When she shared about the timing of the book being delivered to her, I went back and checked the date of her first letter to me. It had sat in my post office box for three weeks! And, it had taken me a few days to write Michaelene and send the book—yet it had arrived at exactly her moment of need.

After reading her letter, I confess—I was still skeptical. So, I sent her a different book using the same method of shipping. It came right back to me, unopened and stamped "Contraband Material." Then as if to seal the doubt forever, I received an e-mail from a staff member at the prison asking me to give a talk at a pre-release prison, sharing the story about Michaelene and me. It turns out it was the same lady who first gave Michaelene a copy of *Chicken Soup for the Grieving Soul*. She had witnessed the huge change in Michaelene, verifying how strict the mail policy is for the mental health ward and how God had used Michaelene's story to bring several people to the Lord—even to revitalize her own faith.

I shared this story with a newspaper reporter friend. She loved it and published it in the paper. A member of my church read it and stopped me, introducing herself as Pat Collins, a jail ministry board member. Pat believed God was calling us both into prison ministry and offered to take me under her wing, inviting me to get involved in the local jail first.

Fast-forward to today, and I, too, am a board member of the jail ministry and involved in the volunteer programs. God has drastically changed my heart toward prison ministry, and I am so glad he did. Michaelene and I are good friends. I visit her regularly and she writes faithfully—still encouraging me to keep writing inspirational works.

See, I am doing a new thing! Now it springs up; do you not perceive it? I am making a way in the wilderness and streams in the wasteland. ~Isaiah 43:19

CONSEQUENCES

Dijuahn Robinson, Arizona

MY FIRST encounter with Christ happened at a Baptist-run Vacation Bible School. I was eight and sensed God calling me to preach. However, in high school, peer pressure got hold of me. I joined the "Bloods" gang. I hit the prison yard for the first time for my criminal activity in 1993 and did two-and-a-half years on that tour. After being home ten months I got in trouble again.

My wife and I had an "altercation." When this policeman arrived, he was on high alert. I was on the phone and being obnoxious to him. He saw I had a weapon and drew his. I reached to hand my gun over to him when he squeezed off five rounds into my chest.

Both my lungs were punctured. Doctors removed my spleen, reconstructed my stomach, repaired a damaged liver, and did their best with a severed radial and ulna nerve in my left arm. It's a miracle I survived. Doctors told me I would never walk again and I spent six months in the hospital recovering.

Police arrested me while I was still hooked up and recovering. They moved me to the isolated portion of the hospital for security reasons. I had to recover without any family or outside visits. I couldn't walk. Nursing staff bathed me. I was crying. I couldn't eat, I was helpless. I had no strength. I couldn't sit up.

The legal results of that evening included ten-and-a-half-year and two-and-a-half-year sentences for aggravated assault against a police officer and another related charge. Once I weaned myself off the powerful medications, it finally occurred to me I was on the wrong track. God started reminding me of stuff, that I had a purpose. He used the strangest people to remind me of that.

Aside from the pain of my injuries and overall helplessness, I felt very alone. I really had no one to talk to all day. A female officer came by my room and asked, "What's wrong?" I told her the short version of my injuries. She propped me up and said, "Without incriminating yourself, tell me what's happening."

She listened patiently and said, "God has a purpose for your life and the Lord put me here today for this." She immediately got me out of the isolation cell and put me in a medical pod where I could talk with other people, which improved my attitude greatly. From then on, God started opening doors not just to my physical recovery but to the greater need—my spiritual recovery.

> Have mercy on me, LORD, for I am faint; heal me, LORD, for my bones are in agony. ~Psalm 6:2

WALKING THE YARD WITH DAD

Dijuahn Robinson, Arizona

MY FATHER didn't raise me, so I grew up early. He spent his life in a gang and in prison. I was really angry at him because he hadn't been in my life. Yet, God made a way so we'd be together when he died February 3, 1997, at the San Juan Unit (now called the Lumley Unit) of the Perryville prison.

That weekend my mother and my wife came to visit us. He was acting weird. Turns out he had a brain tumor they couldn't remove and he was HIV positive. On my first prison tour I was locked up with Dad's best friend. I was very disrespectful to my dad in front of him. He told me, "No matter what it is, he's still your father. You need to sit down with him and find out why he wasn't there."

Years later, I was given just such an opportunity. He opened up and shared things that helped me to forgive him. As we walked the yard, I told him about my life, why I was so angry, my decisions, why I blamed him. He took it, accepted it, and was very apologetic. Even though I was in prison with him, he said, "I'm still proud of you and I still love you."

Dad had to be put in isolation. They moved him to the Florence medical unit at the Central Arizona Correctional complex. Some contacts were made by officers and they arranged to transfer me to Central also. They would let me go over to the medical unit so Dad and I could spend his last days together. My dad did come to faith in Christ. We had that conversation on his hospital bed.

Within a few days he was dead. I didn't attend the funeral because we'd made our peace.

I've been in prison my son's entire life. The cycle has repeated itself. I hope it stops for him. He's got some trouble, which is painful, but he never joined a gang or did the things I did. He's been in church and graduated high school. I was able to attend that ceremony just after my release. What a powerful moment for us! He has since watched me graduate from the University of Phoenix with a BA in business administration.

> Therefore, if you are offering your gift at the altar and there remember that your brother or sister has something against you, leave your gift there in front of the altar. First go and be reconciled to them; then come and offer your gift.
> ~Matthew 5:23–24

AUGUST 8

POST-RELEASE STRUGGLES
Dijuahn Robinson, Arizona

MY HOMECOMING from prison wasn't much like *The Shawshank Redemption*. A lot of real life hit me head on. I had a lot of enthusiasm heading out, given all the work God had done with me inside. Almost immediately I connected with a church and started using my speaking gifts to work with youth. Then one of the people I cared most about in my life, my grandma, passed away. Next, I lost my first post-prison job, and my uncle passed away from cancer, all within weeks of each other. That took a lot out of me.

But it wasn't over. I ran into some marital problems followed closely by the biggest blow yet. On May 31, my sister was murdered. That triggered a lot of emotions. Instantly I wanted blood. I was angry at God. I didn't feel I could effectively minister because I had so much anger and rage in my heart, so I pulled back to give myself time to figure it all out. I've been to so many funerals, I've buried so many people, carried so many caskets, but it hadn't happened so close to me until now. I didn't understand. I was serving God whole-heartedly, raising money for ministry, traveling, preaching the gospel. It was very painful—still is. It's led to some discontent.

All those years when I played the tough guy I depended on my strength and size for my identity. I have since mostly recovered from the shooting, but my left arm never fully healed.

When I have a bad day, my arm reminds me. Being in and out of the hospital with my recent stomach issues reminds me—I still need God for my strength. We unconsciously forget all the time. I'm vulnerable and still dependent on God. I remember people celebrating me for my accomplishments, but it was God all the time.

The police found my sister's killer. It's a death penalty case and it is as hard for me now as when I sat in the box and people decided my fate. I'm trying to put myself in the right position so I can heal. I don't want to be too judgmental.

The healing on this will take a lot of time. I know God's holding me, keeping me. I wouldn't have made it these five years without him.

Though he slay me, yet will I hope in him. ~Job 13:15

AUGUST 9

HOPE IN JESUS

Roger Morgan, California

I HAVE BEEN so blessed to be a volunteer chaplain in a state prison. It has been wonderful to share my story with the inmates; I long for it to encourage them and give them hope.

When I was in the military there was never enough money to party the way I and the other GIs wanted to party. We lived for our days off. A friend of mine had a car and that was my ticket to go into the city. One night, I asked my friend for a ride but he said his battery was bad. I quickly came up with a solution—I knew where there were some junk cars off-base, so we did the wrong thing and stole a battery out of one of the cars. We got caught and were sentenced to lose all our stripes and rank, forfeiture of two-thirds of our pay, six months at hard labor, and a bad conduct discharge.

We were in jail about four months when our superiors came to us and said they thought we were able to be retrained. They asked if we would go through a six-month retraining program. We accomplished that and were reinstated back into service.

God got my attention and now I share my incarceration stories with prison inmates while volunteering for prison ministries. Although they laugh at my measly six months of service (most of them are sentenced to life), it doesn't matter. Even if you only served a week, losing your freedom really stinks.

I told the prisoners that although the courts sentenced them to life in prison, God is still the Judge, Jury, and Creator. I invite them to look at Peter's and Paul's lives for encouragement. Peter was in the bowels of a prison, chained to Roman guards, and God released him. Paul was in and out of prison several times, but kept his faith and kept encouraging others to keep their faith, too. I tell the inmates I visit that God may or may not choose to release them early, too, but they can still be spiritually free right where they are. It all starts with being truly repentant and choosing to serve God.

> The Lord lifts up those who are bowed down, the Lord loves the righteous.
> ~Psalm 146:8

AUGUST 10

SHARE YOUR PAST— FOR GOD'S GLORY

Roger Morgan, California

PRIOR TO becoming a volunteer chaplain inside a men's prison, I had been raised in the church. I had heard God's Word, and knew right from wrong. We lived in abject poverty, surviving in the shacks of West Virginia. My mom and I left the coal mines and moved to Baltimore when

I was fifteen years old. We moved there because my mom had to get away from my father, an abusive husband.

It was then I realized there was a life outside of "the Holler." I forgot my church background and went wild doing all the wrong things: literally, "sex, drugs, and rock & roll."

I now often share with the inmates something Paul said—of all sinners, he was the worst. Paul also said that if God should have turned his back on anyone, it was he. But Paul became a new creature in the Lord. God completely forgave him of killing Christians, and God can forgive each of us, too. The Lord gives us free will—free will to choose a life of destruction, or to choose him. It's all ours for the asking. Once we use the free will he gave us to turn our life over to him, he promises to never leave us or forsake us.

I believe that even the bad parts of our life can be used for good. My past experiences give me some credibility with those I counsel. They listen to me because I've been there.

I have a niece who got hooked on OxyContin and was literally a walking dead person. She had to be hospitalized for thirty days to get flushed out. I would try to visit her every other day.

While the nurses were tending to her needs, I would go over and talk to her roommates. One young Asian lady said she was in for a transfusion and would be going home the next day. I asked if she would mind if I prayed with her. I did pray for her but she never left the hospital. She died overnight. During those thirty days I prayed with another roommate and she never got out of the hospital, either.

Someone said I should not have prayed with them because I jinxed them. That's not true. God never promises our next breath in this short life we live. Sharing Christ with those ladies gave them a chance to talk with God. We need to take advantage of every opportunity the Lord gives us, whether we're stuck inside a prison or visiting someone in a hospital.

By the way, today my niece is a changed person. She is now happily married with a beautiful baby boy.

> He said to them, "Go into all the world and preach the gospel to all creation."
> ~Mark 16:15

A DESPERATELY WICKED HEART

Joe Miller, Florida

IT DIDN'T matter that I was raised in a good home, or took advanced college prep courses through high school with people who became professors at Johns Hopkins and state's attorneys. It didn't matter I was on the state championship track team in Sayre, Pennsylvania. It didn't matter that I went into the Air Force as a surgery tech for four years.

When I got out someone hired me as a surgical assistant. None of those things mattered when I came face-to-face with my own darkness and evil. I'd never committed a crime before, not even speeding.

I was going through a separation and divorce while living with my girlfriend. I knew a guy who read through the Bible each year, so I picked one up to try it myself. I was hit with an overwhelming conviction: I'm living in adultery. Here's where the weakness in my own character happened. I can't tell her we can't live together. It will devastate her. I wasn't saved and decided it was worse to hurt her emotionally than to not listen to God. God dealt with me and I didn't follow.

I'd lived in a protected environment all through high school—super achievers with great families. Now I was with people who didn't have good morals. You know the crowd-pleasing, trying-to-get-along-with-everybody deal? I was unprepared to handle it. I'm not blaming them—I made my own choices.

Unless we're born again and cooperating with what God wants to do, there's no telling what we'll do in a day's time. When the sheriff's deputy read, "two counts of murder one, two counts of kidnapping in the first degree, midnight burglary," life as I knew it ended. I had killed two men.

Sitting in a Florida county jail overwhelmed, I remembered my grandmother, who took me to a Vacation Bible School when I was nine or ten. She put an "ABC" on the feltboard: A is ask, B is believe, and C is confess. But I had a difficult time with God forgiving a murderer. I was devastated and in despair.

Someone gave me a Gideon New Testament including the Psalms, which I read. Romans 8:1 gave me great hope. However, by the time I finished I was in Psalms. King David said a lot of things about what God should do to those who shed innocent blood—none of it good. That scared me.

My cousin's pastor came to visit me. He asked me if I knew Jesus and I said, "Yeah?" with a confused look.

He asked, "Well, what's wrong?"

I was raw honest in my despair. "Does he forgive a murderer?" I asked.

The pastor answered, "Yes."

That didn't satisfy some intellectual curiosity between my ears. There was a power of God in that answer. That's when I was changed. I started seeking ways to learn about God in the Bible day and night.

Still the court gave me four mandatory twenty-five-year-to-life sentences.

> The heart is deceitful above all things and beyond cure. Who can understand it? ~Jeremiah 17:9

ENVIRONMENT SHAPES WILL?

Joe Miller, Florida

THEY SENT me to the Rock for my first ten years. I did see a lot of bad events. Even though it might seem like hanging with the wrong crowd would be unavoidable in prison (we're all criminals), you can still make positive choices.

I heard a guy give a talk who said, "Environment is stronger than will." The books you read, TV or movies you watch, are all environments. Whatever environment you spend a lot of time in will powerfully impact your choices. You will be swayed. We must change our environment, what we think about, who we spend time with. For me, I went to church inside, cultivating relationships with guys who were going in the right direction.

That makes a difference when trauma enters your life. I felt very bad for my parents. I'm sure their hopes and dreams for me were shattered and they were publicly shamed. I wanted to get out and prove to them I was born again, really saved, and pursuing God.

In prison when they call you to the chapel, it's usually not a good thing. I was in the band room with Jack Murphy doing music stuff. Earlier my father had crashed his motorcycle through a barn. He was in a coma for three months. I knew he'd been struggling since then. So I'm telling myself, *It's not bad news, not bad news.*

When I arrived, it was really bad. Dad had used a shotgun to kill himself. I was so overwhelmed. I went back to the dorm numb, then started crying. I was in a good dorm with Cooper (page 76) and Murphy. Each one of the guys in my Kairos group came by at lunch time—which they never do because we all respect that as a time of privacy if you want it. Some hugged. Some cried. Some gave advice. One guy didn't know what to say. He just stood in my doorway. Just being there means a lot sometimes.

It made a real difference having Christian brothers to relate with at that moment. I could have easily gone the other way in my grief, the way of prison life. For many it feels like another nail in their coffin of despair and compounds their hatred for the world. I had a bond when I needed it.

> Finally, brothers and sisters, whatever is true, whatever is noble, whatever is right, whatever is pure, whatever is lovely, whatever is admirable—if anything is excellent or praiseworthy—think about such things. ~Philippians 4:8

AUGUST 13

STABBING ON THE RUNNING TRACK

Joe Miller, Florida

ONE AFTERNOON I found myself in the library with a new Bible. It was small enough to fit in my pocket and had a special cover I admired a lot. A friend of mine, Ron, walked in when I heard that gentle, quiet voice of God say, "Give him your Bible."

The next voice was my own: "But I don't want to!"

I walked over to Ron anyway to say hello. He noticed the cover and commented on how nice it looked. I asked him if he'd like one.

"Oh yeah, I'd love one like that."

"Here, it's yours." He was so happy to get that Bible. I was less than happy. I had no concept why God would ask me to do something such as that. *There are plenty of Bibles to be had. Why mine?*

Later on, Ron and I were at different prisons for about five years before he was transferred back to where I was at Tomoka.

He caught up with me jogging one afternoon and asked, "Do you remember that Bible you gave me?"

"Sure." Next he told me an unbelievable true story.

"I was up at the Rock running. I jogged around a corner where a couple of guys tried to rob me. I started to fight them off when one pulled a knife and stabbed me. The blade punctured the Bible in my front pocket and left only a tiny nick in my chest. They left and didn't take anything. I carry that Bible everywhere now."

With that one act, I had saved a man's life. I could have been selfish. Who knows the consequences of being selfish even in a little thing? When God says do something, no matter how small, just do it.

> Whoever has my commands and keeps them is the one who loves me. The one who loves me will be loved by my Father, and I too will love them and show myself to them. ~John 14:21

AUGUST 14

LIVING WITH THE PAST

Joe Miller, Florida

I DIDN'T SPEND a lot of time rehashing my crimes during my long years in prison. I couldn't change what I'd done. There were times when I gave a testimony and I would experience an overwhelming remorse. I'd choke up, start crying, my throat hurt, my eyes burned. It was embarrassing.

After my arrest I tried to commit suicide. They served TV dinners in aluminum foil but it just wouldn't cut the skin. I made the mistake of talking about my crime with one of the runners—I didn't know anything about jail or that they told everything they heard to others. Next thing I know, I wasn't getting those dinners anymore. When I got to the county jail they assigned a counselor to see me. I asked him—if possible—to let the families know how sorry I was. I'd give my own life just to have the victims back. I don't think he did.

At my parole hearing thirty-five years later, the brother and sister of one victim were still showing up to oppose my release. But when authorities granted parole, the brother at the last moment said he wanted money for funeral costs. It sounded to me like ongoing resentment. I absolutely understand why they've hurt so long, but it hurts me to see it.

My wife and I gathered the resources we had and paid off the small amount immediately. I was glad to do it because it was some form of connection to say, "I wish I could do more." I knew I wasn't allowed to talk to them, but I was thankful for this one thing I could do. It was symbolic, but it was a big deal to me. I still pray for them, to see them saved. I hate to see their lives ruined by bitterness and resentment.

You do worry sometimes you will become calloused to the harm you've done. I don't ever want that to happen. Jesus never forgot the cost of sin and kept his nail-scarred hands. Certain wounds, even after being transformed by grace, remain burned in the memory. It's part of being human.

Periodically the story of David baffled me. After the evil he did, how could God say David was a man after his own heart? I meditated on that a great deal. A priest recommended I read St. Augustine's story, since he thought our lives were so similar. *Confessions* is a powerful read.

Having the light of God shining on the event helps take a little of the sting away, but you can't say, "That's over" and forget it. You have to decide how to carry on with the rest of your life.

> Therefore I despise myself and repent in dust and ashes. ~Job 42:6

THE PLEASURE
WAS ALL MINE

Dave Myers, Ohio

I WAS TWENTY-FIVE in 1983, and in private sector law enforcement. It was also the year I asked Jesus into my heart. Sadly, I chose not to walk with him, and in my early forties I found myself facing a five-year prison sentence.

While in jail awaiting my sentence, a Christian man befriended me. Before going to prison, he led me back to the Lord.

When I left jail I went to the Correctional Receiving Center. I was terrified. It was like "boot camp," only with mean guys—inmates *and* staff.

My first bunkie (cellmate) was twenty-year-old Mike—a kid who had lived on the street all his life. He was tough—hated everyone, especially me. Mike warned me that first day to sleep with one eye open.

I prayed for him from the moment we met. Finally I asked, "What have I done to you?"

"Nothing; I hate whoever I room with. You need a different cellmate," he said.

It took no time for Mike to prove he hated me. Together we went to the CO and asked for different bunkies.

"Do you think this is the Hilton, where you can switch rooms if you aren't comfortable?" The officer scowled. "The best I can do, Myers, is put you in the hole."

I didn't want any dings on my record, so I decided I'd just have to trust God to get me out alive. We went back to our cell and I told Mike, "I am making it a goal that I will shake the hand of every bunkie I room with, before we part ways. I'm also gonna tell them it was a pleasure spending time with them." I don't know where that came from, but I had peace as soon as I said it.

As Mike continued pacing the cell, swearing and complaining constantly, I stayed calm and upbeat, reading my Bible and praying. He finally asked what I was reading and I told him. He kept asking questions about Christianity—never having heard that Jesus loved him and died for him. One awesome day, he asked me to lead him to the Lord.

Not long after, we were awakened at 5 a.m. It was time for Mike to go to his parent institution. I watched him pack his two bags and head for the door. He stopped, dropped both bags, and turned around. Walking back to me, he stuck out his hand and I shook it.

"Dave," he said. "It's been a pleasure spending time with you. Thanks, man."

I choked back tears . . . the pleasure had been all mine.

> Those who go out weeping, carrying seed to sow, will return with songs of joy, carrying sheaves with them. ~Psalm 126:6

AUGUST 16

THE WRITING ON THE CEILING

Gary Benjamin, Pennsylvania

I SPENT FIVE years incarcerated in West Virginia. My first night in the DOC (Department of Corrections) I was placed in "the hole." When I got ready to go to sleep, I glanced up at the ceiling and saw some writing. I was amazed that someone had been able to write that high from the floor. And, they had written not one, but two, verses from the Bible. The first verse, Jeremiah 33:3, read, "Call to me and I will answer you and tell you great and unsearchable things you do not know." The other verse was Habakkuk 1:5: "Look at the nations and watch—and be utterly amazed. For I am going to do something in your days that you would not believe, even if you were told."

Those verses really touched me and gave me hope. I felt they were a direct sign from God for me and I took their meanings to heart.

After I was released I went to Ready, Pennsylvania, to the New Person Center (NPC). I was a resident there, and after participating in several programs I owed more than $2,000 in program fees. Thankfully, while in the DOC I had obtained my master certification in Microsoft Office. So, the executive director, Rev. John Rush, found some work for me to do around the office to help pay back my fees. It felt good to be working and to pay off my debt.

283
❧

Then, after about six months, I was moved to another house in the NPC program. This time I was made a house trustee. It really boosted my self-esteem to know others trusted me and counted on me.

In September 2009 I was thrilled when NPC promoted me to house manager for the only house we had in the program. I've held that position a few years, and now I am preparing to move to a different part of Pennsylvania to start another Christian transitional program. It makes me proud to be giving back and helping others.

God is doing exactly what the writing on the ceiling said he would do, those many years ago.

Call to me and I will answer you and tell you great and unsearchable things you do not know. ~Jeremiah 33:3

PARTNER TO THE UNTHINKABLE

Dawn Anderson, New Mexico

AS THE women's chaplain I see many sad inmates, but Susan's* withdrawn demeanor made me suspect she had been abused. She eventually told me her background. I cringed as she described being brutally beaten by most of the men in her life. Stories poured forth of being strangled with electrical cords, receiving blows to the face, losing teeth, having hair pulled out, and being sexually assaulted in evil ways. Susan had been caught in a cycle of abuse at a young age and now, far from home, she was facing murder charges.

Greg*, the man she had been involved with, convinced Susan to go out of state where he had plotted to kill an acquaintance for money. It was a brutal murder. At Greg's command, he forced Susan to help wrap the dead body in a tarp, drag it outside to a barn, and set the corpse on fire. When Susan shared with me the sketchy details of this crime that gained media attention, she also added that she loved Greg enough to take the fall in order to spare him life behind bars. Turning this inmate around was not going to be easy.

Greg was arraigned first and sentenced to twenty-five years to life, in spite of his desperate attempt to place the blame on Susan. Behind bars, he continued to harass her with letters, but more and more she began to let go of the fear, and trust Jesus.

The day of Susan's sentencing I was nervous. She, too, was looking at twenty-five to life for conspiracy to commit aggravated murder, tampering with evidence, and abuse of a corpse. During the proceedings the judge, who was well known for his stiff sentences, asked the prosecutor for final remarks. To the surprise of everyone, including Susan's court-appointed attorneys, the prosecutor told the judge how he had witnessed an extreme change in Susan from the time he had begun to interview her months prior, until now. He spoke of her abusive past and how he sensed a kind, but wounded, soul in this dear woman.

No one was more shocked than Susan herself at the prosecutor's recommended sentence of ten years with possible judicial release in three. To everyone's amazement, the judge took the recommendation and handed down the sentence.

I will say of the LORD, "He is my refuge and my fortress, my God, in whom I trust." ~Psalm 91:2

A WEEK I WON'T FORGET

Dawn Anderson, New Mexico

"MOM, CHRIS never receives mail. Would you please add him to your list and write to him?"

This was a snippet of the telephone conversation I had with my son one Saturday afternoon while he was serving time in prison.

Growing up, most mornings I would wake up and wander into the kitchen, where my mom would be sitting at the table writing letters. I'm forever thankful that what seems to be the lost art of letter writing was passed on to me by her faithfulness to keep in touch with others. There's something to be said for taking time to select stationery, the right pen, and then actually handwrite the letter. It doesn't include the expense of buying stamps and envelopes, or the time walking or driving to a mailbox. Yes, it takes some effort, but I guarantee that inmates appreciate every piece of personal mail they receive. And Chris was no exception.

Adopted at a young age by older parents, now that he found himself behind bars, they were unable to make the drive to visit him at the out-of-county location. And with their limited income, the expense of writing and sending prepaid stamped envelopes was more than their Social Security budget would allow.

So, I agreed to honor my son's request and began to correspond with Chris. Our friendship grew over the years and I loved being able to share my faith with him. Likewise, Chris seemed to enjoy telling me about his everyday life in prison, mixed with an occasional story from his childhood.

One year in early spring, I experienced a week like no other. On Saturday our son had an accident in his new vehicle. Thankfully, he wasn't hurt, but the vehicle was totaled. On Monday, we had a fierce rainstorm and our sump pump burnt out, flooding the basement and resulting in $5,000 worth of damage. On Wednesday, my nephew attempted suicide and was fighting for his life in the hospital.

Feeling as gray as the cold March weather, the following Saturday I received an unexpected collect call from a correctional institution. It was Chris. He quickly got to the point, simply stating, "I'm turning thirty next month; my life is a mess. I'm ready to surrender to this Jesus you've been telling me about for the last three years."

And there on the phone, I was able to lead him in the Sinner's Prayer.

My rough week was suddenly completely forgotten for a while—and joy filled both our souls.

In all their distress he too was distressed, and the angel of his presence saved them. In his love and mercy he redeemed them; he lifted them up and carried them all the days of old. ~Isaiah 63:9

MAKING A PROMISE

Christopher Dunn, Missouri

ALL MY life I'd been at the center of ridicule, rejection, and abuse. I hated my life; I hated everything about who I was. I prayed so many times asking that God would take my life. Being the only son of a woman who cared only for herself, I was rejected and unloved. I was never accepted as my sisters were. There was physical abuse, too, for not wanting to participate in her manipulative games with men. She would try to claim I was the son of different men, but I always knew that the man who lived with me, who played with me, who taught me, and who loved me was my father. After being rejected so much by my biological mother, I created my own little world. But, as it's been said, all things happen for a purpose.

My father was all I had. Even as a child I was not allowed to have friends or play sports. My father tried to be there for me, but he was not always there to protect me. I never used drugs or drank; I promised my father I wouldn't. I had been baptized in a good Christian church when I was a baby. Because of mixed religions and conflicting family structure, I was confused about God. What little I knew, I learned from my father. As I grew up, I learned to follow "the code of the streets" of St. Louis, Missouri.

I was raised in and around poverty, oppression, violence, and death. My life took a turn for the worse after the deaths of some of my relatives, including my father's passing in 1989. I believed I had lost the only family I would ever know. I attempted suicide several times. I wanted so much to leave this world, to forget it all and be free.

But then my hell got even hotter. In May 1990, police came to my mother's home and arrested me for a crime I knew nothing of. I was convicted and sentenced to serve the remainder of my life in prison.

Now in prison, I was again contemplating suicide when I got to thinking about my father and the promises I made to him. I sat down and asked God to come into my life and accept me as one of his. I promised God, as I had my dad, I would live my life fully until I was able to see them. I realized then that Someone wanted me to live, but for what reason, I had to wonder.

But if from there you seek the Lord your God, you will find him if you seek him with all your heart and with all your soul. ~Deuteronomy 4:29

GIVING BACK

Christopher Dunn, Missouri

AFTER I asked Jesus into my heart, I started to go through a spiritual transformation. I joined the prison churches and became active in every program offered. I started to work on my own personal problems and in the process I was able to assist others. I learned the powerful truth about God and the Lord Jesus Christ. God was working in my life.

Then, on December 11, 1992, I received a letter and two birthday cards from a woman named Elizabeth Michael (see Jan. 9, Beth Michael). It was the day before my birthday and those cards I will never forget. I wrote her back and thanked her, not knowing then that we would be writing for more than seven years. She and her husband did something I couldn't believe: They became my new family and accepted me into their lives. I felt the concern, love, and support of those two and I remember her scolding me for wanting to give up my fight to regain my freedom. I started to fully open up to them and then I knew that God had sent them to me.

I wanted to spread the love and the joy that I have come to know, feel, and accept from them and the Lord. My eyes opened wide with the possibilities of beginning a pen pal program to help other inmates throughout the incarcerated communities. I presented the idea to my "Mama" and "Pops" and they agreed. Mama and I were already planning and compiling a prisoner resource directory for helping with needs in various fields. We placed our Pen Pal Connection information in the directory and started sending it to prisoners and chaplains.

Another reason for this was to involve the people of society; they fail to realize that we are human beings, too. Someday we will return back into society. While most people give credit for the lower crime rates to the government and to the politicians (due to harsher laws and punishments), it is really the volunteers in ministry who make the greatest difference. These volunteers have given us hope and love through their prayers and sharing Jesus.

As God opens my eyes and heart, I give thanks to him each and every day. I was once blind and bitter, but now I am what God wishes for me to be—his child. God has entered my life and I want to never disappoint him. THANK YOU, heavenly Father!

... because we have heard of your faith in Christ Jesus and of the love you have for all God's people ... ~Colossians 1:4

288

WAKE UP WITH A PUNCH

Billy, Texas*

FOR SOME reason my bunkmate transferred out of our cell. He forgot his wooden cross up under my bunk. A neighbor of mine a few cells down found it and took it. Later, I saw my former bunkmate in chow hall and he asked me if I could get his cross back to him.

When I next found the neighbor and told him John was looking to get his cross back, he replied, "He left it, that's it."

"OK, I'll tell him."

I had just reclined in my bunk and closed my eyes for a short catnap when I felt several sharp blows to my face. This neighbor came down on me with everything he had, putting his fist into my face. I shot up and looked at the guy and said, "What do you think you're doing?"

"Nobody tells me what to @#^% do!"

"Look, bro, all I did was tell you the fellow wanted his cross back, but God bless you." He stumbled back a few feet with a funny look on his face.

"You don't like what I did, you better take care of business," he snarled.

"I'm a Christian. I'm not going to fight you, but I *will* pray for you." He left, but came back forty-five minutes later. I asked him, "Are you all right?"

"Yeah."

"You had no right to do what you did, but I forgive you," and I stuck out my hand to shake his. We shook. A while later he ended up apologizing to me. But that night I prayed, "Let there be peace between me and this man. Either move him or move me." The next morning, he was gone. Transferred because of some trouble he'd been in. That's the closest I ever got to a fight in thirteen years, which is not a bad record with a crime like mine.

> If it is possible, as far as it depends on you, live at peace with everyone.
> ~Romans 12:18

FOCUS ON WHAT IS REAL

Billy*, Texas

M Y CRIME was horrible; the perverted, sick piece of scum I was. I deserved every day of prison time I got and probably more.

That's where Christ comes in: his comfort, his forgiveness. That's why I can't focus on what people think. You can't please everyone, so I focus on pleasing the Lord. Don't worry about what people think. What the Lord thinks about you is important. That's focusing on what's real.

People consider sex crimes worse than murder and those who commit them are treated worst of all—by parole personnel, by police, by society. How am I able to live with society's lack of forgiveness? Because I know who I am in Christ. If people don't want to forgive me for something I didn't even do to them, it's on them. I practice loving them regardless of how they treat me. You can't be a people pleaser. That's why I tell people a short version of my testimony. You got a problem with it? I understand. God bless you. Hope I can help you overcome it if you choose to be my friend.

You have to be a prudent man in those matters. You use the wisdom God gave you. You don't throw it out to just anybody. I want friends to know so they can make a decision right then so they don't feel deceived. I do let other people get to know me a little bit before I reveal the past.

If you don't want to try, I'm going to keep you in prayer. I'm not going to hate you or be mad at you. I don't get my feelings hurt over it. It used to hurt at first—ain't no doubt. But the more I come to know who I am in Christ, the better I handle my "scarlet letter."

It's a terrible thing to live without forgiveness. I've been on both sides of the track. From the age of four to eleven I was molested by males and females. I've been there. It messed my mind up, which is not an excuse. There is no excuse for what I did.

I called up an old friend in Corpus Christi, Texas, when I got out. He and his wife are Christians. They know me and why I went to prison. He was my fishing buddy. They told me I should come over. I said, "I just wanted to call and make sure I was welcome."

They answered, "You know what? You did the crime, you did the time. You're forgiven."

The big difference is having people in your life who know the Lord. The Bible says no one is good, not one. Everybody sins. How does each of us deal with it? I know of only one perfect Person who never sinned.

> For I will forgive their wickedness and will remember their sins no more. ~Hebrews 12:4
>
> [God] endured with much patience vessels of wrath prepared for destruction, . . . in order that He might make known the riches of His glory upon vessels of mercy, which He prepared beforehand for glory. ~Romans 9:22–23

AUGUST 23

"SLAM 'EM DOWN" SINGS

Billy*, Texas

I ACQUIRED A nickname inside. Drink pitchers are not allowed in chow hall except for servers because prisoners will use them to fight. So, if you want a refill on your drink while I'm going between tables, I'd tell them, "slam it down if you want another round," and I'd refill the cup before moving to the next table. So they started calling me "Slam 'Em Down."

I also love country gospel music. Often while getting ready in the kitchen I would sing either a song I'd heard, or something I made up. I've written more than one hundred of my own songs. It just puts me in a great mood to sing something about the Lord. I suppose, as with most kinds of music, some people appreciated it, but others didn't.

So this big black dude, 6'4" and twenty-nine years old, worked in chow hall and called over to me.

"Look, I wrote my mom and told her how I've accepted Christ because of you."

He completely surprised me. "What do you mean?"

"Those songs you sing every morning before we open chow hall, if I'd seen you on the streets, a white boy singing country gospel, I'd have slapped you and told you to git out of here. I don't like country. But the way you sing, I've heard the gospel through your singing. Because of you, I've given my life to Christ."

We hugged and cried. You can imagine that doesn't happen normally—blacks and whites hugging and crying in prison. Those are the joys. I'm riding with Jesus and I'm not tired yet.

> Let the message of Christ dwell among you richly as you teach and admonish one another with all wisdom through psalms, hymns, and songs from the Spirit, singing to God with gratitude in your hearts. ~Colossians 3:16

STORYBOOK ENDINGS

Misty Wieging, Ohio

AS A stay-at-home mom, I longed to serve in ministry but knew my options were limited. So, when the opportunity came to serve in the prison, I couldn't wait for my clearance to go through.

While waiting, I received an e-mail from my friend Deb about a program at the Franklin Pre-release Center called Aunt Mary's Storybook Project. Deb shared what she knew about it; the women could pick out a children's storybook and we would record the women reading the books to their children. We would then mail the books and the tapes to the children as a gift from their moms.

At the end of the e-mail she simply asked, "Is this something you might be interested in?"

My heart practically leaped out of my chest with excitement! What Deb did not know is that I am a children's storybook "junkie." At the time she sent the e-mail, I had more than three hundred children's storybooks on my bookshelves! Some of my sweetest memories from raising my own kids include bedtime reading, because I always tucked my kids in with a storybook.

I immediately e-mailed her back and then called my husband—I was so excited! The Lord had found a perfect place for a woman like me (who had nothing special to give by the world's standards), to bless these women separated from their children.

Over the years, this "mother's heart" connection has given me the privilege to pray for women and share the love of Christ with them. It has also given these mothers the opportunity to "tuck their children in" with a storybook each night.

Someday, for those who have put their trust in Jesus, we will all have storybook endings and live happily ever after, with our King.

> Blessed are those who have learned to acclaim you, who walk in the light of your presence, Lord. They rejoice in your name all day long; they celebrate your righteousness. ~Psalm 89:15–16

SHATTERED

Mike Martin*, Indiana

I GREW UP in a good Christian family. I had a younger sister and brother. Everyone adored my baby brother, John, including friends, family, teachers, coaches, and peers. He was kind, helpful, and always looked up to me. We were a tight-knit family.

As the years went by we all married and began our families. Then, in 2006, tragedy struck when my mother died. She had a strong faith and I struggled with how God could take her so soon. Before I could process her loss, my father-in-law passed away. Both were in their fifties. I became angry with God. Why hadn't he healed them?

In the summer of 2007 we bought a large wooded lot to build a house on. John worked side-by-side with me clearing the lot. That was the kind of person he was; he would do anything for anyone. We became even closer as brothers and best friends during that time, as we spent hours together, talking about life.

Just a year later the unthinkable happened. John was attacked and killed by his drug-addicted friend. John's wife was attacked, too, but thankfully survived.

My heart felt as if it had been ripped out of my chest. I was totally numb, yet felt indescribable pain at the same time. Our family was shattered and would never be the same.

From the moment I learned about John's death I became full of rage. It didn't matter to me who had killed my brother; I was bent on retribution. I became obsessed with revenge. Time did not heal—rather, it made me worse.

I now understand how a sane person can become so consumed with rage they could commit murder. My mind was going down a dark path. I had no thought for myself or even for my family, and began smoking and drinking heavily. At the same time I tried to maintain an image that I was spiritual and thinking clearly. I wanted others to believe I was okay, yet, my thoughts were continually on killing my brother's murderer. I visualized stabbing him to death, the same way he killed John. My inner core was filled with hate and resentment.

Along with the bottled-up hatred was incredible guilt; I couldn't forgive myself for not being there for my brother when he needed me most. The madder I got at myself, the more I hated the killer. It was becoming a vicious cycle and I saw myself becoming the person I despised the most. I had put myself in a prison.

> Refrain from anger and turn from wrath; do not fret—it leads only to evil.
> ~Psalm 37:8

AUGUST 26

A WORK IN PROGRESS

Mike Martin*, Indiana

I STAYED BUSY in an attempt to deal with the anger by seeking the death penalty for the murderer. I also helped John's wife and daughters and worked full-time. I completely withdrew from my immediate family. When my wife told me I was ignoring her and my daughters, I lashed out. I thought she was being selfish and did not know what I was going through. My priorities had become very messed up.

294

Strangely, in my moments of need, family or friends showed up or called, intervening just when I was at my lowest. It was the same people who kept showing up: our pastor, church members, friends, family members, and co-workers. They did not judge, or preach to me, they were just there. They brought meals, prayed, and listened to me cry. As the weeks turned into months, they were still there. They handed me songs on CDs, or mentioned books that might help. Each would end up being exactly what I needed to hear or read. Slowly, God worked through them to soften my heart.

The healing came in stages. I came to realize God does not make bad things happen; rather he gives us the freedom to live our lives, all the while wanting us to come to know him and love him of our own free will. I also realized I had to let go of the hate and anger. I had to forgive, and that is probably the hardest thing to do, especially when the person who has wronged you shows no remorse and doesn't ask for forgiveness.

For me, forgiveness was letting go of my rage and anger and not letting the killer keep me in a prison of hatred. Forgiving means I get to leave my prison of rage and, through the eyes of Jesus, I see the murderer as a broken person and a work in progress, someone God could still use for good on this earth.

This is a huge leap of faith for me. I am a work in progress, too. I've learned that God can change anyone's heart, but we have to first give it to him.

> Though you have made me see troubles, many and bitter, you will restore my life again; from the depths of the earth you will again bring me up.
> ~Psalm 71:20

FISHING FOR MEN

Rocky DeYoung, Minnesota

I MADE A crazy commitment when I became a Christian at twenty years of age. The first two books I read as a believer were about Hudson Taylor and George Müller, two nineteenth-century missionaries. Therefore, my concept of following the Lord meant to go wherever he takes you.

After living overseas for quite a while as a missionary, I returned to Minnesota and pastored a church for ten years. Then it seemed to me I'd paid my dues and it was time to do what I wanted to do—become a professional fishing guide! But I made the mistake of visiting the InnerChange Freedom Initiative (IFI) program at Minnesota Department of Corrections (MDOC)–Lino Lakes. I'd been working as a volunteer in a prison near where I've lived for seventeen years before I visited. I knew lots of guys in the system. I knew all the mistakes you can make, too, because I'd made them all. When I visited the IFI, I thought, *This is how it ought to be done.*

A program manager essentially stalked me until I caved to his offer to come on board. I took a significant pay cut in favor of having peace of mind, which was better than sitting on a lake pretending to be happy.

IFI has a ninety-day chemical-dependency education program as part of a longer eighteen-month pre-release program that assists MDOC in reaching all the men who are required to receive this treatment while incarcerated. I think 80 percent of the state's inmate population of 9,500 are required to get some sort of treatment, but the state is not equipped to meet a fraction of that number. We do it from a biblical perspective. You don't have to be a Christian and every participant is a volunteer.

My job as reentry manager is to help them with their release plan during the two years we have them. I work with case managers on the inside, parole officers on the outside, housing and jobs counselors—the people who will be in their circles. It's very rewarding.

In 2012 the MDOC crunched seven years of data to study our recidivism rates, which indicate the percentage of inmates incarcerated again within three years of release. Prisoners who finished the program, but didn't necessarily stay with their mentor 100 percent on the outside had a 2.4 percent recidivism rate. If an inmate finished the program and stayed with his mentor, the rate fell to .8 percent.

The state's comparable rate is 50 percent. They know that IFI works. They love us in this facility and we work well together.

I have always had a missions mindset, and prison is a mission field. I go to a different country (prison) where authentic change occurs every day.

Each of you should use whatever gift you have received to serve others, as faithful stewards of God's grace in its various forms. ~1 Peter 4:10

SPIRITUAL CRIMINALS

Rocky DeYoung, Minnesota

THE RISK of what we do here is the possibility that guys volunteering for the program can learn all the songs, all the Bible verses, all the material, and in the end become spiritual criminals twice as bad as when we started. We do everything we can to avoid that, so we try at every possible point to test their faith.

For example, let's say an inmate tells a staff member, "I want to follow Christ and have him run my life." The first test we'll put him through is honesty. He must lay out the factors surrounding his crime—all of them. We deal with his criminogenic behavior and thinking. If he does lay them out, we know his baseline for building a new life. If he wants to hide something, we know it because we have studied his case file extensively.

That's what makes working in prison difficult for outside volunteers because they don't really have that level of knowledge. They see prisoners one way when they pop in for their weekly or monthly visit, and we do see benefits from that participation. But spiritual criminals know how to manipulate the uninformed. They can't do that in our program.

We get countless opportunities to deal with guys who are playing spiritual games. Are they stealing stuff out of the kitchen? Are they selling things? We have to break that prison culture mind-set not once, but repeatedly over eighteen months. If a guy doesn't change inside the program's counterculture environment, he won't be changed upon release.

Spiritual criminals will get in a church and think, *Look at this fresh group of people I can use.* When you're entrenched in criminal thinking you love *things* and use *people. They'll ask me to give my testimony up front because it sounds exciting. Then I'm in and I can start manipulating.*

There are tipoffs we look for. We regularly recruit new classes of thirty to fifty guys. We pull all the classes together every day for community. I like to put a microphone up front and say, "Any of the new guys got anything to say?"

The first three men to stand up have signaled their first red flag. They can't help themselves. They think, *Here's a fresh group and I've got to start establishing my place in the pecking order.* Usually those guys don't make it.

> Then Peter said, "Ananias, how is it that Satan has so filled your heart that you have lied to the Holy Spirit and have kept for yourself some of the money you received for the land? Didn't it belong to you before it was sold? And after it was sold, wasn't the money at your disposal? What made you think of doing such a thing? You have not lied just to human beings but to God."
> ~Acts 5:3–4

AUGUST 29

RED FLAGS
Rocky DeYoung, Minnesota

IT'S TEMPTING to set people with dramatic conversions on a pedestal, but we have to be realistic about their behavior as much as our own. The red flags "regular" people deal with are the same as those of ex-prisoners, but usually with far heavier consequences in the case of the ex-prisoners.

The first big red flag for our men is women. As soon as *she* comes into the picture, before or after release, inmates are done thinking. They'll adjust *anything* to accommodate her. We battle it constantly. We're not telling them they can never have a relationship with a woman. However, it's worth doing the right way. It's not a separate issue, but part of the whole Christian-life package.

I have a couple of guys who were married when they came in or did this crazy thing of getting married when they were in prison. They were married, we dealt with it. We asked them not to go home with her when they got out. Instead, they went to a halfway house to learn how to date her and court her. They argued, "She'll never go for it," but we said, "You have to sell it—it's all about her. You're going to woo her and learn to treat her like a lady. Who's going to refuse that?" It worked out well for the few who tried it.

I'm not suggesting an Adamic "It's her fault" blame game. It takes two to tango. However, we must live in reality. We tell the guys, "You can't afford to be around a woman who would exercise such poor judgment as to hang around you." It sounds mean, but it's true.

I don't know any mothers who raise their daughters and recommend they find a nice guy in prison. A woman seeking romance from a prisoner is a red flag. He's got three things on his mind—a cigarette, a job, and sex. The flesh is very powerful and these red flags together nearly always result in problems that recently released prisoners can ill afford. That's why we recommend a one-year waiting period to give them a chance to get on their feet.

Two other giant red flags: When they isolate and when they get bored. If either of those things occurs, it's back to the old ways. "What's your plan when you get bored?" Doing the right thing can be boring. Prisoners are used to drama and chaos. Now they have to be content with mowing the grass or fixing the plumbing. Entertainment choices can be a trap, as can be lack of hobbies. Eighty percent of the guys I ask can't think of a single hobby. Downtime can lead to another downfall.

> Be very careful, then, how you live —not as unwise but as wise, making the most of every opportunity, because the days are evil. Therefore do not be foolish, but understand what the Lord's will is. ~Ephesians 5:15–17

AUGUST 30

LEARNING FROM MY MISTAKES
Rocky DeYoung, Minnesota

ONE REASON I know what works so well is that I've made all the mistakes myself. I've picked up a few timeless lessons that help me set and keep proper boundaries.

First, you can't work any harder than the inmate does on their situation. If I find myself at home thinking about his situation I'm way too invested. He'll try to do this with you all the time. He'll begin by trying to elicit some emotional attachment on your part. Then he'll start working you. If you're not aware of it, you're no longer in control. You can't teach it. You have to fall into it enough times before you can recognize the pattern. The answer is not shutting him out, but responding in constructive ways.

For example, I knew ex-prisoners who told me they had nowhere to live. I said, "You need to come live with me." We don't do that anymore. They have places to go. Often the reason they want to live with me is that they think there will be less accountability because of the friendship. At a halfway house they will have to work to follow house rules. The emotional leverage isn't there as it is in our friendship. They buck against the need to follow authority, but it's good for them. It's part of transition.

A second principle involves my attitude about full disclosure. I used to have this theory that I don't want to know an inmate's crime because then I'll be thinking of that when I work with him. I think a lot of volunteers have that perspective. That'll hurt you in the end when prisoners are released. If I don't know the history and a prisoner goes back to those things outside, then I'm just an enabler. You never start a prisoner relationship as a volunteer with "Hi, what are you in for?" but you eventually need to get to it and you want him to self-disclose.

Prisoners who shade the past, excuse the past, or are unwilling in the proper context to discuss their past are holding onto "Plan B" in their back pocket. That is a sure path back to prison. When you think about it, the same is true for anyone unwilling to be transparent and accountable to a trustworthy brother or sister in Christ. We all have sin to deal with. We avoid dealing with it at our peril.

I gave an account of my ways and you answered me; teach me your decrees.
~Psalm 119:26

LIVING OR DYING

Jeff Peck, Virginia

IN ONE of the many emotionally tugging scenes in *The Shawshank Redemption*, the two key characters, Andy and Red, sit against a wall and discuss their situation. For Andy, prison has been extremely brutal. Coming off an extended stint in isolation, he dreams of escaping to a little patch of paradise in Mexico. Red is resigned to his existence as a lifer with some clout, as the man who "can get things," but with no chance at surviving on the outside. He's institutionalized and that's about all there is to it.

Red chastises Andy for his escapism, reminding him he's stuck for the duration and that kind of escapist thinking just adds to the depression. Andy replies with determination, "It comes down to a simple choice: Get busy livin' or get busy dyin'."

The fictional movie was inspired by the real-life choices facing inmates today. A lifer I came to know in the Pennsylvania correctional system decided he could not live caged up the rest of his life. Franklin planned to stab an officer and die in the lethal response that would surely follow. He chose to get "busy dyin'." The officer survived and the professional staff threw him into four years of solitary confinement, where he found new life in Christ. That's when he got "busy livin'."

Franklin will never get out of prison, but has dedicated his life to serving his fellow inmates by assisting them in their education, their legal needs, and other ways in which God calls him. He even wrote a telling article in which he reminded his fellow prisoners that "life" is the first part of a "life sentence."

In one of the many paradoxes of Scripture, God calls us to lose our lives in order to find them. He commands his followers to deny themselves to find true life, meaning, and purpose. Paul went so far as to say, "For me to live is Christ, to die is gain."

The redemptive themes in *Shawshank* owe all their power to the Bible's emphatic proclamation of victory over sin and death. "Get busy livin' or get busy dyin'" didn't point to the cross, only to either despair or a humanistic hope of a peaceful beach away from life's pain and tribulation.

Prisoners and those of us who have never been caught each face a similar choice each day with one slight alteration: "Get busy livin' *and* get busy dyin'"—dying to self and all its flawed desires so in Christ we serve those still dying in the shackles of sin.

> I have been crucified with Christ and I no longer live, but Christ lives in me. The life I now live in the body, I live by faith in the Son of God, who loved me and gave himself for me. ~Galatians 2:20

MY UNEASY FEELINGS

Jeff Peck, Virginia

GOING INTO prisons across the country always meant I'd be meeting new prisoners for the first time. The reasons for my travel always involved getting stories or photos, which meant I'd be wading into the prison population, making me the target of many curiosity seekers.

While I was walking a medium-security unit in California for a yard event, camera in hand, an inmate strode up to me and challenged, "I'll bet you won't take a picture of me!" Every square inch of his exposed skin was inked with tattoos—including his face and skinhead. Prominently displayed on his forehead was the Nazi swastika. I did snap a shot, but he quickly retorted, "You'll never use it."

In Missouri's Petosi prison I met four inmates, each with a death sentence, but who were, until their day of execution, running a hospice care center for other inmates. I got to know them and their individual stories.

During Easter services at Angola, where Charlie Daniels fiddled and Chuck Colson preached, I walked among literally thousands of inmates seated in the rodeo arena. Some eye-balled me with cautious looks, while others welcomed me with warm smiles, high fives, and handshakes.

In these instances and many others I could never quite shake a certain tension. It was not about physical safety. When I shook the hand of a man sentenced to die or anyone else inside, the words, "Glad to meet you," didn't come easily. Why not?

My heart struggled with letting God dispense his grace as he wishes. If a man has repented and dedicated what life he has left to serving Jesus, who am I to question God's wisdom? But moral pride still whispered, *How can he smile and have joy knowing the pain he's inflicted? You and your family have been victims of crime.*

It's a form of spiritual prejudice, I confess. I do not struggle with it nearly as much today. God has used prisoners to humble me.

On a Florida yard one brutally hot, humid day, I brought some of Prison Fellowship's *Inside Journal* newspapers to pass around and take photos of men posing with them. After an hour or so, an inmate walked up to me holding one of the papers.

"You might want to take this one home. I don't think you want it circulating around here."

303

I was floored. I had snapped up a bunch from my office without realizing one had my home mailing address on it. That personal demonstration of concern for me from a man I had just met personified the gospel. Here is a brother in Christ looking out for me. Thank God for grace and mercy!

> Accept one another, then, just as Christ accepted you, in order to bring praise to God. ~Romans 15:7

SEPTEMBER 2

GOD'S LIGHTNING BOLT
Will Olsen, Pennsylvania

AS THE chaplain, I went in to the private counseling room to speak with Antoine*. His long hair didn't bother me, his tattoos didn't bother me, his piercings didn't bother me. His countenance did. I asked, *Lord, am I going to be able to get through this?* I've met a lot of inmates and heard just about everything one can hear, but his demeanor . . . he just looked as if he belonged to Satan. He wasn't very emotional, but withdrawn, downcast.

"Something's bothering you," I told him. "I'm here to help in any way I can. Is there anything you'd like to share with me?"

There was a long pause. Then he said, "My life is a total mess, a disaster. I'm really screwed up." I hear that a lot in a place like this.

"Do you know about eternal life? Do you believe in God? Heaven and hell?" His answers gave me an inkling he was involved in some kind of satanic group.

"Where are you now with all this?"

"I'm on my way out," he said flatly. That was the door God opened, so I walked through.

To my surprise, as I shared with him, tears started pooling on the table. It really looked as if there was genuine sorrow for the way he'd been living. He prayed with me to receive the forgiveness afforded by Christ on the cross and follow him.

A few days later Antoine told me, "Chaplain, I want you to know the day you came in, I was planning to commit suicide, but you were my lightning bolt. I was a member of Satan's church and if you would have looked at me on the street I would have ripped your face off. I thank you for what you did. I'm praying that God will help me become a counselor."

Then he asked if I could baptize him. I reviewed the meaning of baptism, what it stands for, and what it is not. Since we don't have baptismal fonts in prison, we get creative. I had two fellow inmates hold him in a dunking position as if we were in a pool. As he bent down, I poured water on him from a Styrofoam cup.

Four other prisoners were so inspired by his example, they came forward to be baptized, too. Antoine became a regular at our Bible studies, and was released about four months later.

I received a letter from him thanking me for our time together, and affirming over and over that his change was real. He was dedicated to serving the Lord and stated the name of the church he attended. He had offered his services to the pastor for anything he needed (even if it was scrubbing toilets) and he began leading a Bible study and serving the homeless.

> For God, who said, "Let light shine out of darkness," made his light shine in our hearts to give us the light of the knowledge of God's glory displayed in the face of Christ. ~2 Corinthians 4:6

SEPTEMBER 3

OVERWHELMED BY WHAT I LOVE

Will Olsen, Pennsylvania

I WAS HAVING a melancholy day, feeling overwhelmed really. The heaviness that gets to me most is due to seeing guys come back, numerous times. For example, I know a man who came back nine times. I visited with him that ninth time and just stared him in the eyes. I said to myself, *I'm not going to say a word until I hear him say what we both know: 'I'm tired of all this and I'm ready to talk about God.'* I know in my head that

God's ways are not mine, but a person still gets down from time to time living around so much brokenness, despite his best efforts to extend hope and healing.

So I paused and said, "Lord I need help, it's a lot to do, I love what I do, but sometimes it's overwhelming."

Immediately in my spirit he told me, "Stop. Pull all those notes out of your drawer and put them up." My drawer has been filling up with "thank you's" for years and I just never took the time to do anything with them.

"Lord, that's going to take a while."

"Put them up. Then read every one."

"That will take a couple of hours!"

"Put 'em up. Read every single one."

God is so patient. It took me close to three hours before I finished gathering the notes and found a way to organize them all on my office wall. Sure enough, I didn't just tack them up, but I started reading and remembering all those men and women with whom I had an opportunity to do or say something for Jesus that helped them. Most of the notes came from ex-prisoners who were doing well in their freedom.

I told God I was done and I heard him say, "Now, that's why you're here."

> Let us not become weary in doing good, for at the proper time we will reap a harvest if we do not give up. ~Galatians 6:9

SEPTEMBER 4

ATTEMPTED MURDER

Ted Shaw, Florida

WHEN YOU'RE lost, your thinking really is twisted. My logic only worked by first assuming a lot of wrong things. I burglarized people who "made it too easy" by leaving keys in the car or tool sheds unlocked. I did two short stints in jail for that. Then I moved into marijuana hunting.

My partner and I reconnected after my second jail stint. We located small farms growing patches of weed. We took it and added to that by robbing drug dealers.

Even though you're living wrong, your conscience still talks. I'd get so scared before a job I'd throw up. Once the fear passed, the adrenaline kicked in and I would do things I didn't think I was capable of doing. This went on for three years.

In June 1983 we kidnapped and robbed a drug dealer. He convinced us he was not the main man and could get us more money from his partners, if we let him go. We did. He disappeared.

Not long after, my partner spotted the dude's vehicle two counties over. After a few days of surveillance we grabbed him in his carport and hauled him into the backyard, where he started struggling. I was high on cocaine and had been drinking. He grabbed a gun, I grabbed mine and we wrestled until the guns went off. He was shot twice, but survived. Shocked, I retreated to my secluded residence deep in the woods.

Police from two counties swooped in and arrested us. My partners all turned against me. The police charged my girlfriend as accessory after the fact. She didn't know anything about my crimes so I made a deal: I'd cop out to the attempted murder charge as long as charges were dropped against her. Ten days later, after sawing through the seams of reinforced window plating with a smuggled tool and homemade paint to cover the cracks, I escaped the detention center.

I ran to West Virginia still living my lifestyle, but returned to Florida after a year-and-a-half to reconnect with my girlfriend. I can't say for sure what was happening to me, but I was getting tired of it all. Maybe it sounds strange, but I wanted to turn myself in.

I called a trusted police officer who was a family friend. He was also captain of the Criminal Investigative Division (CID). When he picked me up he didn't bother to handcuff me. Before taking me to jail, he took a detour to a special building for investigators. He ushered me into a room full of men and women, all with shoulder holsters, in the midst of something very important. They looked a little upset we had interrupted. After walking around the table greeting folks, on the way out, he stopped at the door and turned around. He announced, "Just checking on y'all, and by the way, this is Ted Shaw." These people were the task force set up to track me down because they had heard I was back in the area.

The judge gave me seventy-five years for attempted murder, but no one ever charged me with the detention center escape.

> For although they knew God, they neither glorified him as God nor gave thanks to him, but their thinking became futile and their foolish hearts were darkened. ~Romans 1:21

MYSTERIOUS WORK

Ted Shaw, Florida

GOD WORKS in mysterious ways. On March 6, 1992, I got off early from my prison work and returned to my cell at 3 p.m. Nobody else was around.

In the cell there was a book I hadn't noticed before about evolution. The basic story line: It took millions of years for a cell to become man. I just threw it in the corner and said, "What kind of belief is that?!"

Then I heard in my head, *What do you believe?* Suddenly I became convicted of all the things I'd done, but I came up with excuses. *How am I going to give all this up?* What will so-and-so think? Then I see my situation. I have nothing. I'd only done seven of a seventy-five-year sentence. I'd never been to chapel except for the mandatory AIDS class. I didn't know any Christians, and didn't want to. I was in my own world and figured I was okay.

That day the Holy Spirit of God convicted me. After wrestling for hours I said a prayer: "Lord, I believe in you. If you'll have me and accept me, I'll do what you want me to do." No lights or sirens went off. I just went to sleep. Most peaceful sleep I've ever had. Next morning, I knew it was real. It would change my life and thought patterns.

I found the chaplain, who set me up with a Bible and baptized me. I also found a Bible study that took me three years to complete and was critical to my growth. Finally, I started going to church services.

A few weeks after this all happened an inmate named Pappy* swung by and said, "I got us." I knew what he meant. He was making good after bumming a big joint of reefer from me some time ago. It was unusual for Pappy to ask me for reefer because he had six officers bringing him dope. When we finished smoking that time he promised, "I'll getcha." He was one of the biggest dealers the chain gang ever saw.

So he saw me and said, "Come on."

"I don't smoke it no more." He looked at me funny.

"What happened?"

"Lord saved me."

"Well, I'm saved, too."

"That's between you and the Lord, but I don't want it anymore." And I didn't. The Lord knew I couldn't win that battle in the flesh—he just took it from me. From the day he saved me to this very moment I've never even wanted marijuana, nicotine, or any other drug. That was the biggest miracle God performed at the time of my salvation. I know he doesn't do it that way for everyone. He took it from me and people were shocked.

My friend Adams* was into the same thing I was, but he was a businessman selling it. He noticed he and I were talking less. The Lord gave me new friends, a new crowd, and that's who I was hanging out with. I'd catch him looking at me sometimes because we were in the same dorm. Finally he came down and said, "So you're saved, huh?"

"Yeah." I was studying the Bible.

"I'm all right with the Lord."

"Okay. I am, too." I don't know what it was, the life I was living maybe, but he got convicted. Not long after, he ran up to me shining like a new guy, to tell me he now really had found Jesus.

Unless I go away, the Advocate will not come to you; but if I go, I will send him to you. When he comes, he will prove the world to be in the wrong about sin and righteousness and judgment: about sin, because people do not believe in me . . . ~John 16:7–9

SEPTEMBER 6

HE'S GOT YOUR BACK

Robert McDonald, Tennessee

I FEEL LOUSY admitting this, but I never really gave much thought to the impact my incarceration had on my family. While locked up I was too busy just trying to exist.

I've never been in the military, never fought in a war, yet I was in a constant spiritual battle while behind steel doors. Those "battles" were everywhere and at all times of the day and night. My mantra quickly became, "Jesus, keep my back!"

When walking in the "yard" I would have to stay alert, being careful to avoid clusters of men; when I entered a classroom I would quickly scan the seats, careful of whom I sat beside; during my job in the kitchen I tried to remain silent and dutiful. Worship service on Sunday morning should have been my favorite hour of the week (unless I got a visit from the outside—those supersede everything), but I quickly learned that even worship services were meeting grounds for gang members. I could never let my guard down; there was never any true relaxation or respite behind that barbed wire.

It was only in the months following my release that I came to realize what torment I had put my loved ones through, especially my mother. I am sure she asked herself, "Where did I go wrong?" I never will have a true grasp of the pain I caused her. All I know is that I want to try to make it up to her. I desperately want to change, and I know that is what she wants, too.

While I can testify that Jesus did have my back while I was locked up, I also know he will continue to protect me, as long as I give him first place in my life. It's not gonna be easy. Temptation is all around me. The spiritual battle is not over, but with Jesus by my side I will prevail. I know now how important it is to keep Jesus first—doing so is the only hope I have of staying clean and free.

Not only do I want my life to glorify the Lord, but I also want to make my momma proud. I never want to hurt her like that again.

The LORD is good, a refuge in times of trouble. He cares for those who trust in him. ~Nahum 1:7

SEPTEMBER 7

THE POWER OF PRAYER
Maggie Cochran, New York

DESPITE THE governor commuting her death sentence to thirty-three years to life and giving her a chance at parole, Donna remained mean, bitter, and angry. She claimed she was born again eighteen years earlier and that Jesus was her Lord, but still her mean streak remained.

Whenever she passed by anyone she deemed a hypocrite (which was usually everyone), she'd say something nasty to them, adding that they were "going to burn in hell."

I, along with hundreds of others, dreaded seeing her coming. For several years the sight of her made my heart pound and my anxiety level drastically increase. There was just no way to get along with Donna.

You'd think that getting off death row after committing multiple murders would have made her more grateful, but it did not. Even after participating in several ministries her tirades continued.

Last winter, while looking through an old issue of an inspirational magazine, I read a story about a man whose family and friends said that, despite decades of prayer, he remained mean and hateful over perceived injustices. His presence made people tremble in fear and dread. In this way, he sounded just like Donna.

For more than twenty years this man's family and friends prayed faithfully for him, and one day, to the astonishment of his wife, he announced he would like to go to church with her. Amazingly, he eventually came to ask Jesus into his heart and even became an active Christian, happily assisting others.

Many of us had been praying for Donna for almost two decades. Knowing there is strength in numbers, I wrote to the magazine and asked to have Donna put on its prayer list, specifying her anger problem.

A few weeks later Donna walked up to me and I froze, expecting a verbal barrage to be unleashed. Instead, I was shocked when she most sincerely said, "Maggie, I don't know why I can't get along with you. I've searched for a reason and just can't figure out why you make me mad." Then, she suddenly began to cry. "Can you please forgive me?"

Shocked speechless, I finally replied, "Of course I forgive you, Donna."

We hugged and Donna walked away. I had to sit back down . . . stunned.

A few weeks later, Donna overheard me asking the chaplain about the Bible-based Anger Resolution Seminar coming soon.

"Sign me and Maggie up so we can be 'anger buddies' and go through it together," Donna said.

We did, and it's been a few weeks since the class ended. Donna is a different person now—she's dealing with her past, is turning to God daily for patience, and is trusting him with her future. She is a constant reminder to us of the power of prayer.

If you believe, you will receive whatever you ask for in prayer. ~Matthew 21:22

PRESSING ON

Pat Collins, Ohio

ALMOST FIFTEEN years ago I wrestled with the challenge to go inside our local jail and minister to the ladies there. I admit I was afraid. However, I knew I needed to be obedient, so I signed up for orientation at the jail. It was a little overwhelming, but I was reminded by the staff I could not get lost or go anywhere I wasn't allowed—the halls and doors were all locked and monitored.

I kept having doubts in my mind, such as, *This isn't your calling,* and, *You'll say the wrong thing.*

A few weeks after orientation I learned that my background security check was finished. I could now go inside the jail and meet Cathy*, my first inmate.

When I arrived at the jail, I sat outside in the parking lot and prayed. I longed to hit it off with Cathy right away and encourage her in the Lord.

"What if she doesn't like you?" the Enemy whispered in my ear.

I fought the fear and went inside. After signing in, I showed my badge and told the officer I was there to visit Cathy.

"Go on up to the visitation room. It's empty," he said.

To get to the room I had to take the elevator. I wasn't sure which floor I needed, but then I remembered I couldn't get lost. Someone would direct me.

Once inside, the elevator door didn't want to shut. I tried every button.

"This is a sign," I heard the Enemy taunt.

When at last I made it inside the visitation room I waited several minutes. No Cathy. Finally, an officer came to the door and said exactly what I had been dreading: "I'm sorry, but Cathy does not want to see you."

Again, that pesky voice: "This is not for you."

I scooted my chair back.

"But," the officer continued, "if you don't mind, there is another inmate who is having a tough time right now. Would you mind seeing her?"

"Sure." I was there to help, after all. It really didn't matter who it was.

When I met Danielle my heart instantly melted—she looked so sad and couldn't stop crying. She told me "something was missing" in her life,

312

and we talked. Eventually I asked her if she wanted to invite Jesus into her life. When she tearfully said, "Yes," I knew this was God's divine appointment. And I knew with certainty, this ministry *was* for me.

> . . . that our God may make you worthy of his calling, and that by his power he may bring to fruition your every desire for goodness and your every deed prompted by faith. ~2 Thessalonians 1:11

HOOKED ON JAIL MINISTRY

Pat Collins, Ohio

AFTER THAT first visit I knew I would be back—I had found my calling. And now, fifteen years later, I've been going inside the jail on Sundays and leading two, sometimes three, sessions of women's worship services. I share the truth of God's Word with female captives, hopefully setting at least a few free. It is a spiritual battle and I, like all Christians, am on the Enemy's "list," so to speak. As in any ministry, it's imperative to be in the Word and in prayer every day. The battle is the Lord's, but we still have to put on our armor to be able to stand against the attacks.

Most Saturday afternoons I lock myself in my office to hear the message the Lord wants me to share on Sunday. One Saturday, though, God was silent. I ended up recycling bits and pieces of previous messages and did not have my usual peace about it.

When I arrived at the jail lobby I prayed with Caroline, the guitarist who led the worship music, but I still felt unsure of the message. I was desperately begging God to show up.

While Carolyn and I greeted the women as they filed into the classroom, my heart filled with compassion for them, moreso than usual. There was an unmistakable heaviness in the air. As they shared about their week—their family concerns back home, their upcoming court battles, their shame and embarrassment for having been arrested—my burden for them only increased. "Lord, show me how to help these ladies."

Suddenly I knew what God wanted me to do. It was plain and simple: Forget the message. Pray.

I walked around the room, obediently laying hands on each of the ladies and praying for the specific needs they had shared. By the time the forty-five-minute session ended there wasn't a dry eye in the room. In place of the heaviness from earlier was a new hope—and unexplainable joy. We all sensed it and knew—God had been in our midst.

> Put on the full armor of God, so that you can take your stand against the devil's schemes. ~Ephesians 6:11

OUT FOR GOOD

Mary Booth, Ohio

I HAD A LONG history of incarceration—in jail at least ten times. Each time I swore it would be my last. Most of my offenses involved stealing.

Around my third time in jail I decided to attend the Sunday afternoon worship service led by Pat Collins. I had been far from God and wasn't sure he was even interested in a wretch like me. Still, I felt nudged to go. At the least, it got me out of the module and my cell for a while.

I liked Pat's inspirational messages and kept going back. Pat and I became friends. She was also in the Be-a-Friend program and started visiting me every week. I was impressed with her strong, unwavering faith. And, she didn't judge or scold me each time I got arrested.

A few years ago, while out, I ended up falling for the wrong guy. He was hooked on cocaine and I got hooked, too. I lost everything: my home, my belongings, and worst of all, my family. I have three wonderful daughters and ten grandkids whom I love very much. I couldn't believe the hold the drug had on me. I became homeless for several years and stole things to get money for the drugs. I slept under bridges and in cornfields. My daughters put up with a lot from me and tried to get me help, but eventually they had to exercise tough love toward their mom.

When I got arrested for drugs it ended up saving my life. Pat was a Be-a-Friend to another lady, so she sent a new volunteer, a good friend of hers, Connie Cameron, to see me. When Connie appeared I had been feeling real bad. I had desperately called out to God to please send someone to me soon. Then she showed up, just when I thought he had abandoned me.

Connie and I became good friends, too. I looked forward to seeing both her and Pat every week. They helped me grow in the Lord, they prayed with me, and they went to court with me. When I finally got out five years ago, they both stayed in touch. When I moved into my first home, they and the ladies from their church gave me my first housewarming. I couldn't believe that total strangers brought me gifts and food.

I've stayed out of jail ever since and have remained drug free. I'm thrilled to say my kids and grandkids have witnessed the change in me, too, and they are all back in my life.

I'm not sure where I would be right now—probably in prison or dead—if it weren't for the Licking County Jail Ministry. God used them to get my attention and to help me get my life turned around. I am forever grateful.

> If you repent, I will restore you that you may serve me. ~Jeremiah 15:19

SEPTEMBER 11

A DEADLY BROKEN PROMISE
Samuel Pitts, Florida

I CAME INTO this world to alcoholic sharecropper parents in 1938. Naturally I fell in line with the drinking-and-fighting lifestyle, but did finish high school before going into the Air Force. I returned home prematurely with an undesirable discharge for my drinking and raising Cain.

I married, and when our fifth child arrived I had a serious accident on the job. They put a plate in my head and at age twenty-eight I fought to walk and talk again. Lying in my hospital bed I wondered what was going to happen to my family, so I did what a lot of desperate people do. I said a little prayer: "God, if you'll let me get out of here, I'll never drink again." Two weeks later I hobbled out holding onto my wife and a walking stick.

For the next twelve years everything I did prospered. I went into business for myself and made a lot of money building and selling homes. We had six daughters and three sons. I really thought I was somebody. I forgot about my promise.

One afternoon I finished a job for a contractor. He came by and asked me for the bill.

"I don't have it figured out yet. I'll find you in a couple hours." He asked me to meet him at a certain address. I got a haircut, found the place. No one was there except a bartender who asked, "What'll you have?"

"Can of Budweiser."

Twelve years of sobriety didn't matter. The moment I put that can to my lips, it was on. I knew I'd get drunk. I drank from 1 p.m. until 8 p.m., when I drove to another beer joint and stayed until they closed. I met a man there. I thought he did something that he hadn't done. In the drunken confrontation I killed him. Next morning I was in the county jail for first-degree murder.

My family all about went into shock. I did, too. I hired a good lawyer and was gullible enough to think if you tell the right lies, you'll win your case. But you can't fool everybody. My next shock was prison. I realized the wrong I did and wanted to make amends for it, but didn't know where to start. I thought, *Oh, boy! You lied to God and this is what you get.*

A lot of folks say they're Christian, but they're playing games. I was thankful for the healing and the twelve years of career success, but I never *knew* God or served him. It was all about me, the money, and the good times. In an instant I wrongfully took a life and, at the same time, threw my own away.

> Many will say to me on that day, "Lord, Lord, did we not prophesy in your name and in your name drive out demons and in your name perform many miracles?" Then I will tell them plainly, "I never knew you. Away from me, you evildoers!" ~Matthew 7:22–24

THE SLOW PROCESS
OF CHANGE

Samuel Pitts, Florida

I SPENT ALMOST a year in jail during the trial phase. A priest from my neighborhood came to visit me quite frequently. He, more than anyone else up to that point, led me to Christ. But I was like a child in my understanding, with no one to teach me.

Facing twenty-five to life in prison sobered me up. In jail there are not very many people who can lead you. I'm the perfect example of a bunch of folks with crazy lives and crazy ways of thinking. At first you don't trust anyone, especially where they put me—UCI Raiford, "the Rock."

So I'm surrounded by a new world of regular violence. I don't really know or trust anyone. I've made a decision to change my life through Christ, but still have a lot of the old self controlling my thoughts and actions. I think it's amazing that God was able to deal with my situation just fine despite my confusion.

That's where I first met Mr. Ken Cooper—a middle-aged bank robber. There was something different about him and the guys he was hanging out with. He seemed to really know Jesus more than anyone else around me. He turned a lot of young men to Christ. He had a magnetism. When he latched onto someone, he never gave up.

We became friends. He never tried to ram Christianity down my throat, but he helped me in every area he could. It was slow learning, but I'd gain a little every time. I had so much of the old ways in me, so much rotten stuff to get out.

Prison is not the easiest place to break old habits. Christians do catch a lot of flak. They're made fun of, jumped on sometimes. I did seven years at the Rock before the DOC transferred me to Appalachia Correctional. They released Ken early and he started developing programs for prisoners. He'd encourage me when I saw him occasionally as he came through my prison.

The support from other Christians is vital to making it. Many claim to be sincere like Ken, but only a few are, and they seek you out. One thing that sincere believers do is stick with you through your life even if you don't have it all figured out just yet. I had much to learn, and my new friends didn't sugarcoat anything I was still doing wrong. But they were faithful and I'm grateful to them. I think that's how God means it to be.

Better is open rebuke than hidden love.

> Wounds from a friend can be trusted, but an enemy multiplies kisses.
> ~Proverbs 27:5–6

SEPTEMBER 13

GREED

Samuel Pitts, Florida

OF ALL the stuff I needed to get rid of, greed hung on like a cancer. I justified my dealings because my family needed it. They were really suffering. When I gambled, loan sharked, or whatever I did, I gave some to them—that made it okay in my mind. That's the ruination of a lot of men—the value they put on a dollar.

Among other things I did for income, I made rings using materials normally found around the dental lab where I worked. People legally make rings all the time except for one thing: In prison it's against the rules. As we know, there are no big rules or little rules. You have to observe them all. There again was my thinking: *I've got to make a dollar.*

I felt I could not turn money down. I needed it. I justified it like during Christmas. I could slip some money to my children and grandchildren that would buy them dinner—that made me feel good and them, too. The ends justified the means. It also gained me quite a bit of respect on the yard. I made some good bargains because other prisoners knew I wouldn't tell officers. All this is wrong as it can be, but at the time I felt it was a must. It was greed.

I heard people preach—like Ken Cooper—who said, "You don't need it." Jesus has what I need—doing things my way only leads to trouble. As long as I had money, thieves were trying to get it, too. I worked to keep it hidden from them and the police who did shakedowns of our cells. Avoiding detection always eats at you.

It wasn't until I went to another prison I got serious with God about this. I planned to put in for a pardon. My older sister told me she and

Mama would hire a lawyer. Then surprisingly she confronted me by saying, "If you're going to keep on sending us money, we know you're doing wrong. We'll be wasting any money we spend on a lawyer because this will come out."

> Whoever loves money never has enough; whoever loves wealth is never satisfied with their income. This too is meaningless. ~Ecclesiastes 5:10

CONFESSIONS
Samuel Pitts, Florida

THAT STARTED it. I slowed, then stopped, my loan sharking business. It took a few years to quit the gambling. The harder I prayed, however, the more enjoyment I got out of life. All of a sudden, I realized I had what I needed regardless of what amount of money I had. I also pushed aside those problems hiding my sin. It opened a new level of freedom I had never experienced.

I recently wrote a letter to the parole board about a fellow I left behind at the program we had done together. I first met him in the early eighties when he was a crooked, no-good scoundrel. If his name ever came up I thought of him as nothing but trash. He owed me $500 when we parted ways. And oh! I was mad about that. We had a deal going on to make us a lot of money. It didn't pan out. Most of them don't.

Twenty years passed before I saw him again. We were both attending the transition program for lifers. So I went to see him, still a little bit angry. He spoke to me first.

"Sam, I'm so sorry things worked out the way they did. I don't get but about $25 a month, but I'm going to go to the store and buy you something."

I just blurted out, "Tex, I've been out that money twenty-five years. I'll keep doing without it. Debt's paid. Had I not been doing wrong, you couldn't have gotten a penny. My greed is what caused this—not you." I felt a big relief telling him that. It felt so good to turn some old garbage loose. I asked him, "You seem a bit different—have you considered going with Christ?"

"Already got him, Sam." We started hanging out. He would beat me to our program meetings and set up two chairs at the front since neither one of us could see or hear very well anymore. So we had a better friendship than we had the first time. The first time wasn't really friendship. I used him. This time, it was genuine brotherly love.

> Therefore confess your sins to each other and pray for each other so that you may be healed. ~James 5:16

SEPTEMBER 15

HOW I STOPPED CUSSIN'

Samuel Pitts, Florida

LIVING AT the Rock had many problems, dangers, and temptations. But one of the first things I realized I needed to do after giving my life to Christ was to break my cussing. That was something inside me that had to come out. It made no difference where I was living. Cuss words just flowed out of me like second nature. Mind you, I didn't know much about the Bible yet, but something inside me knew it didn't wash with God.

It took me eight months to stop using the Lord's name in vain. Every time I would say it or think it, I would say "Praise God" three times. I did it silently at first, then out loud. People would hear me and say, "What are you talking about?"

"If you or I cuss God once, I'm going to praise him three times." One day we had to change our bunks around in the cell. I lifted up the top bunk when it somehow bumped the light fixture, which came down and knocked a hole in my head. It stung something fierce and I shouted "God Almighty!" Instantly I knew I was done cussing.

> But now you must also rid yourselves of all such things as these: anger, rage, malice, slander, and filthy language from your lips. ~Colossians 3:8

OWNING UP TO FICTION

Samuel Pitts, Florida

IT'S NOT easy to talk about what I did. At first, I tried to justify it. He did my family wrong and he got what he deserved. It's easier to see yourself as defender than murderer and I wanted to avoid the death penalty.

As time goes on and you keep feeding yourself this fiction you start to wonder if it's really true or a lie. I realized I had to quit lying.

I can't just clean up the living room. The whole house must be clean if I'm going to be with Jesus. I started accepting the fact that I was wrong, 100 percent wrong. The man shouldn't have been killed. I shouldn't have done it. For a time I could not forgive myself.

I prayed about it and asked God to forgive me. That's all I could do to make amends. No one ever came forward on my victim's behalf to speak against my release at parole hearings. We always look for that. This man was not from the area. He was a drug-headed drifter. No one knew him. It makes the tragedy that much worse. It gave me a lot of relief to tell God I was wrong and accept 100 percent responsibility for it.

> Then I acknowledged my sin to you and did not cover up my iniquity. I said, "I will confess my transgressions to the Lord." And you forgave the guilt of my sin. ~Psalm 32:5

TIME WARP

Samuel Pitts, Florida

I LEFT PRISON July 12, 2011, after more than twenty-seven years inside. The entire world had changed. It's like a caveman stepping out into New York City. In my hometown near Gainesville, Florida, there are so many new highways and buildings, I can't find anything. Nothing looks the same. Street names I recognize that used to be dirt roads are now six- or eight-lane highways.

Most of the people I grew up with and went to school with are dead. Two of my sisters and a brother are dead. My 100-year-old mother is still alive, but she's out of her mind with Alzheimer's.

Everything is different. The prices stagger me. I can't bring myself to pay $5 for a gallon of milk. The last gallon I bought was 99 cents. A loaf of bread was 35 cents. Now they cost close to $10 for two items. I didn't use to care about the price of things back when I was living my life without Christ. If I wanted it, I bought it. Now I pay attention because I'm on a very limited income. Sometimes people take me out to eat and they'll spend $80 or $90 for the group tab. That used to be two weeks of work for me.

I don't expect I have that much time left, so I believe that God would have me doing just what I'm doing now: telling folks, especially young people, about their choices. Explaining how I landed in prison and how easy it is to fall into it. I have a great audience to start with—my grandsons, my sons, and others I meet around the neighborhood. Word gets out in the community you're from prison and folks don't always listen.

One grandson told me he wanted to be just like me. I said, "No, you don't! Five minutes is about all you'll want and all you can take."

I also attend AA meetings. People hear my life story there and want to ask questions about it. I enjoy doing it. Cooper has also set me up with a few speaking opportunities to share what God did in my life. I understand why a lot of people don't quite appreciate the price I paid for my crime nor what my family suffered for my actions. We ex-prisoners deserve the suffering we got and, for those of us who took a life, it's hard to see how anything could pay for the damage of that act. It's true.

But I think, too, the gospel asks each person to think about what we deserve in front of a holy God. I agree with God about the many things I've done wrong throughout my life. I also thank him there's blood on the cross enough to cover them all.

NOTE: Sam died of health complications in the spring of 2012.

> He is the atoning sacrifice for our sins, and not only for ours but also for the sins of the whole world. ~1 John 2:2

FROM "MISSION"
TO "GRACE"

Carol Davis, California

AFTER SEVEN years of ministry as the founder and executive director of the Mission of Grace Foundation, I began feeling a significant change coming—a change from a focus on mission to a focus on grace. I wasn't sure what that would mean, but I felt it strongly.

Our speaking and teaching ministry's primary audience was church leaders and Christian professionals seeking clarity of purpose and direction for their lives and ministries. For years, participants successfully emerged from our classes with written mission, vision, and goal statements. But something new was brewing inside me.

One night I had a dream I was walking through a field of huge snakes with an employee in my husband's construction business. This man had been in and out of prison in his younger years. Initially, I thought I was being called to walk with him to help slay some "spiritual snakes" in his life. He had been physically free from prison for more than twenty years, but he still wasn't free in his heart, mind, and soul. However, I would soon learn it wasn't this man God wanted to deal with, so much as it was me! Each time we walked through an issue in his life, God would speak to my heart, "Carol, you have the same problem."

My knee-jerk reaction was, "How could you compare me to a former felon?!"

God quickly showed me sinful things about myself I had never seen. I had never struggled with receiving God's love and grace. When I slipped into a depression, feeling incredibly inadequate and unworthy, he showed me my desperate need for his grace and forgiveness.

During these two years of struggle our teaching ministry came to a standstill. Then, after an intense healing journey, God invited me back into ministry—same content—but a new audience—prisoners! The first prison ground on which I stepped was the same prison where the employee had been incarcerated.

Prison is the ultimate place for grace. Many male inmates have made first-time decisions for Christ through our "Passport to Purpose" program. Our team of volunteers making this possible is composed of former officers, inmates, and everything in between. And now, many inmates and paroles are living their mission *with intention* from the foundation of God's grace!

> For you, O God, tested us; you refined us like silver. You brought us into prison and laid burdens on our backs . . . but you brought us to a place of abundance. ~Psalm 66:10–12

THE SMOKING BIBLE

Carol Davis, California

THE FIRST time I attended chapel in the highest-security yard at California State Prison, Solano, I wasn't sure what to expect. I had been asked to consider teaching our Passport to Purpose program to the men on this volatile yard, but I wondered whether I could make a difference. Were their hearts too tough to penetrate?

To answer my question, the Lord used the testimony of a man named Willy to touch my own heart. In 1973 Willy was sentenced to sixteen months in a California state prison. But, at the end of his sentence, things took a different turn and he ended up serving eight more years. Then, right before he was paroled, he gave in to violence and earned another fourteen years.

Willy was devastated. He felt he couldn't handle doing any more time and made a rope to hang himself. He set the date to end his suffering— December 13, his birthday. That date seemed to make things whole.

On December 11, somebody slipped a little green Gideon Bible across the floor, under his cell door.

"Normally, I would've used the pages to roll and smoke weed," he said. "But that day, that Bible smoked me!"

As Willy began to read, he began to see his need for a Savior. The words began penetrating his mind and his heart.

On his birthday, instead of grabbing his rope, he grasped hold of his newfound hope in Jesus. From that point on, Willy was on fire for the

Lord! He told anyone who would listen about his new friend Jesus, and even boldly told those who *wouldn't* listen.

After many years of walking with Jesus, Willy made parole. In the end, he spent more than thirty-five years in prison, rather than sixteen months. Despite the huge difference in time, amazingly he was not bitter, but thankful, giving all the praise and honor to God for rescuing him that fateful day through his little green Bible.

> For the word of God is alive and active. Sharper than any double-edged sword, it penetrates even to dividing soul and spirit, joints and marrow; it judges the thoughts and attitudes of the heart. ~Hebrews 4:12

SEPTEMBER 20

THE ONE PERCENT
Carol Davis, California

GOVERNOR JERRY Brown Affirming More Releases of Killers," threatens the front page of a California newspaper. "High Number of Violent Parolees Live Downtown," warns another headline. Scary stuff to citizens fearful for their families.

At one time, the release of more "killers" would've alarmed me. But now, after being involved in prison ministry, I see with new eyes.

In California, non-lifers serve their sentenced time, then are released. Lifers (those with open-ended sentences, i.e., twenty-five years to life) serve their minimum time, but then must demonstrate their rehabilitation to a parole board, which determines whether they are still a threat to society. Many of these lifers are the same "killers" referenced in the newspaper headline, although not all lifers have killed someone.

A couple of years ago, I was taken aback when I reviewed the list of lifer inmates scheduled for parole board hearings at the prison where I teach. Shockingly, I knew almost all of them! Most had been devoted small-group facilitators in our one-year Passport to Purpose program. These high-caliber men of faith certainly were not the scary type of people I imagined lifers to be.

Over the years, I have found most Christian lifers, who are near, at, or past the end of their minimum sentence, to be deeply committed to personal growth with a burning desire to make a positive difference in the lives of others. They often feel compelled to focus the rest of their lives on giving back after taking so much from their victims, families, and communities. But, despite their efforts to make amends, they're still usually only remembered for what they've done, not for who they've become.

According to the California Department of Corrections, in the past twenty-one years, only 0.06 percent of California's paroled murderers returned to prison due to a new felony—that's right, far less than 1 percent!

Contrast that fact with the alarming newspaper headline about the release of more "killers." In actuality, the threat to society is pretty minimal. However, because of the severity of their past crimes, people are afraid to help them, house them, employ them, befriend them, or even worship with them.

In the life of the early church, there was a killer many Christians were terrified to encounter, even after he had a radical conversion experience. Just imagine if the early church had refused to embrace the transformation of the killer Saul into the apostle Paul. We would have missed so much!

If the apostle Paul was redeemable, maybe there are some others deserving of another look, another chance, and another life.

> ". . . he tried to join the disciples, but they were all afraid of him, not believing that he was really a disciple." ~Acts 9:26

SEPTEMBER 21

GRACE GIVERS OR GUILT TRIPPERS?

Carol Davis, California

PETE, WHY don't you tell us a little about yourself?" said the Bible study leader to the newest participant joining the group. Pete, a clean-cut, nicely-dressed gentleman, looked around the circle as his heart pounded against his ribs. With all eyes focused on him, he replied, "What would you like to know? Where should I begin?"

In an attempt to relieve the pressure of the moment, someone in the group popped off, "Why don't you start by telling us about your prison record?" Laughter erupted throughout the room.

Pete smiled, and then dropped the bomb. "Well—I actually was released just six weeks ago."

Silence. Complete, deathly silence.

All eyes fell to the floor as a thick cloud of shame and embarrassment descended upon the room. Everyone who had previously laughed now felt incredibly insensitive.

Pete, on the other hand, while slightly uncomfortable, now felt completely liberated! In agreeing to come to this Bible study he had wrestled with how he would ever tell his new group about his life journey. He didn't want to be in a group where he couldn't be authentic and real. God had miraculously protected him through his incarceration and he wanted to be able to share about his struggles and victories. Little did he know that God was going to solve the problem for him on the first night by providing him an unexpected opportunity to share his testimony!

For many former prisoners, if not most, this would have been a debilitating moment, serving as an excuse to never return to any group, especially a church group. Fortunately, God knew it was just what Pete needed. However, it was a good reminder that we need to be sensitive to visitors, making them feel comfortable in our midst.

According to the Pew Center on the States, one in one hundred Americans is incarcerated, and one in thirty adults is on parole or probation residing in our communities. Former inmates live in our midst now—we just don't realize it. Many former prisoners (and their family members) suffer silently and alone, especially in the church. They desperately need someone to walk alongside them to encourage and uplift them, but they are terrified to let the real truth out due to shame and fear of rejection. When the right people don't embrace them, often the wrong ones do, starting them down the path back to prison.

As God brings people into our midst, let's strive to be warm and welcoming—to be grace givers, not guilt trippers!

> He who conceals his sins does not prosper, but whoever confesses and renounces them finds mercy. ~Proverbs 28:13

THE NEW JIM CROW

Carol Davis, California

"COLORED WAITING Room," stated the sign boldly posted on the office wall of an African American pastor. I was meeting with this pastor in regard to our prison ministry. Previously I would've pretended I hadn't seen the sign in order to avoid an awkward, uncomfortable conversation. But there was no hesitation, even though it was the first time I had seen such a sign.

I had recently attended a criminal justice gathering in Jackson, Mississippi, with Dr. John Perkins and a group of denominational leaders. Our goal was to wrestle with the grim realities presented in attorney Michelle Alexander's recently published book, *The New Jim Crow: Mass Incarceration in the Age of Colorblindness*. Before reading her book, I sheepishly admit, I wasn't really familiar with Jim Crow.

Throughout our gathering, we discussed such statistics as: America, "Land of the Free," has 5 percent of the world's population and 25 percent of the world's prison population. There are 7.3 million people, or 1 in 31 adults who are under some type of correctional supervision: incarceration, parole, or probation (per a 2009 study by the Pew Center on the States). Broken down by race, that's 1 in 45 whites, 1 in 27 Hispanics, and 1 in 11 African Americans!

Why the huge difference in ratios? Alexander argues that the escalating trend of mass incarceration, with a disproportionate number of black and Hispanic men, began with the 1980s War on Drugs. Even though the percentage of drug users/dealers/traffickers was virtually the same among people of color versus whites, the war was fought primarily in impoverished non-white communities.

The laws pressed upon former felons as they return to society are strikingly similar to the Jim Crow laws pressed upon African Americans as they emerged from slavery, thus the title of Alexander's book. She states,

> The 'whites only' signs may be gone, but new signs have gone up – notices placed in job applications, rental agreements, loan applications, forms for welfare benefits, school applications, and licenses informing the general public that 'felons' are not wanted here. A criminal record today authorizes precisely the forms of discrimination we

supposedly left behind – discrimination in employment, housing, education, public benefits and jury service. Those labeled criminals can even be denied the right to vote.

The pastor I met with, a superintendent of a large denomination, had other pictures on his wall as well—of his family, his diplomas (including a Ph.D.), and—of his former prison cell. Discrimination has been overcome by people who spoke up, spoke out, and stood up with him. But despite his success, he is still required to check the "felon" box and face its consequences.

> Speak up for those who cannot speak for themselves, for the rights of all who are destitute. Speak up and judge fairly; defend the rights of the poor and needy. ~Proverbs 31:8–9

SEPTEMBER 23

CHAPLAIN LIFE

Danny Croce, Massachusetts

MY LIFE changed forever through Jesus twenty-six years ago as an inmate at Plymouth County Correctional Facility. Then I became its chaplain sixteen years ago.

In 1992, they built a new multi-use facility so that now we have county, state, and federal inmates awaiting trial and serving sentences. We're one of the top-security facilities in the area with a maximum possible population of around 1,600. We have all kinds of people—including a lot of ICE (Immigration and Customs Enforcement) inmates, because of the crackdown on immigration—serial killers, the infamous Whitey Bulger, and of course other New England locals.

I teach five Bible study classes, counsel people individually, listen to staff, and on Thursdays lead a special spiritual growth class for the serious guys who can't get enough. They ask about church history, Greek, apologetics, hermeneutics, theology—stuff you'd get in a Bible college. I don't just lead prisoners to Christ—I have them for a year or two, so I really want to equip them to become men of God. The world, the flesh, and the devil are waiting to drag them away after release.

DANNY CROCE

I'm on call if there's a death or suicide and usually meet families in the hospital. I visit inmates in hospitals who are leaving this life. I don't get paid by the government so I raise my own funds.

We spend a lot of time preparing for release, starting with discussing how they got into trouble. We've seen a few of the same guys come in and out two or three times and for the Christians it's always the same reasons—stopped reading the Word, stopped going to church.

Ninety percent of the time if they don't get plugged into a Bible-based church *immediately*, their days of freedom are numbered. The pattern is predictable. Usually there is an old flame, she's using drugs, he's done. If you grab the same old barfly, you'll be back. They think they'll go out like a knight in shining armor to save her out of that pit. But it's a lot easier for her to pull him down.

Not every church with a cross on it is Christian. There are places that if they found out you're an ex-prisoner they'd give you a look that says, "Please leave." I ask them to tell me where they're going to live and I give them a few recommendations about a church.

Some officers ask, "Why do you do it, Chap? They're going to come back." They see inmates go to Bible study for two months and they're "shocked" when they don't make it. First, attending a Bible study—I don't care who you are—is no barometer of spiritual health nor is it a magic bullet. So much more goes into a healthy Christ-centered life. Second, you can't pass judgment on the whole because of the few. If they all came back I'd get out of this business and hang iron. It's a way of life, not an 8 to 5 job. You love it or you don't.

WORLD IMPACT FROM PRISON

Danny Croce, Massachusetts

THERE'S A cycle of ministry that begins with new men striking the "impress me" stance at the back of the chapel. I ignore them. Sooner or later I strike a nerve during the teaching and they start staring at me. Gradually they sit down . . . in the back. Then a few weeks later they move up to the fourth row. They find a Bible and move to the front row and start taking notes. Finally they bring their friends, the chapel gets packed to capacity, and officers have to turn inmates away. A bunch get released, we start over.

Jesse was typical. I spotted him in back with long gray hair and a big moustache. He worked his way up as described and one day caught me alone. He asked, "I've been listening to what you say about Jesus and I believe he died for my sins. I've asked him to come into my life. But what if you've done something *really* bad?" You could see tears welling up in his eyes.

I know this guy was a leg breaker. I think he wielded the ballpeen hammer. I told him, "Listen, if Hitler had bended the knee, asked for forgiveness, and followed Christ, he too could have been saved." Jesse left the Hell's Angels.

I've led men to Christ from Lebanon, George, from Africa, and another from Belgium who spoke seven languages. When I preach, some-

331

times I ask for an "Amen." He would clap and say "Bravo, Chaplain Danny, Bravo." All these men returned to their countries and started churches or ministries. They were on fire.

Prison really is a unique place to share the Good News because they all accept the truth about the bad news first. They have no problem admitting their sin and that it is against a holy God. They agree with the penalty, too—eternity in hell.

Yes, at first, sin blinds them. Jesus said after John 3:16, "Light came into the world, but men loved darkness because their deeds were evil." But many become sick and tired of hurting people, lying, and stealing. Sin isn't fun anymore once they see the price Christ paid—raw hamburger on the cross.

Some people do look at you crazy because sin blinds them. But others are attracted and want to know the truth about what makes you different. Jesus told the disciples he'd make them fishers of men, so I go to the toughest fishing hole in town. The fish are biting there.

Jesus is not lost—we are. When he finds us it's the greatest thing. We have no purpose, reason, or hope before Jesus. Inmates ask, "Would it matter if I opened my eyes tomorrow? Would anyone notice?" The only One who can change that attitude is God. When that happens, it's everything. Without God you just exist.

> "Now is the time for judgment on this world; now the prince of this world will be driven out. And I, when I am lifted up from the earth, will draw all people to myself." He said this to show the kind of death he was going to die.
> ~John 12:31–33

SEPTEMBER 25

"CONTROL" IS JUST AN ILLUSION

Kim Hricko, Maryland

IT WAS ALL over for me. I was utterly broken and without a shred of hope. My life had been irrevocably destroyed—and I had no one to blame but myself. I was in prison and the life I had known prior, for thirty-two years, was gone forever. I was convinced I would no longer be able to fulfill my role as a mother, wife, daughter, sister, or even good friend. With those roles I had always defined myself—now, I was defined by a number. I could not think of one single reason to stay alive. I wanted to die—I deserved to die.

As a girl in junior high school I sensed that nagging in my spirit for the Lord, and gave my heart to Christ. But shortly after I graduated from high school, I chose to walk away from that relationship. I foolishly believed I could live life as I wanted, on my own terms, being accountable to no one. I felt certain I knew right from wrong. And besides, a little sin here and there wasn't too bad. Surely I was strong enough to negotiate life on my own.

The truth was, the control I imagined having over my life was just an illusion. My independent attitude only left me wide open for everything Satan would sling at me. One by one, all the things I had said I would never do became mundane to me. I was going through life at such a fast pace I didn't even look around to see the path I was on until it was too late. My foolish choices destroyed me, as surely as they destroyed my entire family, and another family. I was ultimately arrested and charged with . . . my husband's murder.

Alone in my prison cell, curled up on my bunk, I knew that no one could ever love me again. I didn't deserve love, not from family and certainly not from God. The weight of my sin was too much to bear; suicide seemed the only way out. Again, Satan had me convinced of wrong thinking.

And then suddenly, unexpectedly . . . one short phone call changed everything.

> For I know my transgressions, and my sin is always before me. ~Psalm 51: 3

READ THE PSALMS AND SEE

Kim Hricko, Maryland

PRIOR TO my sentencing, I attempted suicide at my friend's house. Thankfully it did not go as planned, but it did land me about a year at the Perkins State Hospital, a maximum-security mental health facility in Maryland, for treatment.

One day, lying on my bed and feeling especially low, an officer called me to the phone. (Inmates are not allowed to receive calls at prison unless it is an extreme emergency, but I was at a hospital where there was a pay phone and I was allowed to receive calls there.) When I answered the phone and heard my mother's voice, I broke down.

"Mom, do you still love me?" I bawled.

She replied loud and firm, "Yes, and so does God." My mom gave me the best advice anyone could get for any problem—she told me to get a Bible and read it!

After we hung up, I found a Bible and instinctively turned to the book of Psalms. Psalms is located smack dab in the middle of the Bible, and years ago I would always open it to that book. Those verses always comforted me.

In psalm after psalm I read words that seemed to be pouring out from my own broken heart. Several written by David are about how he had sinned against God. David had messed his entire life up and, like me, was responsible for murder. David thought it was over for him, but David also knew the Lord, and knew from whom his redemption would come.

Gently and tenderly, through David's own words and story, God reassured me he wasn't done with me, either. His personal message to me was that he loved me, and even though I had rejected him for so long, he was still the God of redemption, and of second (third, fourth, . . .) chances. God's love never ends. He has a purpose for every life he has created.

I have been in prison for fourteen years now. The lies the Enemy told me about life being over for me have been put to death. I am blessed to have family and friends who love and care for me. I daily rely on God for guidance and encouragement. I will not take my eyes from him again. I will always hurt for the victim's family, but I pray that they forgive me and that they, too, know the love and comfort of God.

I consider it a privilege to share with others that no matter what they have done, God still loves them. I tell them to read the Psalms and see for themselves.

Have mercy on me, O God, according to your unfailing love; according to your great compassion blot out my transgressions. ~Psalm 51:1

A LITTLE CHILD
SHALL LEAD US

Lois Wolf, Pennsylvania

THE PHONE rang at our Pennsylvania home as I was getting ready for Sunday school that morning of February 15, 1998. With a strange tone of voice, my son David told me Steve had died. It took a moment for me to realize that "Steve" was my son-in-law.

Through tears, I immediately called my prayer partner, Gail. I knew I needed spiritual support to get through this. Gail dashed over to help me pack, since my daughter Kim wanted me to be with her in Maryland.

I was grateful my husband drove. And I was amazed at how the Lord gave me great peace during the ride there, even though I still didn't know all the details.

We had Steve's funeral in State College, Pennsylvania. The pastor did a wonderful job. It was obvious to all that Steve was dearly loved, there were so many people there. When the Lord nudged me to stand up and share about Steve's salvation, I was (thankfully) unaware both the crew from the television show *Hard Copy* and the state police were in the crowd. Already they were after Kim for his death. I had no clue what was going on.

A few days after the service the police phoned Kim to come see them so she could get Steve's wedding ring. The Holy Spirit alerted me to put her on our prayer chain.

Late that night, Kim still had not returned and I didn't know where she was. I had just tucked my eight-year-old granddaughter, Anna, into bed and prayed with her when I heard a knock at the door. To my utter astonishment there were about eight Maryland state policemen standing there. I let them in and asked if I could call my prayer chain. Unknown to me, our phone was already tapped.

I then asked why they were there and an officer replied, "Your daughter is wanted for Steve's death."

What? How can this be? I wondered frantically.

I was mortified—completely in shock. They escorted Anna and me downstairs while they searched the home. They were seizing Steve's computer and searching every crevice of the townhouse Kim and Steve had recently purchased.

I remember asking for my Bible. Precious Anna requested that I read Ephesians 2:8–9. The cop that stood guard beside us got to hear a gospel message, and to see our good God using a dear child to speak truth and peace at such a moment.

Because of the Lord's great love we are not consumed, for his compassions never fail. They are new every morning. ~Lamentations 3:22–23

IN CHRIST YOU ARE FREE
Lois Wolf, Pennsylvania

IN ALL the chaos, my blood pressure hit the ceiling. My son, David, came over with a friend of Kim's and took me to the emergency room. Another relative came to take Anna.

Throughout this whole ordeal I saw God's hand move in amazing ways. I was able to drive and follow David home to his place in Maryland, and that night sleep like a baby. I was thankful I could do both.

The next morning, my first thought was, *God, where is my daughter?*

I decided to start with the local police and incredibly they knew where she was—just three blocks from me at the detention center. It was Wednesday and I was told I couldn't see her until Friday. But God intervened and I got to go right over, thanks to the power of prayer and the obedience of those from my church—many of whom were lifting up this entire situation to the Lord.

I learned that God's hand had moved again when I found out he had spared Kim's life. Earlier, she had gone to a friend's house intending to kill herself. She slit both her wrists and took a whole bottle of meds. Her friend walked in and found her in the bathtub and called for an ambulance.

When it was time for Kim's trial I was not only able to see her, but I could lean over the stairs and give her a quick kiss. Again, God's favor. At her sentencing, there were dozens of letters written from people who knew her. I believe it helped and that's why she got life with possible parole. It could have been much worse.

Even the guard let me hug Kim later (not normally allowed). My last words to my daughter before they took her to prison were, "I don't care where you are; in Christ you are FREE!"

Steve's parents were going to raise Anna, but again I asked for prayer as I wanted her raised in a home where she heard the Word of God. Soon, his mom called me and asked me to come and get her. I am a nurse, but I chose to quit my job and be there for this precious child. Anna had lost her mom and dad, school, friends, and home, such huge losses for anyone, but especially for a young child. But God has been faithful and has provided wonderfully for us.

Instead of my faith wavering, it was cemented. The lesson ingrained in my heart was: As long as we remember to keep Jesus first, everything will work out all right.

> The salvation of the righteous comes from the Lord; He is their stronghold in time of trouble. ~Psalm 37:39

ASHAMED OF OUR PAST

Larry Johnston, South Carolina

I HAVE BEEN involved in the prison pen pal ministry for many years. I have seen lots of inmates come and go; some were released from prison and some, unfortunately, will never leave due to their crimes.

James is a young man with whom I currently write. I always try to find a few things out about those I am matched up with, things they are willing to share.

I saw something he had in common with many other inmates: Sometimes we are so ashamed of our past that we are blinded to the depth of God's love and forgiveness. Instead of turning to the Lord for help, we look for means of escape to deal with life. The drug user uses drugs, the alcoholic uses alcohol, and some have eating disorders.

James was a hurting soul. He used to be a "pew warmer" Christian. Growing up he gave lip service to the hymns on Sunday morning and put a dollar or two in the plate when it went around. He even did good deeds;

he took a Saturday afternoon once to help the pastor paint the balcony of the church.

But when James wrote back the first time, he said, "I am playing with fire and I feel I need to get my life right with God. I know *of* Jesus' and the Father's love, but I don't know it personally."

I immediately wrote James back and said, "My friend, if the good Lord is speaking to your heart, then it is time to listen." I included Scripture passages that directed him deeper into the precious Word of God. God's Word is powerful and able to cut through the noise and static of this world. James needed to see how deep and wide was the Father's love for him.

Thankfully, he heeded my advice.

> . . . our gospel came to you not simply with words but also with power, with the Holy Spirit and deep conviction. ~1 Thessalonians 1:5

SEPTEMBER 30

CHOICES

Larry Johnston, South Carolina

THE MORE James read about God's undying love for him, the more his eyes were opened.

One of the Scripture verses I sent to James is Jeremiah 29:11: "For I know the plans I have for you," declares the Lord, "plans to prosper you and not to harm you, plans to give you hope and a future."

It was like turning on a light in a very dark hallway. James shared he was lost and blinded. Like many of us, he thought his sins were too great for God to forgive. He wrote, "Now I know this is not the case. From the foundations of the world the Lord saw who I was, who I chose to become, yet he loved me anyway. Larry, now I see that God chose me to exist in the first place. I was the one who made the bad choices to go in the direction I did—away from him."

Another person in prison ministry sent James a card he still had. He thought it was cute because it had children from all over the world, different races, holding hands and encircling the globe. Inside the globe was the babe Jesus wrapped in a manger. The words at the top of the card were, "For God so loved the world that He gave His one and only Son, that whoever believes in Him shall not perish but have eternal life" (John 3:16).

Words can't express the joy I had when James wrote informing me he knew the true Jesus. He could feel the warmth of the Father's love.

Today, James is taking a Bible correspondence course and is hungry for a closer walk with Jesus. You see, just as with James, our Father's plans are great for each of our lives. But, it is *what we do* with what he gives us that is up to us—our choice.

I love how James signs his letters to me now. It is with this Scripture:

Choose for yourselves this day whom you will serve . . . as for me and my household, we will serve the Lord. ~Joshua 24:15

TIME TO GRIEVE

Connie Cameron, Ohio

THE FIRST time I meet with a new inmate through the Be-a-Friend program inside the Licking County Jail, it is always an anxious moment for both of us. I always pray and ask God to help me be a good listener, and to be a light in that dark place. My heart's desire is to encourage and build up, to share God's love and offer hope.

I always long for the two of us to "click," but sometimes that does not happen, at least not at first. But this day, as soon as I saw Jennifer's sweet smile, sparkling eyes, and beautiful golden-red curly hair, I *knew* we would hit it off and become good friends.

After our introductions, I shared with Jennifer the purpose of the ministry. I was there to be her friend, to encourage and pray for her. It took me aback for a moment when she was sincerely appreciative to have someone from "the outside" come to see her. Seldom do we see such gratitude. But then, the more she talked, the more I realized there was something different about her. Jennifer had a unique sweetness about her. Twice during our visit two officers walked by the glass-enclosed room we were in and flashed sincere smiles when they saw her. She gave them big, bright smiles in return. She was obviously well liked.

Then, after I shared a little of my testimony, Jennifer's sparkle disappeared and her bright eyes suddenly filled with tears. She said her father died when she was young and her relationship with her stepfather had not been good. Due to her own actions, her sisters had pulled away from her also. And . . . her mother had died just a year or so earlier.

"I was with my mom," Jennifer sobbed, "when she passed. I was her caregiver. We were best friends." She wiped her eyes, adding, "Everyone said we were joined at the hip." Amazingly, Jennifer still tried to smile in the midst of such obvious pain.

Oh my . . . not even thirty years old and no longer having her mother—the rock in her life.

I could understand wanting to numb her pain with drugs, but that is never God's plan. God wants us to turn to *him* in our grief. He can, and will, mend our broken hearts, comforting us no matter where we are.

For he has not despised or scorned the suffering of the afflicted one; he has not hidden his face from him but has listened to his cry for help. ~Psalm 22:24

IT'S NOT ABOUT ME

Connie Cameron, Ohio

THE NEXT week when I returned to the jail for another visit with Jennifer, I was again impressed by her positive attitude and bright smile. She made it easy for me to look forward to our visits.

While catching up, Jennifer nonchalantly mentioned she had discovered the "inspirational" book section at the jail library.

"I don't know what has gotten into me," she exclaimed, "but I no longer enjoy romance novels—they just don't hold my interest anymore. Instead, I'm longing for books that encourage me and challenge me to grow in the Lord."

I sat back, crossed my arms, and smiled. This was music to my ears. Then, it suddenly dawned on me that our jail ministry provides complimentary copies of *The Purpose-Driven Life* by Rick Warren. They are available to any inmate upon request. I asked Jennifer if she'd ever heard about the book.

"No, what's it about?" she asked.

"Well . . ." I smiled ". . . it's not about you."

She gave me a strange look. "Actually, Jennifer, those are the opening words in the book. We all assume life is about us, but we were created by God for *his* purposes, not our own. Our main purpose is to have a personal relationship with him."

"Oh yeah, I'd love to have a copy of that," Jennifer responded.

I made the request to our jail chaplain and by our next visit she had read the first several chapters—and couldn't stop talking about it.

"Wow! That book is awesome!" Jennifer exclaimed, her golden curls framing her face, adding to her glow. "Every day I can't wait to get off work in the laundry room so I can hurry back to my room and read some more!"

It was thrilling to witness the change in her over the next few weeks as the drugs wore off, allowing her true personality to shine through. Added to that was the joy of seeing her grow in her relationship with Jesus, allowing him to be her Comforter.

Jennifer would need God's strength to endure the disappointment right around the corner. . . .

Therefore, since we have these promises, dear friends, let us purify ourselves from everything that contaminates body and spirit, perfecting holiness out of reverence for God. ~2 Corinthians 7:1

DISAPPOINTMENT AND ACCEPTANCE

Connie Cameron, Ohio

IT WAS two days before Thanksgiving and I had many things to do. I told Jennifer I would try to make her court appearance that morning. She was hoping to be released and then be accepted into a local halfway house. But when I became delayed, I decided to pray continually from home for Jennifer and ask God for wisdom for the judge. We were hopeful she would be released and sent to a treatment center, yet how many times had I seen it go the other way?

A few hours later, curious as to how court went, I got online and looked her up. *Ugh.* The poor girl got three more months in jail and was ordered to take drug intervention classes.

Knowing that Jenn would be devastated, I went to see her and encourage her. All the way there I prayed for the right words. But when I finally saw her, her unmistakable peace was surprising.

"Ya know," Jennifer said, staring off into space. "Some of the girls in here were saying, right before I went to court, that they didn't know how they would cope without me here. They said they looked forward to my bright smile and positive attitude; that I helped them endure this place."

"Yeah, I can see that," I quietly responded, sensing her pain and disappointment over the judge's ruling.

"And there's this one girl who used to tease me about being a 'Bible thumper.'" She smiled weakly. "She just found out her boyfriend had been cheating on her. The same 'boyfriend' who got her hooked shooting meth. She just came to me for advice."

Jennifer smiled again and continued, "I told this girl, 'You probably don't want to hear this, but I don't know what else to say to you except you need to pray about it.' And guess what, Connie? That very night she was in Bible study."

Wow, I was suddenly very glad I had taken time out to come to the jail. What a blessing! It was obvious God wanted Jennifer to remain here a little while longer to get her heart turned more to him, and to continue using her to help others.

Many are the plans in a person's heart, but it is the Lord's purpose that prevails. ~Proverbs 19:21

"ALL SUICIDE BEDS ARE FULL"

Connie Cameron, Ohio

DURING THIS same visit with Jennifer at the Licking County Jail I suddenly remembered something from our recent jail ministry board meeting. Our chaplain, Scott Hayes, had asked for prayer for the inmates and staff because he had been told, "All suicide beds are full."

There was a moment of silence after he spoke—each board member processing his words. "It's the holidays," Scott somberly added. "We need as many volunteers as possible to go inside the jail or to write to the inmates and encourage them."

I reflected on Scott's words during my visit with Jennifer. She had just shared about the girl who had called her a "Bible thumper," when I suddenly locked eyes with her. My mouth opened and, even though I had no idea what I was going to say, these words came out: "Maybe this is why God is not releasing you from here yet. I've told you before that you have something different about you that others sense, including me. The ladies here are attracted to your positive attitude and are comfortable with your sweet personality. You've shared that some of the girls search you out to tell you what a big smile you have and how you make them feel better just by being there."

My eyes filled with tears as chill bumps rolled over my skin. "The suicide rooms are full here and the holidays are coming. Maybe, as Rick Warren says, 'It's not about you.' Your sentence may be for the benefit of some of the others. I believe God wants you here to use you to help the other girls, and in the process he will bless you and grow you closer to him."

I remembered my earlier prayer for the right words. For several long seconds Jennifer and I stared at each other, unblinking. Her eyes were full of tears and she seemed hungry for more confirmation.

Wiping my eyes, I whispered, "I feel God's presence here with us."

"Me, too," Jenn whispered back, stretching her hands out for prayer.

During the long drive home I sang Christmas carols and thanked God for nudging me to visit Jennifer. I knew she would be okay, and I knew everything would get crossed off my "to-do" list—in God's perfect timing.

. . . just as the Son of Man did not come to be served, but to serve, and to give his life as a ransom for many. ~Matthew 20:28

THE OPPORTUNITY
OF REHAB

Jennifer Williamson, Ohio

WHEN I found out I could have a "friend," a volunteer from the jail ministry, visit me inside the jail, I jumped at the chance. When you live with the same people every day, it gets old fast. Having someone from the outside come in to visit is like a breath of fresh air (those are rare here, too, especially since I work in the laundry room and usually miss the few opportunities to go outside in the enclosed area).

We are permitted to have visits with family and friends, but it's not in person, rather through a monitor. Not that I'd had any other visits, except for a social worker and my Be-a-Friend volunteer, who comes in about once a week. The only relatives I have are my two sisters and they are probably mad at me, because I haven't heard a word from either of them. I don't have a husband or boyfriend, either. I've never been married, nor had kids, so with my parents gone now I've been feeling pretty much alone in the world.

It's been about a year since my mom passed—I miss her so much. Watching her decline was heartbreaking, but I didn't want a stranger to take care of her, and my sisters weren't able to do it. My stepdad walked out on her in the last year of her life. My mom needed me, and there was no place I'd rather have been than by her side.

I wasn't "hooked" on drugs before Mom passed; I just enjoyed them occasionally. But when the waves of grief came after she died I wanted to numb myself. That's when I got arrested.

At first, like most of us who get caught, I was angry at God. *How could he allow this to happen to me?*

I was also very disappointed with myself, until I read *The Purpose Driven Life*. It was then I realized God had, indeed, intervened. If I hadn't been arrested I'd probably still be doing drugs, still covering up my pain, still not caring about life. But here I've finally gotten clean and . . . I like myself. I've attended drug abuse classes and AA classes (Narcotics Anonymous is currently not offered). Both have helped a lot.

One day I surprised Connie by telling her my two sisters never got the "opportunity" to go to rehab as I have. Connie complimented me on having a great perspective about being here. She told me, "God is on your

345

side. You are very special. Keep trusting him with your future. He has an awesome plan for your life."

Gradually, I'm starting to believe it.

> Trust in the LORD and do good; dwell in the land and enjoy safe pasture. Take delight in the LORD, and he will give you the desires of your heart. ~Psalm 37:3–4

OCTOBER 6

LEARNING MY "PURPOSE"

Jennifer Williamson, Ohio

I WAS STARTING to grasp this "relationship with God" thing I had been reading about. But I also found that it takes a lot of discipline to read my Bible every day, and to remember to talk to God about everything, instead of getting mad or upset that life isn't going my way.

It helps, too, that I have a job in here. I'm one of the fortunate inmates in that I get to work in the laundry room on day shift. I don't get paid for it, and it can sometimes be kind of gross, especially when you have to wash the clothes of inmates who have lost bodily control due to heavy drugs leaving their system, but the laundry job gets me out of the module and gives me something to do. And, I get to encourage the deputies, too.

The day of my court visit when I found out I had to stay here for a few more months, I was pretty down. Connie came to visit me that day and her words felt like they were directly from God. When she returned a few days later, right in the middle of the visit I saw Stephanie, an inmate who had been released for a while. When Stephanie walked by, escorted by a deputy, I felt so bad for her. She was returning to finish her sentence, but she had a young daughter and would now be away from her during Christmas. I told Connie and she responded with a powerful message.

Connie looked me in the eyes and said, "You're on, girl."

I stayed quiet, absorbing her next words with all my being.

"Jennifer, remember what I said the other day, when you didn't get released like you hoped? Remember you said that the girls in Bible study kept telling you God put you here for them? This could be God's confirmation of the gift he has placed inside you; your purpose. God knew Stephanie was coming back . . . and she would need you."

Connie keeps telling me God has gifted me to be a good listener and encourage others. I'm starting to believe she might be right. We also talk about my future and how I think I should use my gifts when I get out. I loved being my mom's caregiver and felt I was good at it. I'm thinking about pursuing caregiving of some sort.

It's been a while since I've thought seriously about my future. It feels amazing to have hope again. I feel like a new person.

> . . . each of you has your own gift from God; one has this gift, another has that. ~1 Corinthians 7:7

MORAL REHABILITATION VERSUS PUNISHMENT

Burl Cain, Louisiana

IN THE nineties the Louisiana Secretary of Corrections Jimmy Leblanc and I, the senior warden at the Louisiana State Penitentiary (aka Angola) conducted a difficult execution. The man being executed was a released prisoner who had committed another heinous crime.

When it was all over, we looked at each other and said, "We failed miserably. We are not supposed to let this happen. We've got to do everything in our power to change the way we run prisons." That was a profound experience for us both.

Adult corrections means to correct deviant behavior. It doesn't mean lock and feed. Therefore we should never allow prison to become the "devil's playground."

People come to us broken, distressed, and many times very angry. We have to look to Scripture that is very helpful on this. Philippians 3:13 says we can't change the past. All we can do is look to the future. Based on that Scripture, I run this prison. I try to get the inmates to forget the past, move forward, and not do it again.

To accomplish this we need a big dose of morality because moral people don't rape, kill, steal, and break the law. Therefore we need morality-based programs and education because without the moral component we just make smarter criminals. If we have the moral component we change lives. And morality is found best in religion. I don't care if you're Buddhist or Muslim. Most religions advocate high standards of morality. The immoral commit crimes. We're all immoral to a degree, but not to a degree where we hurt others and have to go to prison. Prison is supposed to be a place that promotes morality, change, forgiveness, and redemption.

I'm responsible that people who leave my prison do not hurt someone again. That is my responsibility alone. If I run a place that is lock and feed, torture and torment, then I have not met my obligation to society. This is why I exist on this earth. I take this job very, very seriously. So many in my profession have not a clue as to what they are really supposed to be doing. It's very disappointing. Do the traditional thing, get the traditional outcome—high recidivism rates. Do the nontraditional thing—what I'm talking about—you get nontraditional outcomes and low recidivism rates.

I do not consider myself yet to have taken hold of it. But one thing I do: Forgetting what is behind and straining toward what is ahead, I press on toward the goal to win the prize for which God has called me heavenward in Christ Jesus. ~Philippians 3:13-14.

THE WAY WE DO IT HERE (PART 1)

Burl Cain, Louisiana

AS THE warden at Angola I'm responsible for 5,309 inmates with only 1,600 cells, 1,500 officers and staff, and very few weapons. We could never accomplish what we do without culture change. But you have to understand the hole we started from.

Angola was built on a foundation of oppression. It was known as one of the bloodiest prisons in America before my predecessor and I took over. The amazing thing about this place is that the prisoners we take in are no less violent and dangerous than they were thirty years ago. We just changed the culture.

This prison only has men convicted of murder, rape, and armed robbery, and are habitual felons. If you have 50 years or less on your sentence I don't even keep you here. I'm going to send you to another prison unless you're very violent. I have more than 4,000 lifers. The average sentence is 93 years. Therefore 94 percent of the inmates are going to die here. This is real hard-core, with a lot of bad people in one place.

I instituted a rule when I arrived that there will be no profanity in this prison. We do not curse. The officers do not use profanity toward the inmates or each other. The inmates don't use profanity toward each other or the officers or they get punished. That sets up an environment for rehabilitation, because we recognize that spewing profanity is not conducive to moral rehabilitation.

How do I boast we don't have profanity? It's by the grace of God. We are not oppressive to the inmates, including the way we speak. Oppression only breeds hostility and takes the culture in the wrong direction. What we say and how we say it is where a lot of trouble starts, isn't it?

The absence of profanity creates a safer environment. Inmates like that, too. Prison is their community. We tell them there are no rats in our prison. If you see or hear someone doing wrong in your neighborhood, you call the police. It's the same in our prison community. At nearly any other prison, the person "ratting" risks their life for telling on the person doing wrong. You can't build a safe community and culture with that environment.

The words of the reckless pierce like swords, but the tongue of the wise brings healing. ~Proverbs 12:18

349

THE WAY WE DO
IT HERE (PART 2)

Burl Cain, Louisiana

M OST OF our innovations come from God. I'm not that smart. And when God's ready, we innovate again. All these things have a profound impact on the inmates and culture.

I've trained the inmates to hand me notes—good or bad—as I walk among them. I read and answer them all myself. I know their problems. They often connect with me in church. If I'm in church, they'll attend to pass notes, and then hear something useful.

In addition to a massive farm and ranching system that feeds the entire Louisiana state prison system—which gives people productive work—we have hospice care and a special funeral process.

Hospice care is for the terminally ill. Men know they have access to counseling and care by trained ministers. They're not going to be left alone. When they die, they know they will be buried in prisoner-crafted pine caskets, carried by a horse-drawn carriage, and buried in hand-dug graves at the prison cemetery with dignity. Chuck Colson was buried in one of our caskets. Why do we do all that? It fights oppression by injecting respect and dignity for prisoners who are used to getting none their whole lives. It changes them.

We give the hardheads light at the end of the tunnel. We talk to them in their cell blocks as we wait for them to calm down. We ask, "When will you quit doing this to yourself? You keep resisting authority and living a demonic life. When are you going to let me let you out of this cell?" Eventually they take the offer, join the double-bunked dorms, and quit causing trouble.

This place is probably safer than your city. When women walk in here there are no whistles or cat calls. We have neither graffiti nor gangs in this prison. It *can* happen. We ignore political correctness and anything else that gets in the way of maintaining the moral culture we've created.

This place is safe enough to let women guard inmates. We posted a little twenty-year-old woman just out of high school in a dorm where 25 percent of the inmates are aggravated rapists. She's going to guard them? That's a joke. They let her guard them. She just has eyes. She can't control them. Yet we have peace and harmony. One lady had a seizure and passed out. An inmate went up to molest her and three or four others stopped him and called for help. That's the environment we have here.

I think God changed this prison, because it has the worst of the worst. If it can change, how can someone from another prison tell me, "We can't do what you did"?

> If your enemy is hungry, give him food to eat; if he is thirsty, give him water to drink. In doing this, you will heap burning coals on his head, and the Lord will reward you. ~Proverbs 25:21–22

OCTOBER 10

THE HEART OF CULTURE CHANGE
Burl Cain, Louisiana

THE COMPONENT critical to our culture change had to be when we established the fully-accredited New Orleans Baptist Theological Seminary on prison grounds. This, in turn, helped us raise $3 million to build six churches on the different yards.

No tax dollars went into any of our religious programs. The state of Louisiana got a tax-free educational program (through the seminary) it could never have afforded itself. The religious community pays for tuition and keeps the library going. Everybody brags about it. It's politically correct in Louisiana to be for Angola.

Here's the key to why the seminary and the church are at the heart of what we do. Every other week we close Angola to outside prison ministry to let the theologically-trained inmates do it. Inmate preachers have their own congregations, some numbering as many as 200. They have ushers and assistant pastors and I go to church with them. They preach and I listen. When you have inmates preaching to other inmates you're going to have a culture change.

When a prisoner's mother dies, and you let an inmate who has four years of seminary training and knows all about grief counseling sit on the bed with him all night, then you're going to have a more effective program. When you have an inmate teaching anger management you will be more effective because he feels the other inmates' pain. When you have inmates running a hospice program and they are the caregivers loving on them, wiping behinds, and giving baths to their brothers then you have an effective program. Inmates are preaching the funerals. Missionaries get things started, but the local people must eventually own it and spread it amongst themselves.

We also send our inmates out as missionaries to other Louisiana prisons. We saw the violence drop 42 percent at Dixon Correctional Institution six months after our two missionaries arrived. They are even way more effective at evangelizing each other than outside ministry. This whole thing is common sense.

If you attended a church with a preacher who left after morning services and didn't come back until the next Sunday—he didn't do any weddings, funerals, counseling, anything else—you wouldn't have a viable church. Why should you expect different in the prison? We have people come in from outside and preach and drive home. Inmates know that those preachers are not in a cage, not staying in this place for decades. But when the one preaching to them is living in the cage with them, they relate. That's why I block every other week to outside ministry to give the inmates a chance to grow and develop into mature ministers themselves.

> Do your best to present yourself to God as one approved, a worker who does not need to be ashamed and who correctly handles the word of truth.
> ~2 Timothy 2:15

OCTOBER 11

GOING BEYOND THE TESTIMONY

Mayra Alemar, New York

MY LATE husband, José, and I were rescued from our drug-addicted lives through Prison Fellowship's Angel Tree® program. That is how we came to Christ and saw our entire family transformed.

Before José came home from prison, I started visiting the church that ministered to our family. The pastor took me into Rikers Island Jail in New York City—the place I had spent a short time for a drug sale conviction— to share my testimony. I went every second Sunday of the month.

When José came home we started New Cornerstone Adoption Program (a 501(c)(3) non-profit). It focused on bringing women prisoners the Word of God, helping them with basic needs (like toiletries), and just hugging and crying with them. We also helped their children on the outside with food and clothing.

In 1991, an inmate challenged us. She was angry at herself, the world, the system, at God. She said, "All you Christians talk about is 'God is good,' and how you want to help by telling us how you changed your life! But what can you do *for me?* I don't want this child that I'm carrying." She had plans to abort. We talked to her and convinced her that if she carried the baby, we would care for him or her until she came home. It took many visits to gain that trust.

I physically couldn't be a mom again (I already had three children). But this woman presented the opportunity to have another baby at home, and I was very happy about it. On December 18 Isaac joined Mencia (11), Alex (10), and Ricky (6). The social worker knew our story, and our pastor, and backed us up.

The birth mother had another two years to do. She fell in love with Isaac and wanted to have him. We brought the baby to visitation those years so she could play and bond. She went into Teen Challenge for Women for eighteen months after her release. We continued to bring Isaac for visits until she finished.

She decided to start over by moving to Florida and said she would send for him when she was ready. We stayed in touch for a while by phone. Then she disappeared. Isaac was three. She reestablished contact when Isaac turned 14 and wanted to live with him. It was a tough time. We never hid anything from him. He called me "Mom" and I gave him all the love and nurture he needed. Her lifestyle was different from ours. She was drinking and smoking so Isaac started smoking. He only spent a few months before deciding it was not going to work at all.

He came home for good and we formally adopted him soon after.

> Religion that God our Father accepts as pure and faultless is this: to look after orphans and widows in their distress and to keep oneself from being polluted by the world. ~James 1:27

GIVING JESÚS BACK

Mayra Alemar, New York

W E MET Darla* in the nursery at Rikers, where mothers can stay with their babies for up to eighteen months. She was seventeen and an undocumented Mexican immigrant. She loved her baby. However, she had to finish the last year of her sentence at Bedford Correctional. The state planned to step in and take the baby into foster care. They couldn't send the child, Jesús, to Mexico to be with family because he was American born.

Darla cried daily knowing the separation was nearing. We tried to contact her parents in Mexico and a sister, none of whom could come because of their immigrant status. Finally she asked if I would take the child. We were glad to do so.

We went to court this time and acquired guardianship of Jesús. They took our references and jobs, our whole situation, into consideration. It's still unusual for the state of New York to even consider people with our backgrounds to be entrusted with children. The judge questioned us for hours. She warned we could not get public assistance for the child. We didn't want it. We just wanted to help. By human standards we probably shouldn't have qualified, but God kept making a way, because our hearts were open to helping as many children as we could.

Darla did well at Bedford. She earned her GED, went to Bible study, and followed the Lord. The United States deported her and we had to take Jesús to Mexico. That was a condition in the paperwork.

José flew down first to get pictures to prove residence and title of home before we could release Jesús through the Mexican government. It was all approved. Next, I flew to Mexico with Jesús, who was three. I organized his passport, social security card, and papers from the judge, and took him to his mommy. It was emotional to leave him there. I had him a couple of years and he called me "Mommy." She was not jealous, but rather so humble even at seventeen.

I still speak to her today. She lives with Jesús and her parents in Mexico.

The LORD hears the needy and does not despise his captive people.
~Psalm 69:33

RESCUING KEVIN

Mayra Alemar, New York

WHEN WE started taking kids into our home as a way to temporarily help moms get through jail time and still keep their families intact, we had no idea where God would take us.

Janet* called me her godmother. We were ministering to her as we were so many moms at the Rikers nursery and she, too, asked us to take her boy, Kevin, for a time. The original plan involved her sister taking Kevin, but her sister got sick. So I was asked if I would take him until she recovered.

A new official at the nursery recommended we get formal custody of Kevin. It's a lot of paperwork, but we did it. It seemed like a lot of trouble, when we fully expected to hand Kevin over to his aunt very soon.

The sister recovered and requested Kevin come live with her. We returned to court to make it legal, but the judge refused the transfer. She had four other children and no job. The judge thought Kevin would be better off with us. Janet understood this. We discovered just a few months later that her sister's kids were taken away from her. We were so glad to have custody for Kevin's sake.

Kevin grew up with us until he was two, when Janet came home. She found an apartment and a job at a fast-food place, and was doing well. We went back to court and released custody back to her. Everything seemed to be working out and we were glad.

After three months, Janet was back into the drug world. There was a shootout in the apartment because she owed money to drug dealers, so Janet went on the run.

The sister called us in the middle of the night urging us to come to the Bronx and pick up Kevin. She couldn't get in and knew he was alone in the apartment. We couldn't believe it!

José dressed and left our home in the projects. No police were around to help so he broke through the window. He found two-year-old Kevin sitting in the bathtub with his big dog, Max, faithfully watching over him.

José took Kevin, the sister took Max, and the police got involved. Later, Janet showed up at our apartment wanting Kevin back, but we refused. She was not in good shape from the drug abuse and really needed help. The court agreed and gave us permanent custody. That brought the number in our family to seven living in our little two-room apartment. Today, I can hardly believe that Kevin has begun preparing to go to college.

> But he lifted the needy out of their affliction and increased their families like flocks. ~Psalm 107:41

WHEN GIVING NEVER ENDS
Mayra Alemar, New York

JANET LATER gave birth prematurely to Mookie, whom she abandoned in the hospital. Social Services called us since we had Kevin, his brother, and asked if we would take him before he went into foster care.

At that point I was determined to not take any more kids. Already twelve children had come through our house. José was quick to say, "We'll take him."

"No, we're not! I'm tired. I need to think."

Because Mookie was twenty-six weeks old and only 1.5 pounds with complications, it would be three months before he could leave the hospital. I really prayed about taking him home. I asked the Lord if he wanted me to take this child, please reveal it to me. I finished praying and the phone rang. A social worker urged me to come to the hospital and see him.

I went with my oldest daughter and José. We were shocked when we saw him and we cried—such a tiny, fragile human being. All you could see were big eyes and a big belly because they had operated on his intestine. I said, "We're taking him."

At that point New York City put us through another thorough investigation even while we took Mookie home from the hospital. After all these years, they made us official foster parents.

Our joy was tempered by Mookie's crying all the time. José and I took turns staying up all night. It was exhausting. Doctors told us, "It's colic." My mother's heart didn't believe it.

We finally got an appointment with a neurologist. When we arrived the doctor saw a red mark by his right eye. The medical staff knew we were foster parents and immediately ordered us to the ER. They thought we'd been hitting Mookie.

The police were waiting with a social worker. I was told to sit down and stay put while they took Mookie through a full exam. We explained that he had fallen asleep against a piece of Velcro in his high chair.

The exam confirmed our explanation, but then they hit us with a body blow—he had severe brain atrophy. He had mental retardation, the brain of an 80-year-old man, cerebral palsy, and he was blind. We had never been told any of this before. All we could do was cry.

That started the roller coaster for us. After ten years he's had seven surgeries. He has three different meds to control his seizures and needs 'round the clock care. I had help from José, but now that he's no longer around it falls on me. It's overwhelming sometimes. An agency sends me a girl five hours a day, which helps. Even so, he smiles when you call his name. He laughs when he knows I'm near. I love this boy. José used to say, "Mookie has a complicated life, but he's happy."

We've done all this not just to tell incarcerated women of the goodness of God, but to demonstrate it. God instituted the family. We want that to be the first thing so more children don't end up in prison as have their parents.

> She opens her arms to the poor and extends her hands to the needy.
> Proverbs 31:20

FINDING THEIR FATHER

Linda Fowler, California

OVER THE past fifteen years I've had the privilege of holding weekly Bible studies at our local county jail, and also facilitating weekly church services at one of our state prisons. Many individuals have touched my life. I have seen in them God's manifestations, which are hard to put into words. But, over the years, I've come to see a common link . . . the absence of a father. Even though many of them had a mother present in their life, they were not always the best role models, as they had their own personal struggles and addictions. Some had other relatives, such as grandparents, who stepped up to help out, but not enough.

One female inmate told how she had been brought up in a drug-addicted family. Drugs were the acceptable norm. She did not know her father—her mother was the only parent she had. And, due to drugs, her mom was unavailable to give her guidance and direction in life. She witnessed her mom turning to drugs when she was happy, sad, worried, or mad. She saw drugs as the way to cope with life. Subsequently, she began running with the wrong crowd, became addicted to the fast life, and got involved in drugs, too.

Eventually her lifestyle caught up with her and she is currently serving a sentence of life in prison. At first, she spent most of her time in solitary confinement reading. One day she selected a Bible from the library cart. She read it through many times. She became hungry to know even more about God.

At the same time, her mother was realizing she had failed her daughter and knew she needed to be strong for her. This caused the mother to cry out to God for help, too, and she accepted Christ.

The mother shared with her daughter all about how God was changing her. And now, with God's grace, both women have turned their lives around and are choosing to live for Christ. Both have come to know they've always had a "Father," and are learning how to trust him.

> Jesus replied, "Anyone who loves me will obey my teaching. My Father will love them, and we will come to them and make our home with them." ~John 14:23

OCTOBER 16

REMEMBERING CHUCK COLSON

Jeff Peck, Virginia

ON THE morning of May 16, 2012, thousands gathered to honor, mourn, and celebrate the life of Charles W. Colson. In the media-saturated, attention-deficit world we live in, the news spike reporting his death lasted about two days, hardly equivalent to other famous people who died, such as Steve Jobs.

But the legacy of Chuck Colson far outweighs the brief mention of a busy world. Though most of the secular press could only see the former Nixon "hatchet man" who went to prison for a Watergate-related crime, the movement he launched continues to impact innumerable lives.

Perhaps the most tangible expression, completely missed by press accounts, were those in attendance at the National Cathedral service in Washington, D.C. Republicans and Democrats, Catholics and evangelicals, wardens and ex-prisoners, people of all races, celebrities and nobodies—they all came because this former Marine captain turned Republican dirty-trickster, turned prisoner, had spoken into their lives.

Chuck's message consistently anchored itself in the Christ who went to the cross for us. His more than twenty books—many now must-reads—pointed to that reality. Chuck spent every Easter since his conversion preaching the gospel in prison—a witness that made a profound impact on the warden of Angola, who continued to transform his institution into what can only be described as the gold standard of corrections. Chuck prayed through food slots, hugged prisoners with AIDS, argued persuasively in the public square for revealed truth, and set fire to a prison ministry movement that has established roots in more than 110 countries.

Chuck knew the heights from which he'd fallen, which gave him the desire and ability to break through the fog of fame (even Christian popularity) and be personally interested in everyone he met. I don't say this from the distance of an admiring fan who treasured his writings or snagged an autograph. I watched him shake thousands of hands, listen to millions of stories, and wade through countless editorial meetings, all the while showing respect and concern for all those people. He not only reviewed the work I did as a member of the Prison Fellowship staff, but he asked me how I was.

I'm not worried, nor is it my job to ensure this lion of the faith is remembered. He never bothered with it himself because his focus never shifted from honoring the One who saved him in the midst of a political meltdown. I simply find that in remembering the man I knew, I see the mark of Jesus on a life well lived. Heroes of the faith are important, for they remind us of the possibilities when we fully submit our hearts to him who went to the cross for us.

> For the message of the cross is foolishness to those who are perishing, but to us who are being saved it is the power of God. ~1 Corinthians 1:18

DEATH BY COP

Steve Silver, Oregon

I GREW UP as part of the Oregon foster care system, went to juvenile detention, then to a state institution after several crimes. I was nineteen when I went in charged with unauthorized use of a vehicle, kidnapping, twenty-three counts of theft, and twenty-seven counts of burglary.

There was a lot of violence inside to say the least. I weighed 160 pounds, blonde, with blue eyes. You can paint the picture from there. Sometimes I lost.

After my release I was driving around Salem with my girlfriend and using a false name. I had tried to write phony checks using my own name and decided that wasn't so smart.

One evening, police officers pulled me over in the parking lot of a Safeway store. I had already decided I was never going back to prison to risk facing the trauma I had experienced. I knew how to do "suicide by cop." That was my plan if they tried to arrest me.

In my heart I didn't want anyone else to get wounded. I casually asked my girlfriend if she would be willing to get me a pack of cigarettes. The police agreed to let her go. While I'm standing there talking to the cop, giving him my fake identification, I saw other police cars pull into the parking lot and position themselves on the perimeter, which made me nervous.

Two more cruisers rolled up on us and a field sergeant approached. The first cop returned to his car and the sergeant started talking to me. After fifteen minutes I was shaking like a leaf, knowing I was done. The first officer returned with his ticket book. He was writing me up for no driver's license, no insurance, and other violations.

Then the sergeant said, "I know your name is not Sean. I know your real name is Steve. I'm going to tell you, I don't know why I'm doing this, but I'm giving you these tickets and letting you go. If you don't show up for court, I'll hunt you down and drag you back to Oregon."

Then they let me go. The girl I had sent into the store was a Christian. She told me later she stood at the window watching and praying. God had laid it on her heart that if she did not pray and intercede for me, I was going to die at that moment.

We left the state. The girl and I married, but it wasn't a Bonnie-and-Clyde adventure. She ended up taking me to a church where I got saved.

> As for me, far be it from me that I should sin against the LORD by failing to pray for you. And I will teach you the way that is good and right. ~1 Samuel 12:23

OCTOBER 18

I HAVE NO DEFENSE

Steve Silver, Oregon

DURING THE next year-and-a-half every sermon or message I heard pointed me to the fact that as long as I was on the run from the law, I was also on the run from God. I couldn't fully commit my life to whatever God's purpose was for me.

I recognized God prompting me to return to Salem and turn myself in. Growing up in the system, with the life I had lived, I trusted nobody. God was asking me to place my life back in the hands of a system that had destroyed me.

I couldn't keep running, but I feared prison for what had happened to me there. I drove back to Salem and looked up a former foster parent at the police station who gave me the details of the court I needed to appear in. I took a deep breath and entered.

As I waited my turn to go before the judge, I watched other cases. The judge handed out prison sentences for the same things I was facing. Someone with no driver's license got a year in jail. Another with no insurance gets six months. For lying to a police officer the judge dishes out four months, and for not turning yourself in on a warrant a guy got a year.

I'm thinking, *I'm toast. The judge is going to bury me.* I prayed before hearing my name called. The judge read the charges and asked me to plead.

"Your honor, I have no choice but to plead guilty."

"Do you have anything else to say before sentence is imposed?"

I prayed, "I can make excuses, Lord, but you have to be my defense." The answer he gave was, "You have no defense." When I had been a former criminal I had to try to justify my behavior. I had to have an excuse for why I had acted so stupid. For the unrepentant, it's never their fault. But God wouldn't grant me permission for the smallest of excuses.

So, that's what I told the judge: "I have no defense."

He looked at me. "Here's what I'm going to do: one year for the first charge, six months for the second and third . . ." He gave me jail time for all five offenses *and* a fine! Then he suspended all of it and set me free on probation.

I couldn't believe it. Other people who received real jail time gave all kinds of excuses, none of which impressed the judge one bit.

As I was falling apart afterward, God was telling me, "That's trusting me." That changed my life as I finally learned to listen to that still, small voice even if it's telling me to go against everything I've ever learned.

> The LORD is my strength and my defense; he has become my salvation.
> ~Psalm 118:14

HONOR AMONG CHOICES

Steve Silver, Oregon

THE CRIMES that put everybody in knots—offenders, victims, the system, families—are sex offenses. I've been walking in my faith for twenty-two years and those affected by sex offense are the people with whom I now work. But it didn't happen overnight.

The horrific things I experienced in prison were merely the culmination of a life of sexual abuse in the foster system. My stepfather sold me as a young boy to his cocaine buddies as a prostitute.

Fast forward to the time of my miracle court hearing. I'd been living in a parked bus, working a part-time job, and riding my bicycle everywhere. My first wife had left me, I was dirt poor, and wondering, *What next?*

I opened a can of cream of mushroom soup for dinner one evening while listening to the radio when I heard one of Chuck Colson's Breakpoint commentaries. I don't remember the topic, but I know what went through my heart. *The only reason Colson has that prison ministry is that he had the money to finance it.*

That's when God interrupted my thoughts with, "Go sign up." I spent three days arguing with God. I thought prison ministry meant *only* that people went behind the walls. I still didn't want to go near a prison and I believed (incorrectly) that my record would shut me out anyway, given regulations about ex-cons.

You can never win an argument with God. Since 1991 I have volunteered or worked in some capacity dealing with prison ministry. Around 1994 I shifted my focus to prisoner reentry because I kept seeing guys going back into prison. There are many reasons but a big one is there are few known places to go that accept them.

Prior to my current position as director of Stepping Out Ministries I used to do odd jobs on the side. I married an amazing woman who was eager to do ministry with me. We were full-time foster care parents for high-needs children. We started a lucrative landscaping business, kept up with another part-time job, and volunteered with prison ministry. The schedule-juggling became a nightmare.

God wisely asked us to focus—he would honor whatever choices we made—but we couldn't do them all. The landscape business was making more than $125,000 annually. I weighed it against the prison ministry and we gave the business away. Next I stopped the part-time job. The hardest choice was between foster care and prison ministry, especially for my wife. We really believed in early intervention, but we stepped out on faith and decided to go all in for prison reentry with a focus on sex offenders.

God has provided our needs and I am using the darkness of my past in a redemptive way bringing people closer to Jesus and benefitting public safety. It's tough work, but I think that is where God is most glorified and we find joy.

> Whoever serves me must follow me; and where I am, my servant also will be. My Father will honor the one who serves me. ~John 12:26

REACHING OUT TO THE DESPISED

Dan Flemming, Arizona

AFTER EIGHT years as the pastor of a small church in a high-crime area of Phoenix, Arizona, my heart beats for missions, especially to the immediate community. If a church does not minister to its neighborhood then it's largely irrelevant. For us, we have a lot of unemployed people living in low-income housing, and people who have been to prison or have friends and family in prison.

My efforts to build a framework for ministry to prisoners and ex-prisoners have not been an overnight sensation. Success, though, is not always measured by how fast or how many. We're called to do what we can with what God provides.

The Bible has some interesting things to say about prison. In his famous remarks in Matthew 25, Jesus gives us a list of good works that demonstrate the inner character of those who really believe in him. It's clear that "the sheep," as he calls his own, are quite unaware of their activities. That is, they're not doing them to earn salvation. They're just doing them out of an irresistible urge to do what Jesus would do after they've given their lives over to him, by his grace.

And look at the list: feeding the hungry, giving drinks to the thirsty, clothing to the naked, aiding the sick, offering hospitality to strangers. I think most churches are well on board with these kinds of ministries. Most provide some food and clothing bank services, nursing home ministry, and so on. But then we get to this odd one: "I was in prison and you visited me." In the first set of deeds we resonate with the plight of the needy. Life's been tough on them. This last bit about prisoners takes us into more difficult territory.

Prisoners are despised. Some have referred to them as the "new lepers" whom society shuns. Looking at their tough, mean, hardened exteriors can lead to fear, suspicion, rationalization, and a quick decision to let others deal with them.

Yet the Bible is full of crime and imprisonment: Samson, the thieves hanging on crosses next to Jesus, Jeremiah, Joseph, Paul and Silas, Jesus' disciples, and those who should have done some time for their crimes such as David and Moses, who both committed murder.

Our little church has a ministry of writing letters to inmates and taking community service individuals to work around the facility. We are preparing to take in ex-prisoners, mentor them, and get them on their feet.

As a pastor, I have a diverse congregation who all have needs, but I am challenging us to include within our group the people most unlikely to darken our door unless we reach out. So, we're visiting prisoners.

The King will reply, "Truly I tell you, whatever you did for one of the least of these brothers and sisters of mine, you did for me." ~Matthew 25:40

KATY'S* STORY

Dan Flemming, Arizona

IT ALL started with her children. A teacher invited them to attend our church. Pretty soon, Katy started coming as a way to see them while they were in Child Protective Services. Her limited visitation rights allowed it.

But Katy was always strung out on meth and couldn't sit through a Bible study. We got to know her a little—her street life, her dysfunctional relationships with men, the meth lab they ran, the guns they kept for protection, the jail time, and the kids.

She started talking to our janitor, DK, who is also in charge of our community service projects. Occasionally DK gave Katy things to do like picking up trash and vacuuming.

After a year of slow but steady loving on her, she surrendered her will and heart to Christ and was baptized. Then she started marriage counseling with her boyfriend. He also made a profession of faith in Christ and was baptized, after which they got married. He has now held down a real job for four years—a first—given he used to "earn" his living cooking meth.

Katy became involved in Celebrate Recovery—a biblically-based twelve-step program for addictions. She is being loved and ministered to and working her way back to sobriety.

During a park bench conversation with her in our courtyard, she told me she knew that the church cared for her. She said, "The church cared for my kids when they arrived barefoot, dirty, unwashed, and snot running down their noses." She saw the church hug her dirty kids. If they could do that, maybe they could love her, too.

We praise God for the family's growth. It is not over. Their lives still run into chaos here and there—not completely surprising. The journey continues with new trials, but we stay faithful to our calling and remember that her story is just one of many that still need to happen.

> A new command I give you: Love one another. As I have loved you, so you must love one another. ~John 13:34

OCTOBER 22

THY WILL BE DONE

Heather Shaw, Ohio

KARLA FAYE Tucker's story began like many others on death row. Her childhood was marked by abuse, drug use, prostitution, and a broken family. Her life of desperation and hopelessness culminated in the brutal murder of two people in 1983. Then, Karla was led to Christ through a local prison ministry while awaiting trial in a county jail, and her life was transformed.

Karla spent fourteen years on death row. She renamed it "life row," and it was there, in the midst of hopelessness and death, that Karla radiated the peace and joy of God to everyone she met. In an interview with Larry King, Karla explained her upbeat mood in the face of her impending execution:

> It's called the joy of the Lord. When you've done something like I've done and you've been forgiven for it and you're loved—that has a way of so changing you. I have experienced real love. I know what forgiveness is, even when I've done something so horrible. I know that, because God forgave me when I accepted what Jesus did on the cross. When I leave here I'm going to be with him.

Karla hoped and prayed for her sentence to be commuted, but she also accepted that God's will would be done no matter the outcome. In a video she left for her friends in the event of her death, Karla exhorts, "We pray and we believe God is going to do it our way. But if his way is to call me home, we have to accept that. We have to have peace with that, too."

In her life and in her death, it was Karla's desire that Christ be glorified. By her willingness to carry her cross and die to herself—both spiritually and physically—she became a shining light, a comfort, and an example to those imprisoned by bars or by sin.

> For we who are alive are always being given over to death for Jesus' sake, so that his life may also be revealed in our mortal body. So then, death is at work in us, but life is at work in you. ~2 Corinthians 4:11–12

OCTOBER 23

"DO SOMETHING!"

Linda Kesterson, Tennessee

I HAD BEEN praying for God's intervention in the life of my son for some time. Josh had a history of drug addiction when he was younger, but at twenty-five I thought he had put that all behind him. He was "settled," or so I thought; he was in church and had a wife and two sons, whom he adored. Then, something drastically changed.

It was obvious to me he was growing away from God and he was involved in some dangerous behaviors. I watched as he became very irrational, couldn't get to work on time, wasn't paying his bills, and most disturbingly, had lost a great deal of weight in a short period of time. Every time I tried to talk to him about what was going on, he got defensive and angry. I knew from past experience that this was a sign he was using again.

My prayers to God were simply, "Do something!" My pleas to Josh were, "Please stop whatever you are doing and get your life back on track before something happens that can't be fixed." Josh was about to lose his home, he had already lost his job, and his wife was at the end of her rope. I tried to get through to him but something had such a tight grip, I couldn't get anywhere.

Josh would cry out for help, but always he returned to the drug he thought was his lifeline. On June 24, 2011, I watched in despair as my son was taken away in the back of a police cruiser. I didn't know what he had done or how serious the charges were, I just remember seeing his grossly-thin face peering out the back window at me, yelling at me, "Do something!"

I would have done anything to keep him from spending even one night in jail. But there was nothing I could do but keep praying.

> Know then in your heart that as a man disciplines his son, so the Lord your God disciplines you. ~Deuteronomy 8:5

OCTOBER 24

GOD HAS A PLAN
Linda Kesterson, Tennessee

I KNOW IT was God's hand that drove the events that followed. Bail was set high, and while I could have come up with the money if I had really tried, I wasn't sure if it was the right thing to do. I was hopeful Josh's upcoming hearing would bring a reduced bail.

When the day of the hearing arrived, my mother's heart was determined to do whatever I could to get my son out. However, when the judge stated his bond was *doubled,* I was shocked. Suddenly, posting bond was no longer an option.

Three months later, when I sat in a courtroom and watched in horror as Josh, my only son, was sentenced to prison, it was almost surreal. I had gone there so confident God would move in a miraculous way; that I would bring him home. I had trusted God's purpose and made the decision not to post bond. With godly assurance, I had resisted the urge to bankrupt myself in an attempt to provide the finest legal representation money could buy.

As I sat in that courtroom with my daughter-in-law by my side, I was paralyzed by the judge's ruling.

How could this happen? Even men with no faith in God are being set free for more serious charges. After all the prayers . . . after standing in faith . . . after declaring his freedom . . . how could this be happening?

In the days that followed, time seemed to stand still. It was like everything froze and there was nothing I could do. There were so many thoughts spinning in my head of what I should have done and how I might have stopped this. But ultimately, I had to return to the position of faith. I had to accept that I had not, indeed, heard wrong. Just because things didn't go the way I planned, doesn't mean I should not have followed what I believed to be God's direction. I had to settle into the assurance he had a plan and that regardless of the outcome, he is still God.

"I the Lord do not change." ~Malachi 3:6

OCTOBER 25

A TIME TO TRUST

Linda Kesterson, Tennessee

THAT DAY following the court hearing, Josh called me from jail. He sounded so frightened and confused, I wanted to talk to him for hours. I wanted to tell him what to do and what not to do. I wanted to quote all the Scriptures I thought would carry him through, and tell him everything God had ever taught me in an attempt to prepare him for this next step. Even after I hung up the phone there was a whirl of motherly advice filling my mind—things I should have said, and would definitely say the next time. I was anxious and scared for my son.

Then—that blessed still, small voice that so often comes out of nowhere whispered to my heart that this was a time to trust. I've had plenty of opportunities to speak before; so many chances to prepare my children for life's difficult times; so many days God had set aside for me to arm them with the tools they would need for tough times. I had poured into my son's life in the past, but today was a time to trust. A time to "Be still and know that he is God."

I couldn't fix this. I couldn't even make it easier. All I could do was trust that God would give Josh strength and wisdom, and that not one minute of this ordeal would be wasted. I could take comfort in the ways I knew I had spoken into his life in the past, and I also repented for the times I had neglected to do so. I prayed for Josh's safety, and for his spiritual growth. I remembered that God is not so concerned with my son's physical comfort, as much as he is with the condition of his soul. God knows what is needed to get each of us to turn back to him.

For now, all I could do was love and support my son, and trust my heavenly Father.

> There is a time for everything, and a season for every activity under heaven.
> ~Ecclesiastes 3:1

PLANTING SEEDS OF FAITH

Linda Kesterson, Tennessee

ONE OF the little frustrations of having a son in prison has been the responses of well-meaning family, friends, and strangers, who sympathize with his two young sons. I know it's with a compassionate heart, but it seems the world is writing off the lives of these two little guys as being forever scarred and doomed to turmoil. My heart cringes as I almost hear a sentencing spoken over their lives in the whispers of, "Their father is in prison."

As I pray over my grandsons, I remember that "my God works all things together for good for those who love Him" (Romans 8:28). I fully expect God will use these difficult times to strengthen and grow them into young men who hunger after his heart. It may not be easy to see, but I know that the hand of God is on us all.

Due to Josh's incarceration I am with my grandsons quite often. I know someday I will look back on these days with fondness for all the time I've had my grandsons to myself, with the opportunities to speak into their lives the plan and love God has for them. I pray for his divine protection over them, and I refuse to buy into the assumption that they, too, will travel down a road to self-destruction.

Early in this ordeal we decided to be truthful with five-year-old Juelien about where his father is and why. He, in turn, has announced the situation to more than one unprepared stranger. Not quite knowing how to respond, they will look to me for some sort of guidance. With a reassuring smile, I always try to ease the awkwardness of the moment and take advantage of the opportunity to share a testimony of how great God has been to us. God has provided for us all, answering prayer after prayer.

It is not only a welcome relief for the unsuspecting strangers, but with each declaration of God's sovereignty, I hope to plant seeds of faith in their hearts, as well as in my grandkids'. Speaking faith into the situation will hopefully also push out any thoughts of self-pity or hopelessness that might have been sown by well-meaning acquaintances. With absolute trust I believe, as Paul exhorted us to persevere in our trials and hardships knowing that God will use them to refine us as silver in the fire, he will not fail these littlest victims.

Even our own childhood disappointments, in the potter's hands, can be made into a masterpiece. It's never too late to turn our heartbreaks over to the God of Glory who promises to exchange our ashes for beauty.

> ... bestow on them a crown of beauty instead of ashes, the oil of joy instead of mourning, and a garment of praise instead of a spirit of despair. ~Isaiah 61:3

OCTOBER 27

OUR SOVEREIGN GOD

Linda Kesterson, Tennessee

GIVEN SOME time to dry out, Josh soon realized his arrest and time in jail probably saved his life. Had he continued on the path he was on, he would have likely died of some complication of starving himself, never sleeping, or putting dangerous drugs into his weakened body. And if the drugs didn't kill him, some crazy attempt to get them, or driving under the influence, might well have done him in, and possibly other people.

Along with the gratitude Josh has for God's saving grace in his life, as well as in his marriage, he has a new appreciation for the dangers of living a life divided. So many of us have been guilty of dabbling in our sin of choice, all the while believing we can keep it under control and avoid any real consequences. In fact, can't the downfall of the human race be traced back to the belief that the wages of sin really aren't death? But, we can rest in the assurance we not only have a God who forgives, but One who pursues us in our sin and will go to great lengths to bring us safely back to him.

As I look back over these months I remember that first day, feeling as if I couldn't bear to have my precious son spend a weekend in the county jail. I remember fearing for his safety and wondering if his wife would stand by him through this. Their marriage was already shaken and I couldn't blame her if she decided to cut her losses. I knew Josh could lose his family in the process, and I could lose my grandsons. But, as the weeks turned into months, God's amazing grace has become evident in every day. My daughter-in-law, who I had never really had the opportunity to bond with, came to live with me. She began to attend church and dug into God's Word as I have never seen anyone do. My grandsons now walk around singing contemporary Christian music and Juelien, upon seeing some men arguing on the street, announced that they just needed to "cry out to Jesus."

The changes in them, and in me, have been miraculous. And I don't believe twenty years of Sunday services at the local church would have produced the growth I have seen in Josh.

God heard our cries. He answered my prayers. To God be the glory!

> He upholds the cause of the oppressed and gives food to the hungry. The LORD sets prisoners free. ~Psalm 146:7

OCTOBER 28

A CHANGE OF HEART

Michael Brown, Oregon

I HAVE A ministry writing to inmates. I write personal letters, and my wife and I send out monthly newsletters, too. Recently, we mailed 122 newsletters.

It is important to me to keep each letter personal. I want each individual to know they are not just some random forgotten number, placed on them by society. If they are saved through Jesus then they are in right standing with God, and to him they are Number One!

These letters I write are friendship letters. I show the inmates godly love and godly grace, and befriend them as if they were a new neighbor who moved in next door. I have become very close to these guys who write back every week; many are "closer than a brother."

I have to admit, though, that at first I had trouble writing to the men who had committed sexual crimes. But God used a man from Kansas named Richard* to help me in this area. Both Richard and I were molested as young boys. I chose to become a child advocate, and Richard wanted to be a child advocate, but sadly was attracted to young people. He knew these thoughts were wrong, but he could not control them. He faithfully prays for his victim and hopes he didn't scar him in any way. Richard sought help in overcoming this, but even a minister ran him off.

I knew God gave me Richard's name from the pen pal ministry to teach me about the problem from a psychological aspect. I asked Richard to be patient with me and work with me. I needed to understand all this in order to be able to walk in true agape love—from my heart.

During this same time I spoke with another man, Gordon, who had earned his doctorate in theology while inside prison. I shared with Gordon how I was struggling with sexual predators, and told him I felt guilty cheering Richard on in the Lord while I knew he had victims out there scarred for life!

Gordon wrote back such words of wisdom: "Michael, God has sent you to reach out and love and encourage this man from your heart! So you don't have to feel guilty for doing this because God will send someone to help and minister to the victim as well. It's the same as you sowing into somebody's life, then down the road someone else waters."

I've learned two important things from this situation: 1) I've learned how to have compassion for sexual predators, and 2) Gordon reminded me God connected Richard and me. God loves Richard so much he sent me to him, and he certainly has enough love to send somebody to the victim as well!

I planted the seed, Apollos watered it, but God has been making it grow.
~1 Corinthians 3:6

NINETEEN YEARS

Mahluli Guilford, California

NINETEEN YEARS, for some, could seem like a lifetime. Unfortunately, it has proved to be just that for a great number of people. For example, nineteen years is the average age of our military personnel, many of whom have lost their lives in war by that age. It is the same age at which countless young people have fallen at the hands of rival gang members. And, by nineteen, many are tied to the nation's penal system. For me, personally, nineteen represents the number of years I spent ducking the call of Jesus on my life, while in prison.

My family had abandoned me, although my crimes were not against them. I found myself facing the reality of a "twenty-five-years to life" sentence alone. Still, when Jesus called—I ran the other way. One depressing day the realization set in that I despised my life; the best I had done with it was to get myself sentenced to possible life in prison. I could list myriad reasons as to how this sentence came about, but the truth is that I had a faulty core belief system. I managed to reason with myself it was okay for me to take what I wanted, when I wanted it; and that it was permissible for me to administer retribution for things done against me. It may be difficult for some to relate, but this was the law of the land where I came from. Sure, I understood right from wrong, but I would rationalize my bad behavior into acceptable behavior.

After nineteen years in prison, I was transferred to California Men's Colony (CMC), where I immediately became active in a peer-based group called Yokefellows. It is a Christian group in which I made a point to share upfront I was not a Christian, nor did I have any interest in becoming one. They welcomed me anyway.

For five months I reminded everyone of my non-Christian status. In December of 1998 while speaking to the group, I noticed everyone staring at me strangely. I can't tell you what I spoke about, but I do recall that when I finished, one of them said, with the biggest grin I've ever seen, "Sure sounds like a Christian to me."

Everyone laughed and praised the Lord. I simply sat there stunned, and for the first time ever I was at peace with being referred to as a "Christian."

Later that day, while reflecting on the meaning of the day's events, I accepted Jesus as my Lord and Savior. Though I can't say it's been effortless, I can definitely say it has proven to be the best decision I ever made.

> The Lord, the Lord, the compassionate and gracious God, slow to anger, abounding in love and faithfulness, maintaining love to thousands, and forgiving wickedness, rebellion and sin. ~Exodus 34:6

OCTOBER 30

A MIGHTY MAN OF GOD

Sharon Hill, Texas

EVERYONE KNOWS a *prodigal*, someone who is running from God. It could be a son, daughter, spouse, friend, or co-worker. This prodigal has led a lifestyle of making poor choices, causing them and you years of devastating pain.

Such is the case with my son, an alcoholic. I have been crying out to God for his deliverance for more than thirty years. My son does not have a violent bone in him. He is a kind man with a tender heart . . . but stuck in a painful past. As he grew to become a teenager and then a man, it was as though he was always looking into a rear-view mirror—unable to move forward in life. He lived stuck in his past.

This led him to make many poor choices, including use of alcohol and other drugs. Those poor choices resulted in painful consequences: years of on-again, off-again incarceration. He received more than fifteen drunk driving convictions. My son says he has been in more jails and prisons than he has toes and fingers to count—sad, but true.

Visiting your child behind bars, talking through glass partitions, guards constantly nearby, are heart-wrenching experiences. No matter the age of your child, isn't it true the labor pains never seem to end? The heartstrings never untie?

Today, my son is forty-seven years old and through the power of prayer is becoming that *"mighty man of God"* I have spoken over him all his life! He has been out of prison four years, and I am finally seeing the "fruit of my labor." God has proved faithful—he heard my cries.

After many years in prison my son got used to the loud noise and cannot sleep in silence. He now listens to an audio Bible each night when he retires. How blessed it makes this momma to know that God's Word will not return unto him void.

God loves my son! Indeed, he loves all of his children.

> Praise the Lord. Blessed are those who fear the Lord, who find great delight in his commands. Their children will be mighty in the land; the generation of the upright will be blessed. ~Psalms 112:1–2

OCTOBER 31

TURNING PAIN INTO PURPOSE

Michelle McMorris, Illinois

FOR FAR too many years my son had been getting in trouble with the law. What started out as a slap on the hand eventfully turned into every parent's nightmare.

The first time my son served time behind bars I wrestled with the idea of visiting him. One may think that's a no-brainer, an easy choice. Though it may be for some, it wasn't for me. I knew the right thing to do, yet my heart ached at the thought of what I'd see.

Finally, I gathered up the courage to visit him. The chair scraped across the floor as I pulled it back to take a seat in front of the thick sheet of glass that would divide us. A phone receiver hung on the wall beside me. As I waited for my son, I glanced down the row of sectioned-off visiting areas.

It was empty.

That moment it struck me. I was here for my son, but how many inmates didn't have a loved one visiting them? The thought was heart-wrenching.

Sadly, my son continued down the wrong path. We encountered many trials and tribulations. In my deepest pain, when I thought I could stand no more, I cried out to God. I yanked open my Bible and my eyes landed on Matthew 7:7. As I read the words, God spoke to me. Though I thought there was no hope, this verse told me differently: "Ask and it will be given to you; seek and you will find; knock and the door will be opened to you."

Over the next several years my faith grew as God worked in my life. The day I first visited my son, God had planted a seed in me. I, a stay-at-home mom without much money, brainstormed ways to serve the Lord inexpensively from home. It soon came to me to write to the incarcerated.

In 2004 I wrote my very first letter. Today I write to several pen pals. I'm now the coordinator for the pen pal program through my church. I also serve in the prisons and jails, and I began, and now co-lead, a family support group for those who have an incarcerated loved one.

I know that if it were not for the path my son's life took, as hard as it's been, I would not be the person I am today. I'm using the gifts God has blessed me with, and following the passion and calling for my life.

I knocked, and the door opened wide.

> Ask and it will be given to you; seek and you will find; knock and the door will be opened to you. ~Matthew 7:7

THE COST OF CRACK

Dale Rouse, Pennsylvania

WE DID a man wrong. First, he was a friend. He had a business and wanted to help me and my wife. He gave us funds and we used them to pay for room and board, then blew the rest getting high on crack cocaine. That had been our pattern of living for many years.

Things took a turn for the worse—as they always do—when my "ex" broke into this man's place and stole some checks. She wrote checks to me and I had an ID to cash them. We got caught. My arrest, along with a bunch of outstanding warrants, kept me in jail long enough for my little girls to be taken into Child Protective Services. I tried to get them back, but couldn't.

While in jail I met some volunteers who led Bible studies. I really desperately wanted to make a change and I believe God started showing me a little about himself. But when I got out on bail, I took back control of my life. Everything went downhill.

I returned to a shelter after my release and got sober while I waited on my "ex" to be released. We tried again to make our lives work, but the addiction roared back. She always threatened that if I quit the drugs she'd be gone. I was lost and believed I couldn't handle that scenario. But now, all our children were gone. We'd lost the first three of them years earlier to the custody of my parents, courtesy of the same crack addiction cycle.

We lived day-to-day staying in hotels, stealing stuff from stores, and selling it to pawn shops—whatever it took to get through the next twenty-four hours. It was never less than $150 a day.

I also found out my "ex" had met somebody during her last jail stint and was seeing him. It just tore me up. I wanted to get out, but didn't have the strength. For the last year of my addiction, we got high every day until the money was gone. I would lay my head on my pillow and cry myself to sleep. On December 15, 2005, I prayed to God to take this away from me or take me away from this.

The next morning, I had no desire for cocaine. The desire was gone.

You see, at just the right time, when we were still powerless, Christ died for the ungodly. ~Romans 5:6

THE SEESAW OF SURRENDER

Dale Rouse, Pennsylvania

MY EX-WIFE didn't want to quit the drugs and I knew she was still seeing another guy. So I told her we were done and to have this guy pick her up.

I knew I still had to face the music for the stolen checks, breaking and entering, criminal trespass, forgery, and unlawful taking. I knew my "ex" had already been in jail three or four times by now. I figured I'd never been in trouble before in Pennsylvania, where we now roamed. The judge would probably give me probation, something short. I'd get my life together and move on. I told the lawyers I'd take the heat for all of it. I wanted to quit.

That night, however, as things sunk in, I thought of taking my life. I realized I had nothing left. My family wouldn't talk to me, my kids were gone, I ended my marriage, and I had no job. My mom had also been admitted to the hospital recently so I called to say goodbye. My sister, whom I hadn't spoken to in more than a year because of my lifestyle, picked up instead. The first thing she said was, "What's wrong?"

I just broke down. "I can't do this anymore," I told her, and explained my situation. She told me to stay put, she was on her way. We talked for a little while, then she left. Exhausted, I went to sleep.

The next morning I actually talked to my mom, who told me, "You pack your stuff. Dad will be there to pick you up."

I stayed with them a short period of time before I found a place close by so I wouldn't create problems with authority with the kids. I spent a lot of time with the kids. I wanted them to continue listening to my parents while I got my feet on the ground. I also started going to church. Earlier, when my "ex" had been locked up, I met Chaplain Will in the jail parking lot while visiting her. He had invited me to his church—better late than never.

Finally, the time came for me to go to jail. I told the district attorney I would plead guilty for my actions and testify against my wife for what she did. He said, "We don't need her, we got you." I got fifteen to sixty months.

Seek the Lord while he may be found; call on him while he is near. Let the wicked forsake their ways and the unrighteous their thoughts. Let them turn to the Lord, and he will have mercy on them, and to our God, for he will freely pardon. ~Isaiah 55:6–7

MAKING THINGS RIGHT

Dale Rouse, Pennsylvania

I'VE SEEN so many kids wake up their first morning in jail, realize where they are, and the life just drains out of them. It was the same for me. You think, *There's no hope.*

I found the will to ask the officer in charge for request slips. I put them in with Chaplain Will, asked for a Bible, and to sign me up for every Bible study he had. I also signed up for every class offered in the jail—life skills, everything. I began to change. I let God do the changing. I was not capable. The chaplain provided me with a lot of literature, and he was there for me. He told me straight how it is, and backed everything up with Scripture. I kept reading and trying to understand, but I realized you begin by believing it's true; understanding comes later. Finally, certain things started making sense.

The key idea I needed to connect with was that God loved me. He tells you how many times in the Bible? I asked God to forgive my crimes, my failure as a father and husband, my rejection of everything holy and good, and he forgave me. How do I know? He told me in the Bible. When it first happened, I couldn't forgive myself. It took longer for that to sink in. When it did, it became easier to ask forgiveness from others.

The first person I needed to talk to was the man from whom we stole and whose trust we betrayed. I called, asked him not to hang up, and said, "I need to ask your forgiveness." I explained my addiction, but not as an excuse for the things I did to him. I was truly sorry. Then he interrupted.

"Stop. I don't want to talk about the past anymore," he said. "Let's talk about how you can move on." I stole from this man and the first thing he wants to know is how he can help? I didn't deserve that. He opened the door for me to write and call him while I was incarcerated.

This is how God showed his love among us: He sent his one and only Son into the world that we might live through him. This is love: not that we loved God, but that he loved us and sent his Son as an atoning sacrifice for our sins. 1 John 4:9–10

BEING THERE
WHEN IT COUNTS

Dale Rouse, Pennsylvania

ONE OF the hardest things to deal with while incarcerated is that you have no control over anything happening outside. Your opinion doesn't matter to anyone. Life isn't waiting just because I got myself in jail.

While I was inside for crimes technically committed by my "ex," she regained custody of our three older children. Then officers broke the news that my kids, ages seventeen, fifteen, and thirteen, were now in the custody of Adams County and in foster care. That's a bad day.

I set a goal to never be in this position again and to prove I wasn't a failure anymore. It would be hard to prove to anybody, especially my kids. Things got worse. Authorities terminated my parental rights for my two youngest daughters after my "ex" also lost them for failing drug screenings.

I appealed the decision, but the judge did nothing for eight weeks. Time was of the essence because they were up for adoption. All I wanted was visitation. Finally a letter came, "petition dismissed" because someone had adopted the girls. They shut me down before I got my fifteen minutes in court to argue my side. I live with that every day.

In September I felt a little hope. My son played football and on Friday they would observe Senior Night. Senior players get introduced, you hear their goals in life, and they are escorted onto the field by their parents.

I stopped the warden on Tuesday and asked, "I know this is far-fetched, but do you think I could go to his game? My son's mom is not in the picture. His grandmother who raised him most of his life just passed away. It would mean a lot to both of us if I could be there." I was trying my best to participate in the life of my children and do the right things after a lifetime of letting them down.

The warden looked at me like I was crazy. I'd already had three furloughs to see my mom just prior to her death and for her funeral. Still, he agreed to pass it up to the judge. Friday at 12:30 p.m. some officers showed up and said, "Pack your stuff, you're going to your boy's football game."

Never in the history of Adams County Jail has someone been let out to go to a football game. I showed up early at the field and saw them practicing. Matt measures 6'3"—one helmet above his teammates surrounding him. I walked out onto the field and started hollering his name. He looked around, found me, and broke into a big smile. His teammates starting hitting him on the pads and clapping. We hugged and talked. The moment we walked on the field together just prior to kickoff made for one of my best days ever.

Where do I deserve any of that? That's God and his grace. Since my release my son and I have stayed close. I talk to him about every other day. He's saving money and hopes to go to college.

I'm not proud of my past. It's humiliating. It's degrading. I lost my family, my wife, my kids, my homes, my cars, my possessions, my freedom. But God allowed me to go to jail to give me my life back.

> Take delight in the LORD, and he will give you the desires of your heart.
> ~Psalm 37:4

A MOTHER'S HEART

Janell Michael, California

LAST DECEMBER, a group of us from Ebenezer Outreach Ministry sang at the Sierra Conservation Facility in Jamestown, California. This is one of our favorite places to go. The male inmates there are on fire for Jesus. It's exciting to watch, and to also be a part of a worship service with them. It would be a day I would never forget.

During the second service the men's choir sang. What a glorious thing to witness! These men had more sincere desire to bring true praise to the Lord than is seen in many churches. They sang and danced with absolute joy and abandon. I was overwhelmed with what I saw. I could not have been more delighted if I had been watching my own son perform.

Suddenly, I felt nudged to ask Kim, our director, if I could say something to the men in the choir. She said she would have me speak later in the service.

I wasn't sure what I was going to say to them. I just knew I wanted Jesus to speak through me—I wanted his words.

When it was time for me to approach the microphone, the message suddenly became clear to me. I was to talk to them about a mother's heart and how that applied to them.

I told them I'm a mom. I have a nineteen-year-old son. He is the light of my life. He loves to tease me because he can now reach things on the top shelves that I can't. We are very close. My husband actually asked me if I was going to go to college with him when he leaves soon!

Reality tells me, though, that at some point I have to let go of him. In the same way, the men I was speaking to have gone through the same thing with their mothers. Their moms had to let go of them, too. When our kids leave, it doesn't stop us as moms from loving them or caring or worrying about them. We still want the best for them, no matter what circumstances they may find themselves in.

As I continued speaking, I was amazed at how the Holy Spirit took over my mouth. The words of compassion that came out next seemed to bring much hope and comfort.

> Be devoted to one another in love. Honor one another above yourselves.
> ~Romans 12:10

A MOTHER'S LOVE

Janell Michael, California

SO, AS A mother," I continued, "I ask that you men, if for just this one moment in time, would allow me to be your mom. I realize I probably don't look like your mom (this brought a chuckle). And my eyes may not be the same as hers or the color of my hair. But, as a mom I have to tell you how proud I am of each and every one of you for choosing to be with us today in church. I know how much it would mean to me to see my own son worship as you are. I also know what a privilege I have been given to see you praising the Lord. I know that I am getting to see something within these prison walls that your own mothers will never get to see."

With tears streaming down my face, I felt as if the Lord was allowing me to deliver a Christmas present to each man straight from Jesus.

I couldn't help but be reminded of another mother who had to let go of her son. Mary was with Jesus from the time the angel Gabriel declared that she would give birth to the Son of God, to the day she saw Jesus hanging on the cross, ultimately conquering death forever. Mary was there, physically, with Jesus from the beginning to the end of his time here on Earth. She was a witness to Jesus' life, treasuring in her heart many memories of their time together. Can you imagine the pride she must have felt as she saw the miracles Jesus did, knowing he was her son? Or the anguish she also endured when Jesus was so unfairly persecuted? She may not have approved of, or understood, every decision he made, and she was most likely afraid for him at times, but even Mary, ultimately, had to let go of Jesus.

As I looked out over that sea of blue, I was stunned to see men crying. God's words of love had reached their mark. It was an incredible moment. Turning to join my group, I heard a man yell, "Thanks, Mom!"

But it is I who is most thankful—for the opportunity to have been there that day, to witness what "true church" is all about.

> But Mary treasured up all these things and pondered them in her heart.
> ~Luke 2:19

NOVEMBER 7

ON TOP OF THE WORLD

John Leone, Virginia

IN THE early 2000s I was riding on top of the world as a mortgage broker leading a wonderful life. I was rising as a leader at the bank when one day a loan issue popped up that I didn't know how to solve. I went to a vice president who had been in the business a long time, a respected member of the bank's community. He said, "Just do this."

"What do you mean, just do that?"

"Everybody's doing it. Don't worry about it. Just put it in the folder. That folder will go somewhere in Iron Mountain storage never to be seen again." It was obviously cheating and I was uneasy about it, but I did it maybe twenty times among thousands of loans processed over a few years' time.

Lo and behold, during an internal investigation, it turned out to be *not* okay! I committed wire fraud—lying on applications to approve mortgage loans. The bank fired me.

I was a community leader and solid citizen. I can't go to 7-11 without some kid yelling "Hey, Coach Leone!" I didn't even have a traffic ticket in twenty years.

I spent four years going from one job to another, not happy necessarily with my career, but doing okay. Then in 2010 the FBI knocked on my door. I thought I was in the clear by this point. I had actually started with a good company I liked and felt things starting to take off, but the world fell apart from there.

Between August 2010 and September 2011, I spent a year in agony. I confessed to everything. I'm not going to lie to the FBI. The judge sentenced me in June 2011 to sixty days in minimum security and four months of home confinement. I had to wait until September, the day before my fifteenth wedding anniversary, to go to prison.

The John Leone before his first day inside was a shattered mess. I was forced to resign from that good job. I couldn't be a loan officer anymore or start a new career knowing I'd have to ask a new boss for two months off to serve my sentence. I also had to leave football coaching midway through the season.

I lived with high uncertainty and anxiety, paired with drinking lots of alcohol almost every night. My wife was obviously upset with me, knowing where I was going. Our kids looked at me as if I were a loser. I can't go to Home Depot, restaurants, or the grocery store without seeing lots of people I know. Complete shame is there.

That's the misery I was going through. When I see any story on TV about somebody going to prison now, I wonder if he's a guy who just made a couple of bad decisions and had his whole life turned upside down.

> People who have wealth but lack understanding are like the beasts that perish. ~Psalm 49:20

WAKING UP AT FCI SCHUYLKILL

John Leone, Virginia

MY FATHER drove me the surreal three hours from Virginia to self-surrender at the prison in Pennsylvania. We talked about the directions one takes, trying to have a heart-to-heart and answer life's questions. He handed me a new Bible in plain English. He knew I had resisted my faith for years.

I'm probably a fairly typical Catholic, having been raised in Catholic schools. My faith was fairly important to me during those years, but around sixteen years old I just started falling away. Church doctrine was so strict with rules and regulations. I thought, *God didn't make these rules. Somebody else made these up along the way to suit the power structure.* I'm ashamed to say it now, but I really believed that the story of Jesus was not much different than the Easter Bunny and Santa Claus. *It's just a way to galvanize kids around a wonderful story.*

Now I'm processing through FCI Schuylkill minimum-security camp. Each unit has four ranges with twenty-eight to thirty prisoners in their cubicles.

I spent only two nights in overflow before they assigned me a bunk. It was a sleepless night. I woke up in the morning completely fuzzy. Everything was humid and moist. People were milling around. Opposite my row a prisoner named Joe asks, "Hey, you want a cup of coffee?"

"Boy, I'd love a cup of coffee." They don't serve coffee in prison. You have to buy your own. He made some and said, "Let's go for a walk." We went and sat in the rock garden and just talked. Joe was raised in the same environment as me. We talked about our families and children. Joe was the kind face you meet when you're the new kid. Soon, he'd have me regularly attending inmate-led Bible studies and reconsidering my positions on Jesus. We became good friends.

A few days later I finally visited the doctor to discuss my hypertension. I'd been treated for it for a few years, but you can't bring pills into prison. He took my blood pressure and reported it to be completely normal. All the high anxiety prior to prison had just fallen away.

No wonder—life in camp was a big slowdown. I didn't even get a job because I was only going to be there for sixty days. You can sleep all day if you want and turn into a blob. I walked five to seven miles a day.

Like others, prison gave me a healthy dose of humanity. The kindly way inmates were leading their lives surprised me. This fellowship of Christians—of all backgrounds or none—led by example. It became the catalyst for me to discover true faith.

> In the same way, let your light shine before others, that they may see your good deeds and glorify your Father in heaven. ~Matthew 5:16

NOVEMBER 9

THE RETURN

John Leone, Virginia

PRISON STARTED me on a path to understand how God sent his son to suffer and die for me. A lot of people skip past that because it happened 2,000 years ago—it's just a story. That's what I told myself for years anyway. Now I see it's *the* story—*History*. I know this probably never happens to anyone else, but while I enjoyed the Bible study groups inside with sincere believers, a lot of them got off track. I can't say I put it all together doctrinally.

When I got home, my friend Gerard helped me figure out the rest. The rules of home confinement mean you don't get out much except for a job and a single weekly religious service. With no job in my first month, I did what I could around the house. Gerard was so excited to help that he loaded me up with DVD messages by Louie Giglio.

I painted my basement and listened to Louie for six hours straight. He's that good—an absolutely gifted teacher of the Bible and just what I needed during Part 2 of my prescribed sentence "time out." He opened my heart and mind to who God is and how I relate to him.

I also decided to spend my only religious slot going to Gerard's men's study group. It has been a way to get into fellowship with men grounded in their faith.

This prison episode continues to have an impact on me and my family spiritually. I've moved from "Jesus and Santa are equally nonexistent," to "Why me?" to "Okay, God, I don't know why, but I know you're doing it. Help me get down the path you want me to go." High blood pressure and anxiety have been replaced with smiles, knowing there is a plan for my life.

Other important things are changing, too. My wife and I used to wind down around 9 p.m. Typically before prison, I went downstairs to watch TV by myself and the kids would pile in the bed with her and watch their program. It bothered me, but I didn't do anything about it. Now, I'm always with them watching whatever they want. I wouldn't give that up for anything—the four of us laughing while my 75-pound Labrador tries to sit on top of me.

It's sad so many of us have to suffer and cause others to suffer before seeing the light. But thank God, he lets us see it even when we don't deserve it.

> I run in the path of your commands, for you have broadened my understanding.
> ~Psalm 119:32

NOVEMBER 10

THE LETTER

Kim Rojas, Oregon

THE LETTER sat on my desk, unopened. I stared at it, afraid to open it. Why? Because I knew—I knew there was some secret in that letter I didn't want to read, didn't want to tackle.

The sender was an old family friend with a history of attracting trouble. Maybe that was why I hesitated. How was I to know, though, that the pages of that letter would forever change my life? That reading the enclosed handwritten words would lead to a ten-year conflict that would change my view of my God, myself, and my life forever?

He was a prisoner, a regular guy who served a series of short sentences for petty crimes. Since I was active in our church's prison ministry, I had seen no risk as a woman in writing an initial letter of encouragement to him. His name was Donny. His return letter arrived just days later.

Oh, just open it, I convinced myself. *You don't have to do anything but read it.*

I breathed out a quick prayer and tore it open.

By page 4, I was glad I had opened it. He was funny, honest, and humble. He headed up a Bible study on Tuesday mornings in the prison and told amazing stories of conversions. By the end of the letter, his tone had become serious. "Before we get reacquainted, there's something I need to tell you," he wrote. I was impressed with his candidness, and the more I tried to resist it, the more I realized how much I liked and respected this old family friend.

I read on. "I'm HIV positive."

Strangely, that's when I knew I would marry him.

I worried I was making the wrong decision. My pastor cautioned me, my friends were uncertain, and my family never knew I was becoming involved with an HIV-positive man. But, God knew. In his Word I had read that he would direct my path. Somewhere deep inside me, that same place where faith must live, I felt safe. It would work out, somehow.

> See, I lay a stone in Zion, a chosen and precious cornerstone, and the one who trusts in him will never be put to shame. ~1 Peter 2:6

NOVEMBER 11

CHAIR MAN OF THE LORD

Kim Rojas, Oregon

HE WAS a modern-day leper, an outcast scorned. He was called the Alphabet Man with Hepatitis B, Hepatitis C, and HIV. He had early signs of cirrhosis and other ailments. No one said it, but I could see it in their faces—my friends thought I was crazy. I liked him before I knew about the HIV, and I liked him after the fact. I didn't know what God had in mind, but I trusted my God and I trusted what I read in the Bible.

We wrote letters for a year getting to know each other as friends. Shortly after Donny's release, we were married. We reached out in many areas in the community looking for what God might have us do as a couple—in ministry. Though we volunteered at hospitals, homeless shelters, and youth programs, nothing hit home like the first time we did prison ministry.

Donny stopped short at the door before we entered; he had a look I'd never seen before. And then, he smiled. "This is the first time I'm going through these doors round-trip."

And it wouldn't be the last. When Donny would preach to these men he'd take his rap sheet (history of arrests) from his youth with him. Donny had more than five hundred entries—a huge pile of pages. We taped them together, end-to-end and rolled them up like a roll of paper towels. It literally dragged on the floor. Donny would stand on a chair, one arm in the air and the other with the rap sheet. As a result, he became known as "The Chair Man of the Lord." God had truly delivered him from his old life. Several men gave their hearts to Christ after hearing Donny's bold testimony.

Everywhere he went Donny told people about his Lord and Savior, Jesus Christ. And people believed. One time at a medical office, he frankly asked the doctor, "Do you believe that God has given you the gift to heal with your hands?"

The doctor smiled. "I suppose so."

"Good, then put your hands on me and let's ask God to heal me."

And the doctor agreed. This simple act of faith made me realize how many opportunities are available to share Christ. It's not about another "notch in the believer's belt," but more like, *Whom can Jesus touch today?*

If I would only step out in faith . . . as Donny did.

Now fear the LORD and serve him with all faithfulness. ~Joshua 24:14

THEY TOLD ME SO

Kim Rojas, Oregon

THE FIRST five years of our marriage worked. As marriages do, ours began to have problems. I thought his initial drug relapse was a one-time mistake and could not believe it when his second relapse happened about a year later. I knew I had to forgive him because he was truly sorry.

I wondered if being closer to his family would strengthen him. Since we were both from the same small town, we packed up and made the three-thousand-mile trip home. Donny returned to the hospital where he had originally been diagnosed with HIV a decade earlier when he was a prisoner. He now stood clean, sober, and free. Some of the same medical staff from his past cheered him on. This was a good move.

For a while.

His next relapse ended him up at the hospital. When I got the call, my thoughts instantly were full of fear, thinking, *Oh no, they're going to tell me the worst.* After I learned he was alive, then I felt so betrayed; he had lied to me again. Anger filled the center of my body and I didn't know what to do with it. The emergency room doctor's voice was smooth and even, as he told me that in his twenty-seven years of emergency medicine, he had never seen a body more ravaged by drugs and alcohol.

Oftentimes, we hide our pain behind a smile or a nod. Not until the pain is so great does it show in our physical being. And suddenly, I thought of Donny's pain—his unimaginable pain— and my heart ached for him. The constant war of the many diseases in his beaten-down frame, coupled with battling addiction, must have been unbearable at times. This experience was beyond my human ability to comprehend. I caught a glimpse inside someone's soul, past all the dirt and the sores, the disease and the motive. That day, I learned why Jesus Christ died for me, the same way he died for Donny. And I loved him.

> And so we know and rely on the love God has for us. God is love. Whoever lives in love lives in God, and God in them. ~1 John 4:16

NOVEMBER 13

REMEMBERING THE VOW

Kim Rojas, Oregon

WHEN WE exchanged vows, Donny's Scripture passage was Matthew 25:35–36: "For I was hungry and you gave me something to eat, I was thirsty and you gave me something to drink, I was a stranger and you invited me in, I needed clothes and you clothed me, I was sick and you looked after me, I was in prison and you came to visit me."

And now, seven years later, after the umpteenth relapse, I continued to forgive him, but things still got worse. He began getting motor vehicle violations and landing in jail. Our marriage had long been destroyed. Because of his drug use, his infected body had declined even more. He lost twenty pounds and could not hold down food. He spent a lot of time in bed, and, finally, the relapses stopped because he simply could not leave the apartment. His T-cell count had dipped below two hundred, which meant he now had transitioned from HIV to full-blown AIDS.

One day, from his sweaty pillow, he clutched my arm, a tormented look in his eye.

"I'm so sorry. You've given me the best life I could ask for and I've ruined yours."

My mind wanted to justify those words; I had a mental list just waiting to spew forth detailing how badly he had hurt me, incident after incident, time after time, but I just couldn't. Instead, I thought of Jesus. Another passage (Matthew 18: 21–22) popped into my mind. Those verses came rushing with such force; they were thoughts I did not put there! I knew it was the Holy Spirit speaking to me through the power of God's Word. I knew God wanted my attention, and he had it. "Then Peter came to Jesus and asked, 'Lord, how many times shall I forgive my brother when he sins against me? Up to seven times?' Jesus answered, 'I tell you, not seven times, but seventy times seven.'"

Heavy conviction fell upon me; it felt as if a part of me died.

> But love your enemies, do good to them, and lend to them without expecting to get anything back. Then your reward will be great, and you will be children of the Most High, because he is kind to the ungrateful and wicked. Be merciful, just as your Father is merciful. Do not judge, and you will not be judged. Do not condemn, and you will not be condemned. Forgive, and you will be forgiven. Give, and it will be given to you. A good measure, pressed down, shaken together and running over, will be poured into your lap. For with the measure you use, it will be measured to you. ~Luke 6:35–38

NOVEMBER 14

MY TURN TO DIE

Kim Rojas, Oregon

WITH A good diet and careful medical attention, Donny's numbers began to rise and he was soon back to church, back to work, and . . . back to his old life in the gutter. He was beyond the point of no return and so was I. For all my faith, for the risk of contracting HIV, the hospital calls, the wasted money, broken trust, a failed marriage—this was my lot in life?

It had been seven years since I opened that first letter. From deep within me came the wicked truth. My heart hardened, violent and evil, I looked him in the eye and said, "With all my heart, I want you to die."

That sentence didn't faze him, but it devastated me. I couldn't believe not only that I said it, but that I meant it. Did it take this much for me to see my own wickedness; my own sinfulness?

Then one day, the hospital called. He was in a coma again. This time it was a bicycle accident that damaged his spleen. I went to the hospital in case this was the time he was going to die. But, it wasn't his time; it was mine again.

We laughed together like old times and I pretended that the tears rolling down my cheeks were from the laughter.

"You're a really good person, ya know," he said. "I'm going to put in a word for you when I get to heaven."

And though I wanted to hate him, I couldn't. And I saw him that day through the eyes of God. I ached for him and I ached for me, because I was much more sinful than he and because he really knew how to forgive.

A couple of years later, a letter arrived for me from the county jail. I didn't recognize the name. Odd. I tore it open. In a few paragraphs from a regular guy, the writer described his cellmate, Donny. I rolled my eyes. I couldn't believe Donny had given a stranger my address.

He said Donny had shared his heart with him and he had accepted Jesus. Now, the two studied every night. This prisoner said Donny had a strange glow in his face. My heart sank; I wasn't leading anyone to Christ. And again heavy conviction. Another part of me died.

A few days later, I got the call that Donny had passed away in prison. I sometimes think what would have happened and what different paths my life would have taken had I not read that first letter a decade ago. Should I have left that letter unopened?

I think not.

Come to me, all you who are weary and burdened, and I will give you rest.
~Matthew 11:28

FROM RAGS TO RICHES

Jerry Smith, Illinois

EVER WONDER what life would be like homeless, sleeping under a bridge in the cold winter months? I don't have to wonder—I lived it for ten long years. It ended when I was arrested and sent to Cook County Jail in Chicago, Illinois.

I had turned to theft to support my forty-three-year alcohol and crack cocaine habit. I don't view getting arrested as a bad thing, though. No, I was rescued by the Lord. With my life spinning out of control, I was on a suicide mission—one that could only be averted by divine intervention.

On December 13, 2010, a church from the area came to Cook County Jail for a Christmas celebration. This service was optional for the inmates. But thankfully, I chose to be there.

A pastor came with the group and when he spoke of brokenness, it pierced my heart. I felt the Holy Spirit touch my very soul. For once, I was coming face-to-face with myself, having been running from myself for more than four decades. Halfway through the worship songs, I broke down and cried. At that moment, I not only realized there was a God, but I also knew he loved me and wanted to lead me to a much better life.

Later, when I went back to my cell, it was as if a ton of bricks had been lifted off my shoulders, heart, and soul. I'm the first to admit I'm a hard-headed, stubborn man, yet it was no accident I was in that room that night. I believe that God sent his loving and obedient servants to sing songs of worship and deliver a message straight from the Lord to touch my soul.

When I'm released I plan to attend that church, get baptized, and serve the Lord in the church. For now, I'm reading all the books on faith and how to grow spiritually I can get my hands on.

I know this journey won't be easy; God doesn't promise us it will be. But I truly believe, all things are possible with him in my life.

For the wages of sin is death, but the gift of God is eternal life in Christ Jesus our Lord. ~Romans 6:23

RETURNING HEARTS CELEBRATION

Callie J. Bond, Illinois

EACH YEAR, AWANA* puts together an amazing event at Angola State Penitentiary, in Angola, Louisiana. Returning Hearts Celebration is an event where the incarcerated men of Angola have the opportunity to spend a day with their loved ones.

As a volunteer, the day before the event I was given the rules, shown around the grounds, and told what to expect the following day. The volunteers could pick from a handful of jobs, such as helping with check-in, running the games, or being a Family Assistant.

I chose Family Assistant. My job was to stay with the inmate and family member(s), whether that was their grandchildren, nephew or niece, or their children. The agenda for the day involved playing games, face painting, having family photos taken, and eating lunch.

On the day of the event we gathered at the rodeo grounds with volunteers on one side of the bleachers and the inmates on the other. After the children were checked in, they entered the field and gave the name of the person they were there to see. When the inmate's name was called, he'd jump up from his seat and dash across the field. Once the kids spotted him, they'd often take off running, jumping into his arms as he smothered them with kisses. For some, this was their first time meeting. For others, they hadn't seen one another since the last Returning Hearts event.

As I spent the day with the family, I saw the love the children had for their fathers, grandfathers, or uncles, as well as the love the inmates had for the kids. I witnessed lots of laughter, smiles, and hugs.

Saying goodbye is never easy, but when you have to say goodbye to a loved one you may not see again for an entire year, the goodbyes can be almost unbearable. Hugs and tears were abundant from inmates, kids, and volunteers alike.

What an amazing blessing the inmates and children were given that day! I ended the day humbled and with a deeper love and appreciation for my own children. But mostly, I was in awe of God's splendid mercy and love.

> And he will go on before the Lord, in the spirit and power of Elijah, to turn the hearts of the parents to their children and the disobedient to the wisdom of the righteous—to make ready a people prepared for the Lord. ~Luke 1:17

*AWANA (Approved Workmen Are Not Ashamed) is an international evangelical nonprofit organization whose mission is to help churches and parents worldwide raise children and youth to know, love, and serve Christ.

NOVEMBER 17

MANIPULATION

Marcus Baird, Colorado

CHAPLAINS SERVE Christ in ministering to the incarcerated, but it's also a job. Part of the job stress we endure involves dealing with inmates' different personalities seven to twelve hours a day.

A lot of guys try to play the chaplain and take advantage of him. They'll test to see how far they can push. I'm privy to a lot of their games. As a former prisoner, I used to play them myself. Many don't realize that, so it gives me an advantage. You're constantly contending with fallen people who have been manipulators most of their lives. It's deeply ingrained in their character. They believe they must do it to survive. I have to help them know that God desires to give them a new heart and change their attitude about how to treat people.

A Christian inmate who had been locked up most of twenty-four years was transferred to my unit. He really wanted to join our inmate praise team. He came into my office with an upbeat attitude, then subtly worked the praise team into the conversation and all the things he could do to "fix" it. He tried to assert leadership over the others, too.

Eventually he wanted to be the one shaping the style and song choices alone. I'm about holding people accountable, especially Christians. I said some things to remind him of his place.

We passed each other a day later and I asked how he was doing. He gave me that mean, nasty convict look. Everyone tries to have things his way, and uses manipulation to get there.

Another inmate who helped me a lot complained about head congestion. I asked if he got anything from the medication nurse. "Yeah chaplain, I got it, but is there any way you could bring me something that's, you know, a little more effective?"

"I can't believe you even asked me that." It's completely against the rules and we both knew it. Inmates have desires and try to get them fulfilled in an inappropriate way. That doesn't count the times I get requests for favors like letters to judges to help guys with their cases and other situations that are not only inappropriate, but unethical, or rule violations.

That's a side of offenders many volunteers don't see. Whether Christian or not, everyone puts on the face they think you want to see to try to get something out of you. That doesn't mean the Christian inmates are practicing "jailhouse religion." It just means they have work to do on their character as do the rest of us.

The reality as a chaplain in prison: You live eight-plus hours a day inside and see the good, the bad, and the ugly. I also get to see them change, which is exciting.

> You were taught, with regard to your former way of life, to put off your old self, which is being corrupted by its deceitful desires; to be made new in the attitude of your minds. ~Ephesians 4:22–23

NOVEMBER 18

I DON'T ALWAYS HAVE AN ANSWER

Marcus Baird, Colorado

DEATH NOTIFICATIONS unleash stress possibly more than any other role for a chaplain. It's a moment of ultimate truth for everyone, but for prisoners it carries extra burdens due to the physical separation. Death, like nothing else, makes us want to be together in those dark hours of loss.

One prisoner called his family from my office to learn a close relative had been murdered. The inmate began bawling, fell out of the chair, and rolled about on the floor. I've never seen anyone react that physically. When he settled back into the chair we started processing it together.

Not all death notifications affect you. You keep some distance because it's your job, but some sneak through the firewall and you feel like crying with them.

The shift commander from a medium-security facility called to tell me an inmate's wife and son had been in an accident on their way to church. His wife was killed and the ten-year-old son was in critical condition (later paralyzed for the rest of his life). Could I come by and deliver the news?

That was my most difficult emergency notification in seventeen years. My son was also ten, which brought it home. Heart-wrenching barely works to describe it. Even prison staff were affected. This prisoner had been a Christian before his incarceration, but was caught for something related to taxes.

First, I'm not sure it's the wisest use of public dollars to lock up a non-violent offender who hardly fits into prison society as we know it today. He made a mistake, but had been raising his family well. Now he faces the most devastating news a father and husband can hear from prison.

Not everyone wants to hear about God, believer or not, after something like this happens. You have to allow people to vent and express their anger and confusion toward God. I tell the guys, "It's okay, God already knows about it. It doesn't offend Jesus to express anger."

We need to be upfront with the emotions God's given us. He allows us to wrestle with these things. Commonly I have to say we don't always understand what God is doing. I just direct the conversation toward God's grace.

This prisoner hung on to his faith through a lot of tears. It certainly challenged me. Despite the mistakes people make that lead to prison, they still bleed, suffer, and grieve. Some people may think that's okay because they've messed up and they deserve it. I think that's a little misguided. Paying for your crimes is one thing. The suffering that comes with life happens to us all and should not keep us from stooping to aid and "love our neighbor" as Christ did for each of us.

Do not seek revenge or bear a grudge against anyone among your people, but love your neighbor as yourself. I am the LORD. ~Leviticus 19:18

ACCEPT YOUR CIRCUMSTANCES

Timothy James Burke, Ohio

I HAVE had a blessed life. It hasn't been without its struggles, setbacks, and unwelcome surprises, of course. I had two loving parents, a safe home, plenty of food on the table, good schools, and pals to play with. Most of the problems I've had I've created myself. However, I didn't always see it that way.

After some experiences of abuse while growing up, I started seeing the world through a victim's eyes. I thought the odds were stacked against me, and that I was somehow marked; that people could identify me as someone to treat like an inferior. What I didn't learn until much later was that, by having that (mistaken) belief, I established the way people would treat me. I created my role in our relationship; it wasn't the other way around.

For example, Jesus never struck me as being a victim, even though he was put upon, chased around, beaten, and eventually killed. He wasn't a victim because he *chose* to accept the circumstances as an opportunity to express himself and his message to mankind. Wow! That is the perfect example of humility and love being transformed into power! And it inspires me to view this experience in prison as a way to become more patient and loving, tolerant and understanding, too. It transforms prison into a place to practice generosity, forgiveness, and courage.

I have come to a point where I am thankful for my hardships and trials, and for the people and situations that test me. I think of obstacles not as problems that hold me back, but as platforms I can climb on. When presented with difficulties, I see them as challenges—as chances to attain new levels of personal growth. The greater the hardship, the greater the opportunity: Like the two sides of a coin, they are inseparable and mutually valuable.

Consider it pure joy, my brothers and sisters, whenever you face trials of many kinds, because you know that the testing of your faith produces perseverance. James 1:2–3

BROKEN DIMPLES

Elsa Kok Colopy, Colorado

S HE WALKED up and placed her warm hands in mine. I noticed her smile right away. Her dimples cratered out, one deeper than the other.

"Wow," I said. "You have beautiful dimples!"

"Uh," she said shyly. "This one's not a dimple. It's a scar from when he pushed me down the stairs."

"Oh." My voice cracked and tears filled my eyes as I asked her how I could pray for her.

"I just want to be reunited with my family someday. I miss them."

I bowed my head. "God, give me words."

I think I prayed for twenty women at that maximum-security prison event in Topeka Friday night. Each one came to me with eyes full of tears, a heart so tender and broken.

Some would say that I held the hands of murderers, thieves, and addicts. I would say I held the hands of moms, sisters, and daughters. Most of them asked for prayer for those on the outside. "I have five children," said one woman who looked no older than my daughter. "Please pray that I can pull my life together and be a mom to them."

By the tenth woman, I had a hard time keeping it together; so much pain in one room.

"Please God," my heart cried, "hear their prayers. Heal their hearts, rescue their children, and bring hope and life where there is only despair and death."

My prayers seemed too small for the bigness of the hurt; a drop of grace in a bucket of sorrow.

The woman with the broken dimple stiffened her wrist as I held her hands. She turned one to the side and I glanced down. A long, jagged scar marked the inside of her arm.

Scars on the outside, scars on the inside.

I have tears in my eyes as I write this. I'm feeling a bit like all I did was place a tiny Band-Aid on their gaping wounds. I feel the weight of their hurt and know there are thousands and thousands just like them all around this country, all around this world.

It makes me cry.

God, use those of us who are able to scoop up the wounded and hurting. Show us how to love with all of our hearts.

Maybe if we each extend a drop of grace, their buckets will fill to overflowing. Maybe if we each apply a tiny Band-Aid, we can bind up their wounds. Maybe if we each carry one soul into God's throne room, he can wrap his arms around them there . . . and turn their broken dimples into joy.

Oh, Lord, may it be so.

(Excerpted with permission from www.godhasdimples.com)

> He heals the brokenhearted and binds up their wounds. ~Psalm 147:3

NOVEMBER 21

IN THE EYE OF THE BEHOLDER
Elsa Kok Colopy, Colorado

THE WOMEN of La Vista Correctional Facility in Colorado filed into the visitors' area for our time together. Some entered with smiles; others came visibly bearing their burdens. While many appeared to be older than their years, several looked fresh out of high school. Blond hair, blue eyes, pretty smiles . . . and prison garb. A few wore orange pants, a signal they had broken a rule and were now separated from the rest of the prison population.

Jodi and Carol, the faithful volunteer warriors who serve the women every week, put on the worship music. The ladies lit up. Hands raised, the inmates began to fill the room with praise.

I closed my eyes. It seemed like a hundred women were singing together, so strong and passionate was their song. I could almost picture the angels surrounding us . . . *mighty* . . . *glorious* . . . *majestic*. It truly felt as if their voices were mingling with our own. For a brief moment, it took me to heaven as I forgot my own cares and concerns and let myself become engulfed in silently praising the Lord with the women. There was such a sweet spirit in the room; tears pooled in my eyes.

I finally opened my eyes and scanned the room, lingering on the heavy metal doors locked from either side. I couldn't help but think, while these women may not be free to come and go as they please, for some, being locked up has given them their first true sense of freedom—in Christ.

To the right of those doors I noticed the bathroom. There was a simple paper sign taped to its door: "Offender Restroom."

I paused on the first word . . . "Offender."

I turned to look at the women. Arms raised in worship; tears on their cheeks. And then back to the sign.

"Offender."

I bowed my head as the tears slid down my own cheeks.

"Offender." Yes, each woman there was serving time for a crime she committed. But, as I watched these ladies worship, a whole different set of words came to mind: *princess, beloved, cherished, redeemed, rescued . . . beautiful.*

(Excerpted with permission from www.godhasdimples.com)

> He brought them out of darkness, the utter darkness, and broke away their chains. ~Psalm 107:14

NOVEMBER 22

THANKSGIVING DAY FEAST

Kym McNabney, Illinois

MOST PEOPLE begin Thanksgiving Day in anticipation of a family gathering in a home with loved ones. On November 27, 2008, I rose in the early hours to visit a place most wouldn't care to visit at all, much less spend a portion of their holiday.

For several years a group of dedicated men from my church have been going into Cook County Jail every Monday evening for Bible lessons with the men on Division 14. These volunteers have a huge heart for those behind bars. Serving in prison and jail ministry for almost a decade, I've been blessed to get to know many of these volunteer men. Because of that, I was asked if I wanted to serve with a team to bring a Thanksgiving meal to the men of Division 14.

This was not the first time I'd been inside a facility, although it was my first time at Cook County Jail. I wasn't sure what to expect, but I have a strong faith and I trusted God. One of our jobs as volunteers was to set up the room for the men to receive a Thanksgiving meal provided with

403

donations. We had the full spread: turkey, gravy, bread, pasta, and stuffing. Several groups of men were invited and would attend in shifts of fifty to seventy-five. There would be singing, words of worship, and a prayer to bless the men, the staff, and, most importantly, God.

The men entered single file and made their way along the table of food. My job was to dish out the mashed potatoes. I greeted each inmate with a smile and tried to make eye contact. They returned a grin, and a heartfelt, "Thank you." Many acknowledged their appreciation for taking time away from our families to serve them.

It was a struggle to keep my tears at bay. Obviously, this was a huge blessing to them.

When the last group of men left with Styrofoam containers overflowing with food, I reflected on the morning. It was well past noon, and though my stomach rumbled with hunger, my heart was full. I hadn't eaten an ounce of a Thanksgiving meal—yet it was the best Thanksgiving I'd ever had, and will remain forever embedded in my heart.

The message of Jesus was never clearer to me—serve one another.

> For I was hungry, and you fed me. I was thirsty, and you gave me drink. I was a stranger, and you invited me into your home. I was naked, and you gave me clothing. I was sick, and you cared for me. I was in prison, and you visited me. ~Matthew 25:35–36

NOVEMBER 23

NECKLACES MADE WITH LOVE

Kym McNabney, Illinois

AS THE coordinator for the Adult Prison Pen Pal Program for Willow Creek Community Church, one of my jobs is to answer any mail that comes in from the prisons and jails. I've read hundreds of letters, many asking for Bibles, Christian books, and study material.

On January 11, 2011, I received a letter from a man incarcerated in Texas. He was asking for a specific book. Unfortunately, Willow, for financial reasons, can't honor every request. However, there have been a few times when I've been prompted by the Holy Spirit to use my own resources.

Clifford's letter was filled with compassion and love for Jesus. I felt a tug to honor his request for the book. Included with his letter was a necklace in the shape of a heart with a cross through the middle. Remarkably, it was made with his own hands from vegetable and garbage bags of various colors.

An idea came to me. If he'd make enough necklaces for my daughter's Sunday school class, I'd purchase him that book. The next letter I received was filled with excitement. He had a purpose and went right to work. When they were completed, my daughter's small group leader passed them out. Each girl had her own questions about the man who made them.

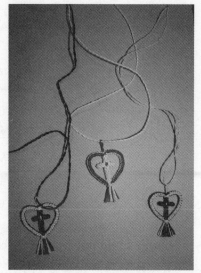

CLIFFORD'S NECKLACES

Clifford wrote them the most amazing letter—filled with words of wisdom and compassion. He didn't want these little girls to make the same mistakes he had, yet he made sure to let them know that Jesus had saved his life.

The girls sat mesmerized as the leader read Clifford's letter. The following Sunday the girls made him the most wonderful cards telling him to hang in there—that Jesus loves him and so do they.

Then, at the start of the Christmas season, the girls decided to make him cards again. The leader didn't realize the strict policies of these institutions. They had decorated the cards with all kinds of things I feared would cause them to be rejected.

But—somehow a miracle occurred and God allowed the cards through. Clifford was so proud of his holiday cards! He hung them on the metal bars of his cell. The guards would pass by and admire the array of red and green paper, decked out with colorful markings and sparkly foam snowflakes. Clifford proudly told them about the hearts of the nine-year-olds from a church in Illinois, hearts that cared for the least of these.

Continue to remember those in prison as if you were together with them in prison, and those who are mistreated as if you yourselves were suffering.
~Hebrews 13:3

LETTER TO A CHILDREN'S SUNDAY SCHOOL CLASS

Clifford Wheatley, Texas

AFTER CLIFFORD received the thank-you note from the girls in the Sunday school class for the necklaces, he sent them the following letter:

To my young friends at Willow Creek Community Church:
Hi from Clifford, the cross maker, in Texas. First let me say that I am very happy to hear that you like the cross necklaces that I made for you. I had fun making them for each of you.

I hear that you are about eight years old, maybe nine. I guess you know that I'm in jail. The reason I'm in jail now at the age of fifty-two is because of decisions, mistakes, and wrong choices that I made, beginning when I was nine years old, your age. Hard to believe that the choices we make at such a young age can have consequences that last a lifetime.

Are you wondering what I could have done at your age that could cause me to be in jail? Well, I was warned by my mother and father not to do it. You are all very smart and I know that your parents and your teachers have told you the very same thing that mine told me when I was your age. You will each have to make decisions and choices just like I did.

What I'm talking about is drugs. I wish I could find the right words to tell you how bad they are and not to ever try them. It's even worse today than it was when I was your age.

Drugs are everywhere. I let an older friend of mine talk me into smoking marijuana. He said it wouldn't hurt me. I wish I would have just said "No." I did say "No" at first, but then I got curious. It didn't seem to be hurting him, so I tried it. That was the biggest mistake of my entire life, a mistake I made when I was nine-years old, a mistake that has cost me everything. It broke my mother's heart, too, and landed me in prison.

Drugs don't get a hold of you all at once—it's gradual. At first it is kind of fun. It didn't seem as bad as they say. I lived in California back then and had a real nice family. I started playing guitar on Christmas

Day when I was seven years old. I loved my guitar and still do. I hung around with older guys who played guitar and they would teach me. They were all using drugs, and I wanted to fit in, so I did, too. Little did I know what my choices would cost me.

> Evildoers do not understand what is right, but those who seek the LORD understand it fully. ~Proverbs 28:5

JUST SAY "NO"

Clifford Wheatley, Texas

CLIFFORD'S LETTER to the girls in the Sunday school class at Willow Creek Community Church continues:

As I grew older I started playing in bands at different places. Everywhere we went there were drugs and alcohol. It took some time before all the bad stuff started happening. It tricked me. Before I made it to college to be a guitar major, several of my friends had died in car accidents due to drugs, but that still didn't stop me. In college there were even more drugs.

One day I realized I was addicted to drugs and couldn't quit. If I didn't have them I would feel really bad. They made me do things I knew I shouldn't do, but my body craved them. That was a terrible feeling and I got scared and didn't know what to do. I was afraid to tell anybody the truth. I was afraid to stop and afraid not to stop. Before I knew it, drugs took control of my life. I had to quit school because I couldn't think and do all my homework. I was failing. I joined the Navy and thought if I moved and quit playing my guitar that would fix things, but it didn't.

I started playing guitar in the Navy band and made two trips overseas while in the band. Everywhere I went there were still drugs. It got worse.

I had two bad car wrecks and by a miracle, didn't die. Then I woke up in a hospital and didn't know what happened. They said I almost died from too many drugs. For some reason God had saved me. But he didn't keep me from jail. I have to pay for my mistakes. God kept me alive though. Maybe it was just so I could write this letter and tell you about the bad choices I made when I was nine years old.

"God, I pray that you will let these special young people learn from my mistakes so none of them will ever go to jail or prison or die from using drugs. Amen."

Thanks for letting me share a little of my story. I don't want to leave you feeling bad or sad though. I'm doing really well here. I'm not on drugs anymore, I have a job here, and lots of friends. My mother is still alive and lives in Oklahoma. We write a lot and talk on the phone. We have been through a lot together. I told her all about y'all and that I got to make you some cross necklaces.

Thanks again. I would love to hear from you. I will be here for a while so let me know if you want more heart crosses. Oh, I learned how to make them in jail.

God bless each of you,
Clifford

Repent, then, and turn to God, so that your sins may be wiped out, that times of refreshing may come from the Lord. ~Acts 3:19

NOVEMBER 26

ANOTHER CHANCE
Robin Schaeferkraft, Ohio

IT WAS August when I came to prison, several years ago. I felt all alone and lost. I cried myself to sleep many nights and believed that even God had forsaken me. I wanted to die.

The sadness wouldn't leave, so that October when I went to Commissary (the store where inmates shop) I bought a bottle of aspirin. When I got back to my room a voice in my head told me to take the whole bottle— and that is what I did. I took 100 aspirin and then I lay down and waited to die.

To my surprise I actually awoke the next day, but I was extremely sick. I went out into the Rec room with my friend, Teresa, and she asked me why I was so sick. I told her what I had done. She immediately went to the corrections officer and he sent me to our medical department. They rushed me to the hospital and I ended up spending five days in ICU. The doctors were worried about my heart, brain, and liver because of the amount of aspirin I took. I began to pray, like I had never prayed before, that I would not suffer what the doctors were testing me for.

Everyone, including me, was amazed that my brain was functioning so well. I was alert enough that a verse from my childhood crept in: "Ask and it shall be given you," from Matthew 7:7. Believe me, I not only asked, I *begged* God I would not have the medical problems the doctors feared. And, praise God—all the tests came back normal! God heard my plea and not only saved me from death, he also saved me from a life of medical problems!

I will always be grateful I was familiar with that Scripture verse when I tried to end my life. The Bible is the most important book there is.

Whenever I get depressed about being in this place, I reflect on how God saved me, and I get the strength to face another day.

God still hears prayers. I am *living* proof.

May the Lord answer you when you are in distress. ~Psalm 20:1

NOVEMBER 27

FREEDOM

Steve Gunning, Minnesota

IN PRISON they say you have "rabbit blood" if you have a history of planning escapes. I did. I spent ten years at Oak Park Heights because of it. Somebody got cold feet and turned himself in, landing me in isolation, where I could hear hell itself. That was early in my sentence. Authorities see that in an inmate's file and know that if you go to a medium facility, there's nothing to stop you if you're really serious about escape. To get me into the InnerChange Freedom Initiative pre-release program they would have to take that chance.

When you're a lifer at a maximum-security prison and are told you will be transferred to a medium it means they are going to let you go free, eventually. Unless you mess up, you're going home. Even non-Christians lose their motivation to escape with that hope dangling in front of them.

I see a lot of irony in my past escape plans and my newfound freedom. My view of God had to radically change. I saw him as a tyrant. I thought the truth would crush me. I'd plunged so deep into darkness I believed that God had to lower the boom on me.

I grew up in a rural Minnesota town with a population of 599 near the Red River Valley. Mom hugged me once in a while, but we did not have a close relationship. It was all about work. I only saw Dad a couple of months a year because he was always away at work. I learned to be self-sufficient and alone.

I developed a secret life of rebellion while I showed people the acceptable hard-working farm boy exterior. The seriousness increased. I masked everything with drugs and alcohol. The one life got so strong, I couldn't hide it. It took over until I committed a murder at thirty-one.

When I look back on the prison I created for myself, it brings tears to my eyes. I put myself in cuffs, leg chain, body chain and the jumpsuit before I spent a day in the Minnesota Department of Corrections.

I didn't realize that, unless you confess the dark secrets, they enslave you and determine the life you live. When something has power over you it's a beast. But if you open up about it, shine the light on it, then it loses its power—especially through Christ's blood on the cross.

God doesn't want to destroy me. He's a loving father who wants to talk with me in intimate relationship. That was a freedom I'd never experienced before. Not long after I started living in that truth, the parole board found reasons to give me a chance at physical freedom.

> The Spirit of the Sovereign Lord is on me, because the LORD has anointed me to proclaim good news to the poor. He has sent me to bind up the brokenhearted, to proclaim freedom for the captives and release from darkness for the prisoners. ~Isaiah 61:1

WANTS VERSUS NEEDS

Steven Gunning, Minnesota

I'M GETTING back up to speed without getting wrapped up in the affairs of the world. There is a war inside. You want everything, but you have to sit back and ask, "Do I need it?"

I did more than twenty-three years and came from a setting where I've been restricted and deprived of many things. For example, I'd like to have a better job and a better-paying job. Currently I work as a janitor from 4 p.m. to about 1 a.m. It's a good interim job, and pays decently. For this season of my life it's exactly what I need until I pass my journeyman electrician's license.

Wants? I'd like to have my own place. The halfway house where I live costs $275 a month vs. $600 a month for a single apartment. I could afford the apartment, but I couldn't put as much into savings. I need to save three months of income and first and last month's rent, so if something happens I'm not without a place to live.

I'd like to have a place to call my own, because I have a roommate in a place the size of the prison cell I just left. It's workable. I've got support and stability. People here care. I need that more than being alone in a new apartment. When I'm alone I can talk myself into anything. I've proven that in the past. Isolation is not a good thing for me.

I was given a nice 1997 Pontiac Grand Am—nothing wrong with it. I'd like a newer vehicle. I'm a motorhead. Instead, I'm going to be stubborn and see how long I can make the car last. A friend invited me to get a Harley to go riding with him. But I need to build up my credit rating so I can think about buying a distressed property, renovate it, then see if I could rent it out. I'm fifty-four and don't really have retirement income. I have to get creative. Buying a Harley isn't a wise decision for me.

Part of me wants to look sharp in newer clothes, but it's not necessary so I shop thrift stores. If people are judging me because of my clothing I don't want to be around them.

Matthew 6:33 absolutely pops me in the face all the time. It's hard to keep your life centered. Everything is designed to draw a person away from God and lessen the time you spend reading his Word. It's hard not to see something to want every day. So it goes like this:

"Lord, you're right, I'm not ready. That beast of a vehicle gets ten miles to the gallon. I'm already filling up twice a week. That would bankrupt me."

> But seek first his kingdom and his righteousness, and all these things will be given to you as well. ~Matthew 6:33

NOVEMBER 29

FIRST MONTH ON THE JOB

Raeanne Hance, Florida

IN NOVEMBER 1999 I started my new position at Prison Fellowship and ran right into a major crisis. Angel Tree® is our big Christmas program where prisoners sign up their children to receive presents and the gospel. We then recruit local churches to "adopt" these children by taking tags off the tree, buying them gifts, and delivering them. The goal is twofold—we reach prisoners with a demonstration of grace by giving their families what they could never do alone, and we reach their families with the love of the local church. But the problem was, with just three weeks before our delivery deadline we still had 5,500 kids to cover in the Miami-Dade area!

We were out of time to recruit more churches and we simply didn't have enough staff to step in and make up the difference. I remember staring at my computer with this mammoth problem, asking God, "How am I possibly going to get this done? We made a promise to the prisoners and their children that we can't break."

The Holy Spirit whispered to me, "Call Joey at FedEx." Next, he reminded me of a friend who works at a bank, which we would need to process $25,000 in transactions. Shortly after I made those calls an amazing donor stepped forward and gave us the money to pay for the gifts!

Yet, can you believe I still had doubts? It takes a lot of people and vehicles to sort and deliver that many gifts to hard-to-reach addresses. I didn't have confidence as to how it would all come together.

On the Sunday before Christmas my husband and I drove down I-95 to the old FedEx distribution center in Miami. We saw a lot of trucks. My husband said, "Look! They are all here for your project."

"No, they're working," I said doubtfully.

"Not on Sunday," he replied. Sure enough, twenty-eight trucks had arrived from all over Florida, from the Keys to Tallahassee. Inside we saw an enormous conveyor belt moving bags of tagged gifts FedEx had sorted. Even a vice president came out and spoke with each driver, thanking them and encouraging them to be safe. He even prayed for our effort. Every driver was a volunteer and FedEx fueled all the trucks. Within four hours every gift was loaded. God shouldered my programmatic crisis to give me the faith I would need not just for the rest of the day, but far into my career.

> Command those who are rich in this present world not to be arrogant nor to put their hope in wealth, which is so uncertain, but to put their hope in God, who richly provides us with everything for our enjoyment. ~1 Timothy 6:17

NOVEMBER 30

SURPRISING DELIVERY
Raeanne Hance, Florida

THE CLIMAX to this huge operation is getting to deliver the gifts. I hopped in a truck with José*. When FedEx announced the need for volunteers, he decided to show up, which is saying something because there was a big Dolphins game that afternoon.

The first shoebox-sized house we delivered to wouldn't open the barred door. It's not uncommon in Miami to see bars on doors and even gates barring access to driveways. José whipped out his phone and called. When they understood we had gifts, they let us in.

Inside we could see a small, sparsely decorated tree and not one gift. The inmate who signed his children up had just been released home a few days earlier and was very glad to see us. He needed a job and asked for our prayers. José watched the gift program in action and especially my praying with the family. His first question when we returned to the truck: "Why did you pray with them?"

I explained what the Bible says regarding prayer—that prayers of faith that line up with the will of God are answered, that we're to never cease praying. Then he stopped me and asked, "What does all that mean?" The surprises just kept coming. I'm focused on the idea that we're bringing the gospel to children of prisoners. But along the way, God interrupted by reaching out to José. By the end of the day, he was so overwhelmed by everything we did, he prayed to accept Christ.

Looking back, that experience sustained me for the next twelve years of ministry. I discovered God is able when I am not. But I needed to truly believe in and rely on God's transforming power in order to work with prisoners.

> You, God, are awesome in your sanctuary; the God of Israel gives power and strength to his people. Praise be to God! ~Psalm 68:35

TORTURED JOURNEY

Mike Ownby, Washington

I HATED the world and everybody in it. I could see nothing good, anywhere. Instead of breaking my heart, this worldview turned it cold, cal-
lous, and hard. I was vehemently opposed to the idea of a God, especially
one who allowed all the suffering I'd seen.

My world was Spokane, Washington, where my father was locked
away for armed robbery. I grew up in poverty, used narcotics, and became
an enforcer for drug dealers. I collected debts by committing robberies
and home invasions. My new girlfriend once suggested we quit our drug
habit. I told her she was crazy. I saw only two possible exits: death or
prison.

Police caught me with assault weapons in the trunk of my vehicle and
off I went for my first stint in jail. When I arrived a fellow noticed me sitting alone. I don't know how I appeared, but he came over and told me,
"You look lonely." You don't tell people you're lonely in prison. It's a sign
of weakness and an invitation to unwanted attention. But in that moment
I looked up and honestly said, "Yes, I am."

"I know a friend to the end. Do you want to know him?" I thought
he's talking about someone to bail me out.

"Jesus Christ is your friend to the end. He'll never leave you or forsake you." He prayed a prayer, which I didn't follow, and then everybody
got locked up. That was the first point at which God tried to get to me.
They released me from jail, but in a few months I'd be back to serve a
longer sentence. During this break, life continued to spin out of control.

Early one evening I blew up at my mom and left in a rage. I walked
in the middle of a dark road and stopped under a street light. I began an
interaction with this God I didn't believe in. "How can you allow all this
suffering?" I was using profanity.

"I will never believe in anything I can't see, feel, or touch! You're God
Almighty and you won't give us a sign? You won't give little bitty me a
glimpse that you're there? If you're real, turn that street light off." I was
way out of line. A few cars go by and the light winks out.

"No. No. The car headlights tripped the sensor into daylight mode
and made it go off. Make it go off when no cars go by." The light went
back on.

I waited ten minutes with a little anticipation in my heart. Doubt crept back. "That's right, you're not real." At that moment, the light went off. It shook me. I wish I could say that was my salvation moment, but I was still very confused. I knew there was a God and I knew Jesus was connected somehow. So that began a journey toward the cross.

> As the crowds increased, Jesus said, "This is a wicked generation. It asks for a sign, but none will be given it except the sign of Jonah." Luke 11:29

GOSPEL OF HATE

Mike Ownby, Washington

DURING THAT first prison stint I tried forms of worship and religion, but really didn't get it. People could tell, too. If you wanted to get drugs, you had to listen to my perverted gospel about Jesus who paid it all—you didn't have to stop your wicked ways. There was no repentance and it drove people crazy, but you had to listen because I had the drugs and guns. It upset my girlfriend, with whom I now had a daughter.

Soon enough I'm back to prison for robbery with a four-year sentence. I wanted to make a promise to my daughter to stop doing drugs, to be a husband, get married, and do right. I'm going to serve God and do right.

Halfway through my term, officers caught me bringing drugs into prison. It destroyed the whole "do good and get out" plan.

I realized I can't do this faith alone. So I prayed that night, "God, if you don't send me somebody, I'm going to walk away forever."

Next morning at chow I sat next to a big guy frustrated by some guards who wouldn't let him use the law library. I knew he'd gone to church. I threw out to him, "What would Jesus do?"

I heard a white supremacist across the way say, "What *would* Jesus do?"

"God calls us to be salt of the earth. What does salt do? It holds back corruption."

We went to the yard and talked. He gave me a white supremacist's view of the Bible, how we were to blow up abortion clinics, kill Jews who killed Jesus, rob banks because they employ usury, and kill the police who protect the system. He used Old Testament stories about a priest who speared some people and David the warrior, who held back oppression.

I wondered, *Is this why I've never been able to follow you? I didn't have the right perspective?*

He took me systematically through the white supremacist gospel. We fasted on Yom Kippur for 24 hours. We talked about what we could do for the kingdom of God.

I got news I was heading back to minimum security, so my new white supremacist friends and I devise an escape plan. I will break out of the less secure facility, contact some people who have missile launchers, and assault the medium-security fence to get them out. It was extreme. I started ending all my former relationships. Anyone not in this gang had to be rejected.

I'd made the decision to live for God. Loving people in this life would interfere with accomplishing God's stuff. I was pretty sure I would die in that effort.

> For the time will come when people will not put up with sound doctrine. Instead, to suit their own desires, they will gather around them a great number of teachers to say what their itching ears want to hear. ~2 Timothy 4:3

DECEMBER 3

SMOKING-PAD CHRISTIANS
Mike Ownby, Washington

THE DAY of my transfer to a lower-security prison came around Christmas. I needed a month to get on the right work crew that would put me outside the perimeter where a white supremacist contact could pick me up and complete the escape. As I wait I'm finding nobody else has the resolve to do something as insane as assault a prison with heavy weapons. Most of the gang who seemed committed to these violent schemes lived in the higher-security prison waiting for me to start the fireworks to get them out.

While the wait continues, I'm often out on the smoking pad keeping to myself. However, I keep hearing the "smoking-pad Christians" talk about the Bible and Jesus. I can't help listening. They talked about love, so I eventually started speaking up, trying to promote this crazy doctrine in which I'd been schooled. I'm using the rhetoric the white supremacists taught me.

"That's crazy!" one inmate said. And they opened the Bible to verse after verse about love, God is love, greater love has no man than this. They had a ton of passages completely opposed to what I'd learned. They wouldn't stop. Every time they saw me they had a new verse. I became very frustrated and confused and privately said, "God, I'm done! This is too much."

He spoke to me in that moment: "You can kill and die for me, but you can't live and love for me." What a heart check! He showed me exactly where my heart was and where it needed to be. In the jumbled mess of religious information I'd acquired, that was the moment real truth asserted itself. I started attending chapel again and went to a Prison Fellowship workshop called "You Are Fearfully and Wonderfully Made."

One guy, Charlie, could hardly speak without tears. He had such overwhelming love for prisoners. It's like he stood next to Jesus. After hearing what he had to say, I got on my knees and gave my life to Christ. That was my born-again experience. I don't really remember what the rest of the seminar was about.

I didn't give my participation in the white supremacist group another thought. I walked away and nothing could stop me.

> Jesus replied, "Very truly I tell you, no one can see the kingdom of God unless they are born again." ~John 3:3

NAME-CALLING AND A BATHROOM BRAWL

Mike Ownby, Washington

THERE IS persecution for following Christ. I had run with a hard crowd. In prison there are some people—often sex offenders of all stripes—who use the church for protection. Like me, some have come to know Christ, but many others are not serious about Jesus. Therefore anyone who goes to church gets tarred as a sex offender, child molester, or rapist.

Chow hall is a big deal. Where you sit is important (it's stupid stuff). Some of the rough crowd watched me once as I loaded my plate. There was an open chair among them and some Christians sitting toward the back.

"Dude, what's up? You gonna come over here and sit?" a guy I knew asked as he gestured for me to sit.

"Nah, I can't do it. I'm going back there."

"You're going to go sit with the rapists! What are you thinking?" But I went and sat down anyway. I'm 6'4", about 260 pounds—no one casually picked a fight with me. I didn't appreciate the slurs.

Like it or not, fighting is part of the landscape even for Christians. I was in the weight room working out and paused to get a drink. A guy blazed past me into the bathroom and takes a fighting stance. A brother, Art, followed him in. They were ready for blows.

Immediately I separated them, and pushed Art out of the bathroom. I could tell he didn't want to fight, but when you're called out you have no choice. If you don't, everybody considers you vulnerable and starts mistreating you. He didn't want to be seen as a coward. He said, "No, no, Mike, don't do this."

"I'm not letting it happen. Get out of here, don't stop walking!"

I turned to the other fellow, "He's not fighting. You want to beat me up, take your best shot." In prison you're not supposed to step in on other people's fights.

The other guy was very mad. A few of his friends noticed and told me to butt out. I didn't budge, "Art is not going down."

They said some things about it not being right and it came to nothing. I don't know why God allowed me to be there, but I knew in Christ that's not how we handle our business. We don't allow ourselves to be tempted into physical violence. We love our captors and live for Christ. Art was a struggling Christian, like I was. I just felt I needed to intercede for my brother.

> Blessed are you when people insult you, persecute you and falsely say all kinds of evil against you because of me. Rejoice and be glad, because great is your reward in heaven, for in the same way they persecuted the prophets who were before you. ~Matthew 5:11–12

LOG OUT OF THE FIRE

Mike Ownby, Washington

I CAME to life in prison. My brothers became my family. I remember a cold Christmas day, when four brothers and I spent the entire day in a small doorway just talking about the Lord—one of the best days of my life. We had such a unity of spirit. I didn't want to leave prison as I got close to release. I knew what awaited me because I'd been through it before.

When I walked out of prison there was a lot of instability. I checked out several churches, but found no connection, no discipleship. I didn't connect with the body and fell flat on my face into drug abuse. When I got to the real world, I was a babe in Christ again—managing bills, making entertainment choices. Community in prison is easier without the same volume of temptations. I had no mentors helping me grow, keeping me accountable.

Mom had been my anchor. She was a successful nurse at a hospital. She planned to provide me a vehicle and housing. I thought I'd make a good start. She went from perfect health to death from cancer in one year. She came to Christ in part from what God had done in my life, but losing her knocked out my most important peg. I was like a log outside a fire. I went cold.

My girlfriend was vulnerable coming out of the lifestyle herself. We had patched things back together after my being under the brief spell of the white supremacists. However, we didn't stay pure. I realized it would wreck me. The Holy Spirit convicted quickly. My girlfriend would ask, "What's going on with you? You get depressed with our choices."

I told her plainly, "We need to get married. I can't live like this. It's not okay. God can't honor it." She agreed. We did.

During this period of faithlessness, I saw grace take over, including several spiritual trips to God's woodshed. If Mike's not following Christ, praying and reading daily, everybody around me is going to know it. My weaknesses don't allow much room for failure, the way someone could ignore their family while pursuing their golf game. It's all sin, just different consequences.

I'm grateful God didn't leave me that way. He turned my whole situation around, again. He showed me that prison isn't necessarily the worst moment, though it can be. Sin can still stalk you and take you down—dramatic conversion or not.

> What shall we say, then? Shall we go on sinning so that grace may increase? By no means! We are those who have died to sin; how can we live in it any longer? Or don't you know that all of us who were baptized into Christ Jesus were baptized into his death? ~Romans 6:1–3

MINING TO MISSIONS
Mike Ownby, Washington

I SAW A TV show about modern marvels featuring the gigantic electric shovel. It lifts 160 tons of ore per scoop. It wields 1,000 tons of torque and can put 300 tons of material in a massive three-story hauler in thirty seconds. One shovel uses the same power as a small city in twenty-four hours. One slight mistake swinging that massive arm and you can hit the back of a 100-ton truck and send it to the ground. I've seen it. It's nonstop, fast-paced for twelve hours to maximize profits.

I thought, *If you've done that, you've arrived.* In prayer I asked God to let me run heavy equipment. While I struggled during that first year out, I did attend a school for heavy machinery training.

I moved the family to Arizona and landed a job at a copper mine. After six months, management put me on the seat of a new $20 million electric shovel. I prayed God would give me the same ability he gave those who built the temple. He did.

My first year out on a very hard mountain I placed third in percentage performance in a field of seventy seasoned operators. I just excelled my way to the top. My pride and arrogance grew to match the size of the machine—massive.

I was living in "Mayberry," with a beautiful double-wide house and no crime—a contrast to our old neighborhood. I was making $80,000 a year. My wife didn't have to work. We were supporting Voice of the Martyrs, missionaries, and generously giving to the church. But my life was mostly work.

Then the Lord says to me, "Is this what you're living for? Is this the top?" I realized God had greater plans. We decided to return to the Spokane we left originally to get away from my criminal past. God sent us back to our mission field.

We founded a discipleship house for anybody in trouble, but focused on ex-prisoner transition. It's all about Christ 24/7 and can take up to sixteen people at a time. Living with people is different than smiling at people once a week on Sunday. One guy told me he couldn't be a Christian six or seven days a week. He left and went back to jail.

While I was doing this, God placed some spiritual heavy-hitters in my life, godly men walking in the Lord for twenty to thirty years who encouraged me and kept me accountable.

Since 2000 I haven't received even a speeding ticket. I manage a sub-outlet of a business. I have the combo to the safe, manage the money, and make sure other people don't steal. I have keys to the church, provide security, and am one of the deacons. God can do a lot even with an ex-robber like me.

> Does the LORD delight in burnt offerings and sacrifices as much as in obeying the LORD? To obey is better than sacrifice, and to heed is better than the fat of rams. ~1 Samuel 15:22

DECEMBER 7

GOD AND SINNERS RECONCILED

Terry Carter, Ohio

ONE COLD night, just days before Christmas while on duty as a cop, I kept glancing into the rearview mirror of the police cruiser. The reflection I kept seeing was yet another sad face in the backseat. I sometimes struggle with this part of my job. The sadness and fear on the faces of the newly arrested made me long to ask if I could pray with them. Seeing yet another person on their way to being locked up, especially during this time of year, always tugged at my heart.

Usually I would say a silent prayer, asking God to show me how I could subtly point them to him, and bring comfort in some small way. This time the answer was clear—sing a Christmas carol.

When another officer was with me, he or she would often get perturbed at my compassion. "These guys are getting what they deserve," was the attitude of most. I struggled with that attitude, because we've all sinned. I know there is a difference between sin and breaking the law, but still, breaking the law boils down to sin, and none of us is immune. Many people behind bars never thought they would end up committing the crimes they have committed, but little sins snowballed in their life.

Sadly, the reoccurring theme in most of these inmates' lives is the breakdown of the family. There was usually no father figure present throughout their childhood. If their parents did get married, they divorced shortly thereafter, and again, very little involvement of the dads.

God often reminds me that only by his grace am I on the enforcement side of the law. Thankfully I was born into a decent family and was given a good start. Had I not been so blessed right off the bat, who knows?

I had to leave the force in my early forties due to disability. I got hurt while chasing a perpetrator. But for months now, I'd been nudged to get inside the jail—but this time in ministry.

Now the inmates don't have to suffer through my singing, and I am able to openly talk to them about Jesus, share my testimony, and pray with them. I am blessed to live in a county where jail ministry is not only allowed, but supported and respected.

Some of the lyrics to a favorite Christmas carol are "God and sinners reconciled." And that's what it's all about: sharing with others, imprisoned or free, about the life-changing love of Jesus. Even those behind bars—they, too, can be reconciled to God.

But he was pierced for our transgressions, he was crushed for our iniquities; the punishment that brought us peace was upon him, and by his wounds we are healed. ~Isaiah 53:5

DISRESPECT OR REPENTANCE

Wendy McDaniel, Illinois

WE HAD arrived at the Stateville Prison in Joliet, Illinois. Our team consisted of Manny, my husband, Tom, and me. We've served with Manny many times, but it would be a day of firsts for me: the first time I ever had a worship service under armed guards, the first time I'd spoken to a room full of rival gang members, and the first time I had a problem with an inmate disrespecting me.

As the men filed in we greeted each of them. One young man stood out, leading me to think he had a high rank in a gang. He took my extended hand. His eyes slowly scanned my body from head to toe. "Nice to see you, too," he said, with a smug grin.

The young man took a seat directly behind me. I could feel his eyes on me when I stood to speak. As I sat back down, I crossed my legs. He called over my shoulder, "Nice socks." I replied I wore Christmas socks to remind me every day was a holiday.

Manny delivered an amazing sermon, Spirit-filled and full of truth. At the end he asked if anyone wanted to give his life to Christ. I turned to see the man behind me stand. As the men filed out of the room, this man headed straight for me. He looked me square in the eye and said, "I'm sorry." I knew what the apology was for.

Two years after our visit I was at Lake County Jail for a Bible study. The officer noticed my Bible cover from Angola Prison and asked how I got it. I explained about the ministry we have there. A voice behind me said, "I know someone who goes there." I asked who, and he responded, "Manny."

"I work alongside him with my husband," I replied. "Where did you see him?"

"At Stateville," the young man said. I looked closer at him and he at me. A smile spread across his face as he blurted out, "Christmas socks!"

This young man read Manny's book, finished a Bible study, and was working on getting his current case overturned. Can God change a heart? You bet he can! He goes down to the bottom of the basket and grabs them all. I consider it an honor to have been part of one of this young man's first acts of repentance.

And if you greet only your own people, what are you doing more than others? Do not even pagans do that? ~Matthew 5:47

THE FRUIT OF THE SPIRIT

Toni K. Cyan-Brock, Texas

ONE MIGHT only look as far as a visiting room, or a tattered letter held in one's hand, to see the fruit of the Spirit working through the people who love us most. How is it possible to feel something for someone you can't see or touch, be it God or man? Yet we do, and when we do, we grow and flower and bear fruit.

The ground is hard in prison, and people will tell you your love will not grow there, that it cannot sustain. But love, and the rest of the fruit of the Spirit, does indeed grow there. Whether inside the prison or outside, it is only through a supernatural strength and grace that we persevere, while others wither and fall away.

The fruit of the Spirit wouldn't seem like something that would grow well in a house of correction. It can be an extreme act of bravery (some may say outright stupidity), to expect these gifts in a penitentiary environment.

While my (someday) husband was making his way through the penal system, I was struggling in many ways myself. It was then I secretly prayed for a husband who would share my yoke and burdens. Just a few days later my childhood friend asked me to marry him, but . . . he was incarcerated.

That night when I went to say my prayers, I remember saying, "God, are you joking me? Seriously? The answer to my prayer is in prison, and he may never get out?"

The fact was—my heart knew it was true. I said, "Yes."

The sorrows we carried as individuals fell away. We are an equally-yoked team and have been for sixteen years. The fruit of the Spirit has replaced the cultivated violence in his countenance with the strength to exhibit kindness, and I have come to trust and have patience that God's will is going to come to fruition in his time. Together we can both see that the Spirit of God moves through us, and everyone with whom we come in contact.

The smallest of seeds turns into a mighty tree, and bears fruit in even the harshest of prison soils.

But the fruit of the Spirit is love, joy, peace, forbearance, kindness, goodness, faithfulness, gentleness and self-control. Against such things there is no law.
~Galatians 5:22–23

LOST CAUSES

Ron Nikkel

THE CARING of people who follow Jesus makes a difference. As the president of Prison Fellowship International I've been in well over one thousand prisons in one hundred countries and I've seen this everywhere I've gone. What kind of difference? In some cases, prisoners are transformed because they come to know Jesus. In other cases, people who had no hope find some measure of hope and meaning, perhaps nudging them closer to knowing God. In still other cases, it becomes a bridge to reconciliation with family and victims and an avenue of restoration. They come out of prison and they have the support, the affirmation, the friendship they need in order to take a different path.

Certainly many people in prison deserve to be there, but they deserve hope and an opportunity to change their ways. Just putting them in prison consigns them to a life of no way out, no exit. Often we treat inmates as lost causes, and people who are repeatedly told that will *act* like losers, too. It makes it nearly impossible to change.

Sure there are a lot of other ministry needs in this world, but I think something that gets to the heart of society as much as any social need is this issue: How do you deal with people who fail in the community—offenders? Failure replicates failure. One thing communities can't do is turn evil into good. From a Christian perspective, prison is one of the most strategic places in any society to bear witness to the transforming reality of Christ. No institution or program can accomplish this. Prisons are the intersection of two failures—individual and social. Recidivism is the evidence of that.

I don't think the impact of prison ministry is measured exclusively in terms of what we call salvation. It's seen in all the ways in which good comes out of a bad situation. To the extent that I love other people, it's not just a means to an end. Some come to a relationship with Jesus, others don't. But, I'm either nudging people toward God and Jesus, or I'm nudging them away. All the positive things we can do for prisoners—improving life, extending a hand of friendship, giving them dignity—nudge them toward good and toward God.

While we were still sinners, Christ died for us. ~Romans 5:8

UNTOUCHABLES REACH FOR THE INVISIBLE GOD

Ron Nikkel

TWENTY YEARS ago, I took Chuck Colson to India and visited the central prison in Trevandrum, in the state of Karola. The inspector general of the prison was a devout Hindu, high-caste Brahmin; very professional. Among prison directors, he's one of the best I've met. He really did seem to care about his staff and institution. He showed us around the prison, maybe 1,500 inmates all dressed in white uniforms. The prison was a remnant of colonialism—overcrowded, no air conditioning, rudimentary facilities, men sleeping on the bare floor or straw. Large cells would hold twenty to thirty inmates. I believe the IG was doing the best he could with the available resources.

At one point he invited us to talk to the men. We said we would love to. We did tell the superintendent, "We are Christians and we're going to talk about Jesus."

He said, "That's okay, it won't hurt them." In his mind, as good a man as he was, they are beyond the vale of redemption. Telling the inmates about Jesus was not an affront to their Hindu way of life—they are "lost causes."

He had all of them assembled in the central courtyard, more than one thousand inmates. They set up a square box upon which we could stand to address them. All the inmates sat on their haunches in a big circle around us. I gave introductions, spoke a few minutes, and then Chuck spoke. When we were done, we waded into the crowd. All of a sudden they stood, surrounded us, reached out and touched us; one after another, not shaking hands, just touching. We wondered what was going on. It took a long time, but they would touch and withdraw.

Chuck talked about the God who cares and loves. It doesn't matter where they came from or what they've done. We concluded that most of the inmates are from the lower castes, the untouchable Dalits, and even if they weren't born that way, when one commits an offense, often his family disowns him completely, due to the shame. We had talked about a Father God who doesn't reject, but embraces. We told the story of the prodigal son. We realized they were touching us to see if it was real. Would we back off as their families had? Is this love real and can it be

427

touched, or are we so untouchable you won't let us touch it? It was a surreal experience to be surrounded by a sea of prisoners grasping, touching, and reaching for a personification of the invisible God. The message has to be made real. Jesus became flesh. He wasn't just an idea.

The Word became flesh and made his dwelling among us. We have seen his glory, the glory of the One and Only, who came from the Father, full of grace and truth. ~John 1:14

DECEMBER 12

GOD CHANGES OUR DESIRES
Pat Brown, Florida

I BEGAN my pen pal prison ministry about seven years ago to share my love for Jesus with those seeking comfort and hope in their desolate lives. Several stopped writing for one reason or another; however, about four years ago I began writing to John Henry, who was in prison for possession of drugs. He served time on several different occasions and came to know Jesus during his last incarceration. He soon began sharing his love for Jesus with others, starting a ministry behind bars. During that time his love for Jesus deepened and his life was changed forever. He promised God that when he got out he would do whatever it took to share God's Word with others.

In 2010, John was released and began his new life in the outside world. He was hired by a trusting employer, married a wonderful woman, and started "Chainbreaker Ministry." The team members in Chainbreaker Ministry are mostly ex-inmates and they visit prisoners in the Texas prison system. They understand the bondage behind bars and wish to bring the Good News that God will "break their chains."

John has seen many men come to know Jesus Christ as their Savior and come to see a deeper meaning for their existence when Christ-followers visit them and offer prayers for them in his holy name. John's life continues to grow and be changed as he watches those he ministers to find peace and hope in the living Word of God.

I continue to correspond with John and each time I receive an e-mail I feel more and more convinced prison ministry is one of the most effective and powerful ministries there is. Sharing Christ with the hopeless, allowing them the chance to ask for forgiveness and become empowered in the Holy Spirit, is so desperately needed for inmates to be able to cope in such an environment as theirs.

What reassurance and joy it is to know that God stands behind his Word and keeps his promises! When you abide in Jesus and ask for things that line up with the will of God, "Your desires shall be done unto you." Only God can change our outlook on life from hopelessness to hopefulness. Only God can make a lasting change in our hearts from sadness to joy.

> If you abide in me, and my words abide in you, you shall ask for what you desire and shall be done unto you. ~John 15:7–8

DECEMBER 13

CHRISTMAS LIGHTS
Geoffrey Fowler, California

ONE CHRISTMAS, I was feeling particularly in tune with the holiday season. Maybe it was the dry, crisp air. Maybe it was the smell of the yule logs burning in the fireplaces of the neighborhoods nearby. Or maybe I'm just getting old and soft.

I am reminded of Christmases long ago when the innocence of childhood lent magic to the season. Sometimes it can be rather hard not to dwell on those elements of the season, elements that, as a prisoner, I am denied. For me, there will be no big Christmas dinner and no presents under the tree.

But what I *really* miss—a huge part of my childhood memories—are all the Christmas lights. I knew it was Christmas when the lights came out. There would be those streets where all the houses were decked out to the max, where people would travel like pilgrims just to stroll and gaze. Christmas lights are so cheerful and colorful.

The Christmas season can affect prisoners in different ways, which I suppose is true for adults outside prison as well. One can easily feel low and distant from the joy that's advertised as being out there somewhere—somewhere we are not.

But the Christmas story is very much about the joy of togetherness. There is the simple, human aspect of a little family, a new family, in humble conditions with meager means—but they are together. The grand aspect is similar: Our heavenly Father comes to Earth to be with us, his children, so we will be together with him forever. Tidings of great joy. We have that wherever we are, inside prison or out.

Imagine the gift we can share once we appreciate what God has given us, that sense of belonging he gives us every day. Philippians 2:14–15 says, "That ye may be blameless and harmless, the sons of God, without rebuke, in the midst of a crooked and perverse nation, among whom ye shine as lights in the world" (KJV).

By reflecting the welcoming love God shows us, we can make someone else's world a little brighter and more colorful. We are each other's Christmas lights—especially needed in a dark world.

> Do everything without grumbling or arguing, so that you may become blameless and pure, "children of God without fault in a warped and crooked generation." Then you will shine among them like stars in the sky. ~Philippians 2:14–15

SEEING THE PATH

Joshua B. Smith, California

NOT LONG ago I was feeling stuck, aimlessly wandering in my walk with Christ. I don't like that—it's very disconcerting. I was being obedient to the call in my life (yes, all inmates have a "calling," to reach out and share Christ with others, including other inmates and staff). So why then, was I feeling a little lost, or even separated, from God?

No matter how many services I went to, no matter how obedient I was in my Bible studies (those I attended or led), I felt there was no fruit being produced. I saw very little, if any, progress being made. I even got to the point where I thought maybe I wasn't doing what God wanted me to do, or that I was moving in the wrong direction.

I know that unconfessed sin can lead to broken fellowship with God (Psalm 32:5), but thankfully, nothing can separate us from his love. So, I searched my soul for sin I had not repented of—and nothing. I finally threw up my arms and told God I was lost! I began begging for a sign or some guidance, but still no answers. I became overwhelmed and discouraged. Even my Christian brothers on the yard noticed the change in my countenance and began to pray for me.

Late one night, not long after they prayed for me, I began just randomly flipping through my Bible. Suddenly, God told me to stop and pray. After a few minutes the Holy Spirit nudged me back to the Word and to 2 Chronicles 15:7. I read it and then read the entire chapter for context. As I read, I realized that as long as I am obedient to do what he tells me to do (regardless of how I may "feel" at any particular moment), then I *am* in his will and doing what I am supposed to be doing. I *am* on the right path, and even if I do not see it right now, fruit *is* being produced. I need to trust God that "my work will be rewarded." Similar to a seed buried in the ground, we don't always see his "behind the scenes" work until it springs forth.

Having done all—stand. Stand on his promises—and your work will be rewarded.

> But as for you, be strong and do not give up, for your work will be rewarded.
> ~2 Chronicles 15:7

DECEMBER 15

JUAN'S FAITH
Callie J. Bond, Illinois

IN 2004 I signed up to be a pen pal to the incarcerated. I started with two inmates, and several months later added a few more. One of the inmates I first heard from was a young man by the name of Juan. When I received Juan's information and read that he was twenty-five and serving a life sentence, my heart stopped. Even sadder, he'd been incarcerated since the age of fifteen.

431

Right from the beginning, Juan openly expressed his faith. As time passed, I learned that not only was Juan a man of faith, he walked the walk. He holds Bible studies with fellow inmates and is steadfast in his pursuit of bringing others to Christ. There are even several times he has ministered through Scripture *to me*, at specific times in my life.

When Juan was first incarcerated, he spoke only Spanish, and had little faith. Now he speaks several languages and surpasses me when it comes to knowing Scripture. God has gifted him with an amazing artistic talent, too, that he shares with others.

If I had to describe Juan, I'd use words like joyful, happy, loving, caring, determined, and a faithful follower of Jesus Christ. Not the typical words used to describe the average inmate.

Many inmates deny their crime and claim to be innocent. Over the years that I've known Juan, I have come to believe he is an innocent man, wrongly convicted. But, he would be the first to say he would not be the man he is today if not for being incarcerated. God got his attention behind bars and saved him.

I've written to many inmates since 2004. Some have been very angry, others full of doubt and discouragement, and some have played the manipulating game, wanting a pen pal for the wrong reasons. Juan has been kind and respectful. He has exhibited the qualities of a true follower of Jesus. Even when things have come down unfairly on him, he has still managed to handle it with a positive attitude, never wavering from his faith.

Knowing Juan has challenged me and made me a better person.

> Jesus replied, "Truly I tell you, if you have faith and do not doubt, not only can you do what was done to the fig tree, but also you can say to this mountain, 'Go, throw yourself into the sea,' and it will be done." ~Matthew 21:21

DECEMBER 16

LOVE IS NEVER WASTED

Duane Grady, Ohio

WHEN I graduated from high school, my sister gave me a card that read, "Now that you have graduated, what are you going to become—older?" Those words prompted me to take a serious look at my life. I was not a Christian at the time—actually far from it—but I still wanted my life to have purpose. Shy and introverted, I was terrified just thinking about giving an oral report in school. I was certain speaking in front of others was not in my future.

After I gave my heart to Christ and married a Christian woman, God started using me. He saw things in me I didn't see in myself. He gave me new desires—including speaking in front of others! For twenty years I was a Sunday school superintendent and even held a district position. I assumed that was my life's plan. But, I became a little restless with it.

Then, two decades ago an overwhelming desire to mentor Christian men began building inside me. I worked on discipleship prospects at my church, but for some reason those dwindled away. I asked, "What, Lord? What is it you want me to do with my life?"

Before long, ministering to incarcerated men became heavy on my heart. After I contacted our local jail chaplain, Mark, he shared with me the many needs in the jail for discipleship.

With the first visit inside the jail I knew that was where God wanted me. And now, seventeen years later, I am an assistant chaplain at the same jail. I have had the privilege to minister to hundreds of inmates who have committed all sorts of crimes and I have learned to just be there for them.

Of course my goal is to share Christ with them, and to encourage those who already know him, but I never realized the impact my presence might have on the staff members at the jail. One young deputy recently told me that my dedication and love for the imprisoned have greatly influenced his life—he had been watching me "behind the scenes." Today he is a wonderful Christian man and has held many important positions in the sheriff's office, dedicated to serving others. I had no idea God was using me to plant seeds in his heart. I truly believe that love is never wasted.

DUANE GRADY IN FRONT OF JAIL IN LICKING COUNTY, OHIO

Today God gives me the strength to speak about jail ministry throughout our community. I thank him for the privilege of getting "older," and also for showing me something in myself that could be used to minister to the least of these.

> Dear friends, let us love one another, for love comes from God. Everyone who loves has been born of God and knows God. ~1 John 4:7

THE BEST CHRISTMAS GIFT EVER

Doug Baumgartner, Ohio

I LEARNED ABOUT Jesus as a child, and was baptized in 1997. Three days after my arrest on December 25, 2010, I gave my life to Christ after speaking with a gentleman named Duane Grady. Duane is an assistant chaplain at the jail. He shared Jesus with me, and I've never been the same since.

I soon signed up for the "Be-a-Friend" program and Bob Geer stepped into my life. One of the first things Bob taught me: As Christians there are no "co-incidences," only "God incidences." I have so many God incidences it is hard to believe! Even though I am in prison, my life has changed a lot and has become very spiritual ever since that Christmas Day. My spiritual eyes were opened and I can now see the true meaning of words like "faith" and "love." I can even experience what they feel like, too. God used the jail ministry to touch my life and now I have everything to live for.

I used to write heavy metal poetry, but now I write Christian poetry. I write at night when it is quiet, and I especially like to write about angels and heaven. The Holy Spirit, living on the inside of me, not only led me to read and write about the Word, but to help others to be touched just as I have been. Over my first month in prison, God would lead into my life three more people who have made a spiritual difference in me, and they still do.

With the Holy Spirit as my guide, I have come to realize that my ways of thinking are the very keys to helping others. I am learning to forget about myself, share the Word with others, and reach out to nonbelievers. It is a big part of my life. I don't pressure them, I just share. God takes care of the rest.

I will never forget that Christmas Day in 2010. God used Duane to give me the best gifts of my life—the gift of the Holy Spirit and the promise of eternity with the Lord.

> I planted the seed, Apollos watered it, but God made it grow. ~1 Corinthians 3:6

DECEMBER 18

DOING MY DUTY

Larry Freed, Iowa

GUARDING PRISONERS is a long way from the sheltered campuses of parochial schools where I grew up. Raised in a farm family in northeast Iowa, I graduated from a large Baptist high school in Waterloo. Then I spent a couple of years at Pillsbury Baptist Bible College in Owatonna, Minnesota, but was not ready for college life. As I joined the Navy for four years, where I picked up much-needed discipline.

I returned to Pillsbury, graduated, buried my father after a terminal illness, and picked up a second degree in police science while I figured out what to do with my life. When Iowa went through a prison hiring boom to staff its nine prisons I jumped in for the pay as much as anything else. I walked a prison "beat" for nine years until my promotion to correctional counselor. I earned a specialized license to help inmates with chemical dependency. There really is something different every day. I will never be at a point where I can say, "I've seen it all."

I learned quickly about the value of my work as well as the opportunities I had to live my faith in a place so foreign to my upbringing. At my prison you'll find every religion, every philosophical perspective, and every political position represented.

I'm obligated—before we talk about the taxpayers or my bosses—to do my job to the best of my ability every day for the Lord. I've worked with a few officers in my career who were professing Christians who felt it was their job to preach the "Romans Road" to every inmate eight hours a day.

However, we're not paid by the Iowa taxpayers to be Dwight L. Moody all day. I'm paid to protect and serve the public by rehabilitating felons for return to society. I do share my faith as appropriate opportunities arise, as with any other job.

A mother of an inmate on my caseload recently asked me, "Are you a Christian?" It caught me off guard. She said, "I could tell by the way my son talks about you in the visiting room." I've never shared my testimony with her son, not that I wouldn't if he asked. We bear fruit nonverbally. When the Lord opens the door I am absolutely ready to talk about what I believe.

Those officers who preached all day, neither one of them is in the system anymore. They probably should have become chaplains instead.

> It pleased Darius to appoint 120 satraps to rule throughout the kingdom, with three administrators over them, one of whom was Daniel. The satraps were made accountable to them so that the king might not suffer loss. Now Daniel so distinguished himself among the administrators and the satraps by his exceptional qualities that the king planned to set him over the whole kingdom. ~Daniel 6:1–3

DECEMBER 19

GOOD AND BAD ADVICE

Larry Freed, Iowa

IF you take away one thing from your career, take this: "There is a fine line between living *in* prison and working *at* a prison." I heard that good advice from a senior corrections officer early in my career. Every one of us has done something where if circumstances had been different, we could easily be wearing inmate blue instead of officer brown. The person named "best in class" during my rookie training at the prison guard academy has now been an inmate on two different occasions. Without humility before God, we can fall as far as the men in the system I work in.

Another supervisor encouraged me to not let intimidation rule me when I come into work. In other words—don't in response to intimidation—turn into Wyatt Earp and bully your way through the day. Some do. I hear the stories. There's no room in the DOC for Wyatt Earps. This is a profession, nothing more or less. Two incidents brought this advice to mind.

My first month on the job I watched an inmate holding a metal mop handle walk up behind an officer, then use the mop handle like an ax to open up the officer's head. I was assigned to ride with the officer to the hospital with a Polaroid camera in one hand and a video camera in the other while an EMT sewed his wound shut. Six months later I showed up in court to walk the jury through those pictures.

Two years later an inmate on my block opened up his wrists with a razor blade. I had to watch and wait for backup because our procedures don't allow me to enter alone. With every pulse of his heart, more blood spilled on the floor. The odor after four hours will stay with me to my grave. Both incidents sensitized me to what people are capable of, but I didn't let it scare or intimidate me in the conduct of my duties.

Some bad advice you hear on the job is "Snitches get stitches." Both sides abide by it, it's cancerous for both. The blue code of silence—you don't tell cops anything. The brown code of silence—you don't tell cops anything. That opens the door for compromise and forces people to cover up for wrong.

My integrity is not for sale. The safety and security of Iowa taxpayers are not for sale. I'm not invited to keggers nor do I go to the local watering hole after work. What others do is not my business. But some of the people who do those things, when they have a serious concern in their life, guess whose office they come to?

> He has shown you, O mortal, what is good. And what does the Lord require of you? To act justly and to love mercy and to walk humbly with your God. ~Micah 6:8

DECEMBER 20

MY PEN PAL, WILLIAM

Sandra Flindt, South Dakota

I "MET" WILLIAM in 2003 after I received his name from the CPP (Christian Pen Pals) ministry. I initially sent him a Christmas card, but now I consider him to be one of my best friends. God is doing such wonderful things in his life, and consequently in the prison where he is serving time.

William actually came to know the Lord one day due to boredom: He asked his cellmate if he had something to read and the cellmate handed him a Bible. William started reading it and subsequently accepted the Lord Jesus Christ as his Savior.

Since then, the Lord has really used William and has blessed him abundantly. William began a Bible study group in his prison. This is a maximum-security prison but the warden allowed the men to meet together for a Bible study. It has grown rapidly, and even includes guards attending at times. William began encouraging the men to sing, too. At first they were very reluctant, but before long, the guards had to ask them to "tone it down."

Well, they don't have to tone it down now. Because out of that Bible study a choir has formed, and . . . they will be putting on a Christmas concert. It has grown in size and popularity to the point that outside guests are invited to attend and even the local TV station will be covering it! A video recording will be made for each inmate to give his family. Since we are William's "family," we will get his copy. We have never even seen a picture of him so this is very exciting for us.

A local church donated choir robes to the prison so they will be wearing those. William said they are really nice and beautiful so they will not only sound like a choir, but look like one, too! Just think of the witness this will be to the other inmates, and to the community. To God be the praise, honor, and glory! He is truly doing great things.

> Hear this, you kings! Listen, you rulers! I, even I, will sing to the LORD; I will praise the LORD, the God of Israel, in song. ~Judges 5:3

DECEMBER 21

FORGIVENESS

Theresa Grace, Arizona

IT HAD been several months since my release from prison. God got my attention one day when I kneeled on that cold cement floor, and I could write pages about how he came through for me while inside. Now that I'm out, he has blessed me with an incredible job, unbelievable experiences, and amazing opportunities.

As I got closer to the Lord the subject of "forgiveness" kept coming up. I knew Jesus had suffered immense pain and torture and died on the cross so my sins would be forgiven. Now God was telling me the only way to truly be set free from my personal bondage was for me to forgive all those who had wronged me.

My spirit had been wounded for as long as I could remember. I had constantly blamed others for their part in hurting me. How could I possibly begin to forgive the men in my life who had taken my innocence as a child, who abused and humiliated me?

Then, one day I read a story about Corrie ten Boom, a Christian Dutch woman who survived a Nazi concentration camp during the Holocaust. Ms. ten Boom described in detail the deplorable imprisonment conditions at Ravensbrück, as well as the horrible treatment she and her sister had received, most often from prison guards.

I read how, years later following a conference in Munich, Germany, Ms. ten Boom found herself in the company of one of the cruelest guards from her past. Memories of brutality flooded back, along with the slow, agonizing death of her sister.

Now, with outstretched hand, the guard was asking for her forgiveness. Corrie stood still, frozen in time, unable to grasp the thought of forgiving this man. She realized, however, forgiveness was not a feeling or an emotion she must comprehend. Forgiveness was a commandment of God. "If you do not forgive men their trespasses," Jesus says, "neither will your Father in heaven forgive your trespasses."

I was astounded. I understood I was not the only one in the world to ever be abused and treated unjustly. So was this woman, and . . . so was Jesus.

Suddenly, the burden lifted. I like how Charles Stanley worded it in *Landmines in the Path of the Believer:*

> We are to forgive so that we may enjoy God's goodness without feeling the weight of anger burning deep within our hearts. Forgiveness does not mean we recant the fact that what happened to us was wrong. Instead, we roll our burdens onto the Lord and allow him to carry them for us.

Bear with each other and forgive whatever grievances you may have against one another. Forgive as the Lord forgave you. ~Colossians 3:13

COMING FULL CIRCLE

Chris Mullen, California

I WAS IN my cell in San Quentin during Christmas of 1989, when a group of people came in to sing Christmas carols. I know now they were Christian songs. I could not see the carolers, but I felt something tug at my heart and a seed was planted that night. I did another prison term after that and continued to use drugs for more than seven additional years, until I came to Christ.

I got clean on July 10, 1997, and began attending church shortly after that. I was out of prison and a co-worker of mine told me her husband had gone into San Quentin and sung Christmas carols. I wanted to do that, to give back, but the man her husband went with no longer went inside the prison, so that door was closed (or so I thought).

I told my boss what I wanted to do and he suggested I call Kevin, a guy he knew involved in prison ministry. Kevin could not help me with San Quentin, but he could get me into CYA, which was the youth prison.

Finally, on December 17, 2011, more than twelve years later, God opened the door for me to sing Christmas carols back at San Quentin. Even though the date had been scheduled for a while, I was still not prepared for what happened that day. John, another volunteer, asked me that day if everything was okay. I told him "Yes," but I know now I was in a state of shock.

I have been to the Chapel at San Quentin many times, but going back into the same cellblocks where I used to live was very different. I did not sing as much as I could have, because I wept in every cell block. The tears wouldn't stop. What kept coming into my mind was how God had taken my life full circle, from a lost inmate searching for him, to having been redeemed and now giving back.

I go into lots of prisons today and give men hope that there is a different way to live. And I get to tell them about the love of Jesus Christ. I am privileged to perform weddings, funerals, and baptisms. I can assure you, I did not see this on the horizon when I was in my prison cell listening to some carolers sing about God's amazing love for mankind—but God did!

They went out and preached that people should repent. ~Mark 6:12

CHILDREN OF THE LORD

George Alfred Roensch Jr., California

I HAVE A dear memory from inside prison in December 2008. It was the year we performed our Christmas play, "Shackled," at our annual banquet to celebrate the birth of Jesus. I was a member of the cast, which included thirteen inmates, for a play that would be performed for an audience of two hundred others.

At the outset, I was not sure if any of us knew what we were getting ourselves into, or what kind of commitment would be required to prepare us for such a daunting task. We were definitely a motley crew, a ragtag bunch. Our differences were extreme: age, ethnicity, background, and education. All of us had many years of incarceration under our belts, but most of us had no theatrical experience. There were some who had learning disabilities (one man could neither read nor write, so he memorized his lines as a friend read them to him), and our eldest cast member had even been on San Quentin's Death Row back in the seventies (his sentence was commuted to a twenty-five-year-to-life term, and he was subsequently found suitable for parole by the parole board). Aside from the standard blue clothing, the common denominator uniting us all was the love of Christ in our hearts.

If memorizing our lines was not difficult enough for us, the play culminated in a musical number as we danced to the Newsboys' song, "I Am Free." Hours upon hours were spent in practice and rehearsal. Thirteen men, once hardened criminals who now possessed soft hearts, were acting and dancing. Our love for the Lord, and for each other, was in action. As I looked around back then, and reflect on it now, I realize that only the Lord has that kind of transforming power. We were willingly and joyfully facing our fears, naively counting on each other, and innocently trusting in the Lord. For this all to work, we, not only as a cast of amateur thespians, but more as a band of Christian brothers, had to come together and care for each other. We were as children in the school auditorium rather than inmates in a prison.

That play will always be a reminder to me we have to become as children before our loving Father. In that simple trust, joy, and love we were able to shine within our smiles and laughter.

Truly I tell you, unless you change and become like little children, you will never enter the kingdom of heaven. ~Matthew 18:3

ROCKIN' THE JAILHOUSE— A CHRISTMAS CELEBRATION

Kym McNabney, Illinois

THIS WAS not my first time in Cook County Jail as a volunteer. I had been a part of the Thanksgiving and Christmas Celebration the men's team from my church puts together. Each time I entered the jail I would think to myself, *The last time I was moved to tears—it's not going to happen again.*

Was I ever wrong.

As the first group of men from Division 14 entered the room, I immediately felt God's love for them. I recognized a few faces from the month before when we served a Thanksgiving meal; a few of them recognized me as well.

The hour began with encouraging words from a volunteer. Next, a group of musicians from church began to play, and voices rang out in song. The men rose from their seats, clapped their hands, putting their whole heart into it. A smile spread across my face as we sang the roof off the jailhouse.

A message was given on how each of us has sinned, yet Jesus came to save us. The message was powerful, reaching many of the men as they called out "Amen!" and nodded their heads in agreement.

Another song rang out, its lyrics so moving that men were raising their hands, while others had tears in their eyes. I glanced behind and spotted three officers, arms together, swaying to the music with tears streaming down their cheeks.

And *that* was when I lost it. My resolve to stay strong completely dissolved.

The service continued as another volunteer spoke on how we all have made promises we haven't kept, and have had people let us down. Yet Jesus is always faithful. His word is his word!

He then invited men who wanted Jesus in their heart to step forward.

One by one, several men made their way to the front of the room. They huddled in a mass of connected arms embracing one another. Tears were flowing from volunteers, inmates, and officers. The presence of God hung in the air.

As the men departed, they shook our hands and thanked us. Some had huge grins and others had red and swollen eyes, but each had a sincerity that tugged at my heart.

I went home humbled to have been a part of a true Christmas celebration—praising our King's birth and witnessing the power of the Spirit to transform hearts.

> Shout for joy to the Lord, all the earth. Worship the Lord with gladness; come before him with joyful songs. ~Psalm 100:1–2

DECEMBER 25

CHRISTMAS TREATS

Ted Shaw, Florida

CHRISTMASTIME really brings a lot of guys down in prison. The "feeling-sorry-for-yourself" blues really takes hold, being far from family; you're stuck inside and you've made a mess of things.

My friend Adams* and I came up with an idea to bring a little cheer and share our faith. We decided to pool what little we had between us and make gift bags for everyone in our dorm—that's ninety-six people. Adams had a job in the canteen, where he could purchase stuff. My boss at the food service contractor would donate small, approved items such as sewing needles and food. We'd throw into the sacks the snacks, sewing kits, and other little things prisoners appreciate but don't have, plus some gospel tracts.

Officers would let us pass them out at count time, but we had to hurry. We flew up and down four wings on the block. Of course we had tried with some difficulty to hide all the goods in our bunks until Christmas.

I don't know that we expected any miracles. We just put it out there for what it was and most of the guys gave us a nod and said they appreciated it. It's really up to God to take what little we could do and touch someone's heart. We provided the goodie bags two years in a row and I have to say, it felt good to be doing something for others.

> Each of you should give what you have decided in your heart to give, not reluctantly or under compulsion, for God loves a cheerful giver. ~2 Corinthians 9:7

DANBURY TRANSFORMATION

Jeff Andrews, Maryland

THE EASIEST time I ever did had to be at FCI Danbury in Connecti-cut. It's ironic that at the time Danbury transformed itself into a tougher prison, God changed me in the opposite direction. Danbury ranked as a level 2, but almost immediately hundreds of Lorton, Virginia, inmates were transferred, more wire and guard towers went up, and so did the tension on the yard. Minimum federal joints in my vast experience are easier to get through, nobody wants to mess up and lose privileges, but this merging of populations changed the dynamic. Guys like my friend Ron Humphrey (page 43) should never have been there.

When I arrived in 1987 I was sporting a long beard and resembled a cross between a mountain man and a hippie from the 1960s. I was "Bobby Bad-A—," always trying to prove something. I had to lift more weights, run faster, win at every physical thing I put my mind to.

So here I was in my private little desert, doing another bit. I'd been running all my life. I had changed identities I don't know how many times, lived in cities all across the country running my con games and selling drugs. I'd seen the inside of twenty-three prisons, but until that time, was never convicted of a single crime. I was so good at covering my tracks and keeping my true identify hidden that authorities always had to let me go because they couldn't positively ID me!

I never got tattoos, but changed my appearance all the time. I'd go to the beauty parlor for half a day to change my hair and my beard; I'd change glasses and clothing style. I could never get away with that in today's high-tech world. I was trying to find out who I was. I liked a lot of the identities I created. They were images of what I thought would be cool, but each time the police would get close I'd liquidate everything and go on the run.

I developed a sense about me that everything was a lie. I couldn't trust anything, I couldn't believe anything. But when the light hits you, it's unmistakable. I recognized Jesus was in the world and he was calling me. I was overwhelmed, a little afraid, but also realized there was no place else to go. Pick up your cross and follow him. Then the eventful night, I got it.

Suddenly I lost the hate that drove me. I had hated myself, my life. Now, all of a sudden I'm comfortable in my own skin. I recognized *whose* I was. I had a new home, a heavenly Father. My life made sense.

> Before the coming of this faith, we were held in custody under the law, locked up until the faith that was to come would be revealed. So the law was our guardian until Christ came that we might be justified by faith.
> ~Galatians 3:23–24

DECEMBER 27

CHANGE I CAN SEE

Jeff Andrews, Maryland

SITTING STILL is not my cup of tea. I'm a "make work" kind of guy. I'm going to go until I can't! You'll probably find me dead in my chair. After my conversion I led a one hundred-man high-impact aerobics class of convicts where we didn't stop for two hours and they had to listen to me talk about Jesus! Just point me in a direction and I'm gone no matter how impossible or foolish it looks. I used to do that for the devil, but now I'm suited up with the army that is going to win.

God knew this about me. And I really needed all that "go juice" to tackle what was waiting for me upon release, which was a mess. My wife of four years had left me—I'd made the same mistakes I'd always made with women. I had $1,000,000 in fines from all the jurisdictions where my seven felonies occurred. And, honestly, you just don't change your behavior to match Jesus overnight, even though a lot of my prayers were impatient requests to fix things so we could go, go, go. It always takes longer than I want.

For example, I still want to take somebody off the road in D.C. traffic when I get cut off. In my wild days I drove like a fugitive because I was one. I just have to cool it and remember how messed up I once was.

When I entered a restaurant I'd start casing the joint looking for the bad guys in case there was going to be a war in the parking lot or inside. I'd be looking for what I could grab to defend myself. I was always ready to go to war because I was always in that type of environment. Now, I don't feel fear or anxiety any longer. I'm not looking for a chair to break.

Another example of change I can see includes the way I treat women. In my previous life I was always on the hunt, always looking for my next move. It was so routine. My new wife (we married after my release) didn't care for that when we were out together. I know I changed because we've been married twenty-four years now by the grace of God.

Would you believe God really changed my work motives? Before, it was about how wealthy I could get to spend on drugs, alcohol, guns, women, and expensive toys. I put my newly-focused energy into a little company that took a chance on me, I paid all my fines, and helped grow IPC Technologies. We're looking at third place in the market for the Shortel product we service.

When I look back over twenty-four years, there have been so many times when I had to lose my pride. I have had to eliminate anything that gives me a podium to stand on.

> The end of a matter is better than its beginning, and patience is better than pride. Ecclesiastes 7:8

DECEMBER 28

NEVER GIVE UP

Callie J. Bond, Illinois

THE FIRST time I visited a prison was in November 2006. I traveled with a small group from my church to the state penitentiary in Angola, Louisiana. That day we went on cell visits, and on one of our visits I met a man named Woodrow.

Woodrow and I talked for a while about a lot of different subjects, including God, one another, and life. I promised to send him information on receiving a pen pal. Woodrow was full of questions, his faith wavering. His baby girl had passed away while he was incarcerated, leaving many unanswered questions for God.

At first, Woodrow and I wrote consistently. He wanted to know about God, about this whole faith thing, prompting me to send him literature to help answer his questions. In time his letters dwindled off, but I never forgot him. God had embedded him in my heart. Each year I'd send him a Christmas card along with a faith-based book. Though he thanked me, letting me know the book was useful, his letters were brief and didn't last. Still, I kept praying.

This past year I received more letters from Woodrow than ever. One letter in particular brought tremendous joy to me as he wrote of confessing his sins to Jesus and asking him into his heart. Woodrow then asked me to keep him in my prayers. I shared he had never been out of my prayers, and Woodrow is most appreciative I did not give up on him. He now attends faith-based classes, reads his Bible diligently, and speaks of growing closer to God. The change is so present in his words it constantly warms my heart and brings a smile to my face.

What greater joy can we experience than to be part of another's journey to receive the Lord into their life? God loves each and every one of us and is waiting for us to come into his loving arms.

> Consider him who endured such opposition from sinners, so that you will not grow weary and lose heart. ~Hebrews 12:3

DECEMBER 29

THE LEAST OF THESE GIVES

Kym McNabney, Illinois

IT'S NO secret that God wants us to be givers, including giving to the church. That principle of giving is clearly stated in the Bible in several places. One powerful verse from Leviticus 27:29–31 stands out: "A tithe of everything from the land, whether grain from the soil or fruit from the trees, belongs to the Lord; it is holy to the Lord."

Many pastors have preached on the subject of obeying God and giving what he lays on our heart to give. An account in the New Testament tells of a woman who only had two coins and gave it all, but there were also those who had much, but only gave a small portion. Many Christians today struggle with giving money for God's purposes.

Several men from our church have been going into the local jail for the past thirteen years for a Bible study. Our church has received many letters of appreciation from inmates about how they've been blessed by the volunteers of Willow Creek Community Church.

One letter in particular stands out. It will remain forever tucked in my heart.

When I picked up the mail for the prison pen pal ministry at our church, I opened the letter, as I've done hundreds of times in the past. Most of the envelopes are stamped, "Inmate Correspondence," as was this one. But what was inside was different. This time there was something included—a check. My breath caught in my throat. After several seconds I opened the letter and began to read.

This man had been in Cook County Jail and had now relocated to another facility. He remembered the volunteers talking about the importance of giving. He went on to say he received some unexpected money from the state and wanted to give Willow Church a gift of part of it.

As you can imagine, most inmates don't have much. Many have no support from the outside world, so the fact that this man made the decision to give some of what may be the last money he would receive, rocked my world.

His obedience to Scripture caused me to take a better look at myself. Seeing his check in that envelope will be forever embedded in my mind, especially in the midst of future conversations or sermons on giving.

I have no doubt God will bless this man. When we choose to do the right thing, God always notices.

Bring the best of the firstfruits of your soil to the house of the Lord your God.
~Exodus 23:19

BE AN OVERCOMER

Mario Ghiloni, Florida

MY NAME has been replaced with a number: R66558. I am currently property of the state of Florida. In the year 2009 I was convicted of driving under the influence and vehicular manslaughter. Drinking alcohol may be okay for some folks who are able to control their consumption. It is not okay for me. I am an alcoholic. Unfortunately, I have only recently convinced myself of that.

In 2001, I had been in a near-fatal car accident. It took the "jaws of life" to get me out. I was life-flighted to a hospital and spent fourteen days in a coma. After four-and-a-half months in the hospital, I was finally able to leave. It then took one-and-a-half years to re-train my brain. I was in a wheelchair and then used a walker. I now walk with a cane. I am still improving in all areas of my life.

I legally obtained my driver's license in 2007. In 2009, I was involved in a fatal car accident. I had been vacationing in Clearwater Beach, Florida, and was driving after consuming two shots of whiskey and one beer. I collided with another driver while traveling at a very low speed as I attempted to turn into a beach parking lot.

I was taken to the hospital and released. I assumed the other driver was okay, too, and never thought any more about it. No one was cited after the accident; both drivers were equally at fault.

Then, after being home for almost a year I received a warrant for my arrest—vehicular manslaughter. The other driver, a young man, had died from his injuries, and my blood had contained .09 percent alcohol.

I received a five-year sentence. I now attend AA meetings weekly while in prison. I know I cannot bring this young man back, and that there is nothing I can do to ease the pain of his loved ones. I've had a lot of downtime to think and to pray. I have gotten closer to the Lord through this and I want my life to count for Jesus. I was selfish and stubborn, but I now want to get on board with living a life that glorifies God.

Have mercy on me, Lord; heal me, for I have sinned against you. ~Psalm 41:4

A NEW CREATION IN JESUS

Timothy James Burke, Ohio

BY OUTWARD appearances my life seemed to be going okay. I was gainfully employed, raising a family, paying the mortgage, and keeping fit. I had the hallmarks of a man with his act together. But I didn't have God in my life. While I acknowledged him, I did not accept him. In the place where I should have kept God, I harbored a secret addiction instead.

When I started coming apart it was like a novice bicyclist losing control, overcorrecting, and crashing horribly. My crash was wildly uncontrolled and in the process I hurt the people I loved the most.

When I called my parents, seven hundred miles away, they already knew. Their anger and disappointment crossed those wires undiminished and there was no mistaking their feelings about what I had done. But, amazingly, it was also clear they loved me in spite of my actions and the pain I'd caused.

I think most people have rough years with their parents as they transition from childhood into adults. My rough years were full of anger and rebellion and grand acts of selfishness and stupidity. When I lived on my own as an adult, I was aloof with my parents. I'd tell my mom that if she hadn't heard from me that was a good sign—it meant I hadn't been found in a ditch somewhere.

My meltdown forced me to reconsider who I am. I tried to live without God and I failed. Three days after my arrest, I accepted that I could not make it on my own and invited Jesus into my life. As soon as I did, I realized he'd been waiting for me to ask all along. I saw, too, that my parents' love had always been there. I hadn't noticed or appreciated it because I was blinded by my diseased choices.

Having a felony is shameful. It stains the family name and casts the light of suspicion on honorable people. Beneath the weight of that sort of disgrace, it would be easy to give up on living, but I don't feel disgraced or dishonorable anymore. I feel loved and appreciated. I feel grateful.

While I long to repay my debts of gratitude to those I have hurt, I realize it may not be possible. Jesus paid for my sins and what happened in the past has passed. I am a new creation, a child of God. Despite my present circumstances, I will choose to live in a way that honors my Father, and my parents.

Honor your father and your mother, so that you may live long in the land the Lord your God is giving you. ~Exodus 20:12

450

ACKNOWLEDGMENTS

CONNIE CAMERON

For the past several years jail and prison ministry have snowballed into a passion in my life. It began with a simple act of obedience on the part of Michaelene Duffy to write to me, and has progressed into a love and compassion for the least of these that oftentimes dominate my thoughts and prayers. From being a volunteer in our local jail, to being on the board of our jail ministry, to co-authoring a book of true stories that reveal the depth and magnitude of God's love, I stand amazed at how God changes hearts—especially my own. My eyes have been opened to the plight of the forgotten, specifically those behind bars who are truly repentant of their sins. They face constant opposition to serve Jesus where they are, and yet choose to remain faithful. God sees you, he is with you, and great is your reward.

It has been a privilege to serve on the board of the Licking County Jail Ministries with Chaplain Scott Hayes and Assistant Chaplains Connie Johnston and Duane Grady, along with the rest of the hardworking, dedicated members. I am thankful for your input for this book and especially for your prayers. To our previous chairman of the board, Pastor Steve Osborne, your excitement for this project has inspired me to persevere on more than one occasion. To board member Ann Kater—thank you for your editorial assistance and your willingness to help out in those final days.

A huge word of thanks goes to the staff at the Licking County Jail in Newark, Ohio, especially Lt. Chris Slayman of the sheriff's office, and Jennifer Eveland, the programs director. God bless you for your dedication to the jail ministries. On behalf of LCJM and the board, we appreciate you and are most grateful for you.

Any endeavor of this magnitude requires lots of help. When I first received the contract I prayed and asked God to connect me to those who shared this passion. I knew many segments had to be represented including those in prison ministry, prison staff members, current inmates, ex-inmates, and loved ones of the incarcerated. I have been humbled and amazed at how God has answered my prayer. He immediately led me to three women I'd never met, but who share the same passion: Carol Davis, Kym McNabney, and Beth Michael. Please know how grateful I am for your input, quick responses, and commitment to this project. How I'd love to hug each of you!

I am more than blessed to have three dear friends and prayer warriors in my life, who share my depth of love for jail ministry: Patricia Collins, Connie Johnston, and Nanette Friend. You have been my rod and staff, holding me up when I was weary and overwhelmed; calling and e-mailing at just my moment of need. I regularly give thanks for you in my life, but never more than these past six months. I also wish to thank Nanette and Connie for temporarily taking over my weekly inspirational newspaper column. You had your own crazy schedules and yet you cheerfully agreed to take on more. What gems you are!

I also wish to thank my church, Vineyard Grace Fellowship, for your support of the jail ministry and for your prayers over this project, especially Brad Kittle. And thank you, Marilyn Schouten, for your tireless postings of prayer concerns and for your love for the "family." You are appreciated!

I have been blessed to have special friends (and ex-coworkers), who for the past two decades have listened to my struggles with writing and shared in my successes: to Elcena (Ross) Wilkes and Maxine Fowler, thank you for encouraging me to keep at it. I treasure our friendships.

Special thanks go to my dear agent, Diana Flegal, for your hard work and dedication to your calling. I appreciate your support, encouragement, and sympathetic ear!

To my amazing family, beginning with my precious mother, Winnie Grimes Jones: You always see the best in others, Mom, and have taught me to do the same. You are a huge light in my life and in the lives of Sue, Tim, and Danny, too. I love and appreciate you more than I can put into words. My wonderful children, Chase Cameron (Elizabeth), Chelsea Wolf (Matt); and Lori Heskett, you are each treasured gifts from God. Thank you for enriching my life and giving me the best grandkids ever! To Elaina, Leah, Nathan, and Amber—you are more lights in my life whom I have greatly missed being with as I pushed toward the finish line.

Special thanks to my co-editor, Jeff Peck. We were both chosen by God to compile and create this labor-intensive, but extremely worthwhile, manuscript. I believe the blend of our two writing styles has added a level of interest and variety to this book that would have been lacking, if not for the other. Thank you for your hard work and dedication to a quality manuscript.

To our gifted copyeditor, Rich Cairnes, and skilled proofreader, Christy Luellen, thank you for cleaning up this manuscript. We hoped we wouldn't give you a lot to do, but you definitely made this body of work shine.

Sincere thanks and appreciation go to our editor, Rick Steele, and all the staff at AMG Publishers, for sharing in the vision of reaching out to "the least of these." This book will offer hope and comfort to a segment of society that is often forgotten, pointing them to a life-changing relationship with Jesus Christ. It has been an honor and privilege to partner with you on this project.

Without the selfless contributors who took the time to share their experiences, this book would not be. Many of you had to press past the pain and open up old wounds, knowing it would glorify God and help others. From the bottom of my heart, I thank each one of you who have contributed your inspirational stories. Your efforts will encourage many, especially lonely, discouraged inmates—and for years to come.

And finally—my dear husband Chuck. I can't thank you enough for encouraging me, over the decades, to keep writing. Your support of me to pursue my passion for writing and for jail ministry has brought me to this book. I owe a debt of gratitude to you. Thank you for picking up the slack at home after long hours at work, and for settling for short visits from me while I finished the race.

But I am most grateful to my Lord and Savior, Jesus Christ. I have leaned on him like never before throughout the writing and compiling of this book, and he has been more than faithful. I stand amazed at how he has come through, time and time again. It is my sincere prayer that God will be glorified in each story, and that his Kingdom will grow as a result of this book. All glory and honor is his.

JEFF PECK

I never imagined when I majored in journalism twenty-two years ago that I would end up in prison, so to speak. I owe a debt of gratitude to Prison Fellowship for the chance to work in this mission field for so many years. I had the opportunity to follow and work with Chuck Colson in prisons around the country and meet so many people whose lives were genuinely transformed by the gospel. That experience matured my own faith and helped transform certain attitudes about "those people." To the greatest co-workers (David, Carlson, Peter Gross, Kerry Morgan, and dozens of others), who shared that journey with me, you are part of this book.

A special thanks to my friends Becky Beane and Kristie Jackson for your insightful comments on the manuscript. No writer can see the forest for the trees after a while and trustworthy feedback not only makes me look better, but gives the reader a far more valuable experience.

Rick Steele and team AMG deserve my gratitude for showcasing these challenging stories and delivering the production labor that every book requires before it can make it to our favorite places to read a book.

I must thank the contributors who dared to open up the ugly past—for publication—in order to further magnify the power of Christ to transform a life. The personal details of those who have lived through an incarceration experience are sensitive and embarrassing. It is truly courageous to speak about them openly, and humbly, for the sake of the One who saved them. I am personally humbled by their trust in me to handle their stories.

My appreciation also extends to the contributors who provided insight into the world of corrections and what happens to families. Their professional knowledge and personal accounts are amazing testimonies of faithfulness and joy in an arena known principally for failure and danger. Thank you for what you do whether you wear a badge, a collar, or volunteer.

A special thanks to my small group (Jacksons, Knotts, Guidis, Dugans, Solomons) who listened to my updates and covered my anxieties with their prayers.

For enduring the tired refrain of "I can't, I've got to work on the book," my son Riley and daughter Sophie each deserve a big pizza and a lot of ice cream. I hope you will appreciate these stories one day, as you wondered why daddy spent so much time going to prisons. Thank you to Mom, Dad, and Lori, who shaped who I am and cheered me on.

Projects like this cut into family time more than I could have imagined. To my amazing wife Marcie, thank you for picking up the slack and giving me the space to do something I believed in. You are an example of God's unfathomable grace to me.

APPENDIX OF
PRISON MINISTRIES

Allison Bottke
Setting Boundaries Books
www.allisonbottke.com

Angel Tree
www.angeltree.org
800-55-ANGEL

AZ Commonground
Azcommonground1.com
602-914-9000

Billy Graham Institute for Prison Ministry
www.bgcprisonministries.com
630-752-5727

Birth Behind Bars
www.birthbehindbars.com
727-934-1267

Christian Pen Pals
PO Box 11296
Hickory, NC 28603
www.christian-penpals.com

Family and Corrections Network
93 Old York Road
Suite 1 #510
Jenkintown, PA 19046
www.fcnetwork.org

Thanks also to Libby's assistant, Kitt Reckord-Mabicka, who helps make all the magic happen.

Dana Trocker and Karlyn Hixson are marketing geniuses, and I'm eternally grateful for their smarts and savvy. On the audio front, Tom Spain, Sarah Lieberman, Chris Lynch, and Elisa Shokoff are thoughtful and proactive about finding just the right people to lend their voices to my words. James Iacobelli and Olga Grlic are responsible for my beautiful covers. They outdid themselves with *The Summer Place*, and I'm grateful that they always make my books look so lovely, and that the women on the covers actually resemble the women on the page. Ariele Fredman is the absolute hands-down most outstanding publicist/cheerleader that any writer could hope to have in her corner. Thanks also to Katelyn Phillips, Lisa Sciambra, Zoe Harris, Chris Lynch, Nicole Bond, Paige Lytle, Iris Chen, Shelby Pumphrey, Vanessa Silverio, Esther Paradelo, Dana Sloan, and Suzanne Donahue. Finally, thanks to Kathleen Rizzo and Lisa Silverman for their careful, attentive reading and for endlessly saving me from myself. Veronica Vega of Salt & Sage was a thoughtful reader. Any mistakes are mine.

Andrea Cipriani Mecchi is a friend and a genius photographer who makes getting your picture taken feel like a party instead of a root canal. I'm grateful to her for making me look good, and for always making it fun.

Jasmine Barta keeps my website looking sharp and my newsletter running smoothly (and if you haven't seen my website or signed up for my newsletter, you can go to www.jenniferweiner.com and fix that right now!).

On the home front, I am eternally grateful to my assistant, Meghan Burnett, whose steadfast good cheer and editorial acumen make my writing life possible, and who kept things on track during a challenging year. Thanks to my daughters, Lucy and Phoebe, for letting their mom sojourn in the neighborhood of make-believe.

This book would not have been possible without the love, generosity, and strategic nonchalance of my husband and first reader, Bill Syken, who is unfailingly kind and supportive and who let me borrow his life-changing orthopedic flip-flops for my novel and didn't complain (much). There's no one with whom I'd rather quarantine.

And finally, thanks to my dear Moochie, muse and companion, the best dog any writer ever had. We adopted Moochie in 2012 and, for most of her life, she was rarely more than six feet away from my side. When I was writing, she'd be curled up on her dog bed beside me. When I went out in a kayak or on a paddleboard, she'd be with me. When I left the house, she'd sit, watchful and waiting, until I came back.

Moochie's heart started failing in the summer of 2020. The vets at the University of Pennsylvania and Queen Village Animal Hospital took great care of her. She hung on and stayed with me until two days after my mother's memorial service on the Cape, when she went out with me on the paddleboard to scatter my mom's ashes in the bay.

Moochie, I hope that wherever you are, you can catch every cat you chase, that you get to eat every chicken wing you find, and that nobody complains when you wake them up in the middle of the night and pretend you have to go out just so you can nudge them out of the warm spot in the bed. I was so lucky to be your person.

The Summer Place

Jennifer Weiner

*This reading group guide for THE SUMMER PLACE
includes an introduction, discussion questions, ideas for en-
hancing your book club, and a Q&A with author Jennifer
Weiner. The suggested questions are intended to help your
reading group find new and interesting angles and topics
for your discussion. We hope that these ideas will enrich your
conversation and increase your enjoyment of the book.*

INTRODUCTION

From "the undisputed boss of the beach read" (*The New York Times*), *The Summer Place* is a testament to family in all its messy glory; it is a story about what we sacrifice and how we forgive. Enthralling, witty, bighearted, and sharply observed, this is Jennifer Weiner's love letter to the Outer Cape and the power of home, the way our lives are enriched by the people we call family, and the endless ways love can surprise us.

TOPICS & QUESTIONS
FOR DISCUSSION

~~~~~~

1. The novel includes very different mother-daughter relationships: Veronica and Sarah, Sarah and Ruby, Annette and Ruby. How are their relationships similar and how are they different? What do you think of Annette's rejection of motherhood? How did it affect Sarah to become a stepmother to Ruby at such a young age? Why do you think Veronica has such a different relationship with Sarah, her daughter, compared to Sam, her son? Are there "right" and "wrong" ways to be a mother?

2. The relationship between Eli Danhauser and his first wife, Annette, was cut short when she left him and their young child, Ruby. Were you shocked by her rejection of motherhood? Did she redeem herself to Ruby at the end? How was this balanced by the stepparent relationship between Ruby and Sarah?

3. This story includes many secrets, some of which are revealed by the end and some of which are not. Do you think the characters make the right choices about which secrets to keep and which to reveal? Is there a right way to share a secret that will change someone's

life? Is honesty always the best policy? How do different backgrounds—such as between generations, or between women and men—affect the decisions made by different characters about their secrets?

4. After we hear the story of Sarah's friend Marni, she thinks to herself that the story is a warning: "End your marriage and you and your children will suffer" (page 140). Do you think this is a common feeling among married women thinking about separation? How about among married men? Discuss the difference.

5. All three women in the Weinberg/Danhauser family have built professional lives around their creative interests: Veronica is a writer, Sarah is a musician, Ruby works in the theater. Both Veronica and Sarah must make choices and sacrifices as they balance their creative lives with their professional and family lives. How do their stories reflect the unique pressures on women who have creative or artistic interests? How do their dreams change as they get older and move into different stages of their lives? Do you think Ruby will eventually make similar choices to those made by Sarah and Veronica, or will she take a different path?

6. After growing up extremely close to his sister, Sam moves across the country for college and ends up staying after graduation. Do you think he felt like he needed to move so he could separate himself from his twin? What did you think of their dynamic?

7. Discuss Sam's journey of sexual discovery after his traumatic experience of becoming a young widower. What was the importance of fanfiction and online dating? In what ways do you think anonymity was both beneficial and detrimental to him?

8. In the Cape Cod community where the events of *The Summer Place* unfold, there is a distinction, sometimes tense, between the "pond people," the families (like Owen's) who have owned vacation homes in the area for generations, and newer homeowners like Veronica and her family. How do the socioeconomic and cultural differences between these groups influence the events of the novel? Do you have any sympathy for the "pond people"?

9. It is revealed that the completed novels that Veronica left behind are based on Sarah's life, but Sarah decides to have them published anyway. What do you think of her decision? Would you have been angry with Veronica? What did you think of her explanation, "that's what writers do"?

10. After Eli confesses to Sarah his own duplicity, she decides not to come clean about her dalliance with Owen. Why not? Do you think she made the right choice not to tell him? Do you think he would have forgiven her? What did you think about Sarah's relationship with Owen? Was he taking advantage of her when they met later in life?

11. At the end of the book, Rosa tells Gabe the full truth about his paternity and her ruse involving Eli. She even introduces him to his father. How would you have reacted to the news? Would you have forgiven Rosa for her lie?

12. Were you happy that they decided not to sell the family home in the end? Do you think it was important to keep it in the family?

ENHANCE YOUR BOOK CLUB

1. In this book, the walls actually talk. Try to imagine what the walls of your childhood home might say about you and your family.

2. The author was inspired by elements of Shakespeare's *A Midsummer Night's Dream* in the writing of this book. In that play, there are missed love connections, love triangles, and even some magic. Read the play or even watch an adaptation with your book group to find the parallels in the stories.

3. Let the Cape Cod setting inspire you! Serve lobster roll sandwiches with crunchy kettle-cooked potato chips. Try out a Cape Cod Cocktail: mix 2 ounces of vodka and 3 ounces of cranberry juice with ice and serve with a lime wedge for garnish. Swap out the vodka for seltzer water for a nonalcoholic alternative.

4. Be sure to keep up with author Jennifer Weiner by visiting JenniferWeiner.com.

A CONVERSATION WITH
JENNIFER WEINER

~~~~~~

Your books always have a fierce, complex woman at the heart of them. Discuss what it was like to write this trio of interesting women who span three generations.

I wrote this book at a difficult time in my life. Last spring, the day before my older daughter turned eighteen, my mom died (on Mother's Day!). My mom was wonderful. She gave me so many gifts, including a love of reading and a level of comfort in my own skin that I wish every girl and woman could have grown up with. Losing a mom when you're in your fifties isn't a tragedy, but my mother's own mother, my Nana, lived to be 101, which meant my mom had her mother until she was in her seventies. When my mom died, not only did I feel very sad, I also felt a little cheated. I'd hoped I'd have her for many years to come, and that my daughters would, too.

My mother died in May. Then, in August, I dropped my daughter off at college in New York City. That was another nontragic loss, because kids grow up and move out. You give them roots, and you give them wings, as the saying goes, and then you watch them leave you.

Those two losses made me realize that the torch had

been passed, and that I was now the matriarch of my family. It made me think about mothers and daughters and the passage of time. As my own first reader, I wanted to write a fun, diverting, juicy book that would keep me entertained and give me some respite from my real life, but I knew it was also going to end up being a story about mothers and daughters and grandmothers and granddaughters; about growing up and letting go of the places and the people we love.

Your characters wear masks and discuss other safety measures, such as quarantine and COVID testing. What was it like to write a book that portrays the pandemic as you were living through it?

If you're writing a book set in the here and now, the COVID of it all presents a challenge. You either have to create an alternate version of history where everything's the same but COVID isn't present, or you have to somehow engage with a pandemic that's been tragic and disruptive while also feeling endless and tedious. I didn't want to write a book that was all about COVID, but I was also really interested in what COVID was doing to romantic relationships, to existing marriages, to families . . . to pretty much everything. I'd read a lot about people who'd just started dating and moved in together when the first quarantines began, and I absolutely wanted to explore what hitting the fast-forward button like that could do to a new relationship. Similarly, I think that COVID lay bare the ways that women were bearing the burden of a household's emotional labor, all of the invisible things that help a family function. I knew what it was like for me when my house suddenly turned into my husband's office, my kids' school, a 24-hour diner/laundry/therapist's office, and I wanted to write about that, too.

You have a sentient house in this book. How did you get into the "mind" of a family home?

Honestly, I think getting into the mind of a house was easier than getting into the minds of some of the male characters I've written!

Architects and interior designers talk about houses with bones and a house's character; houses where you walk inside and immediately have a sense of the people who live there. Between bones and character, you're already halfway to a person! I've also always been struck by the idea that, on a molecular level, houses contain the echoes of every conversation held inside of them, the scents of every meal prepared. It didn't seem to be too far of a leap to imagine a house that not only holds all that history but also has feelings about it. I imagined the house as a protector, the keeper of the family's memories, an entity that knows them intimately and wants what's best for them. Once I had that identity established, writing the specifics wasn't that hard.

In this book, you explore parenting from many angles. There are stepparents, single parents, and even a rejection of the experience entirely. What do you want readers to take away from the book about the expectations of parenting?

I've always been interested in the idea of found families, or how you can make your own family, and it's not necessarily going to include all (or any of) the people who are biologically related to you. I also wanted to celebrate stepparents and the difficult role they have to play. The fairy tales and Disney films might cast them as the villains, but I think that stepparents can have a really lovely, supportive role in a child's life. Like Sarah says, a stepmother or stepfather can be a bonus adult in a kid's life, another person who can provide stability and support. Or, in more dire cases (poor Connor!), a stepparent can be all the stability and support a kid has. I wanted to write a realistic story, not a fairy tale where a stepdaughter instantly and permanently loves her stepmother, or a stepson doesn't have to work through feelings of abandonment and sorrow, but where the relationship takes time and effort on both sides. Most of all, I wanted to show the importance of kids getting love and support and stability from the adults who are around and available to give it to them. I want readers to come away knowing that they have the power to be that stable, loving person in a child's life, even if they don't have the official title of Mom or Dad.

We are truly transported to Cape Cod in the book. What do you find so inspiring about that setting?

The Outer Cape has always been one of my favorite places. It's the place I went on summer vacations with my family when I was a child, the place where I took my own kids. It was also one of my mother's favorite places. She loved to swim, in the ocean and the bay and the freshwater kettle ponds. She loved to ride her bike, and to walk around Provincetown, which is one of the most vibrant, colorful, eclectic towns in the world. I have so many wonderful memories of the time I've spent there . . . and, in the midst of the pandemic, there were so many moments when I wished I was there: that it was summer, and I could feel the sand under my feet and smell the salt water and hear the wind rustling the reeds. I think so many of us needed (or still need) an escape from the world, and if *The Summer Place* gives readers a little bit of that escape and a sense of what it feels like to be in this beautiful, wild, unspoiled place, that makes me very happy as an author.

You pull themes from Shakespeare's A Midsummer Night's Dream *into* The Summer Place. *Talk about the ways that the play inspired you in telling this story.*

I love the idea of enchantment—about people taken out of their familiar surroundings, shipwrecked on an island or lost in a forest, where there are supernatural forces that work to bring lovers together. I love the tropes: Forbidden love! Love triangles! Love potions! And, of course, I love a happy ending.

I've also felt—correctly or not—like the last two years have been sort of like an enchantment (not necessarily a good one!). We've all been pulled out of our familiar lives and "shipwrecked" somewhere else. There are supernatural forces at work, or at least invisible ones, in the form of an ever-mutating virus. We've all started off one place and ended somewhere else, whether it's a happy ending or not.

And, of course, books are their own kind of enchantment. They have their own way of taking us out of the familiar and setting us down somewhere else, where a bunch of actors or players or fairies say, "Let us tell you a story." You bring your own imagination to the table; you work in concert with the storytellers to imagine the setting and the characters, even as you understand that someone else is dictating the action and bringing everything to what's hopefully a satisfying conclusion.

Storytelling is the most human kind of magic. It's maybe even the only magic we have. And to me it feels like that particular kind of magic has never been more necessary.

Veronica Levy is a novelist who pulls back from publishing for a long time. Is it strange to write as a character who is a novelist like yourself? Are there similarities that you share with her? This isn't the first time I've written a character who is a successful novelist whose career goes in a different direction than mine has. Midcareer is an interesting place to be—you're not the ingenue, not the hot young thing, not any big tastemaker's delightful new discovery. I've always tried to push myself, to make each book better than, and different from, the one before it. With the Cape Cod trilogy, I've tried to play with the idea of a "beach book," using the elements of the label that appeal to me (the seductive seaside setting, the idea of romance and happy endings) while pushing the boundaries of the genre. But I think every writer is interested in the road not taken and uses characters to explore directions in which her own life hasn't gone.

With Veronica, I wanted her to make what I regard as the ultimate sacrifice. She's disappointed in herself. She doesn't like the person she's become in success. She wants to make amends. And so she gives up her art, or at least the public expression of her art (it was hard enough to make her give up publishing, and I think that asking a writer not to write is akin to asking her to cut off a limb!). It's a huge sacrifice, but I think a lot of women who become mothers usually do give up something, whether it's in the personal or the professional sphere. I think that Ronnie's story is a version of many women's stories when what they want in the professional world bumps up against marriage and motherhood, and something's got to give. It's my hope that this book will occasion some interesting conversations about how women still seem to have to pick one or the other—being the best mother or excelling at work—while men seem to more easily be able to do both.

Fierce Youth Outreach
P.O. Box 1315
Beloit, WI, 53512
www.facebook.com/fiercey-
outhoutreach

Forgiven Ministries
PO Box 117
Taylorsville, NC 28681
828-632-6424

Fly Right Inc.
P.O. Box 1023
Meridian, MS 39302-1023
www.flyrightinc.org

Good News Jail and Prison Ministry
PO Box 8760
Henrico, VA 23228
804-553-4090

InnerChange Freedom Initiative
www.prisonfellowship.org/reentry

Joe Macdonald Ministry
PO Box 91275
Mobile, AL 36691

Kairos Prison Ministry
www.kairosprisonministry.org

Ken Cooper Prison Ministry
904-859-9780

Koinonia House National Ministries
PO Box 1415
Wheaton, IL 60187

Licking County Jail Ministries
PO Box 535
Newark, Ohio 43055
www.jailministries.org

www.LighthouseNetwork.org
Addiction and Counseling
Helpline: 877-562-2565 x 101

Look Up Ministries
50 O'Bannon Ave.
Newark, Ohio 43055
www.lookupcenter.org

MentorCare Ministries
817-688-4044
Bedford, Texas

New Hope Correctional Ministry
PO Box 1694
Plymouth, MA 02362

New Name Ministries
PO Box 11694
Fort Worth, TX 76110
817-920-5886

Pacific Youth Correctional Ministry
Pycm.org

Prison Fellowship
www.prisonfellowship.org
703-478-0100

Prison Fellowship International
PO Box 17434
Washington D.C. 20041
703-481-0000

Speak Up For Hope
www.SpeakUpforHope.org

Stepping Out Ministries
Salem, Oregon
503-363-2805

Wayside Cross Ministries
Aurora, Illinois
630-892-4239

LIST OF
CONTRIBUTORS

Acuna, Santana - July 14–15

Alemar, Mayra - October 11–14

Anderson, Dawn - January 3–4, August 17–18

Andrews, Jeff - December 26–27

Avila, Grace - June 2

Avila, Joe - May 24–30

Avila, Mary - May 31–June 1

Baird, Marcus - November 17–18

Banther, Janice - January 22

Barnes, Scottie - February 13–19

Baumgartner, Doug - December 17

Beatty, Tom - June 29–30

Benjamin, Gary - August 16

Billy* - August 21–23

Bond, Callie - July 20–23, November 16, December 15, 28

Booth, Mary - September 10

Bottke, Allison - May 8–12

Brown, Chuck - June 21

Brown, Michael - October 28

Brown, Pat - December 12

Burke, Timothy James - April 15–16, November 19, December 31

Bush, Corey - May 16–19

Cain, Burl - October 7–10

Cameron, Connie - January 18–19, February 12, April 25, July 30–31, August 5, October 1–4

Carter, Terry - December 7

Cochran, Maggie - September 7

Collins, Pat - September 8–9

Colopy, Elsa Kok - November 20–21

Colson, Charles - March 11

Cooper, Ken - March 2–4

Cowley, Jack - February 21–23

Croce, Danny - September 23–24

Cyan-Brock, Toni K. - December 9

Davis, Carol - May 1, September 18–22

Deyoung, Rocky - August 28–30

Duffy, Michaelene - August 1–4

Duncan, Brandon - February 8–11

Dunn, Christopher - August 19–20

Flemming, Dan - October 20–21

Flindt, Sandra - December 20

Fowler, Geoffrey - December 13

Fowler, Linda - October 15

Freed, Larry - December 18–20

Friend, Nanette - June 17–20

Ghiloni, Mario - December 30

Grace, Theresa - December 21

Grady, Duane - December 16

Griswold, Bobby - June 28

Guilford, Mahluli - October 29

Gunning, Steve - November 27–28

Hairapetian, Aram - March 12–14

Hamilton, Terry - July 8–11

Hance, Raeanne - November 29–30

Harris, Jim - March 22–26

Hayes, Bernice - April 2

Hayes, Scott - April 3–7

Herst, Lance - June 11–15

Herst, Lance P. - June 16

Hill, Sharon - October 30

Hricko, Kim - September 25–26

Humphrey, Kim - February 3–4

Humphrey, Ron - February 5–7

Hupp, Tara - July 5

Jenkins, Mark - May 22–23

Jenkins, Mryrien A. - May 20–21

Johnson*, Keb - May 2–7

Johnston, Connie - March 18–20

Johnston, Larry - September 29–30

Kent, Carol - January 31–February 2

Kesterson, Linda - October 23–27

Krenklis, Keith - July 16–19

Leonardson, John - March 16–17

Leone, John - November 7–9

Lowe, Steve - April 8–10

Lowry, Johnathan - January 12–17

Mapes, Terry - June 23–26

Martin, Mike - August 25–26

Matesic, Nikola - June 6–8

McCullough, Tom - July 22

McDaniel, Wendy - December 8

Mcdonald, Joe - March 31–April 1

McDonald, Robert - September 6

McMillian*, Myra - April 17–21

McMorris, Michelle - October 31

McNabney, Kym - July 4,
    November 22–23,
    December 24, 29

Meister, Bill - January 5–7

Menard*, Jerry - March 1

Michael, Beth - January 8–11

Michael, Janell - November 5–6

Mill, Manny - March 27–30

Miller, Joe - August 11–14

Morgan, Roger - August 9–10

Mothershed, Bill - March 21,
    April 22–24, June 22

Mullen, Chris - December 22

Myers, Dave - August 15

Nelson, Henry - April 11–14

Newell, Travis - May 14–15

Nikkel, Ron - January 2,
    December 10–11

Olsen, Will - September 2–3

Osborne, Steve - June 3–5

Ownby, Mike - December 1–6

Parsell, Jeannia - January 20–21

Parsell, Scott - July 12

Peck, Jeffrey - March 15, July 21,
    August 31, September 1,
    October 16

Pitts, Samuel - September 11–17

Potter, Bob - July 1–3

Raymond, A. - June 27

Reyes, David - April 26–30

Ricks, Ana - February 20

Robinson, Dijuahn - August 6–8

Robinson, Steve - February 26–28

Roensch, Jr., George Alfred -
    December 23

Rojas, Kim - November 10–14

Rouse, Dale - November 1–4

Russell, James A. - March 7–10

Schaeferkraft, Robin - November 26

Seals, Jose - July 24–29

Sewell, Teresa - January 23

Shaw, Heather - October 22

Shaw, Ted - September 4–5,
    December 25

Silver, Steve - October 17–19

Smith, Christopher - May 13

Smith, Jerry - November 15

Smith, Joshua B. - July 13, December 14

Smith, Vernon - January 1

Spence, Alphonso - February 24–25

Vasquez, EnRique - January 24–30

Walthour, Russell - June 9–10

Wheatley, Clifford - November 24–25

Wieging, Misty - August 24

Williams, Kelon - July 6–7

Williamson, Jennifer - October 5–6

Wolf, Lois - September 27–28

Zamora, Dina - March 5–6